A SPRING
WITHIN US

A Book of
Daily Meditations

Richard Rohr

CAC Publishing

Center for Action and Contemplation

cac.org

Cover and book design by Nelson Kane
Cover image Copyright © Randy Morse, GoldenStateImages.com

Published by CAC Publishing, a division of Center for Action and Contemplation
1705 Five Points Road SW
Albuquerque, NM 87105
www.cac.org

Scripture citations are the author's paraphrase except where noted. Hafiz, "Listen to This Music," excerpt from the Penguin publication *A Year With Hafiz: Daily Contemplations*. Translations and renderings by Daniel Ladinsky. Copyright © 2011 by Daniel Ladinsky and used with his permission. St. John of the Cross, "If You Want," from the Penguin anthology *Love Poems from God: Twelve Sacred Voices from the East and West*. Translations and renderings by Daniel Ladinsky. Copyright © 2002 by Daniel Ladinsky and used with his permission. The excerpts from *The Art of Letting Go: Living the Wisdom of Saint Francis* by Richard Rohr, Sounds True, Inc. 2010, were adapted with permission from the publisher. *Hymn of the Universe* by Pierre Teilhard de Chardin. Copyright © 1961 by Editions du Seuil. English translation Copyright © 1965 by William Collins Sons & Co., Ltd., London and Harper & Row, Inc., New York. Reprinted by permission of Georges Borchardt, Inc., for Editions du Seuil. Excerpts from "Forever Young," "Finding God in the Depths of Silence," and "What Sustains Me: Contemplation," each by Richard Rohr, reprinted with permission from Sojourners, (800) 714-7474, www.sojo.net. Adapted excerpts from *Immortal Diamond: The Search for Our True Self,* by Richard Rohr. Copyright © 2013, Jossey-Bass, San Francisco. Used with permission. Adapted excerpts from *Falling Upward: A Spirituality of the Two Halves of Life,* by Richard Rohr. Copyright © 2011, Jossey-Bass, San Francisco. Used with permission. Adapted excerpts from *Breathing Under Water: Spirituality and the Twelve Steps* by Richard Rohr, Copyright © 2011; *Eager to Love: The Alternative Way of Francis of Assisi* by Richard Rohr, Copyright © 2014; *Great Themes of Paul: Life as Participation* by Richard Rohr, Copyright © 2012; *Jesus' Plan for a New World: The Sermon on the Mount* by Richard Rohr and John Feister, Copyright © 1996; *Letting Go: A Spirituality of Subtraction* by Richard Rohr, Copyright © 2005; *New Great Themes of Scripture* by Richard Rohr, Copyright © 2012; *Richard*

Copyright page is continued on page 428

ISBN: 978-1-62305-037-5
Printed in the United States of America

CONTENTS

FOREWORD

From the many years I've had the pleasure of working with him, I can say one thing for certain about Richard Rohr: He is always ahead of the curve! With his great Franciscan heart wide open to the heart of the world, he seems to have a sixth sense about what's emerging into consciousness and where he is needed next in order to bring real help to a world in which both people and systems are hurting.

Fundamentally, Richard is exactly as he presents himself: a simple, modern-day friar/preacher, deeply rooted in his Franciscan charism and in the Gospel imperative "to bring good news to the poor, to heal the brokenhearted, proclaim deliverance to the captives and recovery of sight to the blind, to let the oppressed go free" (see Luke 4:18). What has set him apart from the pack from the start, however, has been his bedrock awareness that preaching the Gospel is fundamentally not about lip service, but about *changed lives*. The Gospel notion of proclaiming the good news requires more than merely preaching sermons from a gilded pulpit on Sunday mornings. It means confronting whatever stands in the way of liberation, be it personal, institutional, or dogmatic. For more than fifty years, this has been the golden thread in Richard Rohr's ministry, underlying both its consistency and its remarkable innovativeness.

His unique gift has always been his uncanny ability to hold the tension between personal perspectives and systemic ones—or, in other words, between healing and prophecy. As early as the 1970s, he established his reputation for in-the-trenches social activism. But even as he built the Center for

Action and Contemplation into a one-of-a-kind training center for ministry among the most desperately marginalized, he was becoming more and more sensitized to the ways in which the False Self, with its myriad hidden agendas and old wounds, blocked and co-opted the healing energy of liberation. Recognizing that authentic self-knowledge was the missing piece between Gospel imperative and enlightened action, Richard began to address this blockage directly. He was among the first in North America to introduce the Enneagram of Personality as a tool of spiritual transformation, and his bridge-building to the Recovery Movement and inspired work with men's spirituality have set him in a class by himself.

Along with "bring good news to the poor," another Gospel maxim that Richard has lived to the full is "new wineskins for new wine" (see Mark 2:22). This goes with the turf, one might say, since it is not in the nature of the institutional church to change course or *modus operandi* easily. As it became steadily more evident that Richard's teachings were reaching an ever-widening audience, well beyond the boundaries of traditional religious education or formation, the technological reach of the CAC expanded accordingly. Taking the plunge into online delivery systems—webcast, internet, and the phenomenally successful Living School program, inaugurated in 2013—Richard has carried his message of inner transformation in the service of Gospel love to a growing audience of contemporary spiritual seekers.

In 2008, in another brilliantly intuitive, ahead-of-the-curve move, Richard took on the challenge of offering daily meditations in an online format. Today, eight years and some two million words later, these short, deeply luminous reflections have become a lifeline for a worldwide virtual community of spiritual seekers.

A Spring Within Us is more than just a title; it captures the essence of how this book came to be written and the living water you will find here. If I've spent my earlier paragraphs in a brief overview of Richard's remarkably innovative and fruitful ministry, it is in order to better set up my invitation: What awaits you here is the integrated wisdom that emerges out of a life courageously and vulnerably lived. As I browse the pages of this new volume and sense the beauty and profundity of its design (a perspective that is impossible to take when these little gems come flashing across the screen so quickly), I am reminded of one of my very favorite passages from T. S. Eliot's *The Four Quartets*:

Old men ought to be explorers.
Here and there does not matter. We must be still
and still moving into another intensity—
for a further union, a deeper communion.[1]

Whether Richard, my ever-vital and forward-looking friend, would accept the designation "old man," I do not know. But as he traverses his eighth decade, he is definitely now an elder, and the mature fruit of elderhood—"unity attained"—is the fragrance that falls from every page of this book. Indeed, you might say that this is, in fact, a *banquet* more than a book—and even, if you prefer, a wedding feast, in which the water of a life lived with courage, transparency, and fidelity has been transformed into the wine of mature wisdom. And so it is my pleasure now to invite you, one and all, to the banquet table, recalling those immortal words from the Song of Songs (see 5:1):

Eat, friends, drink: Drink deeply of love.

—Cynthia Bourgeault

ACKNOWLEDGMENTS

Since 2008, the Center for Action and Contemplation has been sending my "Daily Meditations" by email to people all over the world. This is a major feat, one I could never accomplish on my own. Generous donors make the infrastructure and technology possible. Many hands, hearts, and minds put the meditations together from start to finish. For the past few years, Joelle Chase has coordinated this effort, working closely with Judy Traeger to sift through my writings and recordings, finding hopeful gems to polish until they shine. Vanessa Guerin offers additional editing and selects companion images for each week of online meditations. Finally, Morgan Overton formats and sends the emails, day in and day out. For all these, and those who have supported us in the past, I am very, very grateful. If only Jesus would have had such on-site secretaries, recorders, and immediate editors!

The theme for the 2014 Daily Meditations, which became this book, grew from Judy and Joelle's inspired idea of bringing together my various teachings on the True Self. In some way or another, many of the concepts I've explored over the years focus on helping people discover and live from their authentic identity, as a unique, one-of-a-kind "beloved" of God. Remembering who we truly are is a gradual, lifelong journey, but there are many ways we can ease and quicken the process. Judy and Joelle organized my work into "a primer for living a whole life," a map to guide us along the circuitous path back to our Source. As a Christian, I fully believe Jesus is a rather ideal summary of the classic life map, but many people come to trust the pattern apart from the "shortcut" that is Jesus. We must be honest about that.

Many teachers—from past and present—have shaped my understanding of human and spiritual development. There are too many to list, but the ones that come foremost to mind are many of the early Eastern Fathers, Francis and Clare of Assisi, Bonaventure, Lady Julian of Norwich, John of the Cross, Teresa of Ávila, Thérèse of Lisieux, Teilhard de Chardin, Carl Jung, Thomas Merton, Ken Wilber, and all teachers of the mystery of death and transformation, including our contemporaries, Mirabai Starr and Kathleen Dowling Singh, along with such brilliant explanatory schemas as the Enneagram and Spiral Dynamics. All of these, and surely many more, have helped me navigate life's stages; I hope I do them justice in sharing what they've taught me as I pass them on to you through my limited lens.

We heard from so many online readers that these meditations were helpful, so we decided to put them into a book—something you can hold, mark up, and return to again and again, year after year, as your life slowly ripens into wholeness. The title locates the true source within you—and not in me.

Of course, I could not help myself and heavily revised the 2014 reflections—after two more years of experience with life and death—so now this book is an original work in its own right! I want to thank Michael Poffenberger, CAC's Executive Director, for initiating the in-house publication of this book. Throughout the process of turning the online meditations into this new form, more wonderful people invested their time and care. I bow in gratitude to . . .

Shirin McArthur, for her thorough and thoughtful editing, for asking important questions, and for clarifying my many revisions.

Lee Staman, for researching and finding reputable sources for the quotations I often half-remember or paraphrase.

Nelson Kane, for the beautiful layout and cover design—I do believe images have as much power to teach and transform as do words.

Sheryl Fullerton, who has edited a few of my previous books, including *Falling Upward*, for graciously reviewing the final manuscript.

Cynthia Bourgeault and James Finley, my colleagues here in our Living School, for their wise and far-too-trustful words at beginning and end of this book. They both continue to be my teachers, not just by their words but, even more, by their persons.

Vanessa Guerin, for bringing together the people, process, and printer to create the lovely book you now hold in your hands.

And I am grateful to you, dear reader, for allowing me to share the lessons closest to my heart. I pray these pages meet you—wherever you are, whatever your age—and help you take the next step forward, ever closer to the Source of Love and Life.

As I love to say, I am never teaching anything totally new, and if any of it resonates with you at a deep level, it is because it has always and everywhere been true—and the Holy Spirit has already taught your hearts this universal truth. We are forever relearning and constantly being "re-minded" of what the soul already deeply knows (see John 14:26). Thank you for allowing me to be a re-minder.

> We shall not cease from exploration,
> And the end of all our exploring
> Will be to arrive where we started
> And *know the place for the first time.*[1]
> —*T.S. Eliot*

Pentecost Sunday, 2016

INTRODUCTION

DAY I
A Primer for Living a Whole and Holy Life

Over the course of these daily meditations, we will follow the trajectory of life from innocent beginning, through inevitable brokenness, to putting everything back together, through ripening into union—with self, God, the world, and others.

I'll begin during the next few weeks by offering an introduction to my methodology: *"Scripture as validated by experience, and experience as validated by Tradition are good scales for one's spiritual worldview."* A balanced and holistic worldview is formed from a non-dual way of thinking and is enlivened by mystical encounter with Presence, always leading to acts of service and charity in the world.

Although each life moves at its own pace, and with endless variety, this growth does follow a common sequence, and we'll look at nine likely stages of spiritual development. Then, as the year progresses, we will dive deeper into each stage and its unique spiritual tasks. We will explore the splits that occur early in our lives and the ways in which we can find healing and wholeness. These meditations will focus on the practical ways in which our spirituality forms our inner lives and is then lived outwardly in the world, which is to live a life of love and justice for others.

The Inner Spring and the Deep Well

In the Christian Scriptures, we have Jesus encouraging a Samaritan woman to draw water on her own from the public well (see John 4:7) and serve it to him. It is at this ancient well that Jesus becomes the receiver and asks the woman to be the giver; the expected roles are reversed. A mutual vulnerability is revealed in one of the most beautiful accounts of the character and shape of Divine transformation. Jesus invites the woman to be both the receiver, but also the "source" and giver, of the gift of living water, in an almost Trinitarian kind of flow. Initial reliance upon outer authority becomes her own inner authority, and this from a less-than-ideal candidate, as we see from the full text of this story. Jesus describes this transfer as a "water that I shall give [which] will be a spring of water within you—welling up unto infinite life" (see John 4:14).

In other words, the ancient spiritual well is fully transferred to the individual person; it is now an inside job and has a "welling-up effect," which is exactly the image that mystics like Francisco de Osuna[1] and SS. Teresa of Ávila and John of the Cross loved so much. This theme is also repeated when Jesus says that "from the heart [of the believer] shall flow streams of living water" (see John 7:38). So hold onto these key ideas: mutuality, the deeper stream, spiritual work, and the transfer from Source to recipient.

But let's also go farther back into Jewish history and find the early foundations for images of a spring or well. They imply hidden depth, the work of digging, and the search for a foundational, life-giving source—all of which are precisely our concerns here. Well is one of those "bookmark" words that we find regularly appearing in the Scriptures, developing a subtle but important theme. First there was Abraham's well at Beersheba (see Genesis 21:25–32), which was a symbol of an early peace treaty or "oath" between the Israelites and the Ishmaelites or Arab peoples. Then there is the very interesting digging of three successive wells by Abraham's son Isaac (see Genesis 26:19–22), called in Hebrew *esek* (quarrel), *sitnah* (accusation), and *rehobot* (room or space).

Only the third well is claimed by Isaac, with the words, "Now Yahweh has made room for us to thrive in this place." But note that, to find this third well, we have to go through the dualistic mind of "quarrel" and "accusation" before we can come to the "open space" of Rehoboth, where we can thrive. Talk about perfect symbolism! We can probably presume this was the well of his son, Jacob, which John's Gospel then uses as a teaching aid (see John 4:6).

And there is one more bookmark: the almost-Jungian symbol of the *bitter* well at Marah (see Exodus 15:22–25), which the Israelites desperately needed to survive in the desert. Yahweh tells Moses to throw a piece of wood in the well, which then turns the waters "sweet." Not all sources become good wells, and some punitive and exclusionary messages in all sacred scriptures must indeed be sweetened and made inviting for the soul. I see this as an early indicator of the need for spiritual alchemy, very real discernment, and the necessary search for a truly helpful interpretation of the well from which you draw. This is what the Jewish people often called *midrash*. Let's try to do just that in this book, and I hope you will find it sweet and refreshing water indeed!

DAY 3

Plumbing the Depths

The Psalms use a wonderful, vague, but oft-quoted line, I suspect because it evokes something true: "Deep calls unto deep" (see Psalm 42:7). Eugene Peterson translates it even more courageously in *The Message*, where he says "chaos calls to chaos." In either case, the psalm points to what we would now perhaps call the unconscious, the hidden, the suffered-toward, or the often-mystical level of meaning. This is the always-forbidding yet *deeply promising darkness* where so much truth, hurt, and real healing are invariably revealed—however reluctantly. Yet this is also where all the joy and all the juice are finally found! We "sin" and do stupid things precisely when we stay on the surface of things. At the depths, even the depths of our mistakes, there is always grace, new space, and more authentic freedom.

It will do us no good to stay at the surface. Simply reaffirming what have become lifeless doctrines, repeating religious clichés that offer nothing to the soul and ask nothing of the soul, giving textbook answers that only strengthen our egocentricity and our fear of change, are not what we are about here. The need for healing and resurrection is great, at every level: personal, familial, ecclesial, political, economic, sexual, and planetary.

I hope and pray we can offer "depth to depth" in this book: the depth of the Great Tradition, of a Franciscan alternative orthodoxy, of modern psychology and quantum science, of cultural critique, of the parallel depth of human, animal, and planetary suffering that is experienced on our earth today. These depths are ready to meet and need to kiss one another.

If this book lessens suffering even slightly, if it can take away some levels of our seeming hopelessness and our obvious cynicism, it will be well worth the time, the effort, the ink and paper that the staff at the Center for Action and Contemplation have so generously offered here. May this book be a kiss of juice and joy to many people.

DAY 4
Life as Participation

When you listen to the news or look around and within you, doesn't it seem we are mostly going nowhere? Each individual is on his or her own to find and create his or her own personal meaning. It seems we are all condemned to start at zero, with no shoulders to stand on, which makes the relatively short human task quite difficult. It basically does not work, especially for the young, or for those who die young. In our postmodern age, we have rejected any strong sense of the common good or any Great Tradition. Thus we are addictively repeating the same patterns that produce violence, suffering, emotional immaturity, low self-esteem, and a far-too-premature death.

We need new ways of thinking and being to engage with others *through our simple humanity*, and even our brokenness, our differences, and our complexity—because these are what we do have in common, if we are honest. Know this: *How we do anything is how we do everything!* How you love yourself is how you love the world and how you love the world is the only way you will know how to love yourself. Our loving is of one piece. That is why we need to emphasize our *inherent human identity as good, and more than adequate*, instead of always creating ever-new contests for success and importance. This is the secret gift of any good spirituality.

For our spirituality to be authentic, we must experience things from the inside out instead of just the outside in, which is the terribly codependent trap of this materialistic and highly overstimulated culture in which we live. We let others define us instead of drawing from our own deep well. (Please do not hear that in an individualistic way; it is finally the exact opposite—which is truly a paradox.) Indeed, the goal of mature religion is to help us die before we die: die to our small self so we can find our Big Self. All major religions describe this (as Jesus does in all four Gospels) in one way or another: A false and largely self-constructed identity must be surrendered before the True Self can stand radiant and revealed. This is basic and essential conversion. Both good religion and good psychology agree here.

Our contemplative practice is a "laboratory" in which we learn to die to our passing identities, emotions, and thoughts so we can receive the always-permanent and perfect mirroring of the Divine gaze. The rest of our life becomes the field in which we live out this participation in Love, bouncing back the gaze of grace to the Other and then having plenty left over for all others besides. *All spiritual knowing is knowing by participation.* Hold onto that, as vague as it might, at first, sound to you, and we will go a long way with it!

Contemplation as Catalyst

Great love and great suffering are the natural gateways to all spiritual transformation and growth, gradually opening us to Divine Union. They are available to all of us if we are willing to be present. Contemplation is a way of maintaining the fruits of great love and great suffering over the long haul. Otherwise, we slip right back into our dualistic thinking and living. The contemplative mind also greases the wheels of consciousness and helps us to be ready and willing to deal with great love and great suffering when they arrive—and hopefully they always will. Otherwise, we face the great tasks of life with only our small and momentary feelings and defenses, which are always inadequate to the task of greatness.

Transformation is always a gift to be received. We can't achieve it; like grace, it is given and can only be accepted. In other words, it is not a matter of intense willpower. We can nurture openness and presence ahead of time so that, when the opportunity comes, we are ready and willing. Throughout this year, there will be consistent invitations to nurture the contemplative mind. In particular, the *Gateway to Silence* phrases, which can be used to focus your mind and spirit, appear at the close of each meditation, beginning today. These are merely suggestions; use whatever words, gestures, or ways draw you into non-dual consciousness, helping you let go of obsessive thoughts and emotions and simply rest in pure and naked Presence. Which leads to one more foundational principle: *You cannot get there; you can only be there.* Trust me, that is not just playing with words.

At the close of each week, I'll also offer a special Sabbath meditation, remembering key teachings from the preceding days and introducing a contemplative practice: an opportunity to allow our monkey-minds to take their rest. This monkey-mind is the part of you that needs to write a commentary on everything (often called "judging"), instead of letting it *rest there as itself and in itself*—without your commentary. Monkeys and minds are constantly self-referential, and that is entirely too small a reference point for any Big Truth or Great Love.

I hope this format and intentional sequence of study will offer a deep and experiential way of daily spiritual formation, not just for your own personal growth, but for the blessing of the world in which you live!

Gateway to Silence: My True Self is Love.

DAY 6

My Religion Is Kindness

I think the genius of the Dalai Lama and of Buddhism is that they do not get lost in metaphysics and argumentation about dogmas and doctrines. They stay at a different level and thus avoid much of the endless disagreements that we find within Christianity. They do not argue about "what" but spend all of their time on "how"—which we have tended to neglect while we argue about "what." As the Dalai Lama says, "My religion is kindness." We could dismiss that as lightweight theology, until we remember that Jesus said, "This is my commandment: You must love one another" (see John 13:34). Kindness is supposed to be the religion of Christians too![2]

As we continue to mature in contemplative thinking, we will come to a sure sense that there is a deep okay-ness to life. "All shall be well, and all shall be well, and all manner of thing shall be well," as Lady Julian of Norwich (1342–1416) put it. We can live more and more within a foundational unitive consciousness and know the Divine Life itself is already flowing through us. *Your life is not about you; you are about Life!* Life, your life, all life, the one life that we all share, is going somewhere—and somewhere good. You do not need to navigate the river, for you are already flowing within it. For some reason, it takes a long time to get where we already are. Our goal is to intentionally participate in this mystery of what has always been our True Self. The Great Ones all agree on this: This one life, this True Self that lasts forever, is already Love (see 1 Corinthians 13:8, 13), because we are created "in the image and likeness of God" (see Genesis 1:26), who is love (see 1 John 4:16).

We are constituted by the same kind of inherent, intimate, completely reciprocal relationships that form the eternal life and the perfect love of the Trinity. That statement, if even slightly understood, could and should change your self-image forever. This eternal participation gives a metaphysical foundation and stable core to the meaning of salvation and holiness, instead of the unstable core of our always-changing behavior and psychic states.[3]

Such intimate good news seems to us almost too good to be true, and we never seem ready to believe it! In the meantime, we must practice believing it, and prepare for an eternity in the bosom of the Trinity by simply being kind and patient with everyone now—and even kind and patient with ourselves. God surely is.

Gateway to Silence: My True Self is Love.

DAY 7
SABBATH MEDITATION

Remember: **Introduction**

We will follow the trajectory of life from innocent beginning, through inevitable brokenness, to putting everything back together, through ripening into union—with self, God, the world, and others. (Day 1)

Hold onto these key ideas: mutuality, the deeper stream, spiritual work, and the transfer from Source to recipient. (Day 2)

"Deep calls unto deep" points to what we would now perhaps call the unconscious, the hidden, the suffered-toward, or the often-mystical level of meaning. (Day 3)

Our contemplative practice is a "laboratory" in which we learn to die and to receive the Divine gaze. (Day 4)

We can't achieve transformation; like grace, it is given and can only be accepted. We can nurture openness and presence ahead of time so that, when the opportunity comes, we are ready and willing. (Day 5)

Your life is not about you; you are about Life. (Day 6)

Rest: **Sacred Time**

I invite you to set aside time for contemplative practice as you begin this year of Daily Meditations. People ask me, "How long should I pray?" I say, "As long as it takes you to get to an emotional and mental 'Yes!'" Many find that they need two periods of twenty minutes a day to come to such surrender. Perhaps it is early in the morning, before your brain has a chance to begin its list-making and judgments. Or, it could be in the evening, which might include an Examen of Consciousness (see Week 12, Day 7), looking for the God-encounters during your day. Maybe it is taking moments throughout the day to pause, breathe, be still, and recognize how you have turned from "yes" and back to various kinds of "no."

The sacrament of Sabbath—keeping a chosen time sacred (though all time is holy; there is no distinction or division between profane and sacred!)—was offered by the Jewish people as a gift for all of humanity.

In our busy, technology-driven culture, it is especially important that we intentionally seek rest and re-creation. It might be a way of saying that *at least* one-seventh of life must be about non-performance and non-egocentric pursuit, or we forget our life's purpose.

Take a moment now. Perhaps breathe in and out with this week's *Gateway to Silence*, "My True Self is Love." Rest in the awareness of Presence and know that you are never apart from it. When this moment ends, Presence will still be here, now, always.

For further study:

The Naked Now: Learning to See as the Mystics See
Silent Compassion: Finding God in Contemplation
Yes, And . . . : Daily Meditations

WEEK 2:

YES, AND

DAY I

Sic et Non: Yes, And

In my formation as a Franciscan, we were told that our job was to somehow make the Word of God accessible to the ordinary person; to invite them into the fullness of their own life and not just talk to the highly educated or church insiders. As Jesus put it, "preach the good news to all creation!" (see Mark 16:15). So many preachers sound like they are still responding to their seminary professors' critical questions rather than talking to the ordinary "person on the street" who needs the Gospel to be relevant to his or her own life. One of the key techniques for teaching good theology is a tradition that in Latin was called *Sic et Non.* It was also the title of a very important book by Peter Abelard (1079–1142), written somewhere around 1100 A.D. *Sic et Non* can be translated as "Yes and No" or "Yes, But" or "Yes, And."

"Yes, And" best describes my own approach. First of all, I want to affirm the Tradition, what is worth saying "yes" to, what is good and perennial and lasting and constant. *And* I complement that Tradition with both Scripture and personal experience in order to form a holistic and balanced spiritual worldview. At the same time, I very often want to add, "*But,* how come no one ever tells us this? Why is this part of the Tradition somehow forgotten or ignored? What might be the biases at work here?"

Spiritual teachings are invariably watered down to be palatable to the ego and to confirm what we are used to hearing. It seems you can only see what you are told to notice, and almost all periods of history have their own selective attention—including ours, I am sure. The only advantage we now enjoy, and it is a big one, is that we have the globalization of available knowledge at everyone's fingertips on the Internet. The days of telling half-truths and getting away with it are over. People are fully ready to return to the wisdom of Abelard and we are now all becoming *Sic et Non* thinkers—otherwise known as non-dual consciousness or contemplation.[1]

Gateway to Silence: Yes . . . and . . .

DAY 2
Wondering or Winning?

Peter Abelard took all of the major theological positions of the Scriptures and the Church and he invited a *Sic et Non* approach to understanding them. Peter Lombard (1100–1164) then wrote a book, building on Abelard's work, called *The Sentences*. It was so influential that, for almost three centuries, in order to get a theological doctorate from a European university, you had to write a commentary on *The Sentences*. The goal of both Abelard and Lombard was not to win an argument or to prove one way of believing. They simply laid out all the arguments on one side and all the arguments on another side and trusted that truth and the Holy Spirit would lead and teach the authentic believer from there.

We no longer enjoy that kind of trust or freedom. In some ways we went backward, especially after the so-called Enlightenment of the seventeenth and eighteenth centuries, which idealized rationalism. We have lost our ability to think and dialogue in this Yes, And way. After the Protestant Reformation, our style of conversation had already become argument and "apologetics"—whose goal was to prove the "enemy" wrong and ourselves right, certainly a form of narcissism. Yet this has been the form of discourse that has held sway for the last five hundred years. We fell in love with a self-serving notion of truth and certitude; we Catholics declared our Pope "infallible" (all evidence to the contrary) while Protestants declared the Bible to be "inerrant" (all evidence to the contrary). We all swam in very small pools of truth and, to make it even worse, truth was always framed as either/or and seldom—very seldom—as both/and. Thus contemplation faded into meaninglessness.[2]

Gateway to Silence: Yes . . . and . . .

The *Questio*

What the *Sic et Non* approach allows you to do, quite frankly, is to be non-reactionary and non-rebellious. You do not need to prove that your statement is the last and final statement, which is what the ego always wants to do. Rather, you just ask others to consider it. Abelard and Lombard laid the foundations for what we call Scholastic philosophy. When Scholastic philosophy was at its best (in the twelfth and thirteenth centuries), the development of an idea proceeded by what the great teachers called the *questio* (Latin, "to seek"). Our English word "quest" probably comes from that understanding. The systematic asking of questions opens up *wonder* and encourages *spiritual curiosity* by drawing out pros and cons for answers to the question, thus refining the question itself instead of just looking for the perfect answer.

Now educators and psychologists both agree that people who ask good questions are much more likely to be intelligent and creative than people who always have answers—which is *not*, in fact, being certain, but too often a cover for low self-esteem, a pervasive fear of vulnerability, and a need to dominate a conversation. None of these are attractive human qualities, it seems to me. Simple curiosity is an infallible sign, not just of intelligence, but of both humanity and humility, and a willingness to engage with reality. Abelard points out that, in Luke's Gospel (see 2:46), the little boy Jesus, symbol of all wisdom and truth, is sitting among the teachers, *listening* to them and *asking them questions*. If Jesus can listen and ask questions, Abelard says, who are we to think we are better than him?[3]

But our need for certitude and closure, very common among the young and uncertain, and frankly among the males of the species, degenerated into insisting on answers, needing answers—and preferably certain answers at that. And, until recently, it was men who did all the preaching in the church. This has not served human conversation or political debate well at all. We moved from wondering to answering, from humble awe to plain awfulness, which has not served religion well at all. This need to be right has reached its nadir in what we today call fundamentalism, common in almost all religions and in most political discourse today.[4] Forgive my lack of patience, but fundamentalists are so lacking in basic curiosity and questioning that they persist in imagining that Hans Christian Andersen's *The Ugly Duckling* is literally about ducks! They invariably miss the actual spiritual meaning of a text in their lust for certitude and quick answers. This has been a huge loss to religious consciousness and the transformation of peoples.

Gateway to Silence: Yes . . . and . . .

The Contemplative Alternative

We need to rediscover the *Sic et Non* approach both in our politics and in our churches. Otherwise, I do not know what we are finally offering the world except violence, because angry conversation creates angry minds and angry hearts and, eventually, angry behavior. It seems to me that we have the possibility, rooted in our own Tradition, of raising up the capacity for humane, dialogical, *Sic et Non* conversations—where I do not need to prove that you are wrong. I do not need to pretend that I am totally right. I can keep my mind and my heart open. It really seems to me that could change the Church, which could then serve its leavening function in changing the world.[5]

What we are enjoying now is a renaissance of the contemplative mind, the one truly unique, alternative mind and heart that religion has to offer the world. Without this new mind, most doctrines, moralities, dogmas, and church structures will almost certainly be misunderstood, misused, and mishandled. As the Apostle Paul said in his famous "Sermon on Wisdom" (see 1 Corinthians 1:17–3:3), we must "know spiritual things in a spiritual way" (see 2:13), and much of our way of knowing has merely aped the rational and proud knowing of the world. Contemplation is a different way of knowing. In the true meaning of the word, it is pure "consciousness" (*con shire* = to know with), which is a humble *participative knowing* with the One who knows all things.[6]

Small people make everything small. Big seers see with the eyes of God. Dualistic people use knowledge, even religious knowledge, for the purposes of ego-enhancement, shaming, and the control of others and themselves. Non-dual people use knowledge for the transformation of persons and structures, but most especially to change themselves and to see reality with a new eye and heart. They hold and "suffer" the conflicts of life instead of passing them on or projecting them elsewhere. When we agree to hold "the whole," eliminating nothing, we are living in the naked now and being present to the moment outside the mind.[7]

Gateway to Silence: Yes . . . and . . .

Jewish *Midrash*

I think we learned the *Sic et Non* approach in the early Christian period from our Jewish ancestors. They called it *midrash*. *Midrash*, as a different way of coming to truth, meant getting together to look at Scripture in a dialogical way, an open—but faith-filled—way. Each participant might offer: "It could mean this. It could mean that. It might challenge you in this direction. It might invite you in that direction."[8]

Jewish *midrash* extrapolated from the *mere story* to find its true spiritual message. We all do the same when we read anyway, but Jesus and his Jewish people were much more honest and upfront about this. Fundamentalists pretend they are giving the text total and literal authority, but then it always ends up looking like what people in that culture would want to believe anyway. (Remember, good Bible Christians in the U.S. Confederacy and in South Africa were quite certain the Scriptures justified oppression and enslavement of black people.) Dualistic or fundamentalist people, who still lack some degree of *real freedom from foundational egocentricity*, always seem to murder, mangle, and manipulate the text for their own purposes.

To take the Scriptures seriously is not to take them literally. Literalism is invariably *the lowest and least level of meaning.* *Serious* reading of Scripture will allow you to find an ever-new spiritual meaning for the liberation of history, the liberation of your own soul, and the liberation of God in every generation. Then you realize the text is true on many levels, instead of trying to prove it is true on only the simple, factual, or historical level. Sacred texts always maximize your possibilities for life and love, which is why we call them sacred. I am afraid we have for too long used the Bible merely to prove various church positions, which largely narrows Scripture's range and depth. Instead of transforming people, the biblical texts became utilitarian and handy ammunition.[9]

Good theology keeps God free for people; good *midrash* keeps people free for God.

Gateway to Silence: Yes ... and ...

DAY 6

The Jesus Hermeneutic

You deserve to know my science for interpreting sacred texts. It is called a "hermeneutic." Without an honest and declared hermeneutic, we have no consistency or authority in our interpretation of the Bible; both believers and preachers can go all over the place with their interpretations, without any solid authority for what they are saying. My methodology is very simple and consistent; *I will try to interpret Scripture the way that Jesus did.* That is probably what we really mean by that common phrase that we should "interpret the Bible through the eyes of Jesus" or even "in the light of Jesus." (That does not mean that I believe or interpret as though the Christian *religion* was meant to replace and supersede the Jewish religion. Both Romans 11 and, more recently, Pope Francis strongly assert this is not true.)

So what does my Jesus hermeneutic mean? Even more than telling us exactly *what to see* in the Scriptures, Jesus taught us *how to see, what to emphasize,* and also *what could be de-emphasized, ignored, or even disagreed with.* Jesus was in no way a fundamentalist or literalist. He was obviously a man of the Spirit, who frankly took great liberties with his Scriptures to make his points, balancing sacred texts with legitimate Jewish tradition and, finally—and quite obviously—with *trust in his own experience of the same!* Just watch and imitate how he did it, and you will gain knowledge and deep respect for his Hebrew Scriptures and for Jewish custom and practice. By the way, Paul did exactly the same thing, and it is ironic that Christians, in much of our history, were taught not to trust their own experience.

Jesus consistently ignored or even denied exclusionary, punitive, and triumphalistic texts in his own Jewish Scriptures in favor of texts that emphasized inclusion, mercy, and justice for the marginalized. He saw, with a deeper and wider eye, those passages that were creating a highway for God and which passages were merely cultural, self-serving, and legalistic additions. When Christians state that every line in the Bible is of equal importance and inspiration, they are being very *unlike* Jesus, because he clearly did not agree. In his "Sermon on the Mount," he distinguishes between "the law and the achieving of its purpose" and then says, six times in a row, "The Law says ...but I say" (see Matthew 5:17–44).

The Bible is a living document for Jesus and grows through context, inspiration, and concrete application, very much as Pope Francis has shown us in our time. This is very different than the strict interpretation of the United States' Constitution, which some Chief Justices assert is a "dead document" that can never be interpreted, but only applied (as if that were possible!). What a sad dead-end, and the rigid result of putting the US Constitution above the active Word of God. This is precisely what we mean when we say that Christ is "The Living Word." We too are called and given permission to be living words, or, as the Apostle Peter puts it, "living stones making a spiritual house" (see 1 Peter 2:5). You cannot build a living dwelling with people merely quoting a now-dead past. The word of God must always be brought to life in the healed and transformed lives of people. In fact, if there is no healing, I doubt whether you have just heard the word of God. Thus Jesus' ministry is almost entirely the interplay of teaching and healing, with the healing illustrating the teaching and the teaching legitimating and inviting us into the healing. Check it out for yourself.

Jesus read and interpreted the inspired text in a dynamic and active way, which is precisely why he was accused of "teaching with authority and not like our scribes" (see Matthew 7:29).[10] The Jewish people in his time had also become used to a "dead" interpretation of their Scriptures, but the Bible, as Jesus taught, was (and is) so much more powerful and alive. It moves toward healing, expansiveness, and the constant renewal of things.

Gateway to Silence: Yes . . . and . . .

DAY 7

Sabbath Meditation

Remember: **Yes, And**

As Franciscans, we were told that our job was to somehow make the Word of God accessible to the ordinary person; to invite them into the fullness of their own life. (Day 1)

Abelard and Lombard simply laid out all the arguments on one side and all the arguments on another side and trusted that truth and the Holy Spirit would lead and teach the authentic believer from there. (Day 2)

The systematic asking of questions opens up *wonder* and encourages *spiritual curiosity.* (Day 3)

Non-dual people use knowledge for the transformation of persons and structures, but most especially to change themselves and to see reality with a new eye and heart. (Day 4)

Sacred texts always maximize your possibilities for life and love, which is why we call them sacred. (Day 5)

My methodology is very simple and consistent; I will try to interpret Scripture the way Jesus did. (Day 6)

Rest: *Lectio Divina*[11]

Read the following passage slowly and aloud four times. With the first reading, *listen* with your heart's ear for a phrase or word that stands out for you. During the second reading, *reflect* on what touches you, perhaps speaking that response aloud or writing in a journal. Third, *respond* with a prayer or expression of what you have experienced and to what you are called. Fourth, *rest* in silence after the reading.

The Shining Word "And"
> "And" teaches us to say yes
> "And" allows us to be *both/and*
> "And" teaches us to be patient and long-suffering
> "And" is willing to wait for insight and integration
> "And" does not divide the field of the moment
> "And" helps us to live in the always-imperfect now
> "And" keeps us inclusive and compassionate toward everything
> "And" demands that our contemplation become action
> "And" insists that our action is also contemplative
> "And" is the mystery of paradox in all things
> "And" is the way of mercy
> "And" makes daily, practical love possible[12]

Gateway to Silence: Yes . . . and . . .

For further study:

Sic et Non; Yes, And
The Naked Now: Learning to See as the Mystics See
Yes, And . . . : Daily Meditations

MYSTICISM: INNER EXPERIENCE

DAY I

A Vital Spiritual Experience

In the early 1960s, Jesuit Fr. Karl Rahner (1904–1984) stated that, if Western Christianity did not rediscover its mystical foundations, we might as well close the doors of the churches because we had lost the primary reason for our existence. Without a contemplative mind, we are offering the world no broad seeing, no real alternative consciousness, no new kind of people, no healing of the past hurts and memories that are closing down history. In fact, culturally religious people, or mere "civil religion," is often worse than no religion, because such religion is commonly used to justify our own cultural prejudices, hatefulness, and violence. This is the history of all religion unless it actually changes and converts people at the deeper levels of consciousness and heals the unconscious.

Until people have had some level of *inner religious experience*, there is no point in asking them to follow the ethical ideals of Jesus or to really under-stand Christian doctrines beyond the formulaic level. At most, formulaic moral ideals and doctrinal affirmations are only the source of deeper anxiety! Furthermore, that anxiety will often take the form of denial, pretension, and projection of our evil elsewhere.

You quite simply don't have the power to obey the law, or any ideal—such as forgiveness of enemies, nonviolence, or humble use of power—or achieve any satisfaction with simplicity and "enoughness," except *in and through union with God*. Nor do doctrines like the Trinity, the Real Presence, salvation, or the mystery of incarnation have any meaning that actually changes your life. Without some inner experience of the Divine, what Bill Wilson of Alcoholics Anonymous called "a vital spiritual experience," nothing authentically new or life-giving ever lasts long or goes very far.[1]

Gateway to Silence: We are one in Love.

DAY 2

Experiencing God

Don't let the word "mystic" scare you. It simply means *one who has moved from mere belief systems or belonging systems to actual inner experience.* All spiritual traditions agree that such a movement is possible, desirable, and available to everyone. In fact, Jesus seems to say that Divine Union is the whole point! (See, for example, John 10:28–38 or John 15:1–9.)

Some call this movement *conversion*, some call it *enlightenment*, some *transformation*, and some *holiness.* It is Paul's "third heaven," where he "heard things that must not and cannot be put into human language" (see 2 Corinthians 12:2, 4). Consciously or not, far too much organized religion has a vested interest in keeping you in the first or second heaven, where all is certain and everything can be put into proper language. This keeps you coming back to church, and it keeps us clergy in business.

This is not usually the result of ill-will on anybody's part; it's just that you can lead people only as far as you yourself have gone. Transformed people transform people. When they talk so glibly about what is always Mystery, it's clear that many clergy have never enjoyed the third heaven themselves. They cannot teach what they do not know. Theological training without spiritual experience is deadly.[2] As Pope Francis said in one of his interviews, such preaching bores "the one who is doing it and also the one who has to listen to it."

As many mystics have intimated, each in their own way, to know God is mostly *to allow yourself to be fully known by God*; they are in the same circuit of the one love. Paul put it quite directly: "I shall know as fully as I am known" (see 1 Corinthians 13:12), or, in another place, "Now that you have come to acknowledge God, although really it is that God has acknowledged you, how can you want to go back [to mere laws and rituals and practices]?" (See Galatians 4:9) Every moment of unitive experience is *primarily God experiencing Godself in us and as us*—and we respond by offering our ecstatic enjoyment to that exchange.

God is always the initiator and we are always the respondents. Even when we think we are initiating a prayer or an act of love, we are just responding to a previous nanosecond of mercy and grace from the Other Side. *Experiencing God is, first of all, allowing God to experience us—fully and freely.* We know one another "center to center," or not at all. In other words, you can never know God as you know any other object. *God awakens you precisely as a fellow subject, and from that honored place you can know and love God back.* We are always and merely closing the circuit of love. God loves Godself in us and we love ourselves in God.

Gateway to Silence: We are one in Love.

DAY 3

A Sacramental Universe

Fr. Vincent Donovan, a missionary in Africa, wrote of working with the Masai many years ago. He said the people were all sitting, very respectfully listening to him as the priest, and he was teaching them about the Seven Sacraments of the Church. When he described a sacrament as *a physical encounter or event in which you experience God, or grace, or the holy*, he said he could tell the old men were not very satisfied that there were only seven such moments. One of the elders finally raised his hand and said, "Father, I thought there would be seven thousand such moments!"[3]

A philosopher of religion said that, if you look at the history of all religions, they almost all begin with one massive mistake. They make a clean split between the sacred and the profane. Then all the emphasis is placed on going to the sacred spaces, creating sacred time and sacred actions, and ninety-eight percent of life then remains "unsacred." This is at the heart of the problem. This is why so many people have such a hard time encountering the holy. They are not insincere; they're people who were told to look for God only in very few places and times. When you build so many churches and shrines, God is seemingly only *there*. When you emphasize holy liturgies, all of life stops being a liturgy. This is simply true in the practical order of perception; it is how we pay attention—and don't pay attention.

The correct distinction is never between sacred and profane, but only between sacred and *desecrated* places, people, and things. It is we alone who desecrate God's one incarnate world by our inability to see truthfully, to see the depth of things, and then to show a reverence that comes quite naturally. When we do see and show reverence, then it is one sacramental universe, and everything—absolutely everything—can be a gate, a window, and a door.[4]

Gateway to Silence: We are one in Love.

DAY 4

God Is Another Word for Everything

The goal of prayer and mysticism is Divine Union—union with what is, with the moment, with yourself, with God, which means with everything.

God is another word for the heart of everything.[5]

St. Bonaventure (1221–1274) said that all of creation is the fingerprint and the footprint of the Divine One (*vestigial Dei*). Everything is the Body of God, which the Apostle Paul locates in three places: in people (see 1 Corinthians 12:12–30), in the physical elements of bread and wine (see 1 Corinthians 11:23–27), and in the entire physical universe (see Romans 8:14–23). All came forth from the Creator and reveal the Creator in some unique way. One would think that the three monotheistic religions would have been the first to see this, and especially Christians, whose distinguishing doctrine is the Incarnation.

When you say you love God, you are saying you love everything. That's why mystics can love the foreigner, the outsider; in fact, they cannot *not* love them, because they see truthfully and fully![6]

Gateway to Silence: We are one in Love.

DAY 5

Union Begets Morality

Almost all people—before they have experienced God's unmerited love—think that their morality will somehow earn them Divine Union. But mystics know otherwise. Their morality is a response to Divine Union. Once you've experienced that you're one with God and your neighbor, why would you steal from her and make her life more difficult? Once you've experienced union with your neighbor, why would you lie to him, or steal his wife? Of course you wouldn't.

But most of us think backward: "If I don't lie, God will like me." No, if you don't lie, you'll like yourself more! God likes you already. *That problem is solved, once and for all and forever.* That's what every mystic knows and enjoys at ever-fuller levels—that you're loved unconditionally, in this life—not in some conditional future heaven.

And that's why mystics are foundationally happy people. In fact, if they're not happy, they're not mystics. If someone is a "sourpuss" (Pope Francis' word!), you know that person is still playing the moral game, which wears them out because it is mostly about willpower, which always fails. That willpower game leads to constant failure, backsliding, and disappointment with the self. Your friends will influence your behavior far more than willpower ever will. Saints are those who really enjoy hanging out with God, with good people, with beauty, and with silence; then their morality flows out of them like syrup from a maple tree.[7]

Gateway to Silence: We are one in Love.

DAY 6

The One Thing Necessary

Mystics are always saying, in one form or another, "Do not be afraid." They know that all is okay. They want you to hear this message so that you can stop fretting and fearing and enjoy Divine Union right now. "Enjoy" is the operative word. Mystical experience allows you to enjoy your own life and to stop creating enemies, people to fear, and nations you have to punish and kill. When you are enjoying deep union, you don't need to create divisions, mistrust, and separation. Conspiracy theories and tabloid gossip hold little interest for you.

True spiritual encounter changes your politics, your attitude toward money, your use of time, your relationship toward foreigners and the weak, your attitude toward war and nationalism. You are a citizen of the Big Kingdom now (see Philippians 3:20) and, when you realize that, you will live very differently. If you are not ready to change, don't seek out God.

Once you have one sincere moment of Divine Union, you will want to spend your time on *the one thing necessary, which is to grow deeper and deeper in love every chance that you get.* Talk to someone who has had a near-death, or nearing-death, experience. In the end, they all agree: It's all about love. It's all about union, and all the rest of what they thought was important was mere window dressing.[8] "Saved" people are just people who learn that earlier than the rest of us. You can either discover the one thing necessary now or wait until later. You could be a lot happier and make a lot of other people happier if you would discover it now. "Martha, Martha, you worry about so many things, yet so few are needed; indeed, only one" (see Luke 10:42).

Gateway to Silence: We are one in Love.

Sabbath Meditation

Remember: **Mysticism: Inner Experience**

We must learn to think as Jesus thought. (Day 1)

A mystic is one who has moved from mere belief systems or belonging systems to actual inner experience. (Day 2)

It is we alone who desecrate God's one incarnate world by our inability to see truthfully, to see the depth of things, and then to show a reverence that comes quite naturally. (Day 3)

The goal of prayer and mysticism is Divine Union. (Day 4)

The morality of a mystic is a response to Divine Union. (Day 5)

Once you have one sincere moment of Divine Union, you will want to spend your time on *the one thing necessary, which is to grow deeper and deeper in love every chance that you get.* (Day 6)

Rest: **Moving Beyond Matter**

Look around you and notice your surroundings at this moment. Let your eyes fall on some object—perhaps a candle, tree, rock, or creature. Simply observe the object, without judging or labeling. Give your full attention, senses, and presence to this object.

Gradually let your gaze soften and take in the more-than-matter-ness that is also here. Deepen your awareness of God's presence within this thing and within you.

Rest in silence for several minutes (or continue with a longer time of contemplative prayer) and then turn your gaze to bless the rest of the room, landscape, and world in which you find yourself—one in Love.

For further study:

Things Hidden: Scripture as Spirituality
The Naked Now: Learning to See as the Mystics See
Franciscan Mysticism: I AM That Which I Am Seeking

THE PERENNIAL TRADITION

DAY I
Everywhere Visible and Revealed

The Perennial Tradition encompasses the following recurring themes in all of the world's religions and philosophies:

- ❖ There is a Divine Reality underneath and inherent in the world of things;
- ❖ There is in the human soul a natural capacity, similarity, and longing for this Divine Reality; and
- ❖ The final goal of existence is union with this Divine Reality.

The "perennial philosophy" or "perennial tradition" is a term that has come in and out of popularity in Western and religious history, but has never been dismissed by the Universal Church. I was trained in Catholic traditional theology, its Second Vatican reforms, and Franciscan alternative orthodoxy; these and the whole Judeo-Christian Tradition taught me to honor the visibility and revelation of God in all the world traditions. For me, the very proof that you have met the Christ is that you then see the Risen Christ *everywhere* else—in gardeners (see John 20:15), people walking on the road (see Luke 24:15), bystanders on the beach (see John 21:4), and, as the oldest Gospel puts it, "He showed himself under another form" (see Mark 16:12). *Christ is not a brand name; it is a universal name for the Divine*

Presence when it is recognized and encountered in the physical/material universe.
If you can *only* see and honor the Divine Presence in Jesus and stop there,
then the Risen Christ has not yet worked his transformative magic in your
mind and heart.

"For what can be known about God is perfectly plain, since God has
made it plain. Ever since God created the world, God's everlasting power and
deity—however invisible—have been *there for the mind to see in the things
God has made*" (italics mine; see Romans 1:19–20).[1] That is Paul's astounding statement of what will become the Perennial Tradition. This pattern of
Divine self-revelation has been available and offered to all sincere seekers,
from indigenous religions until now. It is what Owen Barfield (1898–1997)
called "original participation." How could it not be so?

Some early Fathers of the church, and the Second Vatican Council,
called this phenomenon the *ecclesia ab Abel*, the church that has existed
since the first human blood of Abel the Holy (see Matthew 23:35) "cried
out to God from the earth" (see Genesis 4:10). Even Hebrews says "He was
declared righteous" (see 11:4) simply because he devotedly entrusted his animal offerings to God, yet he was neither Jewish nor Christian, nor Hindu,
nor Moslem, nor Buddhist, nor anything organized. It is time to recalibrate
our understanding and honor God's wholeness, generosity, availability, and
universal efficiency.

Gateway to Silence: That all may be one

DAY 2

The Underground Stream

Simone Weil (1909–1943), the marvelous French philosopher, Christian
mystic, and political activist, stood on the edge of Christianity her whole
life, between Judaism and Christianity, wanting her very life to be a bridge.
She loved both traditions and couldn't choose either of them. She believed
that the trouble with Christianity was that it had made itself into a separate
religion instead of recognizing that the prophetic message of Jesus might just
be necessary for the reform and ongoing vitality of all religions. She did not
believe Christians were to be in competition with other religions but, rather,
our Christ was big enough to complement, and usually affirm, the deeper
stream of all healthy religion.

And to make that very point, to build her brilliant bridge, she never
accepted baptism and chose to live her whole life on the cusp of Judaism and
Christianity, while, in fact, radically following Jesus' teaching. She was a liv-

ing symbol of non-dual consciousness and reconciliation of non-opposites, and yet she was always humbly convinced that, if you were sincerely seeking the truth more than partisanship, you would easily "fall into the arms of Christ." The Christ she references is not a brand name, but a naming of How Reality Works.

Building on Simone Weil, I encourage you not to abandon your own mother tradition; that is where your deepest religious consciousness was first formed. You have to be surrendered to and accountable in one concrete place, exactly as the Dalai Lama and Mother Teresa (1910–1997) have also insisted. Otherwise your ego self is always the decider, and you operate as a loner. You must have a home base that holds you accountable for what you say you believe and a concrete community that daily reminds you that *you still do not know how to love.*

You have to go deep in one place. When you do, you fall into the underground stream that we all share. Simone knew that the Christ was a perfectly adequate name for the underground stream, but she also knew it had become a brand name that encouraged division instead of deep unity. So she lived her life "on the edge of the inside," which is always the prophetic position.

Gateway to Silence: That all may be one

DAY 3

Oneing

The divisions, dichotomies, and dualisms of the world can only be overcome by a *unitive consciousness* at every level: personal, relational, social, political, cultural, and in spirituality and religion in general. This is the unique and central job of healthy religion (*re-ligio* = to re-ligament!). A transformed people unite all within themselves, so they can then do the same in the world.

My favorite Christian mystic, Lady Julian of Norwich, used the Old English term "oneing" to describe what happens between God and the soul. As Julian put it, "By myself I am nothing at all, but in general, *I AM in the oneing of love.* For it is in this oneing that the life of all people exists."[2] She also says, "The love of God creates in us such a oneing that, when it is truly seen, no person can separate themselves from another person"[3] and "In the sight of God, all humans are oned, and one person is all people and all people are one person."[4]

This is the Perennial Tradition. Our job is not to discover it, but only to retrieve what has been continually discovered—and enjoyed—again and again, in the mystics and saints of all religions.

As Jesus put it in his great final prayer: "I pray that all may be one" (see John 17:21). We need to join him in that prayer, always and everywhere, or there is little hope for the world, and little chance that this Jewish Jesus, who praised both Samaritans and sinners, will ever be seen as any possible "Savior of the World" (see John 4:42).[5]

Gateway to Silence: That all may be one

Unity, Not Uniformity

Many teachers have made the central but oft-missed point that *unity is not the same as uniformity*. Unity, in fact, is the reconciliation of differences, and those *differences must be maintained—and yet also overcome, at a deeper level!* This is exactly as in the relationship between the Three Persons of the Trinity, by the way. You must actually distinguish things and separate them before you can spiritually unite them without losing their diversity—but almost always *at a cost to your own feelings of centrality and normality.* Spiritual unity is rooted in the essence of everything, whereas uniformity is invariably about accidentals and incidentals—like clothing and belief systems. If only we had made that simple clarification, so many of our problems—and over-emphasized, separate identities—could have been solved, freeing us to move to a much higher level of love and service. It is only the ego that idealizes uniformity, so that it can give itself the illusion of control, create artificial "normality," and exalt obedience and loyalty as higher values than pure and simple love.

Paul already made this principle of unity versus uniformity very clear in several of his letters. For example: "There is a variety of gifts, but it is always the same Spirit. There are all sorts of service to be done, but always to the same Lord, working in all sorts of different ways in different people. It is the same God working in all of them" (see 1 Corinthians 12:4–6). In his community at Ephesus, they were taught, "There is one Lord, one faith, one baptism, one God who is Father of all, over all, through all, and within all; and each of us has been given our own share of grace" (see Ephesians 4:5–7).[6]

His metaphor of the Body of Christ (see 1 Corinthians 12), with its references to feet, ears, eyes, and hands having different functions but overall unity, is a perfect transfer of his highly Trinitarian spirituality to the human dimension. We, like the Three Persons of God, must be held equally, both in our uniqueness and in our absolute unity, which is rarely achieved today.

Right now, we seem to have moved so far to the individualistic side that we have neither unity nor uniformity; we are not united at our spiritual core and, consequently, we each exaggerate our specialness. Only our Divine Identity allows both to be kept in perfect balance.

Gateway to Silence: That all may be one

DAY 5

Trinity: A Radical Love Union

The doctrine of the Trinity is finally the ultimate Christian source for understanding the principle of unity. Yes, God is "One," just as our Jewish ancestors taught us (see Deuteronomy 6:4), and yet the further, more subtle level is that this *oneness* is, in fact, the radical love union between *three* completely distinct "persons" of the Trinity. What is sometimes called the first philosophic problem of "the one and the many" is overcome in God's very nature. *In the beginning is the Relationship*, we might say, and this relationship is foundational and unconditional love. The three persons of the Trinity are not uniform—in fact, they are quite distinct, as symbolized by the three names—and yet are completely *oned* in total outpouring and perfect receiving, one toward the other, in One Eternal Flow of Life and Love. The only word that the first Christian theologians could think of to describe this was, in Greek, *perichoresis*, which in English we might translate as Circle Dance, Interbeing, or even the Divine Symbiosis.[7]

But, as far as we are concerned, it only gets better because humans are then created in this very "image and likeness" (see Genesis 1:26–27), as is all of reality. Did it ever strike you that the basic building block of the physical universe, the atom, which was largely invisible until the last century, consists of three particles, forever orbiting and circling around one another? Trinity is our universal template for the nature of reality. Destabilization of this essential core, in fact and literally, produces death, or the atom bomb.

Further, our word "person," now referring to an individual human being, was actually first used in Greek-based Trinitarian theology (*persona* = a stage mask or a "sounding through"), and then, later, applied also to us—with its meaning turned around 180 degrees! What was symbiotic life, a person drawing his or her identity *entirely in relationship*, now became a separate individual, a Descartes-like identity, wherein "my thinking makes me me!" The downside implications are staggering, because human persons, like the Trinity, are not autonomous beings, but are foundationally *soundings through* from a much Larger Life and Larger Love. This creates an actual metaphysical foundation for human holiness instead of just a behavioral one, because we as human persons are *constituted at our core by the same relationships of love as the Trinity,* in whose image we were created. This is surely what we mean by the soul. The endless, literally endless, implications of this metaphysical—and thus spiritual—truth will make a mystic out of anybody![8]

Gateway to Silence: That all may be one

DAY 6

A Prayer to Know Presence

My colleague and fellow faculty member of our Living School for Action and Contemplation, James Finley, offers a prayer for us to experience union with Divine Reality. Let me simply offer you this prayer without any commentary:

> May each of us be so fortunate as to be overtaken by God in the midst of little things. May we each be so blessed as to be finished off by God, swooping down from above or welling up from beneath, to extinguish the illusion of separateness that perpetuates our fears. May we, in having our illusory, separate self slain by God, be born into a new and true awareness of who we really are: one with God forever. May we continue on in this true awareness, seeing in each and every little thing we see, the fullness of God's presence in our lives. May we also be someone in whose presence others are better able to recognize God's presence in their lives, so that they, too, might know the freedom of the children of God.[9]

Gateway to Silence: That all may be one

DAY 7

Sabbath Meditation

Remember: **The Perennial Tradition**
There is a Divine Reality underneath and inherent in the world of things; there is in the human soul a natural capacity, similarity, and longing for this Divine Reality; and the final goal of existence is union with this Divine Reality. (Day 1)

You have to go deep in one place. When you do, you fall into the underground stream that we all share. (Day 2)

"By myself I am nothing at all, but in general, *I AM in the oneing of love.* For it is in this oneing that the life of all people exists." —Julian of Norwich (Day 3)

Unity is not the same as uniformity. Unity is the reconciliation of differences, and those differences must be maintained—and yet also overcome! (Day 4)

Yes, God is "One," and yet the further, more subtle level is that this *oneness* is, in fact, the radical love relationship between *three* completely distinct "persons" of the Trinity. (Day 5)

"May we, in having our illusory, separate self slain by God, be born into a new and true awareness of who we really are: one with God forever." —James Finley (Day 6)

Rest: **Centering Prayer**

Contemplative prayer can be traced through the Desert Fathers and Mothers, Pseudo-Dionysius, early Christian and Benedictine monasticism, some early Franciscans like St. Bonaventure, the unknown author of the *The Cloud of Unknowing*, and the Carmelites (Br. Lawrence of the Resurrection, SS. John of the Cross and Teresa of Ávila), but then was largely lost everywhere (Jean-Pierre de Caussade, SJ, being one clear exception). After the dualistic fights of the sixteenth century, it was largely forgotten, with almost no teachers emerging, even in the contemplative Orders. If you learned it, it was by the Holy Spirit, or on your own—by study of the sources above!

In the 1970s, Trappist monks Basil Pennington, Thomas Keating, and William Meninger reintroduced Christians to contemplation through the simple practice of Centering Prayer. Centering Prayer is one good way to draw us into the silence that surrounds and holds us, but of which we are too often unaware. It helps us sink into the wordless reality of who God is and who we ourselves are.

1. Sit comfortably with your eyes closed, breathing naturally, relaxing deeply. Become aware of your love and desire for God in this moment.
2. Choose a word or phrase that expresses your intention to be open to God's presence (perhaps this week's Gateway to Silence—*That all may be one*—or simply *Be one*).
3. Hold the word gently, without speaking, repeating it slowly in your mind.
4. Whenever you become aware of anything (thoughts, feelings, sensations), simply return to the word, which symbolizes your intention.

5. Gradually let the word fall away as you slip into silence. Rest in silence.

6. Continue in silence as long as you wish.

Two periods of twenty minutes each day are recommended for Centering Prayer.[10]

For further study:

"The Perennial Tradition," *Oneing*, Vol. 1 No. 1

WEEK 5:

LEVELS OF SPIRITUAL DEVELOPMENT (PART ONE)

DAY I
Levels of Growth

So many of our problems can be resolved if we understand that people are at different levels and stages of growth. The importance of levels of development has come to be recognized by teachers as diverse as Teresa of Ávila, John of the Cross, Jean Piaget, Lawrence Kohlberg, Abraham Maslow, James Fowler, Clare Graves, Ken Wilber, and Bill Plotkin. Some speak of six levels, some eight, and some ten, but in general they move in a very similar direction and share many commonalities about what we mean by human maturation and growth.

Thomas Aquinas (1225–1274) said, "Whatever is received is received according to the manner of the receiver."[1] As a preacher and teacher, I have found that whatever I teach will be heard on many different levels, according to the inner psychological and spiritual maturity of the listener. It is rather obvious once you say it. Jesus was teaching the same in his parable of the four different kinds of soil that received the seed (see Matthew 13:4–9).

My own attempt to correlate the various schemas of development matches to some extent what some call Spiral Dynamics or Integral Theory, both of which conclude that there are approximately nine levels or stages. I will specifically be applying this, over the next two weeks, to the work of spiritual direction. All of these schemas overlap somewhat, so don't get too rigid about interpretation. The trajectory is what is most important.

And remember that this is merely a teaching tool. In real life, the spiritual journey is much more subtle, personal, and complex. Progress through the stages is not usually linear or completely chronological. Also, there is an inherent danger in teaching about *levels* of growth as the ego will try to use this information to place itself at a higher level than it is! So I invite you to read these meditations with openness, humble honesty, and a desire for the wholeness only God can give.[2]

Gateway to Silence: Open me to wholeness.

DAY 2
Similarities

In the remarkable overlap and agreement among the various schemas of development, psychology and spirituality come together beautifully to show us that growth is going somewhere. The trajectory is toward union: union with God/Reality, with the self (mind, heart, and body), with others, and with the cosmos. All seem to agree that the lower (or beginning) levels are dualistic, while the higher (or perhaps I should say "deeper") levels are non-dual and unitive. The early stages are egocentric, the middle stages are sociocentric, and the later ones are cosmocentric.

On a good day, no matter your stage of development, the most you can stretch yourself to understand is people who are one step beyond yourself. It shows how narcissistic we all are, I am afraid. People at the more mature levels may look ridiculous, wrong, heretical, or even dangerous to people at earlier levels. Now you can see why the Jewish prophets, Jesus, Gandhi, and Martin Luther King, Jr., were killed. On the other hand, people at the higher, non-dual levels have the breadth and the depth to understand, to accept, and to forgive people at the earlier or "lower" levels. Their honesty allows them to see that they were once there themselves, and to recognize how long it takes and how hard it is to grow up.

The way you move from stage to stage is basically by some form of wounding, failure, or darkness. St. John of the Cross (1542–1591) called these experiences "dark nights of the soul." The old system that worked for a while has to stop working for you, and it will, and you will suffer. All seem to agree that you have to go through a period of unknowing (sounds like faith to me) to know at a higher and more mature level. You have to go through a period of confusion and doubt, struggling with your shadow, dealing with your own conflicts and contradictions. Unfortunately, Western religions have given their people little good teaching on how to walk in darkness, which is the very essence of biblical faith. Only the mystics and true prophets are honest about what is involved.

If you do not have someone to guide you, to teach you, to hold onto you during the times of not knowing, not feeling, not understanding, you will normally stay at your present level of growth. That guiding and holding are the work of a good spiritual director or teacher, or even an effective homily. Now you perhaps see why Jesus praised faith even more than love. Love is the goal, but faith is the laborious journey toward it.[3] In my experience, people can and will advance if they have a judicious combination of both safety and necessary conflict. Traditionalism, in many senses, usually provides the safety; progressive thinking allows and encourages the necessary conflicts. Most of us place ourselves on one side or the other, and thus do not grow very much.

Gateway to Silence: Open me to wholeness.

DAY 3
Stage One:
My Body and My Self-Image Are Who I Am

At the first stage, one tends to be totally identified with one's body and body image: "I am my body," the infant believes. Body is not yet connected in any enlightened way to heart or mind. Each part—body, heart, and mind—is limited or even dangerous if it's largely disconnected from the other two. Integration is opening all three spaces so that they can enlighten, inform, and balance each other.

Think of little children. They poop and pee and cuddle and eat without shame or defense. They are their bodies and, in a way, that's what makes them so dear, because they haven't made it complex yet by thinking too much. They run into the room naked with no embarrassment whatsoever. We teach them shame by our shocked reaction.

At the first stage, *my body, its image, and the pleasuring and protecting of it* are largely who I am. Many people in a secular, non-wisdom culture like ours may never move past Stage One. People at this level tend to be preoccupied with the pleasure, security, safety, and defense of their material state. And that extends to their morality: If it makes me feel secure, it is moral. Life is largely about protecting myself. (This is seen in the endless need for war and guns, but little need for education, culture, the arts, and spirituality.) Stage One people are mostly dualistic, either/or thinkers, and frankly represent a rather sizable minority of humans. Their morality largely has to do with maintaining their group, and regarding their group as superior.

I believe life, God, and grace nudge most people at least to the next stage. But first they have to allow some of their security and pleasure absolutes to be taken away.[4]

Gateway to Silence: Open me to wholeness.

DAY 4

Stage Two:
My External Behavior Is Who I Am

Most of human history up to now has been at Stage Two and, frankly, much of Jesus' teaching is aimed at this level because it is all about purity codes, debt codes, dogmas, and external rituals—because that was the stage of most of his listeners. At Stage Two, your concern is *to look good on the outside*. Your concern with pleasing the neighborhood, the village, your religion, or your kind of folks becomes such a way of life that you get very practiced at hiding or disguising any contrary evidence. That's why it is so dangerous.

In Stage Two, the shadow self—your denied motives, your real self—is born, but it is hidden, even from you. You have to start pretending that you *are* what looks good to your group and your religion. Your whole identity becomes defending your external behavior as more moral than other people, and defending your family, your community, your race, your church or temple or mosque, and your nation as superior to others.

This is tribal thinking. It is a necessary stage, however, so that you can feel like you are Chosen, are significant, or have dignity. It gives you a strong sense of your identity and boundaries, which serves you well as a child. But many people remain trapped here, in a worldview of win/lose and good guys/ bad guys. Far right-wing thinking—the false conservative, in any country and in any religion—largely proceeds from Stages One or Two.

Eventually, your own external behavior or group performance will disappoint you and show itself to be phony or self-serving. You will begin to see that you yourself, or some people in your group, are, in fact, unkind, dishonest, or violent. That is the beginning of integrating the negative, a necessary "shadowboxing." If you are incapable of such appropriate critical thinking, you will not go through the darkness, the necessary deeper faith journey that will move you on to Stage Three.[5]

Gateway to Silence: Open me to wholeness.

DAY 5
Stage Three:
My Personal Thoughts and Feelings Are Who I Am

Thank God, many people are nudged by life and by basic common sense and honesty to the bare beginnings of critical thinking. People at Stage Three believe, "My own thoughts and my own feelings are who I am." But we do not yet see that most of our thoughts are self-referentially shaped to our own advantage and reflections of our preferences. Our emotions are usually "all about me." We think things like, "I have read a few books; I can quote some authors; I have become a bit more educated." But we do not really see the Big Picture yet. We are still trapped at an egocentric level without knowing it. At this point, education is usually a substitute for actual transformation. Beware of college students, who are invariably at Stage Three, while thinking they are at Stage Six or Seven! Perhaps you know that sophomore means "wise fool."

If Stage Two is more common among conservatives, Stage Three is more common among liberals. Stage Two creates groups; Stage Three creates individuals, and thus it is very hard for Stage Three people to really work together for long. These individuals cannot die to themselves enough to actually seek the common good; this requires a very real death to the ego self, which most are not yet ready to endure.

Most educated Americans and Europeans are stalled at Stage Three. (I can think of many Democrats, progressive Protestants, and Second Vatican Catholics who are at this level.) They are good people; they are easy to make friends with. They are dialogical and conversational. But do not ask them to go very far beyond their own comfort zone or their own egocentricity.[6] It is probably what we once meant by the *bourgeois* mentality; they know and have just enough to be dangerous and sure of themselves, but are not wise or really compassionate.

Gateway to Silence: Open me to wholeness.

DAY 6
The Liminal Space between Stage Three and Stage Four

A death—a period of darkness and not-knowing—is required between every stage, but an even larger letting go is necessary to move from Stage Three to Stage Four. This is probably why most Western cultures are at Stage Three. Without *great love* (and I mean *great* love of someone beyond the self) and *great suffering*, where there is a major defeat, major humiliation, major shock to the ego self, very few people move to Stage Four. This is the necessary dying that all spiritual teachers invariably talk about. As Jesus puts it, "Unless the grain of wheat dies, it remains just a grain of wheat. But if it dies, it will bear much fruit" (see John 12:24). If you do not surrender to such a minor, but very significant, de-centering of the self, there is little chance you can be prepared for later suffering or actual death.

Historically, classic initiation rites were programmed to move people to *at least an initial experience* of Stage Four. If you can get to Stage Four, normally growth will continue to happen from there, because now you know that dying to self is central and necessary. You have begun to learn the art of letting go. You have learned that you do not need to be certain every step of the way. The meaning of faith, of walking in darkness and trust, is slowly becoming clear for you. You learn a certain tolerance for ambiguity and paradox in the movement from Stage Three to Stage Four. But, to be honest, many backslide from Stage Four when they realize the price they must pay (1960s hippies, broad-minded but arrogant liberals, rigid Evangelicals, etc.). They are just too comfortable in their present state, and there is too much to let go. This is the first minor death of the ego, and they do not yet understand death as expansion instead of diminishment.[7]

Gateway to Silence: Open me to wholeness.

DAY 7

Sabbath Meditation

Remember: **Levels of Spiritual Development (Part One)**

So many of our problems can be resolved if we understand that people are at different levels and stages of growth. (Day 1)

Growth is going somewhere. The trajectory is toward union: union with God/Reality, with the self (mind, heart, and body), with others, and with the cosmos. (Day 2)

Stage One: My body and my self-image are who I am. (Day 3)

Stage Two: My external behavior is who I am. (Day 4)

Stage Three: My personal thoughts and feelings are who I am. (Day 5)

Without *great love* (and I mean *great* love of someone beyond the self) and *great suffering*, where there is a major defeat, major humiliation, major shock to the ego self, very few people move to Stage Four. (Day 6)

Rest: **Ecstatic Dance**

Choose a favorite or new piece of music—classical, world, contemporary; anything that calls you to move!—and find a place in which you can listen and move uninhibitedly, barefooted if possible.

Allow your body to lead, following the invitation of the music. Let your mind take a back seat and tune in to the sensations of each part of your body. Feel your feet connect with the ground. Let limbs and joints turn and bend as they will. Swing and sway your head, shoulders, hips. Sink deep into your body, remembering what it is to be a human animal.

Dance until you are pleasantly tired and then gradually slow your movements, perhaps to another musical tempo. Continue moving in smaller, gentler ways: breathe deeply, stretch your arms and legs, roll your head. Come to a seated position and rest in stillness.

For further study:

The Art of Letting Go: Living the Wisdom of Saint Francis
Where You Are Is Where I'll Meet You
The Naked Now: Learning to See as the Mystics See

LEVELS OF SPIRITUAL DEVELOPMENT (PART TWO)

DAY I

Stage Four:
My *Deeper* Intuitions and Felt Knowledge in My Body Are Who I Am

If you can stay in the liminal space between Stage Three and Stage Four; if you can suffer the shock, humiliation, and necessary failure of your game falling apart without regressing to earlier, more dualistic thinking, you will ideally move to Stage Four.

In Stage Four, your deeper intuitions and the felt knowledge in your body are who you are. People who have been trained to keep the heart and head spaces open and to live grounded inside their own bodies and feel their real feelings are able to pass to Stage Four because they have developed *the capacity for presence*—presence to what actually *is*! You suffer through to Stage Four; you do not get there logically. At this stage, you begin to "wake up," as opposed to just grow up.

For some, this is such a breakthrough—so enriching, grounding, and self-validating, after wallowing around in ego and confusion for so many years—that it feels like enlightenment itself. It's easy to become stymied here and think it's the whole spiritual goal. People at Stage Four have "depth" compared to all these hopeless others around them! *This can lead to isolated individualism, self-absorption, and substitution of inner work for any honest encounter with otherness or with the Other.* In such a state, there is little real social conscience (beyond verbal political correctness) and usually a lack of compassion or active concern for what is happening on this earth. This kind of spirituality is all about *my* enlightenment and *my* superiority. The church itself was often content to get people to this point. They believed they were deep and saved because they had decided they wanted to "go to heaven" (which is still well-disguised self-interest!).

But if you are authentically present at Stage Four, you begin to see your shadow self in sometimes-humiliating ways. Without humility, you will slip back to Stage Three; many do. You'll see your phony motivation: You are not as holy as you think you are; you and your actions are largely preoccupied with your own self-image; you think of yourself as moral, aware, and enlightened. Politeness and political correctness pass for actual love. Ken Wilber calls it "Boomeritis" since it is so true of a certain age-group in America and Europe.

When you face the fact that you are not actually all that enlightened, moral, or holy, that you can't project evil onto other religions, races, classes, political parties, or genders, your struggle and humiliation can lead you to real non-dual thinking. As you grow, you understand that *you* are the problem. You are, in fact, petty, needy, self-absorbed, or whatever it might be. Other people are not your real problem—which you totally believe in the earlier stages.

If you are unwilling to do some shadow work, to wrestle with the shadow and see it in all of its humiliating truthfulness, you will not go to Stage Five.[1]
Gateway to Silence: Open me to wholeness.

DAY 2
Stage Five:
My Shadow Self Is Who I Am

At Stage Five, I become overwhelmed by my weakness, insincerity, phoniness, sinfulness, or whatever you want to call it. It is, I am afraid, a necessary hitting-bottom. This is not an easy time, and thus most avoid it, deny it, or, most commonly today, try to entertain their way out of it by endless distractions and avoidance techniques. If we face it head-on, this is what St. John of the Cross called "the Night of the Senses," but there is little training or understanding of this stage in our consumer and materialistic culture. That is probably why so much of the country has become addictive in one sense or another. At this stage, you meet yourself in your raw, unvarnished, uncivilized state, and by God's grace you start dealing very realistically with your own shadow self, your phoniness, mixed motives, and actual unloving-ness. Now you need some good and mature friends, spiritual directors, or support groups.

As a young man, I thought I had become a Franciscan and a priest to teach and talk about love; that I had left everything to love God and neighbor. But by my forties and fifties, I had to be honest and say, "Richard, have you ever really loved anybody more than yourself? Is there anybody in particular for whom you would die?" My celibacy was based on the utterly false premise that if I did not love anybody in particular, I would automati-cally love God more. I realized that that was not at all true. All I did was love myself more, but in a very well-disguised form. Much of that middle period of my life I spent shadowboxing, seeing my own inability to believe and to practice the very things I was teaching to others. And this continues!

The work of Stage Five can go on for quite a long time, and if you do not have someone loving you during that period, believing in you, holding on to you—if you do not meet the unconditional love of God, if you do not encounter the radical sense of grace that touches your unconscious level—the spiritual journey will not continue. You have to experience God's grace as unearned favor, unearned gratuity now, or you will surely regress.

In Stage Five, more than any other stage, you learn to live with con-tradiction and ambiguity. This is true non-dual, or unitive, thinking. Stage Five allows you to find God in what St. John of the Cross calls "luminous darkness." It is a real darkness, but somehow, inside of the darkness, you find light—a much truer, kinder, and softer light. Mostly, you learn patience and surrender.[2]

Gateway to Silence: Open me to wholeness.

DAY 3
Stage Six:
I Am Empty and Powerless

Alcoholics Anonymous would call Stage Six the First Step! At Stage Six, you realize: I am empty and powerless. Almost any attempt to save yourself by any superior behavior, technique, belonging system, morality, role, strong ideological belief, or religious devotion will not work. It will actually lead to regression. What the saints and mystics say is that some event, struggle, relationship, or suffering in your life has to lead you to the edge of your own resources. There has to be something that you, by yourself, cannot understand, fix, control, change, or even begin to address. It is the raw experience of "I cannot do this." *All you can do at this point is wait and ask and trust.*

This is surely what the Nicene Creed means when it says that "Jesus descended into hell." He went the full distance, he hit the bottom, he learned how to survive at the bottom—which is precisely resurrection, but it takes you a while to recognize such new freedom.

This is where you learn real patience, compassion, and forgiveness. I don't know how else you learn to forgive other people until you see—seventy times seven—your own brokenness, your own incapacity to love, and, in this stage, your inability to do anything about it except throw yourself into the arms of mercy and love (see Luke 7:47).

This is the darkness of faith, and now you can trust that this darkness is a much better teacher than supposed certainty or rightness. God is about to become very real. Some even call this stage God's Waiting Room![3]

Gateway to Silence: Open me to wholeness.

DAY 4
Stage Seven:
I Am Much More Than Who I Thought I Was

When you finally accept your own powerlessness, you learn to plug into a different outlet and draw upon a Deeper Source. This is conversion. This is radical transformation. It is like an identity transplant. The Apostle Paul describes his own conversion in this way: "I live no longer, not I, but I live in Christ, and Christ lives in me" (see Galatians 2:20). You experience a much larger sense of self, and it is not all about "you" anymore!

At Stage Seven, you have a qualitatively different sense of yourself. You might feel that "I am so much more than I thought I was!" *The False Self has died in a significant way and the True Self is starting to take over.* But, because you are not yet fully at home here, this stage will, first of all, feel like a void, an emptiness, but hopefully an okay emptiness. You begin to act for the sake of the action itself because it is true, because it is good, because it is beautiful, and not because it is popular or even because it works! There is no felt consolation most of the time, and there is lessening social reward. Yet there is great peace. You are being weaned of your reliance upon your feeling world, which means very little at this point. Because you are living in the Larger Self, all is okay. You know Another is now holding you. You do not need to hold yourself because, on some level, you know you are being held. You are at the heart of faith and, in a certain sense, *true spirituality* only begins at this point! (Most of Jesus' teaching proceeds from this level or higher, which is why much of the church has not been ready for Jesus.)[4]

Gateway to Silence: Open me to wholeness.

Stage Eight:
"I and the Father Are One" (see John 10:30)

Eventually, you are led by grace into the non-dual state ("not totally one, but not two either!"). I do not know anyone that is in conscious Stage Eight a full twenty-four hours a day. To describe this stage, you probably cannot get much better than John's Gospel (see 14:17), where he says, "Then you will know that he is with you, he is in you!" This is full unitive consciousness, where you can live in conscious, loving communion and trust with yourself, with God, and with everyone and everything else. God is no longer out there or over there or separate from you. Henceforward, as St. Teresa of Ávila (1515–1582) says, "You find God in yourself, and you find yourself in God." This is largely an inner experience, an inner knowing. This is truly *following* Christ in his very identity and not just in occasional behavior; Christ, who is an impossible admixture of humanity and divinity, as you are too. You know that you *are* the Body of Christ and that your source is Divine, while you are still quite ordinary and human. Only grace can make this trust possible.

You see that every other aspect of your persona—your roles, your titles, your functions, even your bodily self—is a passing form, a passing ego-possession. At this point, you know your body is not fully you. You have found your soul, your True Self, who you are "hidden with Christ in God" (see Colossians 3:3), who you are before you did anything right or anything wrong. Frankly, you have discovered your soul, which is that part of you that already knows, already loves, is already in union with and can quite naturally say "yes" to God.

When you learn how to trust this Divine Indwelling (and that's what it is—it's God in you doing the God-thing through you), when you learn how to draw from that place, you can find happiness anywhere, at any hour of any day. You can "pray always." You also realize it is this for which you were created. Heaven is not later. Heaven and salvation are whenever you live in conscious union with God and everything else too—even the negative and unjust and broken parts.[5]

Gateway to Silence: Open me to wholeness.

Stage Nine:
I Am Who I Am

You did not expect this, did you? But this is the final, resurrection stage of our incarnational religion. The Divine Incarnation that began in creation and was personified in Jesus, now continues in your unique personality and life. Wow!

The realizations of Stage Nine are what we mean by the full "freedom of the children of God" (see Romans 8:21, Galatians 5:1). At Stage Nine, *I am who I am.* I have nothing to prove or to project to make you think I am anything more than who I am. Stage Nine is the most radical possible critique of false religion. It sees religion as the fingers that merely point to the moon—now, in fact, I am sitting on the moon! So, thank you, fingers, it was great being a Holy Catholic finger for so many years, but I really don't need to prove that the Catholic Church is the only way to God, because I know better now. I do not need to deplete the resources of the earth and the world to protect the USA, because it is only one small part of God's kingdom.

There is no need at Stage Nine to appear to be anything other than who you really are. At Stage Nine you are fully non-dual, fully detached from self-image, and are living in God's full image of you—which includes and loves both the good and the bad parts of you (see Matthew 22:10). Remember, *to experience God is mostly to let God fully experience you, so that you can "know as fully as you are known"* (see 1 Corinthians 13:12). Think about that for a long time, please. This is total non-duality. You are living in God's gaze: you are who you are in God's eyes; nothing more and nothing less. This is the serenity and the freedom of the saints.

This stage is the goal, yet there is no non-stop flight to get here; you must in some way traverse all eight stages, and you cannot skip one of them! *Don't try to engineer this journey; you are being led, and God will make sure you get what you need, when you need it.* You will only fully know that for yourself at this last stage!

Maybe this is what Jesus meant when he said that "those who become like little children will enter the Kingdom of heaven" (see Matthew 18:3). At this final stage, you return to that early little child that you once were—running naked into the room of life. *I am who I am who I am.* God has accepted me in that naked being, and I can happily give myself back to God exactly as I am. I am ready for death, because I have done it now many times, and it has only led me into larger worlds.[6]

Gateway to Silence: Open me to wholeness.

DAY 7

Sabbath Meditation

Remember: **Levels of Spiritual Development (Part Two)**

Stage Four: My deeper intuitions and felt knowledge in my body are who I am. (Day 1)

Stage Five: My shadow self is who I am. (Day 2)

Stage Six: I am empty and powerless. (Day 3)

Stage Seven: I am much more than who I thought I was. (Day 4)

Stage Eight: "I and the Father are One" (see John 10:30). (Day 5)

Stage Nine: I am who I am. (Day 6)

Rest: **Yahweh Prayer**

A rabbi friend taught this prayer to me many years ago. The Jews did not speak God's name, but breathed it: inhale—*Yah*; exhale—*weh*. God's name was the first and last word to pass their lips. By your very breathing, you are praying and participating in God's grace. You are who you are—living God's presence—in the simplicity and persistence of breath.

Breathe the syllables with open mouth and lips, relaxed tongue:

Inhale—*Yah*

Exhale—*weh*

For further study:

Where You Are Is Where I'll Meet You
The Art of Letting Go: Living the Wisdom of Saint Francis

IN THE BEGINNING

DAY I
"The First Idea in the Mind of God" Is to Materialize

"God has let us in on a mystery: the mystery of God's purpose, the hidden plan God so kindly made from the very beginning in Christ" (see Ephesians 1:9–10). Whenever Paul says "in Christ," he is not talking about Jesus of Nazareth. He's talking about when matter and spirit come together, reveal, and expose one another. Jesus is the concrete personification in time of what has always been true, which is the *Christ* Mystery, or the "anointing" of physical matter with eternal purpose. This hidden plan will become apparent when time has run its course, when we can finally see that "there is only Christ, he is everything and he is in everything" (see Colossians 3:11). Most of us have missed this wonderful news because we have never been told to pay attention to it.

What we call "salvation" is happening to the whole of creation and not just to humans (see Revelation 21:1). Our inability to recognize and appreciate this is a central example of our dualistic thinking and even our narcissism. Why would God's great plan just be about us? The irony, of course, is that we are—by far—the most destructive species on the planet, and refuse to take our proper place in the entire family of things."

The very fact that Christians have fought the notion of evolution shows we did not, even minimally, understand the Cosmic Christ. We should have been the first to recognize and honor evolution. The glory, patience, and humility of God is that *God creates things that continue to create* themselves—from the inner dynamism God has planted within them. Many of us would call this inner creative dynamism the Holy Spirit which "hovers over the initial chaos" (see Genesis 1:2) and then stands at the end of history with a constant and beckoning "Come!" (see Revelation 22:17). These two verses are the two bookends of the Bible.[1] Once God has agreed to "become flesh," then grace is inherent to the material world from the beginning, and not a rare, later additive.

Gateway to Silence: God is all-in-all.

DAY 2

The Eternal Christ

Because the idea that Christ is rather different from Jesus seems so revolutionary and even mind-blowing for many Christians, let me point out that it is really founded and grounded in Scripture. Christ is not Jesus' last name. The classic texts that speak of the eternal Christ, not merely Jesus of Nazareth, include the entirely of John's Gospel, which is summed up in the prologue (see 1:1–18). These verses might provide the single best lens for understanding and deeply appreciating the whole Gospel.

Frankly, many people either dislike or give up on the prologue because of the seemingly cosmic and universal statements, as well as the demanding, dogmatic declarations that he (Jesus? Or is it the Christ speaking?) makes throughout the text. People also question why the vast majority of these statements are not found in Matthew, Mark, or Luke. Is this a different lens? The answer is, "Yes, exactly." This is a cosmic, archetypal speaker of universal truth. In fact, he is speaking in much of the text from "inside the Trinity" and inviting us to unitive, highly symbolic, and mystical knowledge of God. This is no longer Jesus within history, but Christ above and beyond history, calling us to a universal truth about the nature of God and our union with God.

This universal truth is followed up most clearly in five texts (which always appear in the first chapter in each case): see Ephesians 1:3–14, Colossians 1:15–20, Hebrews 1:1–3, 1 John 1:1–4, and Revelation 1:4–8. This cosmic Christology is increasingly seen as a parallel and historic fulfillment of the person of Jesus. It took us two thousand years to get over the scandal of the Word becoming flesh in one man, and finally we appear to be ready for that truth to *universalize*. Most Christians up to now loved Jesus, but very few were taught how to recognize and therefore love the Christ.

Gateway to Silence: God is all-in-all.

The Christ Mystery

"[Christ] is the image of the invisible God, the firstborn of all creation. For in him were created all things in heaven and on earth.... All things were created through him and for him" (see Colossians 1:15–16). Jesus is the microcosm of the macrocosm, and his role is to hold together matter and spirit inside of one concrete person—who looks totally human, just like us. Jesus of Nazareth is saying, as it were, "Matter and spirit *have* always been one. But you can't believe this, so I'm going to ask you to see it, struggle with it, and fall in love with it in me. And then you can extrapolate from Jesus, to Christ, to everything else—and perhaps resolve the dilemma in yourself first of all!" When you understand this, you have the full Jesus-Christ Mystery and can live happily inside the one "Body of Christ." If you still live in a world where matter is over here and Spirit is over there, you're not yet a Christian. That's not a moral judgment about you—it's simply a true statement that you haven't yet recognized or allowed the Great Transformation.

"He holds all things together in unity.... God wanted all fullness to dwell in him. Through him everything is reconciled, everything in heaven and everything on earth" (see Colossians 1:17–20). The Christian God is not just in matter and not just Spirit—but precisely when the two operate as one. In that sense, most Christians are not yet Christian; they just "believe there is a God" and God's name is Jesus. Very few were told about the cosmic "Christ. It seems it took us the first two thousand years just to deal with the shock of Jesus, and now the expanding universe itself is forcing us to recognize a God-figure who is at least larger than what God created." It is probably true that we are still in "early Christianity."[2]

Gateway to Silence: God is all-in-all.

First Fruits

The First Incarnation, the materialization of the Mystery, began approximately 14.5 billion years ago with what we now call "The Big Bang." Romans 8, which might be the most inspired of Paul's writings, states: "The whole of creation is eagerly awaiting the full revelation of its *sonship*" (see Romans 8:19). He is expanding his belief in Jesus as the Son of God. He is telling us that it's not just humans who are sons and daughters of God. As Paul sees it, all of creation is "the Son of God," or the Christ. When you think of it, what else could it be?

Paul says, "From the beginning until now, the entire creation has been groaning in one great act of giving birth" (see Romans 8:22). This is evolution itself. We humans do have the advantage of consciousness, but that doesn't mean that everything else doesn't also share in some rudimentary forms of consciousness. Maybe it's merely a quantitative difference but not a qualitative or ontological difference?

The little dog or cat is obviously a creature of God. We hope she somehow knows it. She's fully resting in it right now, without any resistance to her identity or dignity. Humans alone doubt this. Our role is to consciously recognize and honor the full dignity and sacrality of all of creation, starting with ourselves. We humans have a wonderful role in praising everything, and praising God for everything. *We are official praisers!* Paul speaks of "possessing the first fruits of the Spirit, as we too groan inwardly for our own bodies to be set free" (see Romans 8:23). Note "first fruits," which seems to clearly imply that we are not the one and only fruit! It also implies a costly process of personal realization, a *groaning inwardly*, as he puts it. Is all suffering perhaps this costly process?

What we see especially in Romans 8 is that matter is not *evil*, it is merely *unliberated*, and our job is to join in the liberation of all things toward their full dignity as children of God. We are thus "co-operators with God" (see Romans 8:28), joining in the "repairing of the world," or *tikkun olam*, as the Jewish people beautifully put it.[3]

Gateway to Silence: God is all-in-all.

The Great Chain of Being

Of Christ's fullness, we all have a share. (See John 1:16, Colossians 2:9–10.) The medieval metaphor of the Great Chain of Being was the philosophical/ theological attempt to speak of the circle of life, the interconnectedness of all things on the level of pure "Being." If God is Being Itself (*Deus est Ens*), then the Great Chain became a way of teaching and preserving the inherent dignity of all things that participate in that Divine Being in various ways. It was not intended to teach hierarchy as much as *inherent sacrality, continuity, and communality.* This was also expressed in the biblical *pleroma* or fullness of God that dwells in Christ (see Genesis 2:1, Ephesians 1:23).

Such a graphic metaphor held all things together in an *enchanted universe.*

To stop recognizing the "image and likeness" (see Genesis 1:26) in any one link of the chain was to allow the entire coherence to fall apart and become a *disenchanted universe*. If we could not see the sacred in nature and creatures, we soon would not see it in ourselves and, finally, we would not be able to see it at all (as is the case with modern atheism and negative secularism). The Great Chain of Being resolved the early philosophical problem of "the one and the many" to allow us to live coherently inside of one shared universe of meaning. ("Uni-verse" means "to turn around one thing.") This is the way it was seen:

Link 1   The firmament/Earth/minerals within the Earth
Link 2   The waters upon the Earth (snow, ice, water, steam, mist)
Link 3   The plants, trees, flowers, and foods that grow upon the Earth
Link 4   The living animals on the Earth, in the skies, and in the waters
Link 5   The human species, capable of reflecting on all the other links
Link 6   The world of angels and the perfect communion of those who have passed over
Link 7   The Divine Mystery Itself [4]

Gateway to Silence: God is all-in-all.

DAY 6

Creation Is the First Bible

What can be known about God is perfectly plain, since God has made it plain. Ever since God created the world, God's everlasting power and divinity, however invisible, have been there for the mind to see in the things that God has made. (See Romans 1:19–20.)

Every day, we are given a natural way to reconnect with God that doesn't depend on education. It doesn't depend on getting a degree in philosophy or theology, or living in a particular period of history, or believing in a specific religion. It depends on *really* being present to what is right in front of us. As Paul says, "God has made it plain."

The missing element for many of us in the developed world has been contemplation, which allows us to *see* things in their wholeness and with respect (*re-spect* = to see a second time). Without this, I don't think religion achieves a deep level of authenticity—or joy! Many people don't seem to be highly transformed and therefore seem unhappy. They are stuck in a dualistic belief system that doesn't synthesize reality very well; it just picks fights. But if they were to spend time in nature, alone like Jesus or the hermits or the Desert Fathers and Mothers, they would know many of the same things religion has been trying to teach, but they would know them on a cellular level, on a physical and energetic level. That kind of knowing does not contradict the rational; it's much more holistic and heartfelt. In our Living School, we call this a "contemplative epistemology." This is really the change that changes everything—including people.

This holistic way of knowing and seeing rearranges one's worldview at a level that actually cannot be contradicted by mere logical words or passing fads. Instead of fostering this wonderful transformation, most Western religion has been simply transmitting information, and then arguing about it. What a waste of time. There is nothing that is *not* spiritual for those who have learned how to see. Pray for the grace to see things in their wholeness and not just in their parts, for the grace to reverence things before using them, dismissing them, or even trying to explain them.[5]

Gateway to Silence: God is all-in-all.

DAY 7
SABBATH MEDITATION

Remember: **In the Beginning**

Salvation is happening to the whole of creation. (Day 1)

It took us two thousand years to get over the scandal of the Word becoming flesh in one man, and finally we appear to be ready for that truth to *universalize.* (Day 2)

Jesus is the microcosm of the macrocosm, and his role is to hold together matter and spirit inside of one concrete person. (Day 3)

We are thus "co-operators with God" (see Romans 8:28), joining in the "repairing of the world." (Day 4)

If we could not see the sacred in nature and creatures, we soon could not see it in ourselves and, finally, we would not be able to see it at all. (Day 5)

There is nothing that is *not* spiritual for those who have learned how to see. (Day 6)

Rest: **Wilderness Wandering**

Go to a place in nature where you can walk freely and alone, ideally some place where human impact is minimal—a forest, canyon, prairie, bog, mountain. Tell someone where you will be and how long you expect to be there. Take adequate water and clothing for the conditions.

Begin your wandering by finding or creating a conscious threshold (perhaps an arched branch overhead or a narrow passage between rocks). Here offer a voiced prayer of your intention and desire for this time. Step across the threshold quite deliberately and, on this side of your sacred boundary, speak no words, but only *expect*!

Let the land, plants, and creatures lead your feet and eyes. Let yourself be drawn, rather than walking with a destination or purpose in mind. If you are called to a particular place or thing, stop and be still, letting yourself be known and know, through silent communion with the Other. Before you leave, offer some gesture or token of gratitude for the gift the wild has given you.

When it is time to return to the human world, find again your threshold and cross over—and now you have learned to *expect* God in all things.[6]

Gateway to Silence: God is all-in-all.

For further study:

Soul Centering through Nature
A New Cosmology: Nature as the First Bible
The Soul, the Natural World, and What Is

WEEK 8:

THE TRUE SELF

DAY I
Who You Truly Are

Your True Self is who you objectively are from the beginning, in the mind and heart of God, "the face you had before you were born," as the Zen masters say. It's who you were before you did anything right or anything wrong. It is your substantial self, your absolute identity, which can be neither gained nor lost by any technique, group affiliation, morality, or formula whatsoever. The surrendering of our False Self, which we have usually taken for our absolute identity (yet is merely a relative identity), is the necessary suffering needed to find "the pearl of great price" that is always hidden inside us.[1]

I think the only and single purpose of religion is to lead you to an experience of your True Self in God. Every sacrament, every Bible, every church service, every song, every bit of priesthood or ceremony or liturgy is, as far as I'm concerned, for one purpose: to allow you to experience your True Self, who you are in God and who God is in you (read all of John 14 in this light). Only healthy religion is prepared to point you beyond the merely psychological self to the cosmic, to the universal, and to the Absolute Self. Only great religion is prepared to realign, re-heal, reconnect and reposition you inside of "the family of things." Whatever religion *mirrors you as a Divine Child* is, by that very fact, the "true religion," at least for you.[2]

Gateway to Silence: Becoming who I am

Universal Amnesia

At birth, we are, like Jesus, the One Eternal Christ Child, the Divine Child. Perhaps this is why we love to observe little babies. We can tell they're still living out of pure, natural, and shared being. They can switch from a full-faced, million-dollar smile to crying in one second, because they are not thinking, they are just being. They are in immediate connection with pure being, which is also pure spirit. We can't take our eyes off of little children because we know they're living in connection with the Big Self and their True Self.[3]

But we start losing access to that pureness of being around the age of seven, the so-called "age of reason." I remember hearing a story, reportedly true, about a young couple putting their newborn in the nursery for the night. Their four-year-old son said to them, "I want to talk to the baby!" They said, "Yes, you can talk to him from now on." But he pressed further, saying, "I want to talk to him now and by myself." Surprised and curious, they let the young boy into the nursery and cupped their ears to the door, wondering what he might be saying. This is what they reportedly heard their boy say to his baby brother: "Quick, tell me where you came from. Quick, tell me who made you. I'm beginning to forget!"

Could that be true? Have most of us forgotten? Is this what Jesus was referring to when he would often teach that we have to become like little children to "get it"?

In one way or another, most of the world religions, each in their own way, seem to believe that we have all indeed begun to forget, if not completely forgotten, who we actually are. Universal amnesia seems to be the problem. Religion's job comes down to one thing: to tell us, and to keep reminding us, who we objectively are. Thus, Catholics keep eating "the Body of Christ" until they know that they *are* what they eat—*a human and ordinary body that is also the eternal Christ.*[4]

Gateway to Silence: Becoming who I am

The Mirroring Gaze

I have heard it said that the gaze of delight between a mother and the baby at her breast is the beginning of our capacity for intimate relationship.

We spend the rest of our lives hoping for that moment again: that kind of safety; that kind of security; that kind of feeding; that kind of living inside of one world, where we are treasured and loved; that resting in True Self. Perhaps the most perfect image of this that we can find is the Madonna with the Baby Jesus. This is the most common painting in Western art museums, I am told, probably because there is absolute wholeness mirrored in the gaze of love between mother and child. As Carl Jung (1875–1961) said, *we paint the images our soul needs to see.* (It is equally telling to me that, after the Madonna, the most common three statues in historic Catholic churches were St. Joseph, St. Christopher, and St. Anthony—all holding the Christ child. This is no accident. Many without fathers, or good fathers, also longed to be mirrored by a loving man.)

We become the God with which we connect. That's why it's so important to know the true God, and not some little, punitive, toxic god. If you don't know the true God, you don't grow up, but live in fear and pretense. Contemplation, as Thomas Keating says, is the Divine therapy. We know God and we know ourselves by inner prayer journeys, by inner mirroring, and not by merely believing in doctrines or living inside of church structures. God's way of dealing with us becomes our way of dealing with life and others. We eventually love others, quite simply, as we have allowed God to love us; if we all allowed this love, imagine what a loving world we would create.[5]

Note the sequencing in this wonderful line Jesus spoke of the "sinful woman" (see Luke 7:47–48): "Her sins, her many sins, must have been forgiven her, or she could not have shown such great love. It is the person who is forgiven little who shows little love." One could almost use this as an argument *for* sinning, if the trade-off for forgiveness of sin is that great. But, to state it in another way, we can normally mirror to the degree we have been mirrored—by God, and by others who themselves have been truthfully mirrored as good.

Gateway to Silence: Becoming who I am

DAY 4

Original Innocence

Faith is to trust that an intrinsic union exists between us and God; contemplation is how we can experience this union. The path of fall and return is how we, over and over again, experience this union as pure grace and free gift. I will go so far as to say that *any authentic knowing of God happens when you have just allowed God to know and love you—exactly as you are.* As

Paul puts it, "Then you know as fully as you are known" (see 1 Corinthians 13:12). My experience tells me this is quite unfortunately somewhat rare, as most people dress themselves up for God. As Thomas Merton (1915–1968) so brilliantly puts it in *New Seeds of Contemplation*, "To be unknown to God is altogether too much privacy."[6]

There is a necessary movement between the two ends of the Divine/human axis, between our core and the core of God. We and God only really know one another "center to center." The only real sin is to doubt, deny, or fail to experience this basic axial connection. If we don't have some small mirrors (parents, partners, friends, and lovers) that are telling us we're good, it's very hard to believe in the Big Goodness. So maybe our job is *to make it a little easier for people to love us* (words spoken to me by my Novice Master in 1961; I hope I have learned a little about how to do that!).

The Latin root of the word "innocent" means "not wounded." That's how we all start life. We're all innocent. It doesn't have anything to do with moral right or wrong; it has to do with not yet being wounded. We start innocent and unwounded, but the killing of our holy innocence by power and abuse (as in the killing of the Holy Innocents by Herod [see Matthew 2:1–23]) is an archetypal image of what eventually happens to all of us in one way or another.

Probably this has to happen for us to grow up. We can't stay unwounded. We have to leave the Garden, so to speak (more on that next week). It is this movement out and back, between the loneliness and desperation of the False Self and the fullness of the True Self, that is the process of transformation. That's how we move to consciousness and inner freedom.[7]

Gateway to Silence: Becoming who I am

DAY 5

Love Is Who You Are

Thomas Merton stated that the True Self should not be thought of as anything different than life itself—not just one's little life, but also the Big Life. I'm not going to call the True Self just *life*, nor just *being*, because the deepest nature of this life and this being is *love. Love is the reason you were made, and love is who you are.* Because of our weak Trinitarian theology and practice, we Christians have not really drawn out the foundational implications of being created in "the image and likeness of God" (see Genesis 1:26).

When you live outside of love, you do not live within your true being, you do not live your true life, and you do not live with any high degree of consciousness. The Song of Songs states that *love is stronger than death*. "The flash of love is a flash of fire / A flame of Yahweh Godself" (see 8:6). It's a little experience of the one Big Flame, and we're just a little tiny spark of this universal reality that is life itself, consciousness itself, being itself, love itself, a Trinitarian Flow in one positive direction—infinitely and forever.

Let me define this one love as best I can. Love is known *when we recognize our self in the other. We are then no longer "other" ourselves, and that's the immense liberation and ecstasy of love.* Then we're all together in this thing called life and all competing and comparing is over. We have to start with little others—the earth, trees, dogs or cats, other humans—to be ready for the huge leap into the Great Other. All of life is practicing for this! It amounts to an ongoing mirroring process, and God does it best of all by mirroring us perfectly and with total acceptance. In fact, that is what God alone can do: make us into two-way mirrors that both receive and pass on the One Love.

Paul says it so well: "I shall know even as I am known" (see 1 Corinthians 13:12). In other words, you need to let yourself be known nakedly by God, with no pretense, no dressing up. You are who you are who you are! No trying to make yourself something other than who you really are. All God can love is who you actually are right now, because that's the only *you* that really exists. All the rest is just in your head: self-written commentaries and resumes.[8]

Gateway to Silence: Becoming who I am

DAY 6

Ultimate Mirroring

What's happening in prayer is that you're presenting yourself for the ultimate gaze, the ultimate mirroring, the gaze of God. Little by little, you become more naked before that perfectly accepting gaze. It's like lovemaking. You slowly disrobe and become mirrored perfectly in the gaze of the Supreme Lover. You gradually allow yourself to be seen, to be known in every nook and cranny; nothing hidden, nothing denied, nothing disguised. And the wonderful thing is, after a while, you feel so safe and you know you don't have to pretend anymore. You recognize your need for mercy, your own utter inadequacy and littleness. All pretense becomes unnecessary and unhelpful. You know that the best things you've ever done have been done for mixed and false motives, and the worst things you have ever done were done because you were *unconscious*.

"Someone is giving their self to me! Someone is sustaining me," you feel like shouting. Now this experience of being sustained, being given to without any just cause, knowing you didn't earn it, causes the whole worthiness game to break apart. *The True Self experiences all of reality as radical grace.* Who is worthy? No one is worthy. The True Self knows this and lives quietly, calmly, and contentedly inside of its radical unworthiness. The False Self cannot do that, and has to trump up reasons to justify its importance. You can accept this reality of unworthiness because you ironically know that you *are totally* worthy, and it has nothing to do with you! Your worthiness is entirely and gratuitously given to you, never earned. All true holiness is a reflected wholeness as you gradually learn to trust and return the glance of the Divine Mirror. This is the core and heart of all prayer. Really, prayer has no other lasting meaning.

So many of our saints and mystics, in different ways, say that what is happening in prayer is that you are allowing God to recognize God's self in you, and that's what God always loves and cannot *not* love. This is God's *new and lasting covenant with humanity* (see Jeremiah 31:31) that comes with God's very free choice for us in our creation itself. This is what was promised by the prophets, exemplified by Jesus, and ritualized in the Eucharist. The human problem is thus solved from the beginning, and at its core. We are chosen in God from the first moment of our creation (see Ephesians 1:3–5), and all later assurances of our salvation and goodness are merely needed encouragements to believe what is already true.[9]

Gateway to Silence: Becoming who I am

DAY 7

Sabbath Meditation

Remember: **The True Self**

Your True Self is who you objectively are from the beginning, in the mind and heart of God. (Day 1)

Religion's job comes down to one thing: to tell us, and to keep reminding us, who we objectively are. (Day 2)

We eventually love others, quite simply, as we have allowed God to love us. (Day 3)

Faith is to trust that an intrinsic union exists between us and God. (Day 4)

Love is the reason you were made, and love is who you are. (Day 5)

The True Self experiences all of reality as radical grace. (Day 6)

Rest: **Gaze of Grace**

Invite a trusted beloved (friend, lover, parent, or perhaps yourself through a mirror) to spend a few minutes sharing each other's gaze. Sit facing each other and begin by lighting a candle or ringing a bell. Take a couple moments with eyes closed to find your center, the stable witness. Then open your eyes and simply look at the face of the person across from you.

Give and receive this gaze in silence, being present to the other and to the presence of Love within and without. Let your eyes, face, and body be soft and relaxed while also alert. Breathe. If your attention wanders, bring your awareness back to your partner's eyes and to the presence of Love flowing between you.

When two or three minutes have passed, ring the bell again or bring your hands together and bow to signal the close of the practice. Share a few words, an embrace, or an expression of gratitude.

For further study:

True Self/False Self
Falling Upward: A Spirituality of the Two Halves of Life
Immortal Diamond: The Search for Our True Self

LEAVING THE GARDEN

DAY I
Naked without Shame

The Bible has us begin in "the Garden," where Adam and Eve walk in easy proximity with God and where they "know no shame" (see Genesis 2:25). But soon "their eyes are opened, and they realize they are naked and sew fig leaves to cover themselves" (see 3:7). Even though God refuses to see them as objects, and says, "Who told you that you were naked?" (see 3:11), they have begun to hide from God (see 3:8–9), and really from one another, and probably from themselves. They start scapegoating (see 3:12–13), fearing (see 3:10), and seeking "to be like gods" (see 3:5). The only sin does not seem like a sin at all, but a virtue: "to eat of the tree of the knowledge of good and evil" (see 2:17). Our lust for certitude and our need to be right is what keeps us in conflict. All this sets the plot for the entire Bible and, in many ways, for all religion.

You could say that, from then on, the whole Bible is trying to return us to the Garden, where God knows and loves us, and where we have learned that we are always beginners, perpetual Adams and Eves. By the end of the Bible (see Revelation 21–22), the New Jerusalem descends and there is no need for any temple because the temple is finally seen to be the embodied world. It is one big River of Life and endless Trees of Life (see 22:1–2), where "God lives among humans" (see 21:3). But for all the intervening books, just like our own lives, we fight, retrench, deny, run, oppose, and only occasionally surrender to such a momentous truth. God is seldom "found" because we do not know exactly where or how to look.

God is an "undergoing" to be experienced rather than an object to be found. Biblically, when we are found by God, we have always undergone an operation. The Bible might be described as a rather comprehensive listing of the possible, probable, and needed "undergoings."[1]

Gateway to Silence: Life is one good thing!

DAY 2

The Garden as Unitive Consciousness

The Garden is the symbol of unitive consciousness. We cannot objectively be separate from God; we all walk in the Garden whether we know it or not. We came from God and we will return to God. We must establish the metaphysical basis, a stable core, for holiness and Divine Union, or it always bounces back to the unstable core of human behavior. Everything in our lives is another lesson in the one continual school of conscious loving. The English Romantic poet William Wordsworth wrote so well: "the Child is the father of the Man; and I could wish my days to be bound each to each by natural piety...." We live the rest of our lives "trailing clouds of glory."[2]

Authentic spiritual cognition always has the character of *re*-cognition to it! We return to where we started and, as T. S. Eliot (1888–1965) says, "know the place for the first time."[3] Or, as Jacob put it when he awoke from his sleep: "Truly, Yahweh was always in this place all the time, and I never knew it" (see Genesis 28:16). That is, without doubt, the common experience of mystics, saints, and all recovered sinners (which is the only kind of saint).

Many of our journeys before this recognition are journeys away from the center, where we literally become "ec-centric" and off-balance. Recurring biblical texts tell stories of our human fall and recovery, hiddenness and discovery, loss and renewal, failure and forgiveness, exile and return. It seems to be the necessary cycle of learning and deep imprinting.

Fortunately, grace will always lead us back to our Stable Core, our True Self, to discover who we really are in God—and who we really *are*! God seems both very patient and very productive with the journeys back and forth. Such is the pattern of the soul, of history, and of the Bible: a Divine kind of circuitous progress, just like the Israelites during their forty years in the desert. This keeps the ego from taking any credit (although it will try!).

It is normally three steps forward, two steps backward, and, as Lady Julian of Norwich says, "Both are the mercy of God"![4]

Gateway to Silence: Life is one good thing!

DAY 3

Splitting from Others

Ideally we begin life as "holy innocents" in the Garden, with a primal connection to naked Being Itself, with parents whose loving eyes mirror us as *good, true, and beautiful* (the three essential qualities of Being according to philosophy). Good mothers and fathers give us a primal experience of life as union: "I am good, I am true, and I am beautiful" comes naturally to us. But we have to leave the Garden. We can't stay there, letting mother gaze at us forever. We begin the process of individuation, which includes at least four major splits. They are four ways that the mental ego starts taking control and engineering life. Spirituality, pure and simple, is overcoming these four splits.

The first split is very understandable. We split ourselves from other selves. We see our mommy and our daddy, and they're over there, and we're over here. We start looking out at life with ourselves as the center point. It's the beginning of egocentricity. Ego is the center; what I like, what I want, what I need is what matters. And I'm going to let Mama know what I want!

It is so nice to have a personal slave for a few years. These "highchair tyrants," the cute two-year-olds, are nevertheless totally egocentric. God made them cute and adorable so we would put up with them and feed their need for a "narcissistic fix"—just enough so they are indeed fixed, or then we "entitle" their False Self, which is a whole new set of problems! Still, they have begun living a terrible lie: They believe "I'm separate from the rest of the world." But it seems they have to do it. It's a necessary splitting so they can form an appropriate ego identity and appropriate boundaries.

The price we pay for this individuation process is a kind of alienation, an aloneness, a separation from the Garden. This continues and even builds through the early twenties, or until we finally love one person or thing more than ourselves and allow them to begin to change us and grow us up. During this earlier time, *life is all about me* and searching out what makes me look good, feel good, and keep my sense of safety in body, mind, and soul. I hope you have begun to move beyond this by middle age, but sadly, many never do. It remains "all about them," which is hardly ever true, if we are honest.[5]

Gateway to Silence: Life is one good thing!

Splitting Life from Death

The second split the ego creates is life from death. It comes about when you first experience the death of someone you have known—maybe it's your dog, maybe it's Grandma—and your mental ego starts separating life and death into polar opposites, even enemies. There are living people, and there are people who have already passed over and are gone. So you try to manufacture a life for yourself that will not include *death* (read also: failure, sadness, losing, humiliation, etc.). All the wisdom traditions and spiritual teachers say that death is an essential part of life, or, as the Catholic funeral liturgy puts it, "Life is not ended, but merely changed." It takes a long time for all of us to accept this and know it is true.

Almost all male initiation rites insisted that the boy had to concretely face head-on this kind of daily dying ahead of time so he would not be so afraid of it. So did Jesus, by the way. Sometimes the young initiates actually had to dig their grave and sleep in it for a night in an effort to begin to understand that life and death are not two, but include one another. If you split entirely, you spend your whole life trying to avoid any kind of death (anything negative, uncomfortable, difficult, unfamiliar, dangerous, or demanding). Much of humanity has not gone through this kind of initiation or any real "baptism," which Paul rightly calls "going into the tomb with him and joining him in death" (see Romans 6:4).

That's why Jesus says the rich man has an almost-impossible task in understanding what he's talking about (see Luke 16:19–31). If you've stayed in this split kind of thinking—that your whole life's purpose is to stay comfortable, making five-star restaurants and hotels your only happy places, and never suffering any inconvenience—then you are going to put off resolving this split until the last months, or even days, of life. At some point, you're finally going to have to see that this is not a truthful naming of reality. Life circumstances, if you allow them, will easily teach you this. You just can't always avoid the negative; in fact, those negatives are the good teachers.

Many of the saints and mystics, like St. Francis of Assisi (1182–1226), just dive into facing the unfamiliar, the foreign, and the scary ahead of time. St. Francis called it "poverty," which might not be the way we use the word today. For him it meant facing the "poor" side of everything and even finding riches there. What an amazing turnaround! But if you make that turn, undergo that baptism, failure is almost impossible.[6]

Gateway to Silence: Life is one good thing!

DAY 5

Splitting the Mind from the Body and the Soul

The third split the ego creates is mind from body and soul. You make your mind the engineer, the control tower. You make your mind "you." Almost all people do! As Descartes said, almost summarizing the eighteenth-century Enlightenment, "I think, therefore I am." This is considered the low point of Western philosophy, but actually he was being very honest and observant! Even worse, when you say, "I think," you largely mean only with the highly rational left brain, which has overtaken the Western world since the sixteenth century. Before that, the more creative right brain was dominant in most of the world. The right brain receives reality in a *holistic* way, in a symbolic and metaphorical way. It receives the whole without eliminating the mysterious, the problematic, the dark parts, and the threatening parts. You can see why most spiritual growth stops once this split occurs.

When we split our mind from our body and soul and live primarily in our mind, the body gets underplayed and dismissed, and the soul is not even recognized. Even worse, our sense of shame and guilt localizes in the body. (I'm afraid Paul's unfortunate use of the word "flesh"—instead of "ego"— as the enemy of Spirit may be partly responsible for our thinking of the body as inferior.) Jesus' statement for *wholeness* or *holiness* (and they are the same word), is "You are to love the Lord your God with your whole heart, your whole soul, your whole body strength, and your whole mind; and you must love your neighbor as yourself" (see Luke 10:27). He's clearly trying to describe a very holistic way of knowing God that is now better described as *deep intuition* or "full-access knowing" than anything connoted by words like thinking, logic, or reason (which are precisely not full-access knowing but merely one level of limited access).

In Jesus, there's no enmity between body, soul, and mind (with "heart" referring to the combined working of all three, which is probably why it is listed first). Only later, with the idealization of romantic Valentine's Day notions of love, did heart become sentimentalized and emotionalized in unhelpful ways. Jesus' psychology and anthropology were really quite up-to-date. But, as my wise Franciscan history professor said, "The church has often been more influenced by Plato than it has been by Jesus!" (In Plato's view, body and soul are enemies; in Jesus' teachings, they are one.)

This third split is the very one we try to resolve in contemplation. Deep inner journeys of prayer are one clear and recommended way to overcome this split. (Great love and great suffering are actually the quickest ways, but they normally cannot sustain us at the unitive level beyond the honeymoon or grief period.) Contemplation is the mental discipline that detaches you, even neurologically, from your addiction to your way of thinking in general, and your left brain in particular. You stop believing your little mind is the whole show, you stop trusting it as fully adequate, and you start venturing out into much broader ways of knowing, which frankly are much more compassionate and wise because they are not dualistic.[7]

Gateway to Silence: Life is one good thing!

DAY 6

Splitting the Idealized Self from the Shadow Self

The fourth split is when you split your acceptable self from your unacceptable self. You build a persona, a self-image that is based upon what most people want or need from you; things that your family, religion, or culture admire or reward; and those often arbitrary things with which you choose to identify. To the degree you do this, you will repress and often totally deny whatever opposes it. Many of us now call this your "shadow self." Your shadow is what you refuse to see about yourself and what you do not want others to see (although they normally do!). Jesus simply calls it "the log in your own eye" (see Matthew 7:4). Your shadow is fully there, but you just can't see it.

And, even worse, we see others using that same distorted and blocked vision (which is why we tend to dislike people who are playing the same game we are!). "The lamp of the body is the eye" (see Matthew 6:22), Jesus says, and you need to clean the lens of your egocentric eye to see truthfully. Much of the early work of spirituality is becoming aware of the biases, prejudices, and limitations through which you see the moment. It is a lifetime of painful work. The ego never totally abandons its throne, and its disguises become more subtle and sinister the older you get.

Jesus was a brilliant psychologist. He really was. He said you must clean not just the outside of the cup, but first and mostly the inside (see Matthew 23:26). I would say that the major reason why so much religion is a waste of time is that it is mostly about external actions, rituals, and behaviors, whereas Jesus focused very strongly on the internal (attitude, motivation, intention) and actually minimized the external. Only an inner life of prayer and "a searching and fearless moral inventory," as the Recovery Movement puts it, will help you here.

This split from the shadow self reaches full force in the teenage years, but many never fully move beyond it. Young people are just so eager to be acceptable to their peer group and to "look good," but unfortunately a lifelong game has begun. Both Carl Jung and Ken Wilber say, in their own ways, that people who try to look good outside are still dreaming but people who look inside are awakening.

Both the idealized self and the shadow self can blind us to our best and deepest self. This, ironically, is a "field of both weeds and wheat" (see Matthew 13:24–25) that for some magnificent reasons God not only fully accepts but even loves. We are the ones who refuse to live in this full field of every moment, person, and situation, good and bad. As Rumi, the Sufi poet, referring to God, us, and the field, says so beautifully, "I will meet you there!"[8]

Gateway to Silence: Life is one good thing!

DAY 7

Sabbath Meditation

Remember: **Leaving the Garden**

The Bible has us begin in "the Garden," where Adam and Eve walk in easy proximity with God and where they "know no shame" (see Genesis 2:25). (Day 1)

We cannot objectively be separate from God; we all walk in the Garden whether we know it or not. (Day 2)

We have to leave the Garden. We begin the process of individuation, which includes at least four major splits. (Day 3)

Life and death are not two, but include one another. (Day 4)

In Jesus, there's no enmity between body, soul, and mind. (Day 5)

Both the idealized self and the shadow self can blind us to our best and deepest self. (Day 6)

Rest: **Pranayama, Alternate-Nostril Breathing**

This breathing practice can help restore balance in the brain, stimulating and then relaxing left and right hemispheres. Breathing through the left nostril is calming and accesses the right or "feeling" side of the brain; breathing through the right nostril is energizing and accesses the left or "thinking" hemisphere.

Sitting in a comfortable, upright position, breathe deeply, drawing in air deeply so your belly rises. Exhale completely. Continue breathing naturally and deeply for a few breaths. On your next inhale, gently press against the right nostril with the right thumb and breathe in through the left nostril. With your right ring finger, close the left nostril, release the right, and exhale through the right nostril. Inhale through the right nostril, then close it and exhale through the left. Repeat the pattern for several minutes and then rest in simple awareness of your body's rhythmic breath.

Gateway to Silence: Life is one good thing!

For further study:

Everything Belongs: The Gift of Contemplative Prayer
Falling Upward: A Spirituality for the Two Halves of Life
Franciscan Mysticism: I AM That Which I Am Seeking
Immortal Diamond: The Search for Our True Self
Things Hidden: Scripture as Spirituality

WEEK 10:

THE FIRST HALF OF LIFE

DAY 1

Scripture as Template for Development

Walter Brueggemann, one of my favorite Scripture scholars, discovered that the Hebrew Scriptures, in their development, reflect the development of human consciousness. Before we delve into our examination of the "two halves of life," I think you might find it helpful to use this model as an overview of the whole of life.

Brueggemann says there are three major segments to the Hebrew Scriptures. The first five books, or the Torah, correspond to the first half of life. The Torah is the period in which the people of Israel were given law, tradition, structure, certitude, order, clarity, authority, safety, and specialness. It defined them, gave them their identity, and held them together. This is the easiest way to begin, even if it constructs a tent that you eventually need to enlarge. The psyche needs boundaries before it can move beyond them; or, as many have said in different contexts, you need to know the rules before you can rightly break the rules.

You have to begin with some kind of "Torah" in normal, healthy development, and it helps to believe that you are the "chosen people." That's what parents give their little ones—security, safety, specialness. The possibility of Divine election is first mediated and made possible through someone telling you that you are the best, God's favorite, and you should be proud of your group, your identity, your nationality, your religion, and your ethnicity. You must begin with a foundational "yes" to yourself. It is very hard if you start with "no."

The second major section of the Hebrew Scriptures is called the Prophets. Prophetic thinking is the necessary capacity for healthy self-criticism, the ability to recognize your own dark side, as the prophets did for Israel. It introduces the necessary "stumbling stones" that initiate you into the second half of life. Without that, most people (and most of religion) never move beyond tribal thinking, which is the belief that they and their group literally are the best, and really the only ones that matter. They make themselves the point of reference for Reality, which, of course, is never true. This creates narcissism instead of any possibility for enlightenment. It should therefore come as no surprise that idolatry of some sort is really the only sin in the Hebrew Scriptures: making things God that are not God.

The third section of the Hebrew Scriptures, the Wisdom Literature, represented best in many of the Psalms, Ecclesiastes, the Book of Wisdom, the Song of Songs, and the Book of Job, initiates a movement into the language of mystery and paradox, where God is finally allowed to be God. This is what happens in the psyche in the second half of life. You are strong enough now to hold together contradictions, even in yourself and in others—and you can do so with compassion, forgiveness, patience, and tolerance.

But we can't move around in the second half until we've gone through the first two stages and included the best of both of them. The best sequencing is exactly this: Order-Disorder-Reorder or, if you will, Life-Death-Resurrection. The great difficulty of our age is that many people start in Disorder, with no foundational Order to fall back on. It is creating a high degree of mental and emotional illness.[1]

Gateway to Silence: Receive and reflect

DAY 2

Container and Contents

The task of the first half of life is to create a proper *container* for your life and answer the first three practical and essential questions:

1. "What will make me significant?" (your core identity and self-image question);
2. "How can I sustain myself over the long haul?" (the very basic questions of education, occupation, social skills, and the social access these will give you); and
3. "With whom or with what group will I go forward?" (the foundational

questions of affiliation, core relationships, and companionship). Who you hang out with and how you partner will determine your stable core, your trajectory, and the questions you are able to ask, much more than mere thinking or willpower ever will—although you do not realize that until well into the second half of life. Only now, in my seventies, do I fully realize how my early decisions for celibacy, liberal arts education, and joining the Franciscans determined what I could think and could do for the whole of my life.

If you do not, on some level, answer these three concerns, you will remain preoccupied with first-half-of-life matters and not move forward very much. Identity, vocation, and relationships are your platform, your frame, your delivery system, and can become the basis for launching beyond them. One reason I can talk and write the way I do is that the early "conservative" family and Catholic container I was given was so strong and deep—psychologically, philosophically, and theologically—that it has allowed me to hold a lot of truth inside of it, and also to move beyond it, just like all good parents do. It is best to internalize some good order before you face disorder; in fact, I don't think you can integrate disorder except into a previous sense of order. Otherwise you just become an angry cynic or a reactionary.

The transformative key to our development is the prophetic second stage—a non-reactionary capacity for healthy self-criticism—which implies there is always something that deserves criticism! This is the birth of non-dual thinking but, because we have had so few good teachers here, most people became deeply invested dualistic thinkers, rebels, and antagonists instead of prophets. Except for the mystics, Western civilization and church have shown little ability to integrate the negative, the shadow, the inevitable other side of everything.

Scripture-based wisdom, knowledge of the whole history and the whole Tradition, and the reform-minded documents of the Second Vatican Council gave me the tools *to both trust myself and also critique myself,* along with my religion and my country, from the inside out—by our own inner criteria of truth and holiness. Most of us are not taught how to do that; we hide snugly inside an initial, but largely false, sense of order. Catholicism gave me both roots and wings, just like a good parent does. I had no need or desire to throw the baby out with the bathwater like many progressives do, nor to drown in the bathwater as many conservatives do.

The task of the second half of life is, then, to find the actual *contents* that this container is able to hold and deliver. The container is not an end in itself, but exists for the sake of your deeper and fullest life, which you cannot possibly know about until you discover it. Ironically, the stronger and deeper your container, the more it can hold without breaking or excluding. Only such folks can understand the universal growth principle: Transcend and include. If you cannot include previous stages, you have not transcended very well. Instead, you have just rebelled or reacted, and we have wasted too many centuries on that way of trying to grow up or reform institutions.

The two halves of life are cumulative and sequential, and both are needed for a full life. You cannot take a nonstop flight to the second half of life (from order to reorder) by reading about grace and resurrection. If you try to avoid or deny the lessons of order, you will never see its immense importance, its solidifying gift, and also its dark side. You must then walk through and let yourself be taught by disorder in some way or another. It is almost as if you have to experience disillusionment in order to grow up—and thus learn how to go through it—to learn the light and dark of everything. Even Jesus needed regular opposition, a betrayer, and a denier from his own religion and inner circle! Your first container *must* fail you because it is nothing more than your private salvation project, and your understanding and use of it is still far too small and too self-serving.[2]

Gateway to Silence: Receive and reflect

DAY 3

Knowing Who You Are

The first half of life is of crucial importance. You need boundaries, identity, safety, and some degree of order and consistency to get started, personally and culturally. (Conservatives are much better here, but the trouble is that they stay here!) You have to have boundaries to move beyond boundaries, without dropping the boundaries! This is paradox. It's both/and. You have to have a home to which you can return when you leave. In other words, you need to know who you are, or you use everything and everybody to help you to answer that question—and that only leads to narcissism.

We all need some successes, response, and positive feedback early in life, or we will spend the rest of our lives demanding it, or bemoaning the lack of it, from others. There is a good and needed "narcissism," if you want to call it that. You have to first have an ego structure to then let go of it and move beyond it. Only people who have a sense of boundaries and have internalized some *impulse control* tend to be successful in life, jobs, marriage, and relationships. Yet how young people hate all limits and impulse control, the very things that are primary indicators of later success.

If you are mirrored well by others early in life, you do not have to spend the rest of your life looking in Narcissus' mirror or begging for others' attention. You have already been "attended to." You now feel basically good—and always will—and can attend to others instead of yourself. You are free to mirror others and also to see yourself honestly, humbly, and helpfully. People who have not received such mirroring will usually tend to *over-present themselves* in words, in drama, in dress, in bragging, in resume, in shows of strength, and with general "notice me" behavior, which seldom achieves the desired results. Such over-presentation never achieves the very mirroring they so desire; so, as with all addictive behavior, they double their efforts. Ironically, simple human vulnerability invites a similar response from others, leading naturally to trust, friendship, and spontaneous mirroring. Jesus knew what he was saying when he taught that "the meek will inherit the earth" (see Matthew 5:5).

I can see why a number of saints spoke of prayer itself as simply receiving the ever-benevolent gaze of God, returning it in kind, mutually gazing, and finally recognizing that it is one single gaze received and bounced back. And I do believe some people receive this loving gaze from God, even though they never got it from either of their parents. Their longing and their need is so great, and grace is always there to fill the vacuum.[3]

Gateway to Silence: Receive and reflect

DAY 4

The Importance of Law

I cannot think of a culture in human history (before the present, post-modern era) that did not value law, tradition, custom, authority, boundaries, and morality of some clear sort. These containers give us the necessary security, continuity, predictability, impulse control, and ego structure that we need, before the chaos of real life shows up. It is my studied opinion that healthily conservative people tend to grow up more naturally and more happily than those who receive only free-form "build it yourself" worldviews, which happens so frequently in our time. This is the tragic blind spot of many liberals, individualists, and "free thinkers." Admittedly, the tragic blind spot of many conservatives is that they think law, security, and structure are an end in themselves. You are trapped on either end of the spectrum, and the classic advice stands: *In medio stat virtus*, "Strength/virtue stands in the middle."

Here is my conviction: *without law in some form, and also without butting up against that law, we cannot move forward easily and naturally.* Humans seem to need a very judicious combination of *safety* (the conservative strength) and *necessary conflict* (the progressive strength) to keep growing. The rebellions of two-year-olds and teenagers are in our hardwiring, and we must have something hard and half-good to rebel against. We need a worthy opponent against which to test our mettle. As Rainer Maria Rilke (1875–1926) put it, "When we victorious are, it is over small things, and though we won, it leaves us feeling small."[4]

Cultures that do not allow any questioning or rebelling might create order, but they pay a huge price for it in terms of inner development. Even the Amish have learned this, and allow their teens the freedom and rebellion of *Rumspringa*, so they can make a free choice to be Amish—and most do! Groups and ideologies that only encourage private expression and individuation simply cannot create anything that lasts or offers hope. Correction, rebellion, reformation, and self-assertion are not a full plan of life—there is too much "no" and not enough "yes" in such a worldview.

There is a bit of wisdom that has been making its way around the Internet for more than a dozen years now: "Learn and obey the rules very well, so you will know how to break them properly." This rather succinctly sums up Jesus' teaching in the Sermon on the Mount, and Paul's teaching about law in both Romans and Galatians. But dualistic thinkers always choose one side or the other—all law or all rebellion.[5]

Gateway to Silence: Receive and reflect

DAY 5

Building a Self Strong Enough to Die to Self

You need a very strong container in the first half of life to hold the contents and contradictions that arrive later in life. You ironically need a very strong ego structure to let go of your ego. You need to struggle with the rules more than a bit before you throw them out. You only internalize values by butting up against other values for a while. All of this builds the strong self that can *positively* obey Jesus—and healthily "die to itself." In fact, far too many have lived very warped and defeated lives because they tried to give up a self that was not yet there. I saw this in much old religious life before the Second Vatican reforms, and I see it now in the neo-conservative pushback that usually makes one or two seemingly heroic and sacrificial positions into the whole Gospel (no abortion, no birth control, no gay marriage), while they never seem to notice that the sacrifice is always asked of others rather than themselves. My analysis is that *there is no self there that is strong enough to move beyond itself*, which is also why they cannot see their own egocentric response!

The first-half-of-life container is constructed through training in impulse control, traditions, group symbols, family loyalties, the appropriate use of conformity, basic respect for authority, civil and church laws, and a sense of the goodness, value, and special importance of your country, ethnicity, and religion. For example, the Jewish people's deep respect for the Law, communal ritual, and the traditions of their ancestors has held them together over time like few other groups.

To quote Archimedes, you must have both "a lever and a place to stand" before you can move the world. The educated and sophisticated Western person today has many levers, but almost no solid place on which to stand; most of our people have very weak identities, and often compensate for the deficit with terribly overstated identities. I am not sure which is worse. This tells me we are not doing the first-half-of-life task very well. How can we possibly get to the second?[6]

Gateway to Silence: Receive and reflect

DAY 6

It's All about Me

Most cultures are first-half-of-life cultures, and, even sadder, most organized religion almost necessarily sells a first-half-of-life spirituality. In the first half of life it is all about me: How can I be important? How can I be safe? How can I make money? How can I look attractive? And, in the Christian scenario, how can I think well of myself and go to heaven? How can I be on moral high ground? These are all ego questions; they are not the questions of the soul. It is still well-disguised narcissism, or even sanctified narcissism, which must be the worst kind.

I'm sad to say, I think many Christians have never moved beyond these survival and security questions. Even eternity is securing *my* future, not a common future, or a future for humanity; religion becomes a private insurance plan for that future. It's still all about me, but piously disguised. Any sense of being part of a cosmos, a historical sweep, that God is doing something bigger and better than simply saving individual souls (my soul in particular), is largely of no interest. This becomes apparent in the common disinterest of so many when it comes to Earth care, building real community, simple living, and almost all peace and justice issues. For many Christians—

stuck in the first half of life—all that is important is their private moral superiority and spiritual "safety," which is somehow supposed to "save" them.

Once God and grace move us to the second half of life, religion becomes much more a mystical matter rather than a moral matter. Then it's all about union, and participation in and with God. Indeed, this is the work of true religion: to help us transition from stage to stage, toward ever-deeper union with God and all things. Ken Wilber says that only healthy religion provides the "conveyor belt" through all of the stages of consciousness, to the non-dual and higher stages. We will explore this more deeply in the weeks ahead.[7]

Gateway to Silence: Receive and reflect

DAY 7

Sabbath Meditation

Remember: **The First Half of Life**

The Hebrew Scriptures, in their development, reflect the development of human consciousness. (Day 1)

The task of the first half of life is to create a proper container for your life—not as an end in itself, but for the sake of your deeper and fullest life, which is yet to come. (Day 2)

The first half of life is of crucial importance. You need boundaries, identity, safety, and some degree of order and consistency to get started, personally and culturally. (Day 3)

Without law in some form, and also without butting up against that law, we cannot move forward easily and naturally. (Day 4)

You ironically need a very strong ego structure to let go of your ego. (Day 5)

Once God and grace move us to the second half of life, religion becomes much more a mystical matter rather than a moral matter. (Day 6)

Rest: **Visio Divina**

In the Hindu tradition, *darshan* (or *darsana*) is to behold the Divine or to see with reverence and devotion—but, even better, *it is to let the Divine see you, all of you.* The full practice of *darshan* is quite simply to go to the temple to let God gaze upon you, and to stay there until God can love every part of you. In the Eastern Orthodox tradition, icons are windows into God's heart; they are symbols of deeper-than-apparent wisdom. Approaching images with openness to God's presence is also known as the practice of *visio divina*, sacred seeing. But note that the eyes of the icon are always gazing straight forward—at you, until you fully allow that gaze.

Choose an image (painting, photograph, sculpture, or other artwork). Set aside some quiet time with this piece and begin with a prayer of intent to be open to God.

Look slowly at the image, taking in every detail without critique. Observe the colors, shapes, shadows, lines, empty spaces. Allow your unfiltered response to arise—feelings, memories, thoughts. Notice and welcome these reactions, without evaluation, whether they seem negative or pleasing.

How do these feelings, evoked by the image, connect with your life? What desires are stirring in you? How are you drawn to respond?

Take a few moments to reflect in writing, movement, or sound—whatever embodiment fits your expression. Finally, simply rest in God's presence, fully recieve God's gaze, and then literally bounce it back. This is how we know God—center to center.

Gateway to Silence: Receive and reflect

For further study:

Adult Christianity and How to Get There
A Spirituality for the Two Halves of Life
Falling Upward: A Spirituality for the Two Halves of Life
Loving the Two Halves of Life: The Further Journey
The Two Major Tasks of the Spiritual Life

WEEK 11:

THE FALSE SELF

DAY 1

The Disconnected Self

Your False Self is your necessary warm-up act, the ego part of you that first establishes your unique identity, which is thus experienced as *separate*, especially in the first half of life. In other words, it largely lives entirely on the "manifest" level, to the point of being disconnected with the "unmanifest," or pure Being—God. The reconnection of manifest and unmanifest is the great work of all healthy religion.

Basically, the False Self is your incomplete self, trying to pass for your whole self. We fall in love with the part so much that we deny the Whole. God surely understands this and is undoubtedly glad that we are at least in love with something. Such initial love gets us started until we eventually realize that "God is love" (see 1 John 4:8) and that "love lasts forever" (see 1 Corinthians 13:8). It is the one thing we can forever count on and forever *are* because we are created in "the image and likeness" of the Trinitarian God who is constituted by relationships of eternal, unconditional love.

Your False Self is *not* your bad self, your deceitful self, the self that God does not like or that you should not like. Actually, your False Self is quite good and necessary as far as it goes. It just does not go far enough, and it often poses as, and thus substitutes for, the real thing. That is its only problem, and that is why we call it "false." Maybe *small self* would actually be a better term.

The False Self is bogus more than bad, and bogus only when it pretends to be more than it is. Various false selves (temporary costumes) are necessary to form early identities, and they only show their limitations when they stay around too long. If a person keeps growing, his or her various false selves usually die, and need to die, in exposure to greater light. Good spirituality teaches you how to willingly let them die![1]

Gateway to Silence: I am who I am in the eyes of God—nothing more and nothing less.

DAY 2
The Small Self

Your False Self or small self is your launching pad: your body image, your job, your education, your clothes, your money, your car, your sexual identity, your success, and so on. These are the trappings of ego that we all use to get us through an ordinary day. They are a nice-enough platform upon which to stand, but they are largely a projection of your self-image and your attachment to it. They are the psychological self that you have created, as opposed to the self that was given by God.

When you are able to move beyond your False Self—at the right time and in the right way—*it will feel precisely as if you have lost nothing.* In fact, it will feel like freedom and liberation. When you are connected to the Whole, you no longer need to protect and defend the mere part. You are now connected to something inexhaustible.

To *not* let go of your False Self at the right time and in the right way is precisely what it means to be stuck, trapped, and addicted to your self. (The traditional word for that was *sin.*) The discovery of our True Self is not just a matter of chronological age. Some spiritually precocious children—usually those with a disability of some type, or who are in close relationship with some kind of suffering—see through the False Self rather early, while lots of old men and old women are still dressing up what is soon going to die anyway.

If all you have at the end of your life is your False Self, there will not be much to eternalize. The False Self is always transitory. Its various costumes are all "accidents" largely created by the mental ego. Your False Self is what changes, passes, and dies when you die. Only your True Self lives forever. Your True Self knows that it is a branch of love connected to the eternal Vine of Love, and it happily rests there (see John 15:1–7) for its identity and power.[2]

Gateway to Silence: I am who I am in the eyes of God—nothing more and nothing less.

The Separate Self

Your False Self is who you "think" you are, but your thinking does not make it true. Your False Self is almost entirely a social construct to get you started on your life journey. It is a set of agreements between your childhood and your parents, your family, your neighbors, your school chums, your partner or spouse, your culture, and your religion. It is your "container" for your separate self. Jesus would call it your "wineskin," which he points out usually cannot hold any *new* wine (see Mark 2:21–22). Your ego container likes to stay "contained" and hates change.

Your False Self is how you define yourself outside of love, relationship, or Divine Union. After you have spent many years laboriously building this separate self, with all its labels, agendas, and preoccupations, you are very attached to it—and why wouldn't you be? It's what you know and it's all you know. To move beyond it will always feel like losing or dying.

Perhaps you have noticed that we are not as comfortable with talking about dying as master teachers like Jesus, the Buddha, St. Francis, the "Teresas" (of Ávila, Lisieux, and Calcutta), the "Johns" (the Evangelist, the Beloved Disciple, and John of the Cross), Hafiz, Kabir, and Rumi. They deeply knew that if you do not learn the art of dying and letting go early, you will hold onto your False Self far too long, until it kills you anyway.

I used to think it was negative and morbid when Catholic saints were depicted with the skull at their feet, but now I know it was saying something quite positive and liberating about them.[3]

Gateway to Silence: I am who I am in the eyes of God—nothing more and nothing less.

The Ego Self

It was Thomas Merton, the Cistercian monk, who first suggested the use of the term False Self. He did this to clarify for many Christians the meaning of Jesus' central and oft-repeated teaching that we must die to ourselves, or "lose ourselves to find ourselves" (see Mark 8:35). The self that must die and the self that should live must be distinguished and clarified, or we invariably confuse the whole spiritual journey.

Scripture passages about "losing the self" have caused much havoc and pushback in Christian history because they sound negative and ascetical, and were usually interpreted as appeals to punish, deny, or reject the material world and physical self. But the intent of losing oneself is personal liberation, not self-punishment. Centuries of Christians falsely assumed that if they could "die" to their body, their spirit would, for some reason, miraculously arise. I assure you, this is a waste of time. In fact, Jesus is criticized precisely because he was *not* ascetical (see Luke 5:33), exactly as the Buddha was.

Apart from a general Platonic denial of the body in most religions, Paul made a most unfortunate choice of the word "flesh" as the enemy of Spirit (for example, see Galatians 5:16–24). Today we would probably say "ego" or "small self," which would be much closer to his actual intended meaning. Remember that Christianity is the religion that believes "the Word became flesh" (see John 1:14), and Jesus even returned to the flesh after the Resurrection (see Luke 24:40)—so flesh cannot be bad. In fact, it is the container for our full enlightenment. Remember, the Risen Christ still shares in some unique and expanded notion of embodiment, and we say in the Creed that we "believe in the resurrection of the body." Christianity is all about incarnation, from beginning to end.

If it is in any way anti-body, it is never authentic Christianity, but some form of Platonism, Stoicism, or dualistic Manichaeism (all of which are quite common among Christians). Merton rightly recognized that it was not the body that had to "die," but the False Self or the well-defended ego self that we do not need anyway, precisely because it is only a part of us that tries to pass for the Whole.[4]

Gateway to Silence: I am who I am in the eyes of God—nothing more and nothing less.

DAY 5

The Imagined Individual Self

All mature religion must and will talk about the death of any notion of a separate, and therefore false, self. (Most of the time when you read the word "sin" in the Bible, if you substitute the word "separate" you will understand its importance more clearly.) The True Self can let go of any false autonomy and self-sufficiency because it is radically safe at its core.

The True Self is then like a happy and free baby that can crawl away from its mother (God), knowing fully that she will grab him or her back if there is any danger whatsoever. What confidence and security that gives the True Self—to actually do whatever it is that it has to do. "You may eat of all of the trees in the garden" (see Genesis 2:16), Yahweh daringly tells Adam and Eve. God is surely a great risk-taker. Only the True Self can understand St. Augustine's dangerous line: "Love [God] and do what you will"![5] To tell that to the False Self would be disastrous. It would be like telling a seventeen-year-old boy to trust his hormones.

The separate self *is* the False Self, and this fragile identity needs to define itself as unique, special, superior, strong, and adequate. What a trap. So Jesus must say, "Unless the single grain of wheat dies, it remains just a grain of wheat. But if it does die, it will bear much fruit" (see John 12:24).

Whenever you are loving someone or something else, you have died on some level—and let go of your separate self. As Stephen Levine, a master teacher on dying, taught, our fear of death comes from *an imaginary loss of an imaginary self.* Think about that for the rest of your life.

These seeming losses are not loss at all, but actually expansion. This act of faith will allow you to overcome your fear of death and, for Christians, it is what Jesus promised us in many settings. Our False Self is precisely our individual singularity in both its "Aren't I wonderful!" and "Aren't I terrible!" forms. Each is its own kind of ego trip, and both take the tiny little self far too seriously.

The true saint is no longer surprised at his littleness or her greatness. A mouse in a mansion does not need to take lessons in humility.[6]

Gateway to Silence: I am who I am in the eyes of God—nothing more and nothing less.

DAY 6

The Unaligned Self

In one way or another, almost all religions say that you must "die before you die," and then you will know what dying means—and what it does not mean! Your usual viewing platform is utterly inadequate to see what is real. It is largely useless to talk about the very Ground of your being, your True Self, or your deepest soul until you have made real contact with them at least once. That demands dying to the old viewing platform of the mental ego and the False Self, and drawing from a deeper well, which is the point of our entire book.

If you do make contact with your True Self, you forever know that something is there that can be talked about, relied on, and deeply trusted. You move from religion as mere belief to religion as a new kind of knowing and a new source for loving.

Henceforth, you know you have a soul, and your soul becomes your primary receiver station. Most souls are initially "unsaved" in the sense that they cannot dare to imagine they could be one with God/Reality/the universe. This is the lie of the False Self that dies slowly, very slowly, and only after much testing and denial. Many clergy fight me on the idea of actual oneness with God. It is as if they do not believe in their own product.

The realignment of our selves from two to One through a loving and lifelong tug-of-war is the very dance of transformation. It is a trust walk, a constant testing of the reliability of love and God (which you come to know are the same), which eventually allows us to fall trustingly back into our True Self. Then we are One again. We made so much of Christianity about "atonement" when we should have made it about at-one-ment. What a difference a couple of hyphens make![7]

Gateway to Silence: I am who I am in the eyes of God—nothing more and nothing less.

DAY 7

Sabbath Meditation

Remember: **The False Self**

Your False Self is your necessary warm-up act, the ego part of you that establishes your unique identity, which is thus experienced as *separate*, especially in the first half of life. (Day 1)

Your False Self is what changes, passes, and dies when you die. Only your True Self lives forever. (Day 2)

Your False Self is who you "think" you are, but your thinking does not make it true. (Day 3)

Thomas Merton rightly recognized that it was not the body that had to "die," but the False Self that we do not need anyway, precisely because it is only a part of us that tries to pass for the Whole. (Day 4)

All mature religion must and will talk about the death of any notion of a separate, and therefore false, self. (Day 5)

Most souls are initially "unsaved" in the sense that they cannot dare to imagine they could be one with God/Reality/the universe. This is the lie of the False Self that dies very slowly. (Day 6)

Rest: **Drawing Empty Space**

It's difficult to see what is not manifest, what is intangible and yet the most objective of all reality. Yet we can learn to see differently, to be present to Being. This simple practice shifts our usual way of literal seeing and invites an inner change in how we see ourselves, the world, and the Divine.

Sitting at a table or desk with a pencil and a piece of blank, unlined paper, look at a nearby object. Turn your attention to the empty or "negative" space surrounding the object. Rather than focus on the object's contours, look at the lines and curves of the space butting up against the object, the places in between and around the object itself. Breathe deeply and begin to draw these nooks and crannies of air and emptiness. Keep your focus on the negative space as you draw.

You might draw all of the spaces around the object or spend just a few moments drawing. When your pencil comes to a stop, observe the form and detail of the "nothingness" you've drawn. Know that your True Self, though perhaps less visible than ego and persona, is spacious and objective. Let your inner witness quietly observe the "negative space" within yourself. Rest in this abundant emptiness, full of Presence.

Gateway to Silence: I am who I am in the eyes of God—nothing more and nothing less.

For further study:

Immortal Diamond: The Search for Our True Self
True Self/False Self

DUALISTIC THINKING

DAY 1
Stinkin' Thinkin'

Although we begin life, as very young children, as non-dual thinkers, usually by the age of seven we are all dualistic thinkers and, sadly, many of us stay that way for the rest of our lives. Dualistic thinking is the well-practiced pattern of knowing most things by comparison and then, very quickly, by competition. For some reason, once we compare or label things (that is, judge things), we almost always conclude that one is good and the other is not so good or even bad.

Don't take my word for it; just notice your own thoughts and reactions. You will see that you will move almost automatically into a pattern of up or down, in or out, for me or against me, right or wrong, black or white, gay or straight, good or bad. It is the basic reason why the "stinkin' thinkin'" of racism, sexism, classism, homophobia, religious imperialism, and prejudice of all kinds is so hard to overcome and has lasted so long—even among nice people! We have eaten voraciously of the "tree of the knowledge of good and evil," the very one from which Yahweh told us never to eat (see Genesis 2:17). Such dualistic thinking is finally always "stinkin' thinkin'," to use the common, clever phrase of many people in the Recovery Movement who recognize that addicts are almost always highly dualistic thinkers.

At the risk of being too cleverly alliterative (though it may help you to remember), here is the normal sequencing of the dualistic mind: it compares, it competes, it conflicts, it conspires, it condemns, it cancels out any contrary evidence, and then it crucifies with impunity. You can call it the "seven Cs" of delusion. This is the source of most violence, which is invariably sacralized as good and necessary to "make the world safe for democracy" or to "save souls for heaven."

There is a reason why Jesus and all the great spiritual teachers say, "Do not judge!" (see Matthew 7:1, Luke 6:37) and why messengers in the Bible almost always begin with, "Do not be afraid!" Our violence—and almost all of our unhappiness—emerges from our judging, dualistic mind, which itself comes from deeply rooted fear. Neuroscience now makes very clear that *humans deeply love predictability and fear all unpredictability*, which encourages us to make all kinds of absolute affirmations, especially about fearful or dangerous things, like the end of the world, who is going to be punished and how, and the dates, places, and peoples who reveal the coming of "The Beast" or the Anti-Christ. It does work to localize and thus limit our anxiety, just like abused people who cut themselves. Only unitive, non-dual consciousness can heal this violence and lead us to a rather constant happiness. If dualistic thinking is stinkin' thinkin', then I guess we could call contemplation a melodious mind.[1]

Gateway to Silence: Be not afraid.

DAY 2

The Egoic Operating System

Dualistic thinking, or the "egoic operating system," as my friend and Living School colleague Cynthia Bourgeault calls it, is our way of reading reality from the position of our private and small self. "What's in it for me?" "How will I look if I do this?" This is the ego's preferred way of seeing reality. It has become the "hardware" of almost all Western people, even those who think of themselves as Christians, because the language of institutional religion is largely dualistic itself. Because we have not been doing our work of teaching prayer and contemplation, this very limited processing system has almost totally taken over in Western civilization in the last five hundred years. It has confused information with enlightenment, mind with soul, and thinking with experiencing—but these are each very different paths.

The dualistic mind is essentially binary. It is either/or thinking. It knows by comparison, by opposition, by differentiation. It uses descriptive words like good/evil, pretty/ugly, intelligent/stupid, not realizing there may be 80 or 180 degrees between the two ends of each spectrum. It works well for the sake of simplification and conversation, but not for the sake of truth or even honest experience. It wants answers; it wants to settle the dust quickly; it does not really want perception, much less deep perception. We leave that to the poets, philosophers, and prophets.

Actually, you need your dualistic mind to function in everyday life: to do your job as a teacher, a doctor, or an engineer. It is great stuff as far as it goes, but it just doesn't go far enough. The dualistic mind cannot process things like infinity, mystery, God, grace, suffering, sexuality, death, or love. It pulls everything down into some kind of tit-for-tat system of false choices and easy contraries, which is largely what "fast food religion" teaches, usually without even knowing it. Without the contemplative and converted mind, much religion is frankly dangerous for society.[2]

Gateway to Silence: Be not afraid.

DAY 3

Partisanship

Transformation is a different path than mere education. Someone can be highly educated and still be totally dualistic and egocentric (all their thinking is self-referential and therefore quite limited), while an uneducated janitor or motel maid can be non-dualistic because the suffering of life leads her or him into problems they cannot solve and where they must *trust in goodness, hope for more to be revealed, and love what is.* And yes, those are the only "three things that last," according to Paul (see 1 Corinthians 13:13). Such people often tend to learn surrender to soul much more quickly and easily.

I look at the unbelievably sad and even hateful divide between liberals and conservatives in our church and in our country, and at both extremes I find totally dualistic thinking. You can be dualistic as a liberal, and you can be dualistic as a conservative. They are simply two different methods to be in control, two different ways to be right, and two different ways to look down on other people.[3]

Dualistic or divided people live in a split and fragmented world. Usually, they cannot accept or forgive certain parts of their own destiny and experience. They cannot accept that God could objectively dwell within their weak humanity. This lack of forgiveness-of-reality-for-being-what-it-is takes the form of a tortured mind, a closed heart, or an inability to live calmly and proudly inside one's own body—which has created the many unhealthy psyches we now have in our world.

The fragmented mind and the egoic mind see in parts, and usually antagonistic parts, but never in wholes, and this predictably creates antagonism, reaction, fear, and resistance—pushback—from most other people. It is a double-whammy of despair, and the saddest effect of all is that people living from this divided mind continue to do what makes them so unhappy. Sin and addiction have many of the same characteristics.[4]

Gateway to Silence: Be not afraid.

DAY 4
Splitting and Denying

Dualistic thinking works only as long as you stay on the level of abstraction. Once you go to the specific and concrete, you find that everything in this world is always a mixture of darkness *and* light, good *and* bad, death *and* life. If you're honest about it, you can usually say, "This is what is good about it, and this is what is bad about it." But if you stay at the level of dualistic thinking, you won't allow yourself to hold a necessary and life-giving tension. You'll split to give yourself mental comfort and say, for example, "America is entirely good. America's wars are always good wars." It will give your ego superficial comfort, but there is no truth to it. This is killing us—literally.

The dualistic mind is not adequate to the task of life. It cannot deal with subtlety, it cannot see or deal with the dark side of things, it cannot "discern spirits"—one of the gifts of the Spirit of which Paul speaks (see 1 Corinthians 12:10). The dualistic/splitting mind cannot deal with contradictions, with paradox, with inconsistency, with Mystery itself—which is just about everything. Any honest knowledge of God will always and forever be surrounded by darkness and mystery, and will often appear to be paradoxical.[5]

Ultimate Reality cannot be seen with any dual operation of the mind, where we eliminate the mysterious, the confusing—anything scary, unfamiliar, or outside our comfort zone. Dualistic thinking is not naked presence to the always-available Presence, but highly controlled and limited seeing. Yet, to loosely but fairly paraphrase Einstein, we are trying to solve our problems with the same consciousness that caused our problems in the first place.[6]

Gateway to Silence: Be not afraid.

DAY 5
Both Are Necessary

It is true that we need first to clarify and distinguish before we can subtly discriminate. Utterly clear dualistic thinking sets up the frame: "You cannot serve both God and mammon" would be an example from Jesus' teaching (see Matthew 6:24). But non-dualistic wisdom, or what many of us call contemplation, is necessary once you actually get in the right frame: "Now that I have chosen to serve God instead of 'mammon,' what does that really mean?" "Exactly how do I discern what is mammon?" "What does it mean 'to serve God'?" These much harder questions are resolved only in prayer, over time, and by participation in the larger consciousness we described earlier.

Such discrimination will take the rest of your life. Non-dualistic thinking presumes that you have first mastered dualistic clarity, but also found it *insufficient* for the really big issues like love, suffering, death, God, sexuality, and any notion of infinity. In short, we need *both*. If I said any differently, I would be dualistic myself.

Unless you let the truth of life teach you on its own terms, unless you develop some concrete practice for recognizing and overcoming your dualistic mind, you will remain in the first half of life forever, as much of humanity has up to now. Frankly, it comes down to your capacity to sustain ambiguity, hold creative tensions, and, yes, "suffer"! In the first half of life, you cannot work with the imperfect, nor can you accept the tragic sense of life, nor is your ego structure strong enough to hold paradox and mystery, which also means that you cannot yet love anything or anyone at any depth.

Nothing is going to change in history as long as most people are merely dualistic, either/or thinkers. Such splitting and denying leaves us at the level of information, data, facts, and endless arguing about the same. We yell "My facts are better than your facts!" at ever-higher volume and with ever-stronger ego attachment. This is getting us nowhere, and creating a very unhappy world on all sides.[7]

Gateway to Silence: Be not afraid.

DAY 6

Resistance to Change

Sadly, the mind trapped inside of dualistic thinking is not open to change. How else can we explain the obvious avoidance of so many of Jesus' major teachings within the Christian churches? Jesus' direct and clear teachings on issues such as nonviolence; a simple lifestyle; love of the poor and our enemies; forgiveness, inclusivity, and mercy; and not seeking status, power, perks, or possessions have all been overwhelmingly ignored throughout history by the vast majority of mainline Christian churches, even those who so proudly call themselves orthodox or scriptural. The world is no longer impressed by our supposed orthodoxy and biblicism.

This avoidance defies explanation until we understand how dualistic thinking protects and pads the ego and its fear of change. *The ego hates change, probably more than anything else; it loves the status quo even when that status quo is not working for it.* Notice that the things we Christians have largely ignored require *actual change* to ourselves. The things we emphasized instead were usually intellectual beliefs, or moral superiority stances, that asked almost nothing of us, but required compliance from others: the divinity of Christ, the virgin birth, the atonement theory, and beliefs about reproduction and sex. After a while, you start to recognize the underlying bias that is at work. The ego diverts your attention from anything that would ask *you* to change, to righteous causes that invariably ask *others* to change. Such issues give you a sense of moral high ground without costing you anything (e.g., celibate priests who make abortion the only sin, or who crusade about birth control). Sounds like a well-disguised ego game to me, or, as Shakespeare might say, "They protest too much"—and one knows something else is largely at work.[8]

Whole people see and create wholeness wherever they go. Split people split up everything and everybody else. By the second half of our lives, we are meant to see in wholes and no longer just in parts.[9]

Gateway to Silence: Be not afraid.

DAY 7

Sabbath Meditation

Remember: **Dualistic Thinking**

Dualistic thinking is the basic reason why the "stinkin' thinkin'" of racism, sexism, classism, homophobia, religious imperialism, and prejudice of all kinds is so hard to overcome. (Day 1)

Dualistic thinking is our way of reading reality from the position of our private ego. (Day 2)

The fragmented mind and the egoic mind see in parts, and usually antagonistic parts, but never in wholes, and then predictably create antagonism, reaction, fear, and resistance. (Day 3)

Everything specific and concrete in this world is always a mixture of darkness *and* light, good *and* bad, death *and* life. (Day 4)

It is true that we need first to clarify and distinguish before we can subtly discriminate. (Day 5)

Whole people see and create wholeness wherever they go. By the second half of our lives, we are meant to see in wholes and no longer just in parts. (Day 6)

Rest: **Examen of Consciousness**

St. Ignatius of Loyola (1491–1556), founder of the Society of Jesus or Jesuits, proposed a daily exercise which he called the Examen of Conscience[10]—a simple exercise in discernment. Rather than focusing on what went right or wrong, how you failed or succeeded throughout the day, this exercise encourages you to reflect on moments in the day when you were aware of God—when you were present to Presence—and those times when you were forgetful or distracted. So it is not just about strict moral issues, I prefer to call it the "Examination of Consciousness" itself.

Center yourself in silence and an awareness of God's presence. Recall the day with an open spirit. Notice the emotions, sensations, and thoughts that arise as you review the day's events. Let your attention settle on one of these instances and look for God's presence within it, whether you were aware at the time or not. Pray from this memory and within this present moment. Release the day with gratitude and rest in God's grace.

Gateway to Silence: Be not afraid.

For further study:

A New Way of Seeing, a New Way of Being: Jesus and Paul
Exploring and Experiencing the Naked Now
Falling Upward: A Spirituality for the Two Halves of Life
The Naked Now: Learning to See as the Mystics See

SUBVERTING THE HONOR/SHAME SYSTEM

DAY I

Fragile Dignity

When I was studying theology in the 1960s, the assumption was that, to be a good Scripture scholar, you had to be educated in Greek and Hebrew. There is surely much merit to this—although it does make you wonder why Catholics held onto Latin for so long; none of the Bible was written in Latin and Jesus never spoke it. It was, in fact, the language of his oppressors.

Now we have discovered that one of the very best ways to study Scripture is to use the lens of cultural anthropology; in other words, to learn about the social setting in which Jesus lived and the problems with which he was dealing. What we find is that the Mediterranean culture of his time was overwhelmingly dominated by an honor/shame system largely based on externals. Actually, we still live that way in the United States and Western Europe, although we pretend we don't!

Honor and shame are considered to be personal commodities that you can lose or gain. They're what we would call ego possessions. You don't have them naturally. You have to work for your honor and then show it off and protect it. You have to deny your shame, which is what we would now call the shadow self. At Jesus' point in history, and frankly with many today, there is no *inherent* sense of the self, no sense of natural dignity that comes from within. If the self is about honor and shame, it is all about what is being bought and sold, won and lost—all the time. This creates very weak ego structures, even for the False Self, which is already weak to begin with.

Religion at its best and most mature is exactly what is needed for this problem. Without healthy religion, you have no internal or inherent source for your own dignity and positive self-image, no "stable core." You have to find your status and your dignity externally by what you wear, by your title, by how much money you have, by what car you drive. That's a pretty fragile way to live. You are constantly evaluating, "How am I doing? How am I looking?" And your dignity can be taken away from you in one moment if you lose any of these status indicators. This is the insecure postmodern world in which we live. Low self-esteem is the norm; we just compensate for it in many different ways. Instead of being created in the image and likeness of God, we see human personhood today as a "moveable famine" grounded in a sense of scarcity and "zero sum." If you are up, I am down. Comparison and competition are almost the only games left for the psyche. Only mature religion inhabits the world of abundance and draws upon an infinite abundance where, if you are up, I am up too; and if I am doing well, you share in the One Great Radiance. This is quite rare in a secular culture like ours.[1]

Gateway to Silence: You are precious in my eyes, you are honored, and I love you. (See Isaiah 43:4.)

DAY 2

Interior Poverty

When you're trapped inside a social system where you constantly have to work for your own superiority and can slip into inferiority in a moment, you are inevitably very insecure. You cannot draw your life from your own core, or from an outer inexhaustible Source that many of us call God. Life is always on hold or teetering on the edge of nothingness.

A fully converted believer knows that your stable core is something that God gratuitously gives you from the moment of your conception. You are inherently, objectively, totally, and forever a daughter or son of God. You cannot gain or lose that by any achievement or failure whatsoever. God doesn't participate in the honor/shame system. Christianity's single role is to always tell you that you are objectively a child of God, by whatever words, symbols, relationships, or sacraments it can muster. Our primary job is to keep proclaiming the true identity of things, and not to create contests whereby some few can attain their identity—if they are good enough—and where most lose or give up.

But much of religion has bought right into the honor/shame system. All we did was change the cultural rules to religious rules. Now there was yet another way to be superior—by being pious, publicly religious, and "moral" about one or two things (which are usually not central issues). Yet Jesus' teachings against status-seeking and building up religious reputation tell us again and again, "Don't go there!" (Examine Matthew 6:1–21 and Luke 18:9–14.)

Ironically, even the Franciscan concept of "poverty" can be turned into its own form of self-aggrandizement. In St. Francis' teachings, "poverty" is really his code word for not seeking status and upward mobility. Poverty for St. Francis was not about a material end in itself, but a strategy for the relinquishment of all false power. It seems to me that even some Christian groups (not very many!) have identified with *material* poverty as an end in itself (although we could all stand to seriously simplify our lives); the ego can even seek things like poverty, humility, and simplicity as another form of superiority!

If you don't have *interior* poverty, but need to look good and be admired and think well of yourself, then material poverty or humility is not anything admirable at all. It is just another ego stunt. I have met too many radicals who are very rigid and judgmental, and I've also met very comfortable people who are genuinely and completely poor in spirit. The best is to be both simple in lifestyle and fully open-hearted too.[2]

Gateway to Silence: You are precious in my eyes, you are honored, and I love you. (See Isaiah 43:4.)

DAY 3
The Gradual Purifying of Motivation

Jesus tells us to give alms, fast, and pray—but *secretly* (see Matthew 6:1–6, 16–18). These are the same three religious disciplines honored by most historical religions. Whenever you perform a religious action publicly, it enhances your image as a good, moral person and has a strong social payoff. Jesus' constant emphasis is on *interior* religiosity, on purifying motivation and intention. He tells us to clean the inside of the dish instead of being so preoccupied with cleaning the outside, with looking good (see Matthew 23:25–26). The purifying of our intention and motivation is the basic way that we unite our inner and our outer worlds. (Please read that twice!)

All through the spiritual journey, we should be asking ourselves, "Why am I doing this? Am I really doing this for God, for truth, or for others—or am I doing it for hidden reasons?" The spiritual journey could be seen as a constant purification of motive until we can finally say, "I have no other reason to do anything except love of God and love of neighbor. And I don't even need people to know this." When I can say this, I have total and full freedom. I can no longer be bought off! Finally I realize that my life is not about me; it's about Love.[3]

One simple indicator that your motivation is still in the early stages is if you resent or judge people who are not doing the generous or sacrificial thing that you are doing. Listen to Francis in our *Rule of the Friars Minor*, chapter 2: "I warn all the friars and exhort them never to condemn or look down on people who are wearing soft and colorful clothing, and enjoying luxuries of food and drink, rather we should just condemn and look down on ourselves" for doing this. He really was a religious genius. And, I am sorry to admit, that I now too often wear "soft and colorful clothing."

Gateway to Silence: You are precious in my eyes, you are honored, and I love you. (See Isaiah 43:4.)

DAY 4

Downward Mobility

In most honor/shame systems, which are most often publicly grounded in male values, a "true man" always seeks the best, the top, and the most in terms of roles, power, status, and possessions. This usually sets up the male for spiritual defeat or deceit. Although women create their own honor/shame systems too, up to now this was usually home-, appearance-, and family-based. Now women in overdeveloped countries have largely bought into the outer male system too, which can make them doubly trapped.

Jesus tried to free us from all these traps. Throughout the Gospels, we find numerous teachings promoting "downward mobility." The most familiar of these may be, "The last shall be first, and the first shall be last" (see Matthew 20:16), and Jesus' consistent honoring of the least, the outsider, the sinner, and the handicapped.

Jesus tells us to refuse all storing up of treasures, what he calls "building bigger barns" (see Luke 12:16–21). Does that sound like capitalism? Jesus said, "You cannot serve God and money" (see Matthew 6:24). "It's harder to pass through the eye of a needle than for a rich person to enter the kingdom of heaven" (see Matthew 19:24). Funny, we never told the rich they were unworthy to go to communion, when this warning is much more direct than anything Jesus said about divorce, gay marriage, or even abortion. Pope Francis has also been saying, "Money is to serve and not to rule." In the area of money and justice, Jesus makes his most clear and dualistic judgments. It is almost scary, but I think he recognizes that, if it is not absolutely clear, we will ignore it—just as we largely have done.

Yet, we have given generations of Christians the impression that we can *easily* be both rich and still generous, compassionate, and merciful. I know many who can, but they really work at it. Yet we have preachers on television who tell Americans that the more money you make and have, the more you are blessed and honored by God. They say, if you want to tell an untruth and get away with it, make it a really big untruth and for some reason people will buy it. That seems to be the case here. That is absolutely contrary to the teaching of Jesus, not to mention unsustainable with six billion people—and growing—on this planet. Self-serving ideology will trump the invitation of the Gospel every time.[4]

Gateway to Silence: You are precious in my eyes, you are honored, and I love you. (See Isaiah 43:4.)

DAY 5
Leveling the Field

Some form of the honor/shame system is seen in almost all of history. In such a system, there is immense social pressure to follow "the rules" (almost always man-made). If a person doesn't follow the rules, they are not honorable and no longer deserve respect. And anyone who shows such a "shameful" person respect is also considered dishonorable. (A certain US president, and one pope, could not even talk about people with AIDS, much less help them.)

Jesus frequently and publicly showed respect to "sinners" (see John 8:10–11) and even ate with them (see Luke 19:2–10; Mark 2:16–17). In doing so, he was openly dismissing the ego-made honor/shame system of his time—and ours. He not only ignored it, he even went publicly in the opposite direction. That preachers and theologians have failed to see this is culpable ignorance. Now we have a pope who brings back refugee Moslem families to be his guests in the Vatican. We seem to be finally getting it.

When Jesus was confronted with the dilemma of the woman caught in adultery, he masterfully leveled the playing field of the "honored" and the "shamed." To the men accusing her, he said, "Let the one among you who is guiltless be the first to throw a stone at her" (see John 8:7), and to her he said, "I do not condemn you; go now, and do not make this same mistake again" (see 8:11). What a marvelous consolation for people in all of history who have felt shamed or put down or defeated by others! Yet Jesus also holds the woman to personal responsibility for her actions. This should please every fair-minded person—and yet call us all further.

At the same time, this dilemma was an opportunity for the self-righteous accusers to face their own darkness, their own denied and disguised faults. Notice Jesus does not directly accuse them; he even saves their honor by just "writing on the ground" as they self-accuse and walk away "one by one, beginning with the eldest" (see 8:9). Hopefully they had learned from this necessary ego humiliation. Truly free people are able to embrace their failings and have no illusion or need to imagine themselves as better than other people.[5]

Gateway to Silence: You are precious in my eyes, you are honored, and I love you. (See Isaiah 43:4.)

DAY 6

The Economy of Grace

The key to entering into the new social order described by Jesus is never a discovery of our worthiness but always a surrender to God's graciousness. We are all saved by Divine mercy and not by any performance principle whatsoever. Any attempt to measure or increase our worthiness will always fall short, or it will force us into the position of denial and pretense, which produces hypocrisy and violence—to ourselves and others. The hallmark of every Divine encounter is the absolute and total gratuity of it! If you try to understand it by any ledger of merit, you will never understand it.

Switching to an "economy of grace" from our usual "economy of merit" is very hard for humans, very hard indeed. We naturally base almost everything in human culture on achievement, performance, accomplishment, payment, exchange value, appearance, or worthiness of some sort—what is usually called "meritocracy" (the rule of merit). Unless we experience a dramatic and personal breaking of the usual and agreed-upon rules of merit, it is almost impossible to disbelieve or operate outside of its rigid logic. This cannot happen theoretically, abstractly, or somehow "out there." It must happen to me—and in a very concrete situation!

Our word for that dramatic breaking of the ironclad rule is *grace*. It is God's magnificent jailbreak from our self-made prisons, the only way that God's economy can triumph over our strongly internalized merit-badge system. Grace is the secret, undeserved key whereby God, the Divine Locksmith, for every life and for all of history, sets us free. (See Romans 11:6,

Ephesians 2:7–10.) It is really the biblical "theme of themes," as far as I can see.

Life, when lived fully, tends to tool and retool us until we eventually discover a mercy that fills all the gaps necessary for our very survival and sanity. Without grace, everything human declines and devolves into smallness, hurt, victimhood, and blame.[6]

Gateway to Silence: You are precious in my eyes, you are honored, and I love you. (See Isaiah 43:4.)

DAY 7

Sabbath Meditation

Remember: **Subverting the Honor/Shame System**

Honor and shame are considered to be personal commodities that you can lose or gain. Within this system there is no inherent sense of the self. (Day 1)

When you're trapped inside a social system where you constantly have to work for your own superiority and can slip into inferiority in a moment, you are inevitably very insecure. (Day 2)

The spiritual journey could be seen as a constant purification of motive until we can finally say, "I have no other reason to do anything except love of God and love of neighbor." (Day 3)

Throughout the Gospels, we find numerous teachings promoting "downward mobility." The most familiar of these may be, "The last shall be first, and the first shall be last" (see Matthew 20:16), and Jesus' consistent honoring of the least, the outsider, the sinner, and the handicapped. (Day 4)

Jesus was openly dismissing the ego-made honor/shame system of his time—and ours. He not only ignored it, he even went publicly in the opposite direction. (Day 5)

Grace is God's magnificent jailbreak from our self-made prisons. (Day 6)

Rest: **Affirmations**

The words we use have power—for good or ill. Think of a phrase you have said aloud or thought to yourself, language that participates in the honor/shame system by ignoring your inherent dignity.

Turn it around and say, in the first person, present tense, an affirmation of your God-given value. For example:

I am unlovable. . . . I am infinitely loved.

I don't have enough. . . . I have everything I need.

I am stupid. . . . I have the mind of Christ.

I am worthless. . . . I am precious in God's eyes, I am honored, and God loves me.

Repeat the positive statement aloud, slowly, with intention and trust, several times. Then rest in the awareness that you are, already and forever, without any effort or achievement on your part, a beloved child of God.

Gateway to Silence: You are precious in my eyes, you are honored, and I love you. (See Isaiah 43:4.)

For further study:

Dancing Standing Still: Healing the World from a Place of Prayer
Francis: Turning the World on Its Head: Subverting the Honor/Shame System
The Path of Descent

THE PATH OF DESCENT

DAY 1
Hidden in Plain Sight

The Path of Descent could be called the metanarrative of the Bible. It is so obvious and so consistent and so constant that it's hidden in plain sight. We've overlooked this overwhelmingly obvious message by focusing on other things. Why did that happen? How is it that we were capable of missing what appears to be the major point? I think it has to do with the Spirit patiently working in time and growing us historically, I think it has to do with human maturity and readiness, and I think it has a lot to do with the ego and its tactics of resistance.

The literary and cultural critic, René Girard (1923–2015), said the path of descent puts the Bible in an entirely different category than most of world literature because it consistently gives the victim the privileged position, reaching its full denouement in Jesus himself. Once Christianity became the religion of the Roman Empire (beginning in the year 313), and the clergy and the nobility banded together to seek and protect the top, Christianity began to reflect the dominant culture instead of challenging it. It became largely about ego ascent, not the subtle descent about which all spiritual traditions speak. That suits the ego, which much prefers winning to losing; spiritual climbing to any talk of Exodus or Exile, suffering Job and Jeremiah; and surely no personal application of Jesus' Way of the Cross. No wonder that sincere seekers poured into the deserts of Egypt, Palestine,

Syria, and Cappadocia to seek depth and enlightenment in the fourth and fifth centuries.

God isn't really the great theme of the Bible. God isn't really *taught* in the Bible; God is *assumed*. There's never any question that there is a Transcendent Other. The problem is *whether this God is good and trustworthy* and *how to remain in contact with this subtle Transcendence*. The path agreed upon by all the monks, hermits, mystics, and serious seekers was a path of descent and an almost-complete rejection of the ego's desire for achievement, performance, success, power, status, war, and money. The emptiness, waiting, needing, and expecting of the path of descent created a space within where God could show Godself as good, as loving, and faithful.

Christians called this downward path, the Way of the Cross. The Desert Fathers and Mothers called it the Way of the Desert. In Philippians, Paul called it *kenosis*, the way of self-emptying: "Have this mind among yourselves, which is yours in Christ Jesus, who, though he was in the form of God, did not count equality with God a thing to be grasped, but emptied himself, taking the form of a servant, being born in the likeness of men. And being found in human form, he humbled himself and became obedient unto death, even death on a cross" (see Philippians 2:5–8).

But "the church on the corner," created for mass consumption, did not normally want to take Jesus that seriously. We needed an imperial religion, a fast-food Christianity, whose leaders could see their roles as reflecting prestige, a good career move, and not necessarily any direct following of Jesus. I am not trying to be unkind or unfair; just read Western history, to this day, for yourself.[1]

Gateway to Silence: When I am weak, then I am strong. (See 2 Corinthians 12:10.)

DAY 2

God Chooses the Little Ones

From the very beginning, God is able to use unlikely figures and, in one way or another, they are always unable, inept, unprepared, and incapable. The biblical text often shows them to be "powerless" in various ways: Sarah and Abraham, Moses, Rachel and Rebecca, David, Jeremiah, Jonah, Job, and Jesus himself are some of the clearest examples. God didn't pick the Egyptians; God picked the Israelites, an enslaved people in Egypt. In each case, *there needs to be a discovery of a new kind of power by people who do not have power.*

The bottom, the edge, the outsider, as we see in the Bible, is the privileged spiritual position. In a word, that is why the biblical revelation is revolutionary and even subversive. It is clearly disestablishment literature, yet has largely been used by establishments, which is at the heart of our interpretative problem.

According to Jesus, the so-called "little ones" (see Matthew 18:6) or the "poor in spirit" (see Matthew 5:3), as he calls them, are the only teachable ones, capable of being grown. It seems to be God's starting place, as it is in the Twelve-Step Program, because until we admit "that we are powerless," the Real Power will not be recognized, accepted, or even sought.[2]

Gateway to Silence: When I am weak, then I am strong. (See 2 Corinthians 12:10.)

DAY 3

Stumbling and Falling

Sooner or later, if you are on any classic "spiritual schedule," some event, person, death, idea, or relationship will enter your life, with which you simply cannot cope, using your present skill set, your acquired knowledge, or your strong willpower. Spiritually speaking, you will be—you must be—led to the edge of your own private resources. At that point, you will stumble over a necessary "stumbling stone," as Isaiah calls it (see Isaiah 8:14). You will and you must "lose" at something, and then you begin to develop the art of losing. This is the only way that Life/Fate/God/Grace/Mystery can get you to change, let go of your egocentric preoccupations, and go on the further and larger journey.

We *must* stumble and fall, I am sorry to say. We must be out of the driver's seat for a while, or we will never learn how to *give up* control to the Real Guide. It is the necessary pattern. Until we are led to the limits of our present game plan, and find it to be insufficient, we will not search out or find the real source, the deep well, or the constantly flowing stream. Alcoholics Anonymous calls it the Higher Power. Jesus calls this Ultimate Source the "living water" at the bottom of the well (see John 4:10–14).

The Gospel was able to accept that life is tragic, but then graciously added that we can survive and will even grow from this tragedy. This is the great turnaround! It all depends on whether we are willing to see down as up or, as Joseph Campbell put it, that "where you stumble, there lies your treasure."[3] Lady Julian of Norwich said it even more poetically, but I will paraphrase: "First there is the fall, and then we recover from the fall—and both are the mercy of God!"[4]

Gateway to Silence: When I am weak, then I am strong. (See 2 Corinthians 12:10.)

DAY 4

Exposing the Ego

The Cross teaches us to win by losing, but the ego doesn't like that. The ego wants to win by winning! That's the nature of the human psyche. And when the ego is not exposed for what it is, which Jesus' teaching does very clearly, it simply gets out of control.

In a masterful game of smoke and mirrors, the Christian church has focused for centuries on judging the *shadow self,* where Jesus himself never wasted much time. He put all of his energy into revealing the traps and blindness of the *ego self.* But we have spent most of our time making people feel guilty about their shadow self—the part of themselves of which they are ashamed. For the broken and shamed self, Jesus seems to have great pity, sympathy, and compassion. *Jesus is never upset at sinners; he is only upset with people who do not think they are sinners* (i.e., those who have not faced their shadow and often project their evil elsewhere).

Look at Jesus' parable of the Pharisee and the tax collector (see Luke 18:9–14). The Pharisee's ego had him trying to engineer his own righteousness. He could not see the shadow of his arrogance and judgment. The tax collector saw his sin, and realized his complete reliance on God's mercy. It was the tax collector who went home "justified rather than the other." In this quite extraordinary story, the one who supposedly did it right is judged wrong, and the one who seemingly did it wrong is judged right. This was meant to place a central corrective in the heart of all followers of Jesus.

The commonly accepted version of Christianity has largely developed in response to individual ego needs for worthiness and significance. But in the biblical Tradition, you do not see this self-made, autonomous, "getting it right" agenda that appears in later images of Christian holiness. Biblical rightness is primarily right relationship! There are no Promethean figures in the Bible; even Samson's strength can be lost by cutting off his hair. With the possible exception of Jesus' mother, Mary, and Jesus himself, almost every other biblical character, whether in the Hebrew or Christian Scriptures, is shown as a transformed sinner, as someone who first does it wrong before he or she ever does it right. The Bible is full of flawed, wounded individuals, which is quite different than the later "canonized saint" notion created by the Roman Church, although I do know it was our way of showing proof of actual transformation or enlightenment in the human person.

Surprise of surprises, we don't come to God by doing it right; we come to God by doing it wrong![5]

Gateway to Silence: When I am weak, then I am strong. (See 2 Corinthians 12:10.)

DAY 5

The Power of Powerlessness

Paul's expectations of the Messiah, and therefore of the nature of God, were turned absolutely upside down in his encounter with Jesus. Remember, the Jews had been an oppressed, occupied people. They had never been on the top. They had been waiting and waiting for some great historic figure who would liberate them: who was going to stand up to Rome, to Egypt, and to Syria. They were longing for the Anointed One, the Messiah (translated *Christ*), who would finally give them some dignity in human history.

But in his Christ experience on the Damascus Road (see Acts 9:3–8), the One that Paul encountered is a *crucified loser*! This is no military victor. This is someone who was crucified outside the city walls in the manner that slaves were killed. Paul had to utterly redefine power, leadership, and this new reality into which God is bringing us. Clearly, God descended to get to us; we did not climb a ladder of righteousness to get to God!

Therefore, in his writings, Paul idealizes not power, but powerlessness. "When I am weak, then I am strong" (see 2 Corinthians 12:10). "I glory in nothing except in the cross of Christ" (see Galatians 6:14). Is he a masochist? No; he's found what he calls "the mystery that has been hidden since the beginning of time" (see 1 Corinthians 2:7). The big disappointing turnaround (to those on top) is that we don't break through and transform history from the top down, but from the bottom up—because the mystery is revealed at the bottom, in the wound, from the failure, or, as we say, "on the cross."[6]

Gateway to Silence: When I am weak, then I am strong. (See 2 Corinthians 12:10.)

DAY 6

Going Up Means First Going Down

By the grace of God, saints and holy ones of every century still got the point of the transforming power of the path of descent, but only if they were willing to go through those painful descents that Catholics called the Way of the Cross, which Jesus called the "sign of Jonah," which St. Augustine called the "paschal mystery," which the Apostles' Creed called the "descent into hell," and which we would probably call "hitting the bottom" or "facing our powerlessness." Without these journeys, there's something you simply don't understand about the nature of God or the nature of your own soul.

"Can you drink of the cup that I am going to drink?" Jesus said to James and John, who still wanted roles in his kingdom. "We can!" they responded, and he said, to paraphrase, "Indeed, you will and you must, but roles are not my concern" (see Matthew 20:22–23). *Religion is largely populated by people afraid of hell; spirituality begins to make sense to those who have been through hell—that is, who have drunk deeply of life's difficulties.*

Christians speak of this descent as the "paschal mystery." It first of all refers to the process of loss and renewal that was lived and personified in the death and raising up of Jesus. We can affirm that belief in ritual and song, and thank Jesus for doing this, but until people have passed through their own losses and then experienced God upholding them so that they come out even more alive on the other side, the expression "paschal mystery" is little appreciated as the very shape of reality; it is a mere theological assertion. Ironically, in our time, many physicists, biologists, and cosmologists seem to know about this deep pattern better than many "believers." All, in their own way, are discovering that nothing really dies, it just changes form.[7]

Gateway to Silence: When I am weak, then I am strong. (See 2 Corinthians 12:10.)

DAY 7

Sabbath Meditation

Remember: **The Path of Descent**

The Path of Descent could be called the metanarrative of the entire Bible. (Day 1)

Until we admit that we are powerless, the Real Power will not be recognized, accepted, or even sought. (Day 2)

You will and you must "lose" at something, and then you begin to develop the art of losing. This is the only way that Life/Fate/God/Grace/Mystery can get you to change, let go of your egocentric preoccupations, and go on the further and larger journey. (Day 3)

We don't come to God by doing it right; we come to God by doing it wrong! (Day 4)

We don't break through and transform history from the top down, but from the bottom up. (Day 5)

Until people have passed through their own losses and then experienced God upholding them so that they come out even more alive on the other side, the path of descent is little appreciated as the very shape of reality. (Day 6)

Rest: **Falling and Failing into Union**

In many ways, prayer—certainly contemplative prayer or meditation—is planned and organized failure. If you're not prepared for failure, you'll avoid prayer, and that's what most people do. Prayer is typically *not* an experience of immediate union, satisfaction, or joy; in fact, quite the opposite. Usually you meet your own incapacity for and resistance to union. You encounter your thinking, judging, controlling, accusing, blaming, fearing mind. So why pray?

Julian of Norwich, my favorite mystic, uses the word "sin" to mean a state of separateness or disunion. She writes that you become aware of your state of resistance or separateness, and then when you try to sink into the experience of *oneing*, you realize you can't get there by yourself. You can't make it happen. You can't make yourself one.

Julian writes in *Revelations of Divine Love*, "Only in the falling apart of your own foundation can you experience God as your total foundation and your real foundation."[8] Otherwise you keep creating your own foundation, by your own righteousness, by your own intelligent and holy thoughts. Julian describes this reality in terms of what God does: God reveals God's-self as your authentic foundation.

What we're doing in prayer is letting our self-made foundation (or False Self) crumble so that God's foundation can be our reality. Prayer is a practice in failure that overcomes our resistance to union with Love. Let's fall into and rest in that Love one more time.[9]

Gateway to Silence: When I am weak, then I am strong. (See 2 Corinthians 12:10.)

For further study:

Great Themes of Paul: Life as Participation
The Path of Descent
Things Hidden: Scripture as Spirituality
Falling Upward: A Spirituality for the Two Halves of Life

TRANSFORMATIVE SUFFERING

DAY 1
Transforming Our Pain

All healthy religion shows you what to do with your pain. Great religion shows you what to do with the absurd, the tragic, the nonsensical, the unjust, all of which eventually fall into every lifetime. If only we could see these "wounds" as *the way through*, as Jesus did, then they would become sacred wounds and not something to deny, disguise, or export to others.

If we cannot find a way to make our wounds into sacred wounds, we invariably become cynical, negative, or bitter. Indeed, there are such people everywhere. As they go through life, the hurts, disappointments, betrayals, abandonments, the burden of their own sinfulness and brokenness all pile up, and they do not know where to put it. *If we do not transform our pain, we will most assuredly transmit it*—usually to those closest around us: our family, our neighbors, our work partners, and, invariably, the most vulnerable, our children.

Exporting our unresolved hurt is the most common underlying story-line of human history, and it is exemplified in the scapegoating mechanism. Biblical revelation is about transforming history and individuals so that we don't just keep handing on the pain to the next generation. Unless we can find a meaning for human suffering, that *God is somehow in it*, and can even use it for good, humanity is in major trouble.[1]

Gateway to Silence: God is in this with us.

Partnering with God

Many people rightly question how there can be a good God or a just God in the presence of so much evil and suffering in the world—about which God appears to do nothing. Exactly *how* is God loving and sustaining what God created? That is our dilemma.

I believe—if I am to believe Jesus—that God *is* suffering love. If we are created in God's image, and if there is so much suffering in the world, then God must also be suffering. How else can we understand the revelation of the cross and that the central Christian logo is a naked, bleeding, suffering man?

Many of the happiest and most peaceful people I know love "a crucified God" who walks with crucified people, and thus *reveals and redeems their plight as his own.* For them, Jesus is not observing human suffering from a distance; he is somehow *in* human suffering, with us and for us. He includes our suffering in the co-redemption of the world, as "all creation groans in one great act of giving birth" (see Romans 8:22). Is this possible? Could it be true that we "make up in our own bodies all that still has to be undergone for the sake of the Whole Body" (see Colossians 1:24)? Are we somehow partners with the Divine? At our best, we surely are. But I, like you, will never fully understand this Divine storyline to human history.[2]

Gateway to Silence: God is in this with us.

DAY 3

Holding the Pain

Don't get rid of pain until you've learned its lessons. When you hold pain consciously and trust fully, you are in a very special liminal space. This is a great teaching moment where you have the possibility of breaking through to a deeper level of faith and consciousness. Hold the pain of being human until God transforms you through it, then you will be an instrument of transformation for others.

As an example of holding the pain, picture Mary standing at the foot of the cross. Standing would not be the normal posture of a Jewish woman who is supposed to wail and lament to show her pain. She's holding the pain instead, as is also symbolized in Michelangelo's *Pietà*. Mary is in complete solidarity with the mystery of life and death. It's as if she is saying,

"There's something deeper happening here. How can I absorb it just as Jesus is absorbing it, instead of returning it in kind?" Until you find a way to be a transformer, you will pass the pain on to others.

Jesus on the cross and Mary standing beneath the cross are our classic images of transformative religion. They are never transmitting the pain to others. All the hostility that had been directed toward them—the hatred, the accusations, the malice; none of it is returned. They hold the suffering until it becomes resurrection! That's the core mystery of Christian religion; if you don't get that, you don't get it. It takes our whole life to comprehend this, and then to become God's "new creation" (see Galatians 6:15). The imperial ego hates such seeming diminishment.

Unfortunately, our natural instinct is to try to fix pain, to control it, or even, foolishly, to try to understand it. The ego always insists on understanding. That's why Jesus praises a certain quality even more than love, and he calls it *faith*. It is the ability to stand in liminal space, to stand on the threshold, to hold the contraries, until you move to a deeper level where it all eventually makes sense in the great scheme of God and grace, usually after the fact.[3]

Gateway to Silence: God is in this with us.

DAY 4

Suffering Can Bring Us to God

The genius of Jesus' ministry is that he reveals that God uses tragedy, suffering, pain, betrayal, and death itself, not to wound you but, in fact, to bring you to God. So there are no dead ends. Everything can be transmuted and everything can be used.

After all, on the cross, God took the worst thing, the killing of God, and made it into the best thing—the redemption of the world! If you gaze upon the mystery of the cross long enough, your dualistic mind breaks down, and you become slow to call things totally good or totally bad. You realize that God uses the bad for good, and that many people who call themselves good may in fact not be so good. At the cross you learn humility, patience, compassion, and all of the virtues that really matter.

Jesus says, "There's only one sign I'm going to give you: the sign of the prophet Jonah" (see Luke 11:29, Matthew 12:39, 16:4). Sooner or later, life is going to lead you (as it did Jesus) into the belly of the beast, into a place where you can't fix it, you can't control it, and you can't explain it or understand it. That's where transformation most easily happens. That's when you're uniquely in the hands of God.

Suffering is the only thing strong enough to destabilize the imperial ego. The separate and sufficient self has to be led to the edge of its own resources so it learns to call upon the Deeper Resource of who it truly is: the God Self, the True Self, the Christ Self, the Buddha Self—use the words you want. It is who we are in God and who God is in us. Once you are transplanted to this place you are largely indestructible![4]

Gateway to Silence: God is in this with us.

Redemptive Suffering

The "cross," rightly understood, precisely and always leads to resurrection. It's as if God were holding up the crucifixion as a cosmic object lesson, saying: "I know this is what you're experiencing. Don't run from it. Learn from it, as I did. Hang there for a while, as I did. It will be your teacher. Rather than losing life, you are gaining a larger life. It is the way through."

The mystery of the cross has the power to teach us that our suffering is not our own and my life is not about "me." Redemptive suffering is, I believe, a radical call to a deeper life and deeper faith that affects not only the self, but also others. We should pray ahead of time for the grace to bear our sufferings as Christ bore his for us. It is often hard to do when the suffering is upon us.

Hopefully, a time will come when the life of Christ will be so triumphant in us that we care more about others than about our own selves; or, better, when there is no longer such a sharp distinction between my self and other selves. Remember that conversion is more than anything else *a reconstituted sense of the self*. As Paul stated, "I have been crucified with Christ; it is no longer I who live, but Christ who lives in me; and the life I now live in the flesh I live by faith in the Son of God, who loved me and gave himself for me" (see Galatians 2:20).

The suffering that we carry is our solidarity with the one, universal longing of all humanity, and thus it can teach us great compassion and patience with both ourselves and others. Some mystics even go so far as to say that there is only one suffering; it is all the same, and it is all the suffering of God (see Colossians 1:24).[5]

Gateway to Silence: God is in this with us.

DAY 6

Wounded Healers

Only people who have suffered in some way can save one another—exactly as the Twelve-Step Program illustrates. Deep communion and dear compassion are formed much more by shared pain than by shared pleasure. I do not know why that is true.

"Peter, you must be ground like wheat, and once you have *recovered*, then you can turn and *help* the brothers" (see Luke 22:31–32), Jesus says to Peter. Was this his real ordination to ministry? No other is ever mentioned. I do believe this is the ordination that really matters and that transforms the world. Properly ordained priests might help bread and wine to know what they truly are, but truly ordained priests are the "recovered" ones who can then "help" people to know *who they are*. We have been more preoccupied with changing bread than with changing people, it seems to me.

In general, you can lead people on the spiritual journey as far as you yourself have gone. You can't talk about it or model the path beyond that. That's why the best thing you can keep doing for people is to stay on the journey yourself. Transformed people transform people. And when you can *be* healed yourself and not just talk about healing, you are, as Henri Nouwen so well said, a "wounded healer"—which is probably the only kind of healer! [6]

Gateway to Silence: God is in this with us.

DAY 7

Sabbath Meditation

Remember: **Transformative Suffering**

If we do not transform our pain, we will most assuredly transmit it. (Day 1)

Jesus is not observing human suffering from a distance; he is somehow *in* human suffering, with us and for us. (Day 2)

Don't get rid of pain until you've learned its lessons. (Day 3)

Suffering is the only thing strong enough to destabilize the imperial ego. (Day 4)

The cross, rightly understood, always leads to resurrection. (Day 5)

Transformed people transform people. (Day 6)

Rest: **Meditating on the Cross**

CAC's logo, an oval framing two intersecting arrows forming the cross of Christ, shows a collision of opposites. One arrow leads downward, preferring the truth of the humble. The other moves leftward against the grain. But all are wrapped safely inside a hidden harmony: one world, God's cosmos, a benevolent universe. The Celtic cross also places the vertical and horizontal bars within a circle, embracing the suffering of Christ within our own human context and God's eternal love.

Spend some time meditating on an image of the cross. Allow your body, mind, and heart to be completely present to the suffering of Christ. Welcome your own memories or sensations of pain, sorrow, grief. Hold them gently within the circle of God's presence—God's solidarity with human suffering. Then let go of this suffering, yours and Christ's, and rest in faith that from every death comes new life, and in every wound there is the opportunity for healing and hope.

Gateway to Silence: God is in this with us.

For further study:

The Authority of Those Who Have Suffered
Breathing Under Water: Spirituality and the Twelve Steps
A New Way of Seeing, a New Way of Being: Jesus and Paul
Job and the Mystery of Suffering
Things Hidden: Scripture as Spirituality

WEEK 16:

TRANSFORMATIVE DYING

DAY 1
What Must Die

All the great religions of the world talk a lot about it, so there must be an essential lesson to be learned through death. The problem has been that we might know something has to die, but throughout much of religious history we have been invariably killing the wrong thing and therefore not learning the real lesson.

Historically we moved from human sacrifice to animal sacrifice to various modes of seeming self-sacrifice, usually involving the body self. God was not considered friendly and always needed placating. God was distant and scary. God was not someone with whom you fell in love or with whom you could imagine sharing intimacy. Instead, God was viewed as an angry deity who demanded some sort of sacrifice to keep "him" on your side. Jesus presented a much different image of God, but it seems very hard for people to let go of their punitive ideas of God and to actually recognize the revolution of mind and heart that he offered.

Sadly, the history of violence and the history of religion are almost the same history. When religion remains at the immature level, it tends to create very violent people who ensconce themselves on the side of the good and the worthy and the pure and the saved. They project all their evil somewhere else and attack it over there. At this level, they export the natural death instinct onto others, as though it's always *someone else* who has to die.

The truth is, *it's you who has to die* or, better said, who you think you are. Your False Self, your ego self, your small self, has to die. Even the human Jesus had to die for the Risen Christ to be revealed.

Authentic and mature religion is always about *your transformation*. In its full meaning, it is always saying, "You are the one who must change," but we prefer to sacrifice symbolic things rather than our illusions. Jesus is the death of the old notion of sacrifice and the revelation of this utterly new and very meaningful sense of sacrifice. As Hebrews puts it, "He is abolishing the first to establish the second" (see 10:9). Sadly, much of Christianity still operates out of the first.[1]

Gateway to Silence: I lose my life to find Life.

DAY 2

Collapsing into the Larger Life

You are a son or daughter of a Good and Loving God. The Divine Image is planted inherently and intrinsically within you. You cannot create it, you cannot manufacture it, you cannot earn it, you cannot achieve it, you cannot attain it, you cannot cumulatively work up to it. Do you know why? Because you already have it! That is the reason that the message was first called "Good News."

Our first-half-of-life preoccupation with our False Self gets in the way of experiencing and knowing our deeper reality, which I call The True Self. The False Self is an imaginary self that thinks it's separate; it is *the self that thinks my little life is a proper reference point for Great Reality*. This is what must eventually die in order to find the real Reference Point, which many of us call God.

This God will lead you to that new, transformed place of the True Self if you are just willing to get out of the way. You cannot fully do it on your own; it will be done to you. Don't try to engineer your own death; that just reinforces the ego.

A situation in your life will lead you to a place, an event, a relationship, a failing or falling apart of something wherein you can't control life anymore and you can't understand it. Your little, separate, False Self is simply inadequate to the task, and finally, thankfully, you collapse into a Larger Self, who you are and have always been in God, which is inherently beloved.

You can't make yourself more beloved and you can't make yourself less beloved. You just have to recognize one day that it is true and start drawing your life from that much larger and more benevolent Source.[2]

Gateway to Silence: I lose my life to find Life.

Heaven Is Now and Later

Anyone who wants to save his life must lose it. Anyone who loses her life will find it. (See Matthew 16:25.)

This passage is a pretty strong, almost brutal, statement from Jesus. But it makes very clear that there is a necessary suffering that cannot be avoided, which Jesus calls "losing your very life." False Self is your role, title, and personal image that are largely creations of your own mind and attachments. It will and must die in exact correlation to how much you want the Real.

The Real is that to which all the world religions were pointing when they spoke of heaven, nirvana, bliss, or enlightenment. Their only mistake was that they pushed it off into the afterlife. When you die before you die, you are choosing the Real, or union with God, now—and over your imaginary separation from God. You are surrendering to "the kingdom of God" over your own smaller kingdoms. Heaven is the state of union both here and later. Only the True Self can know that. The False Self is infatuated with here and now.

The lasting question is: "How much False Self are you willing to shed to find your True Self?" Such necessary suffering will always feel like dying, which is what good spiritual teachers will tell you very honestly and, if needed and helpful, even brutally. Only a true friend is usually allowed to do that, so it is unfortunately somewhat rare.[3]

Gateway to Silence: I lose my life to find Life.

The One Big Pattern

I believe that the mystery of the Cross is saying that *the* pattern of transformation, *the* pattern that connects, *the* life that God offers us is *always death transformed.* The only pattern is the pattern of death and resurrection. We learn to submit to it with trust, frankly, because Jesus did.

St. Augustine called this metamorphosis, this transformative pattern that is in all things, the "Paschal Mystery." Catholics proclaim it as "the mystery of faith" at the center of every Mass: "Christ has died, Christ is risen, Christ will come again." Death and life are two sides of one coin, and you cannot have one without the other. It is the cycle of all life in the physical and biological universe.

This is the perennial, eternal, constant transformative pattern. You cannot get away from it. It's like a spiral: each time you make the surrender, each time you trust the dying, your faith is led to a deeper level. The mystics and the great saints were those who had learned to trust and allow this pattern. Now even scientific studies, including those of near-death experiences, reveal the same universal pattern. All the disciplines are coming together to say that there's one constant movement at work in this world. To be real is to surrender to its inevitable flow. It's the same pattern in the atom, as it is in the human body, as it is in the galaxies.

I think this is Jesus' big message: that there is something essential that you only know by dying—to whom you think you are! You really don't know what life is until you know what death is.[4]

Gateway to Silence: I lose my life to find Life.

DAY 5

Transformative Dying

Psychologist Kathleen Dowling Singh writes eloquently on this theme of transformative dying. Her book, *The Grace in Dying*, has changed many a life, and many peoples' attitude toward death.

Meditating on death is one of the special conditions that facilitates awakening.... To take in that we will die and that it is uncertain when—that it could be any time, even today—at the level of the heart is an experiential understanding of the whole being that can actually affect and transform us.

Jesus bore witness to awakening from the dream of self. In Gethsemane, he experienced his humanity—aware of his own singularity, aware of self. Even with the depth of his realizations and the magnitude of his love, he experienced the angst of his own impending death.

Jesus prayed, in Gethsemane, the passageway, through the chaotic mind of clinging and reluctance. Surrendering the exclusivity of self-reference—in love, for love, arms wide open on the cross—he emerged into Christ consciousness, transcending the smallness of self, obliterating the separation self imposes.[5]

Gateway to Silence: I lose my life to find Life.

The Way of the Cross

Following Jesus is a vocation to *share the fate of God for the life of the world*. I don't think it is a precondition for God's love or an entrance requirement for "heaven." It is a free invitation. Jesus invited people to "follow" him in bearing the mystery of human death and resurrection.

Those who agree to carry and love what God loves, which is both the good and the bad of human history, and to pay the price for its reconciliation within themselves—these are the followers of Jesus: the leaven, the salt, the remnant, the mustard seed that God can and will use to transform the world. The cross is the dramatic image of what it takes to be such a *usable* one for God.

These few are the critical mass that keeps the world from its path toward greed, violence, and self-destruction. God is calling everyone and everything into union with God's self (see Genesis 8:16–17, Ephesians 1:9–10, Colossians 1:15–20, Acts 3:21, 1 Timothy 2:4, John 3:17). But God still needs some instruments and images who are willing to be "conformed to the pattern of his death" and "transformed into the power of his resurrection" (see Philippians 3:10). They illuminate the path because they allow themselves to be conformed to the Divine pattern—and thus used for the good of others.

Jesus crucified *and* resurrected is the whole pattern revealed, named, effected, and promised for our own lives. "And" is the important word here. The Jesus story is the universe story. The Cosmic Christ is no threat to anything but separateness, illusion, domination, and the imperial ego. In that sense, Jesus, the Christ, is the ultimate threat, but first of all to Christians themselves. Only then will they have any universal and salvific message for the rest of the earth.[6]

Gateway to Silence: I lose my life to find Life.

SABBATH MEDITATION

Remember: **Transformative Dying**

The truth is, *it's you who has to die* or, better said, who you think you are. Your False Self, your ego self, your small self, has to die. (Day 1)

Finally, thankfully, you collapse into a Larger Self, who you are and have always been in God, which is inherently beloved. (Day 2)

How much False Self are you willing to shed to find your True Self? (Day 3)

You really don't know what life is until you know what death is. (Day 4)

"Surrendering the exclusivity of self-reference—in love, for love, arms wide open on the cross—[Jesus] emerged into Christ consciousness, transcending the smallness of self, obliterating the separation self imposes." — Kathleen Dowling Singh (Day 5)

Jesus crucified *and* resurrected is the whole pattern revealed, named, effected, and promised for our own lives. (Day 6)

Rest: **Meditating as Practice in Dying**

As so many holy ones taught, we must "die daily" to our small and separate sense of self. Kathleen Dowling Singh offers an invitation to practice dying through meditation. In her words, "We can sit to meditate with the intention to let it all go, inspired to explore what lies beyond self."

We sit deliberately, with noble posture and noble attention.

We breathe. Progressively, we free our awareness from sensations. We free our awareness from the "I" we imputed upon the sensations and the "mine" with which we tried to claim them. We relieve ourselves of all of our mistaken identifications, loosening our attachments to them, letting them go.

We liberate ourselves from illusions and, cleared of all that congested weight, the burden of being a self, we surrender, entering awareness that is spacious and quiet and uncongested.

We just die into silence. Die to the past. Die to the future. Die to the breath. Completely let go. The silence reveals itself as refuge, as awareness that can be trusted, tenderly loving and resounding with the majesty and the mystery of the sacred.[7]

Gateway to Silence: I lose my life to find Life.

For further study:

Adam's Return: The Five Promises of Male Initiation
Everything Belongs: The Gift of Contemplative Prayer
Falling Upward: A Spirituality for the Two Halves of Life
Immortal Diamond: The Search for Our True Self
"Ripening," *Oneing,* Vol. 1 No. 2
Things Hidden: Scripture as Spirituality
What Do You Mean "Falling Upward"?

WEEK 17:

THE COMMON WONDERFUL

DAY I
Rites of Passage

Only the non-dual, contemplative mind can hold everything in its wholeness, including both death and resurrection. In my work with initiation, this was key. Such non-dual "wisdom seeing" allows you to hold the full promise of the Real Life, which is big enough to even include death. Death and life are in an eternal embrace. We cannot have one without the other. This is the one common theme at the bottom of every initiation rite I have studied.

Briefly put, initiation rites have long been necessary to initiate men in particular into their True Self, into the flow of reality, into the great patterns that are always true, into the life of God. (Until very recently, women did not need initiation rites; their oppressed position in most patriarchal societies taught them these messages, often in sad and brutal ways.) Classic initiation rites brilliantly succeeded in preparing men for both life stages: training young men for the necessary discipline and effort required in the ascent of the first half of life, and preparing them ahead of time for the necessary descent and letting go of the second half of life.

The entire process that we call initiation somehow made it possible for a man to experience these five difficult truths:

1. Life is hard.
2. You are not that important.

3. Your life is not about you.
4. You are not in control.
5. You are going to die.

Basically, they were taught to die before they died. By the end of the initiation process (and optimally, for every life, somewhere between the first and second halves of life), the necessary deaths led to an inevitable and shared resurrection, which I call "the common wonderful." This week we will contrast these five difficult messages with their positive and wonderful counterparts which make it possible to hear them in the first place.[1]

Gateway to Silence: All shall be well.

DAY 2

Life Is Hard AND "My Yoke Is Easy"

The five *positive* messages of initiation, which I call "the common wonderful," are a cosmic egg of meaning that will hold you, help you grow, and give you ongoing new birth and beginnings (i.e., resurrection). By *cosmic egg*, I mean your underlying worldview, your life matrix, and your energy field—that which keeps you motivated and together for the long haul. If it is true then it must be accessible from all directions, which is why I call it cosmic, and because it is life-giving, I call it an egg. It holds you together in a shell of meaning. Our cosmic egg operates largely subliminally, but very powerfully. It is more caught than taught. I find these messages in Jesus' teaching, but there are similar messages in all the great traditions, especially from indigenous religions, the Islamic mystics, the Hasidic Jews, and the Hindu holy men and women.

The first message of the common wonderful: *It is true that life is hard, and it is also true, as Jesus said, that "My yoke is easy and my burden is light"* (see Matthew 11:30).

Enlightened people invariably describe the spiritual experience of God as restful, peaceful, delightful, and even ecstatic. Seek joy in God and peace within yourself; seek to rest in the good, the true, and the beautiful. It will be the only resting place that will also allow you to hear and bear the darkness.

Hard and soft, difficult and easy, painful and ecstatic do not eliminate one another, but actually allow each other. They bow back and forth like dancers, although it is harder to bow to pain and to failure. You can bear the hardness of life and see through failure if your soul is resting in a wonderful and comforting sweetness and softness. Religious people would call this *living in God.*[2]

Gateway to Silence: All shall be well.

DAY 3

You Are Not That Important AND "Your Name Is Written in Heaven"

The second message of the common wonderful: *It is true that you are not that important, and it is also true that "your name is written in heaven"* (see Luke 10:20).

If you know your original blessing, you can easily handle your original sin. If you rest in a previous dignity, you can bear insults effortlessly. Ultimate security allows you to suffer small insecurities without tremendous effort.

If we cannot trust that we have an eternal identity in God, then we are burdened with creating our own personal importance day after day. Either we are made by another or we must be self-made—or we live in the hall of mirrors of everybody else's image of us. Then we vie with one another for a zero-sum dignity and importance. We become lost in comparison, envy, competition, and codependency.

Authentic spirituality is an experience of abundance and mutual flourishing instead of a limited world of scarcity ("Their success is my loss!"). Only material gifts and ego gifts decrease in this way, whereas spiritual gifts actually increase with each use, in ourselves and in those around us. There is no loss in the world of Spirit, but all becomes an avenue to more.

Your importance is given and bestowed in this universe, which is the unbreakable covenant between you and your Creator. God declares you objectively important. As Isaiah says, "God has branded you on the palms of his hands" (see 49:16). The problem of negative self-image that we try so hard to solve is already completely solved, and most people, sadly, do not know this.[3]

Gateway to Silence: All shall be well.

DAY 4

Your Life Is Not about You AND You Are about Life

The third message of the common wonderful: *It is true that your life is not about you, but rather "Your life is hidden with Christ in God. He is your life, and when he is revealed, you will be revealed in all your glory with him"* (see Colossians 3:3–4).

All the truly great persons I have ever met are characterized by what I would call "radical humility." They are deeply convinced that they are drawing from another source; they are instruments. Their genius is not their own; it is borrowed. We are moons, not suns, except in our ability to pass on the light. Our life is not our own, yet, at some level, enlightened people know that their life has been given to them as a sacred trust. They live in gratitude and confidence, and they try to let the flow continue through them. They know that "love is repaid by love alone," as both St. Francis of Assisi and St. Thérèse of Lisieux (1873–1897) have said.

Your destiny and God's desire are already written in your genes, your upbringing, and your natural gifts. It is probably the most courageous thing you will ever do to *accept that you are just yourself.* Only the original manufacturer can declare what the product—you—should be; nobody else. "Even every hair of your head has been counted," as Jesus stated (see Matthew 10:30). God chooses us into existence, and continues that choice of us every successive moment, or we would fall into non-being. We are interrelated with Essential Being, participating in the very life of God, while living out one little part of that life in our own exquisite form.

Paradoxically, I can say *your life is precisely about you, but now you know who you really are,* and can hold this exquisite fire without burning up and burning out.[4]

Gateway to Silence: All shall be well.

DAY 5

Let Go of Control AND Let God's Life Flow

The fourth message of the common wonderful: *It is true that you are not in control, and it is also true that "For all your worrying, you cannot add a single moment to your span of life"* (see Luke 12:25).

If we cannot control the biggies—life and death—why should we spend so much time trying to control all the lesser outcomes? Call it destiny, providence, guidance, synchronicity, or coincidence, but people who are connected to the Source do not need to steer their own life and agenda. They know that it is being done for them in a much better way than they ever could. Those who hand themselves over are always well-received, and then the flow happens through them, with them, and in them.

When you think you deserve, expect, or need something specific to happen, you are setting yourself up for constant disappointment or even resentment, and you will not be able to enjoy, or at least allow, what is actually going to happen. After a while, you find yourself resisting almost everything at some level in an effort to remain in total control. I think this pattern is entirely common and widespread.

Only when you give up your preoccupation with control will you be able to move with the Divine Flow. Without all the inner voices of resistance and control, it is amazing how much you can get done and not get tired. We have discovered that what people call "burnout" is often the result of half-heartedness more than having worked too hard. Giving up control is a school of union, compassion, and understanding. It is also a school for the final letting go that we call death. If you practice giving up control early in life, you will be much happier and much closer to the truth, to the moment, and to God—none of which can be experienced if you are doing all the engineering and steering.[5]

Gateway to Silence: All shall be well.

DAY 6

You Are Going to Die AND Life Never Ends

The fifth message of the common wonderful: *It is true that you are going to die, and it is also true that "Neither death nor life, nothing that exists, nothing still to come, not any power, not any height nor depth, nor any created thing can ever come between us and the love of God"* (see Romans 8:38–39).

It seems that we are born with a longing, desire, and deep hope that this thing called life could somehow last forever. It is a premonition from Something Eternal that is already within us. Some would call it the soul. Believers would call it the indwelling presence of God. It is God in us that makes us desire God. It is an eternal life already within us that makes us imagine eternal life. It is the Spirit of God that allows us to seriously hope for what we first only intuit. Thus Paul loves to variously call the Spirit "the first fruits," "the promise," "the pledge," "the guarantee," or, as it were, the first installment of what is, in fact, the full and final situation (see John 14:17). All spiritual cognition is actually recognition: The Spirit within you knows the truth, you slowly intuit the truth (see John 14:6), and faith allows you to finally and fully grasp this truth—which cannot be proven, but only experienced.

God, by every religion's best definition, *is* love (see 1 John 4:16). What follows, of course, is that if we are God's creatures, then love is what *we* are too, at our deepest core and final identity. When we live consciously within this love, we will not be afraid to die, because love is eternal, and that core self is indestructible. "Love never ends" (see 1 Corinthians 13:8). The entire evolutionary thrust of time and history is making this very clear. Now we know that nothing really dies anyway.[6]

Gateway to Silence: All shall be well.

DAY 7

Sabbath Meditation

Remember: **The Common Wonderful**

Death and life are in an eternal embrace. We cannot have one without the other. (Day 1)

Hard and soft, difficult and easy, painful and ecstatic do not eliminate one another, but actually allow each other. (Day 2)

Your importance is given and bestowed in this universe, which is the unbreakable covenant between you and your Creator. (Day 3)

We are interrelated with Essential Being, participating in the very life of God, while living out one little part of that life in our own exquisite form. (Day 4)

If we cannot control the biggies—life and death—why should we spend so much time trying to control all the lesser outcomes? (Day 5)

When we live consciously within this love, we will not be afraid to die, because love is eternal. (Day 6)

Rest: **Vinyasa and Savasana**

The word *yoga* comes from the Sanskrit "to yoke"—to join or unite. The intentional movement, breath, and relaxation within yoga provide an opportunity to welcome the seeming contradictions of our life. Muscles are engaged *and* the body releases into deeper stretches. The mind is both concentrated and stilled. Within *vinyasa* the body flows through a series of poses, such as Sun Salutation (*Surya Namaskara*), and then finally rests in Corpse Pose (*Savasana*).

If you are not familiar with yoga, consider joining a class in your area or even find a short video online to lead you through the poses and breaths of Sun Salutations. If you already have a yoga practice, connect the rhythms of this familiar sequence to "the common wonderful."

As you salute the sun, bend and bow in gratitude for the life force that flows freely in you without your striving or control, yet invites your complete participation.

As you inhale and exhale through each of the bends and lunges, challenge yourself to breathe deeper, to stretch more fully, *and* let this practice be easy and natural, without effort or strain.

As you lie on your back and let each muscle in your body—from your toes to the top of your head—relax and sink into the ground, remember that you will die, but there is nothing to fear. Not even death can separate you from Love, and from death comes Life. Rest in this awareness.

Gateway to Silence: All shall be well.

For further study:

Adam's Return: The Five Promises of Male Initiation
Beloved Sons Series: Men and Grief
Exploring and Experiencing the Naked Now

DISCHARGING YOUR LOYAL SOLDIER

DAY I
Lacking True Rites of Passage

If you have ever been to Japan, you will know that it is a country that is ritually rich, with a strong sense of the importance of symbol, aesthetic, and ceremony. At the end of the World War II, some Japanese communities had the wisdom to understand that many of their returning soldiers were not fit for or prepared to reenter civil, peaceful society. The veterans' only identity for their formative years had been as a "loyal soldier" to their country. They needed a broader identity to rejoin their communities and families. You do not know how to be a father/mother or a brother/sister or a husband/wife with a soldier persona. They are very different identities.

So the Japanese created a ceremony whereby a soldier was publicly thanked and effusively praised for his service to the country. After the soldier had been fully honored, an elder would stand and announce with authority: "The war is now over! The community needs you to let go of what has well served you and us up to now. But we now need you to return as a man, a father, a husband, and something beyond a soldier."

We have no such rites of passage in our ritually starved culture, and they are deeply needed to let go of a past marriage, a past identity, or a past failure and move to the second half of life. Otherwise, we just keep living, regretting, or trying to redo our past, over and over again. That must be true of half of the people I have ever met!

I call this process of letting go "discharging your Loyal Soldier." This kind of closure is much-needed at the end of all major transitions in life. Because we have lost the sense of the need for such rites of passage, most people have no clear crossover to the second half of their own lives, and remain stuck and trapped in earlier and only partial identities and personas. I wonder if this is not one reason for the high incidence of Post-Traumatic Stress Disorder (PTSD), and depression in general, in our country today. So many are trying to live a human life with an "unhealed soldier" or earlier stage of life always dragging them down and backward. Their forward thrust is largely inhibited, whereas the full Gospel makes inevitable a forward thrust toward Resurrection.[1]

Gateway to Silence: The war has ended. Go in peace.

DAY 2

Unmerited Mercy

The Loyal Soldier is similar to the elder son in Jesus' parable of the prodigal son. His loyalty to strict meritocracy, to his own entitlement, to obedience, and supposedly to his father, keep him from the very celebration his father has prepared, even though the father begs his son to come to the feast (see Luke 15:25–32). We have no indication the elder son ever came! What a judgment this is on first-stage religion.

Jesus makes the same point in his story of the Pharisee and the tax collector (see Luke 18:9–14), in which the Pharisee was loyal and observant and, yet, Jesus says, he missed the point; while the tax collector, who had not obeyed the law at all, but admits it, is ironically deemed "at rights with God"! These are both examples of Jesus' subversive theology, which was intended to undo our usual merit-badge thinking and level the playing field of salvation. Yet most of Christianity never got the point, and ended up creating lots of elder sons and Pharisees. Both the elder son and the Pharisee are good, loyal soldiers—exactly what most of us in the church were told was the very meaning of religion.

Until we have met the Merciful One, until we've experienced unconditional love, I think we all operate out of some kind of meritocracy: "You get what you deserve, and no more than you deserve." Until we honorably discharge this Loyal Soldier, who knows little about real love, we will find it hard to recognize Infinite Love. The Loyal Soldier keeps many Christians from enlightenment, from transformation, from love, from forgiveness, from grace. The Loyal Soldier wears the common disguise of loyalty, obedience, and old-time religion, which is the best you have until you have experienced undeserved and unmerited love from an Infinite Source.[2]

Gateway to Silence: The war has ended. Go in peace.

Spirit-Taught Morality

The Loyal Soldier is largely what Freud described as the "superego," inner voices of guilt and shame, largely inherited from your first authority figures, that keep you under control and get you safely started in life. He said that our superego usually substitutes for any real adult formation of conscience. It is a preconditioned response, and not all bad, but it is nothing close to a free and empowering God encounter. The internalized superego feels like God, because it seemed as though it was our only guide in our early years. Such a superficial sense of conscience is a terrible substitute for authentic Spirit-led morality, yet it is what much organized religion reinforces. We used to call it "pay, pray, and obey" religion, where maintaining social order becomes the goal instead of transformation of consciousness.

What reveals the bogus character of this level of conscience is its major resistance to change and growth, and how it substitutes small, low-cost moral issues for the real ones that ask *us* to change instead of trying to change others. It often takes the form of "straining out gnats while swallowing camels" (see Matthew 23:24), as Jesus says. (I am thinking of Catholics who are self-centered and live materialistic lives, and the only thing they confess is that they "had three distractions during Mass"!)

God, life, and destiny have to loosen the Loyal Soldier's grasp on your small self, which up to now has felt like the only "you" that you know and the only authority that there is. To let go of the Loyal Soldier will be a severe death, an exile from your first base. However, have no doubt, discharging your Loyal Soldier will be necessary to finding authentic inner morality, or what Jeremiah promised as "the law written in your heart" (see 31:33). Most of us need guidance—and failure—to cross this boundary.[3]

Gateway to Silence: The war has ended. Go in peace.

Listening for the True Voice

The internal Loyal Soldier we developed during childhood (largely from our parents' early warnings) was supposed to keep us safe, creating and deploying whatever strategies were necessary to ensure our social, psychological, and physical survival.

The voices of the Loyal Soldier are pre-rational, immediate, deep, constant, and unconscious, and they feel like absolute right and wrong, determining what we value and what we disvalue. They seem to become for us the very voice of God (resulting in our distorted, punitive images of God). They are usually shame- or guilt-based and very good for social order and control, which are first-half-of-life concerns. Thus they are not subject to rational control or explanation; they largely reside in the unconscious. To move beyond them is not normally a matter of mere education, but of deep emotional *healing*.

There is a deeper voice of God, which you must learn to *hear and obey* in the second half of life. It will sound like the voice of risk, of trust, of surrender, of soul, of common sense, of destiny, of love, of an intimate stranger, of your deepest self. *It will always feel gratuitous, and it is this very freedom that scares you. Love can only increase in the realm of freedom.* You need to discriminate the voices of the Loyal Soldier from the voice of the Holy Spirit. God never leads by guilt or shame! The deeper faith journey begins when you start to listen to and follow God's inner voice, and not just shame-based early conditioning. You must move to higher levels of motivation than mere safety and security. God leads by loving the soul at ever-deeper levels, not by shaming at superficial levels.[4]

Gateway to Silence: The war has ended. Go in peace.

DAY 5

Crossing Over to Life

Normally we will not discharge our Loyal Soldier until it shows itself to be wanting, incapable, and inadequate for the real issues of life—as when we confront love, death, suffering, subtlety, sin, mystery, and so on. It is another form of the falling and dying that we keep talking about. The world mythologies all point to places like Hades, Sheol, Gehenna, hell, purgatory, or the realm of the dead. Even Jesus, if we are to believe the Apostles' Creed of the church, "descended into hell" before he ascended into heaven. *Maybe these are not so much alternatives to heaven as the necessary paths to heaven.*

When you discharge your Loyal Soldier, it will first feel like a loss of faith or loss of self. But this is only the death of the False Self, and can be the very birth of the soul. Instead of being ego-driven, you will begin to be soul-drawn.

The wisdom and guidance you will need to cross this chasm will be like Charon ferrying you across the river Styx, or Hermes guiding the soul across all scary boundaries, or Michael the Archangel slaying your demons. These are your authentic soul friends, what we sometimes call spiritual directors or elders. Celtic Christianity called them *Anam Cara* or "soul friends."

Remember that Hercules, Orpheus, Aeneas, Psyche, Odysseus, and Jesus all traveled into realms of the dead—and returned! When the Apostles' Creed says that Jesus "descended into hell," this means that he destroyed hell. Once Christ is there, it can no longer be hell, but is now heaven! Even Pope Benedict said that in his commentary on the Creed.[5]

Gateway to Silence: The war has ended. Go in peace.

DAY 6

Our Real Protection

Early-stage morality seems to be determined by what some call the world of karma or some kind of equalization between debt and punishment, merit and reward. It seeks to create some "justice" between output and input, so the world can make sense to our small self. The Loyal Soldier voices that developed in our early childhood said, "You get what you deserve. You don't deserve anything more than what you've earned and are therefore worthy of receiving." This simple worldview likes "bad" people to be punished and "good" people to be rewarded; just talk to any ten-year-old child. But because most people do not grow up spiritually, things like capital punishment, oppressive penal codes, torture, and war continue unabated, even in people who think they have experienced the transformation of the Gospel.

For most of us, the world of reward and punishment, law and obedience, is the frame with which we began as children. If I had three screaming kids, I suppose I would be into reward and punishment too! "You only get the lollipop when you're a good girl," or "Mommy punishes me when I'm a bad boy, so that must be the way God is too." Right? No; that is the very program that God has to change by inserting some new and wonderful software. Remember: True Christianity is a mystical matter, not a moral matter. In fact, our early moral explanations normally have to fall apart before we can proceed on the mystical path. Scary, isn't it?

Through prayer, suffering, and/or great love, we eventually encounter the real God who is so much greater than our logic and our retributive notion of justice. The Divine is always an experience of mercy and forgiveness, a warming of the heart, as John Wesley put it. Finally, we start to grow up and move beyond the world of karmic debt—*where everybody actually loses*—to the world of grace—where everybody always wins. If the Loyal Soldier is the protector of the first half of life, Jesus is the protector of the world of grace and freedom.[6]

Gateway to Silence: The war has ended. Go in peace.

DAY 7

Sabbath Meditation

Remember: **Discharging Your Loyal Soldier**

Because we have lost the sense of the need for rites of passage, most people have no clear crossover to the second half of their own lives. (Day 1)

The Loyal Soldier wears the common disguise of loyalty, obedience, and old-time religion, which is the best you have until you have experienced undeserved and unmerited love. (Day 2)

God, life, and destiny have to loosen the Loyal Soldier's grasp on your small self, which up to now has felt like the only "you" that you know and the only authority that there is. (Day 3)

God never leads by guilt or shame, but always by grace and mercy. (Day 4)

When you discharge your Loyal Soldier, it will first feel like a loss of faith or loss of self. But this is only the death of the False Self. (Day 5)

If the Loyal Soldier is the protector of the first half of life, Jesus is the protector of the world of grace and freedom. (Day 6)

Rest: **A Ritual**

In order to move to the second half of life, we must respect, honor, and create closure for our Loyal Soldier. We need to "discharge" the Loyal Soldier because he or she has been in charge for most of our lives. This stalwart part of our psyche has tried to protect us, but the time comes to let it rest so that we can live more authentically in peace and freedom.

Over the next few weeks, take the time to write down instances when you hear the familiar voices of your Loyal Soldier (and perhaps they have come to sound like the voice of God). After a month of recognizing and recording the voices, create a ritual in which you bring them to an altar or special place of prayer.

Acknowledge the ways in which your Loyal Soldier has kept you safe and successful throughout your life (for example, obeying laws and staying within boundaries, repressing displays of emotion, hiding anything that would tarnish the ego's image). Offer gratitude for this great service and assure your Loyal Soldier that you no longer need to be defended.

Name some of the ways in which your Loyal Soldier has had a negative, constricting effect on your life, such as keeping you from fully experiencing joy and intimacy. Speak aloud a prayer or intention: "I choose to hear and follow the voice of Love rather than the small and confining voices of my Loyal Soldier."

Place the papers on which you've written Loyal Soldier's admonitions in an old journal or box of mementos (as relics of your past) or bury them.

From time to time, your Loyal Soldier might need a reminder that he or she is not on active duty. When your Loyal Soldier tries to keep your "enemy" self in shadows, gently repeat the process and live into the freedom of peacetime.

Gateway to Silence: The war has ended. Go in peace.

For further study:

Discharging Your "Loyal Soldier"
The Enneagram as a Tool for Your Spiritual Journey
Falling Upward: A Spirituality for the Two Halves of Life
The Little Way: A Spirituality of Imperfection
Things Hidden: Scripture as Spirituality
Transforming the World through Contemplative Prayer

GROWING IN GRACE

DAY 1

The Great Economy of Grace

It is by grace that you are saved, through faith, not by anything of your own, but by a pure gift from God, and not by anything you have achieved. Nobody can claim the credit. You are God's work of art. (See Ephesians 2:8–10.)

Grace is the Divine Unmerited Generosity that is everywhere available, totally given, usually undetected as such, and often even undesired. It has been rightly defined, even in the old catechism, as "that which confers on our souls a new life, that is, a sharing in the life of God Himself."[1]

Grace cannot be understood by any ledger of merits and demerits. It cannot be held to any patterns of buying, losing, earning, achieving, or manipulating, which is where, unfortunately, most of us live our lives. Grace is, quite literally, "for the taking." It is God eternally giving away God—for nothing, except the giving itself. Quite simply, to experience grace you must stop all *counting*!

The ego does not know how to receive things freely or without logic. It prefers a worldview of scarcity, or at least *quid pro quo*, where only the clever win. It likes to be worthy and needs to understand in order to be able to accept things. That problem, and its overcoming, is at the very center of the Gospel plot line. It has always been overcome from God's side. The only problem is getting us in on the process! That full inclusion of us is the greatest testimony to God's humility, mercy, and love.[2]

Gateway to Silence: Open me to grace upon grace upon grace.

DAY 2

Delight Rather than Duty

A friend of mine shared this story with me. An angel was walking down the street carrying a torch in one hand and a pail of water in the other. A woman asked the angel, "What are you going to do with the torch and the pail?" The angel said, "With the torch, I am going to burn down the mansions of heaven, and with the pail, I'm going to put out the fires of hell. Then we shall see who really loves God."

That's what grace does; it empowers those who really love and trust God, and frankly leaves all others in the realm of missed opportunity. Our image for that missed opportunity has been some kind of hell in the afterlife, but it is primarily and clearly emptiness *now*. In that deepest sense, there are indeed many people in hell right now, and there are also many people tasting heaven today, on this earth. But Divine Love never relents, and never stops urging, expanding, and appealing, so why would it stop after our death? This deep realization became the very poorly defined notion of "purgatory," but the underlying concept is quite orthodox—it all relies on an infinite trust in an infinite love.

Only the theme of grace is prepared to move religion beyond the bad and tired storyline that carries a very static notion of God, grace, and the human person. Up to now, we have largely mirrored ego-based culture instead of transforming it. We need grace to reform religion and to recapture the Gospel. Only the theme of grace can move us from a religion of mere requirements (that is all about counting and measuring) to a religion of Divine Abundance which deeply transforms human consciousness (see Ephesians 4:23–24).

As long as we remain inside of a win-lose script, Christianity will continue to appeal to low-level and self-interested morality and never rise to the mystical banquet that Jesus offers us. It will be duty instead of delight, "jars of purification" (see John 2:6) instead of 150 gallons of intoxicating wine at the very end of the party (see John 2:7–10)![3]

Gateway to Silence: Open me to grace upon grace upon grace.

DAY 3

An Inner Immensity

There is an Inner Reminder (see John 14:26) and an Inner Rememberer (see John 14:26, 16:4) who holds together all the disparate and fragmented parts of our lives, who fills in all the gaps, who owns all the mistakes, who forgives all the failures—and who loves us into an ever deeper life. This is the job description of the Holy Spirit, who is the spring that wells up within us (see John 7:38)—and unto eternal time. This is the breath that warms and renews everything (see John 20:22). These are the eyes that see beyond the momentary shadow and disguise of things (see John 9); these are the tears that wash and cleanse the past (see Matthew 5:4). And better yet, they are not only *our* tears but actually the very presence and consolation of God within us (see 2 Corinthians 1:3–5).

You must contact this Immensity! You must look back at what seems like your life from the place of this Immensity. You must know that this Immensity is already within you. The only thing separating you from such Immensity is your unwillingness to trust such grace, such an utterly unmerited gift. It is an immense humiliation to the ego to know that it cannot earn love, achieve merit, or "get enlightened" by any technique or formula whatsoever. You cannot *get* there, you can only *be* there, as any number of spiritual teachers, West and East, have so widely discovered and now teach. You surrender to love; you do not accomplish love by willpower.[4] Love appears to be planted in all things as an inner engine of evolution and consciousness, similar to the way chlorophyll inside of green plants transmutes sunshine and water into energy for the life and growth of the plant—and the life and growth of those who feed off the plant. It is wonderful to recognize that so many spiritual processes are mirrored in nature. All we need to do is observe and recognize!

Gateway to Silence: Open me to grace upon grace upon grace.

DAY 4

Grace Is God's Name

The goodness of God fills all the gaps of the universe, without discrimination or preference. God is the gratuity of absolutely everything. The space in between everything is not space at all but Spirit. God is the "goodness glue" that holds the dark and light of things together, the free energy that carries all death across the Great Divide and transmutes it into Life. When we say that Christ "paid the debt once and for all," it simply means that God's job is to make up for all the deficiencies in the universe. What else would God do?

Grace is not something God gives; grace is who God *is*. Grace is God's official job description. *Grace is what God does to keep alive—forever—all things that God has created in love.* If we are to believe the primary witnesses—

the mystics, the saints, the transformed people—an unexplainable goodness is at work in the universe. (Some of us call this phenomenon God, but that word is not necessary. In fact, sometimes it gets in the way of the experience, because too many have named God something other than Grace.)[5]

Gateway to Silence: Open me to grace upon grace upon grace.

DAY 5

No Exceptions

Death is not just physical dying, but going to full depth, hitting the bottom, going the distance, beyond where we are in control, fully beyond where we are now. We all die eventually; we have no choice in the matter. But there are degrees of death before the final physical one. If we are honest, we acknowledge that we are dying throughout our life, and this is what we learn if we are attentive: *grace is found at the depths and in the death of everything.*

After these smaller deaths, we know that the only "deadly sin" is to swim on the surface of things, where we never see, find, or desire God and love. This includes even the surface of religion, which might be the worst danger of all. We must not be afraid of falling, failing, going "down," because it is there that we find grace. Like water, grace seeks the lowest place and there it pools. (St. Teresa of Ávila writes in her autobiography that water is the single best multilayered symbol for the entire spiritual journey.)

When you go into the full depths and death, sometimes even the depths of your sin, you come out the other side—and the word for that is resurrection. Something or someone builds a bridge for you between death and life, recognizable only from the far side. None of us crosses over by our own effort or merits, purity or perfection. We are all carried across by an uncreated and unearned grace—from pope to president to princess to peasant. Worthiness is never the ticket, only deep desire, and the ticket is given in the desiring. There are no exceptions to death and there are no exceptions to grace. And, I believe, with good evidence, that there are no exceptions to resurrection.[6]

Gateway to Silence: Open me to grace upon grace upon grace.

DAY 6

God Revealed

There is no way that the Scriptures, rightly understood, present God as an eternal torturer. Yet many Christians seem to believe this, and many are even held back from trusting God's goodness because of this "angry parent in the sky" that we have created. The determined direction of the Scriptures, fully revealed in Jesus, is that God's justice is not achieved by punishment, but by the Divine Initiative we call grace, which enables us to bring about internal rightness, harmony, balance, and realignment with *what is*. We would speak of this as "restorative justice," a very Biblical notion learned from the Jewish prophets and exemplified by Jesus. But we are now suffering from centuries of merely a *retributive* notion of justice—even in the church, which should have known better.

In other words, God "justifies" (that is, "validates") creation, not by parental punishment from without (which really changes nothing except perhaps behavior), but by positive enticement and transformation from within, which is surely a far greater victory and achievement of "justice" on God's part. This concept of grace is first called mercy, or *hesed* in Hebrew, the ever-faithful, covenant-bound, infinite love of God, and all God's power for renewal and resurrection proceeds from this source, never from punishment. Jesus punishes nobody! I would go so far as to call grace the *primary revelation* of the entire Bible. If you miss this message, all the rest is distorted and even destructive. I cannot emphasize this strongly enough.

The only prerequisite for receiving the next grace is having received the previous one. As the mystics have often said, God "hides." Every moment is not obvious as God, as grace; it just looks like another ordinary moment. But your willingness to *see* it as gratuitous—as a free gift, as self-revelatory, as a possibility—allows it to be that way. God's hiding ceases. God and grace become apparent as a gift in each moment. And those who learn how to receive gifts keep receiving further gifts. "From God's Fullness we have all received, grace upon grace" as John puts it (see 1:16).[7]

Gateway to Silence: Open me to grace upon grace upon grace.

DAY 7

Sabbath Meditation

Remember: **Growing in Grace**

Grace is the Divine Unmerited Generosity that is everywhere available, totally given, usually undetected as such, and often even undesired. (Day 1)

Only the theme of grace is prepared to move religion beyond the bad and tired storyline that carries a very static notion of God, grace, and the human person. (Day 2)

The only thing separating you from such Immensity is your unwillingness to trust grace, such an utterly unmerited gift. (Day 3)

The goodness of God fills all the gaps of the universe, without discrimination or preference. (Day 4)

Like water, grace seeks the lowest place and there it pools. (Day 5)

I would go so far as to call grace *the primary revelation* of the entire Bible. (Day 6)

Rest: **Saying Grace**

Many cultures have a beautiful tradition of saying a prayer before or after a meal, expressing gratitude and asking for blessing. If we are accustomed to praying over our food, it may become a rote, almost thoughtless gesture. Yet it is another opportunity to intentionally open ourselves to receive and participate in grace. The food is already blessed simply by its existence. God doesn't require our words of thanks. But it does us good to "say grace," to verbally acknowledge the grace that is everywhere, even and especially in the giving of lives—plant and animal—for our sustenance.

If you have a practice of saying grace, bring greater awareness and presence to it. Find or create a prayer that names your experience of grace. This Hindu blessing is said before meals:

This ritual is One. The food is One. We who offer the food are One. The fire of hunger is also One. All action is One. We who understand this are One.[8]

Indeed, it is all One in the immense and undiscriminating Grace that is God.

Gateway to Silence: Open me to grace upon grace upon grace.

For further study:

The Enneagram and Grace: 9 Journeys to Divine Presence
Francis: Turning the World on Its Head: Subverting the Honor/Shame System
Immortal Diamond: The Search for Our True Self
Job and the Mystery of Suffering
Things Hidden: Scripture as Spirituality

WEEK 20:

SHADOWBOXING

DAY I
Necessary Humiliations

Your Loyal Soldier tells you to be socially vigilant: "How am I coming across? Will people like me? Will this be acceptable? Will this help me succeed?" Your Loyal Soldier can serve you well by giving you some social niceties and protection. But after you've lived out of these niceties for years, they become your idealized self, your persona, your chosen public image, your False Self. To protect this image, all the contrary and negative aspects of yourself have to go underground, hidden from others and even from your own awareness. These forgotten and denied qualities make up what many call the "shadow self."

Frankly, much of the movement from the first half of life to the second half of life is shadowboxing, the process of facing the negative part of yourself that you're not proud of, such as hateful thoughts you have once in a while that you hope nobody knows about, or recognizing the log in your own eye when you're confronted with the speck in someone else's eye. This is humiliating, necessary work in every human life—no exceptions. In fact, the purer and holier your well-maintained self-image, the more inner negativity and hatefulness you are likely to harbor, and hide from yourself and others.

When you get your False Self (and the Loyal Soldier who is protecting this self) out of the way, the soul stands revealed. The soul, or True Self, cannot be worked for or created. It *is*, and always has been. The soul is God's "I

AM" continued in you, the part of you that already knows, desires, and truly seeks God. Ironically, the Loyal Soldier that you mistook for God actually defends you from God! I suspect this is exactly what the Dominican Meister Eckhart (c. 1260–c. 1327) meant when he said, "I pray to God that he may make me free of 'God'!"[1]

Gateway to Silence: Christ shall give you light. (See Ephesians 5:14.)

DAY 2

Let Your Enemy Be Your Teacher

Make friends with your opponent quickly while he is taking you to court, or he will hand you over to the judge, and the judge to the officer, and the officer will throw you into prison. You will not get out until you have paid the last penny. (See Matthew 5:25–26.)

Persona and shadow are correlative terms. *Your shadow is what you refuse to see about yourself, and what you do not want others to see.* The more you have cultivated and protected a chosen persona, the more shadow work you will need to do. Conversely, the more you live out of your shadow self, the less capable you are of recognizing the persona you are trying to protect and project. It is like a double-blindness, keeping you from seeing—and being—your best and deepest self. As Jesus put it, "If the lamp within you is, in fact, darkness, what darkness there will be" (see Matthew 6:23). It is all about seeing—and seeing fully and truthfully. It takes a lifetime.

Your persona is what most people want from you; they will reward you for it, and so you will naturally choose to identify with it. As you do your inner work, you will begin to know that your self-*image* is nothing more than just that, and not worth protecting, promoting, or denying. As Jesus says in the passage above, if you can begin to "make friends quickly" with those who "are you taking you to court" (your "enemies"), you will usually begin to see some of your own shadow. If you don't, you will miss out on much-needed wisdom and end up "imprisoned" within yourself or taken to "court" again later. Eventually you will have to "pay the last penny" to reorder your life and your relationships. In the spiritual life, your enemies are really your friends, and that is not just doubletalk. Also, your friends who only flatter you are not true friends at all.[2]

Gateway to Silence: Christ shall give you light. (See Ephesians 5:14.)

DAY 3
Growth through Shadow Work

Shadow work is humiliating work, but properly so. If you do not work through such humiliations with regularity and make friends with all those who reveal to you and convict you of your own denied faults, you will surely remain in the first half of life forever. We never get to the second half of life without major shadowboxing. And I'm sorry to report that it continues until the end of life, the only difference being that, as you become accustomed to your own games, you are no longer so surprised by your surprises or so totally humiliated by your humiliations! You come to expect various forms of half-heartedness, deceit, vanity, or illusions from yourself. But now you see through them, which destroys most of their destructive power.

The important thing is to learn from your shadow side. Some call this kind of discovery the "golden shadow" because it carries so much enlightenment for the soul. The general pattern in story and novel is that heroes learn and grow from encountering their shadow, whereas villains never do. Invariably, the movies and novels that are most memorable show real "character development" and growing through shadow work. This inspires us all because it calls us all. As Joseph Campbell put it so well, "Where you stumble, there lies your treasure."[3] When we have public figures who totally deny their shadow, projecting it elsewhere, with the population even applauding them for that, a culture is in real trouble. This is much of our political scene today, I am afraid.[4]

Gateway to Silence: Christ shall give you light. (See Ephesians 5:14.)

DAY 4
Salvation from the False Self

When we are young, we all identify with our idealized persona so strongly that we become masters of denial and learn to eliminate or deny anything that doesn't support it. *Neither our persona nor our shadow is evil in itself; they just allow us to do evil and not know it.* Our shadow self makes us all into hypocrites on some level. *Hypocrite* comes from the Greek for "actor," someone playing a role rather than being "real." We are all encouraged by society to play our roles. Until grace is fully triumphant, we are all actors and "hypocrites" of sorts.

Usually everybody else can see your shadow, so it is crucial that you learn what everybody else—except you—knows about you! The moment you become whole and holy is when you can accept your shadow self; or, to put it in moral language, when you can admit your sin. Or, as the Recovery Movement puts it, "Do a fearless moral inventory." *Only then do you move from unconsciousness to the beginnings of consciousness.* There needs to be an ongoing struggle, it seems, because the ego takes increasingly clever disguises the closer you get to the Light.

The saint is precisely one who has no "I" to protect or project. His or her "I" is in conscious union with the "I AM" of God, and that is more than enough. Divine Union overrides any need for either self-hatred or self-promotion. They are both equally unhelpful and unnecessary. Enlightened people do not need to be perfectly right; they know they cannot be anyway, so they just try to be in *right relationship*. In other words, they try, above all else, to be *loving*.

Love holds you tightly and safely and always. It gives you the freedom to meet the enemy and know the major enemy is "me," as the old comic character Pogo said. But you do not hate "me" either; you just see through and beyond "me." Shadow work literally saves you from yourself (your False Self, that is), which is the foundational meaning of salvation. For then "You too (your True Self) will be revealed in all your glory with him" (see Colossians 3:4).[5]

Gateway to Silence: Christ shall give you light. (See Ephesians 5:14.)

DAY 5

Sin and Shadow

The closer you get to the Light, the more of your shadow you see. Thus truly holy people are *always* humble people. As one master teacher cleverly put it, "Avoid spirituality at all costs; it is one humiliation after another!" It could have been a great service to Christians if shadow had been distinguished from sin. Sin and shadow are not the same. We were so encouraged to avoid sin that instead many of us avoided facing our shadow, and then we sinned even more—while still remaining blissfully unaware! *One always learns one's mystery at the price of one's innocence,* it has been said.[6]

Paul put it this way, "The angels of darkness must disguise themselves as angels of light" (see 2 Corinthians 11:14). Any idealized persona does not choose to see evil in itself, so it always disguises it as good. The shadow self invariably presents its own selfishness as something like prudence, common sense, justice, or "I am doing this for your good," when it is actually manifesting fear, control, manipulation, or even vengeance. (The name Lucifer literally means the "light bearer." The evil one always makes darkness look like light—and makes light look like darkness.)

Invariably, when something upsets you, and you have a strong emotional reaction out of proportion to the moment, your shadow self has just been exposed. So watch for any overreactions or over-denials in yourself. When you notice them, the cock has just crowed (see Mark 14:68)!

The reason that a mature or saintly person can be so peaceful, so accepting of self and others, is that there is not much hidden shadow self left. (There is always and forever a little more, however! Shadow work never stops.) The denied and disguised self takes so much energy to face, awaken, and transform that normally you have little energy left to project your fear, anger, or unlived life onto others.[7]

Gateway to Silence: Christ shall give you light. (See Ephesians 5:14.)

DAY 6

The Shadow Side of Everything

Full human life demands some shadowboxing with the shadow side of every reality. If we are not willing to do that, if we want the Republicans or the Democrats to be totally right, or America to be perfect, or our religion to be the only proper path, then we are incapable of depth or truth. When everything becomes a secure "belonging system" instead of a transformational experience, people simply locate themselves inside their little world of shared illusions. The fragile self quickly takes on a sense of identity and power by believing its self-serving illusions. A negative identity is more easily formed than a positive one. It is easier to react than to choose, to know what I am not than to know who I am.

So we slide inside our created identities precisely because we have not found our Real Identity, as Paul says, "hidden with Christ in God" (see Colossians 3:3). Before we meet our own soul, most identities are socially constructed by our family, friends, and culture. Once we find the "inner spring" within ourselves, which is the Holy Spirit (see John 7:38), we finally begin to be who we really are. Usually, that does not happen until the second half of life, after we experience some failure and loss or love someone deeply. Then any contemplative practice will foster this wisdom long-term.

For example, look at the transformation of Saul into Paul. Saul was a "Pharisee among Pharisees" (see Acts 23:6), yet this supposedly righteous man was a murderer of Christians. Saul's encounter on the Damascus Road revealed to him that he was *already* one with Christ and with all people. When his soul-blindness was lifted, Saul, now Paul, realized his true identity as a vessel of love (see Acts 9). Same man, different perception! (In general, the change of names we often see in the Bible indicates the movement from False Self to True Self: Abram to Abraham, Jacob to Israel, Simon to Peter, Saul to Paul, and even Mary to "Woman.")[8]

Gateway to Silence: Christ shall give you light. (See Ephesians 5:14.)

DAY 7
SABBATH MEDITATION

Remember: **Shadowboxing**

To protect your public image, all the contrary and negative aspects of yourself have to go underground, hidden from others and even from your own awareness. (Day 1)

Your shadow is what you refuse to see about yourself, and what you do not want others to see. (Day 2)

We never get to the second half of life without major shadowboxing. (Day 3)

Neither our persona nor our shadow is evil in itself: they just allow us to do evil and not know it. (Day 4)

The closer you get to the Light, the more of your shadow you see. (Day 5)

Full human life demands some shadowboxing with the shadow side of every reality. (Day 6)

Rest: **Shadow Work**

Living in the light is as easy as resting in your given, inborn identity *and* it entails a hard, lifelong task of sparring with your shadow. We call this work shadowboxing because it's as if we're fighting an imaginary, unseen opponent. Our intention is not to conquer the shadow, but to draw it out into the light of our awareness and compassion so we are aware of it.

There are many ways to do shadow work, such as paying attention to our dreams; perhaps the simplest is to observe ourselves in our negative reactions to others. Byron Katie's "The Work"[9] offers a simple process for helping us own and struggle with judgments that are all-too-easily projected elsewhere.

Recall a situation that was stressful for you, whether recent or long ago but fresh in your mind. Revisit that time and place in your imagination. Name your frustration, fear, or disappointment and the object of this feeling in a short statement. For example: "I am angry with John because he never listens to me."

Now, with your statement, ask yourself four questions:

1. Is it true? (Yes or no. If no, move to 3.)
2. Can you absolutely know that it's true? (Yes or no.)
3. How do you react, what happens, when you believe that thought?
4. Who would you be without the thought?

Then turn the thought around in three ways—putting yourself in the other's place, putting the other person in your place, and stating the exact opposite. For example:

1. I am angry with myself because I never listen to me.
2. John is angry with me because I never listen to him.
3. John does listen to me.

Find ways in which each "turnaround" is true in this situation.

This practice brings our nebulous shadow into focus, giving us something tangible to embrace and integrate. Do this necessary work all your life *and* rest in God's love for you as you are now.

Gateway to Silence: Christ shall give you light. (See Ephesians 5:14.)

For further study:

Dancing Standing Still: Healing the World from a Place of Prayer
Discharging Your "Loyal Soldier"
Falling Upward: A Spirituality for the Two Halves of Life
Great Themes of Paul: Life as Participation
Near Occasions of Grace
Things Hidden: Scripture as Spirituality

THE SECOND HALF OF LIFE

DAY I
Unity and Simplicity

So now we move toward the goal, the very purpose of human life, "another intensity...a deeper communion," as T. S. Eliot calls it,[1] which the container of the first half of life is meant to hold, support, and foster. Not the fingers pointing to the moon, but the moon itself—and now including the dark side of the moon too.

A new coherence, a unified field inclusive of the paradoxes, is precisely what gradually characterizes a second-half-of-life person. It feels like a return to simplicity after having learned from all the complexity. Finally, one has lived long enough, and built a strong enough container, to see that everything belongs, even the sad, absurd, and futile parts. The stronger the container, the more it can expand and hold.

In the second half of life, we can give our energy to making even the painful parts and the formerly excluded parts belong to the now-unified field. If you have forgiven yourself for being imperfect and falling, you can now do it for just about everybody else. If you have *not* done it for yourself, I am afraid you will likely pass on your sadness, absurdity, judgment, and futility to others. This is the tragic path of the many elderly people who have not become actual elders, probably because they were never eldered or mentored themselves.

Such people seem to have missed out on the joy and clarity of the first simplicity, perhaps avoided the interim complexity, and finally lost the great freedom and magnanimity of the second simplicity as well. We need to hold together all of the stages of life and, for some strange, wonderful reason, it all becomes quite "simple" as we approach our later years.[2]

Gateway to Silence: "May what I do flow from me like a river, no forcing and no holding back." —Rainer Maria Rilke

DAY 2

Peaceful Change

In the second half of life, one has less and less need or interest in eliminating the negative or fearful, making rash judgments, holding on to old hurts, or feeling any need to punish other people. Your superiority complexes have gradually departed. You do not fight these negative things anymore; they have just shown too many times that they are useless, ego-based, counterproductive, and often entirely wrong. You learn to ignore and withdraw your energy from evil or stupid things rather than fight them directly.

Now, you fight things only when you are directly called and equipped to do so. You do not define yourself by opposition or eccentricity as the young often choose to do. We all become a well-disguised mirror image of anything that we fight too long or too directly. That which we oppose determines the energy and frames the questions after a while. We lose all our inner freedom.

By the second half of life, you have learned that most frontal attacks on evil just produce another kind of evil in yourself, along with a very inflated self-image. They also incite a lot of pushback from those you have attacked. Holier-than-thou people usually end up holier than nobody.

In the second half, you try to influence events, work for change, quietly persuade, change your own attitude, pray, or forgive instead of attacking things head-on.[3]

Gateway to Silence: "May what I do flow from me like a river, no forcing and no holding back." —Rainer Maria Rilke

DAY 3

We Are All in This Together

Life is much more spacious in the second half of life, the boundaries of the container having been enlarged by the constant addition of new experiences and relationships. Now you are just *here*, and here holds more than enough.

If we know anything at this stage, we know that we are all in this together and that we are all equally naked underneath our clothes. When we are young, we define ourselves by differentiating ourselves; in later life, we look for the things that we all share in common. We find happiness in alikeness, which has become much more obvious now; and we do not need to dwell on the differences between people or exaggerate the problems. Creating dramas has become boring.

In the second half of life, it is good just to be a part of the general dance. We do not have to stand out, make defining moves, or be better than anyone else on the dance floor. Life is more *participatory* than assertive, and there is no need for strong or further self-definition. God has taken care of all that, much better than we ever expected. The brightness comes from within now, and it is usually more than enough.[4]

Gateway to Silence: "May what I do flow from me like a river, no forcing and no holding back." —Rainer Maria Rilke

DAY 4

Generativity

At this stage, I no longer have to prove that I or my group are the best, that my ethnicity is superior, that my religion is the only one that God loves, or that my role and place in society deserve superior treatment. I am not preoccupied with collecting more goods and services; quite simply, my desire and effort is to pay back, to give back to the world a bit of what I have received. I now realize that I have been gratuitously given *to*—from the universe, from society, and from God. I try now, as many wise people have said, to "live simply so that others can simply live."

Psychologist Erik Erikson (1902–1994) calls someone at this stage a "generative" person, one who is eager and able to generate life from his or her own abundance and for the benefit of following generations. Because such people have built a good container, they are able to "contain" more and more truth, more and more neighbors, more and broader vision, more and more of a mysterious and outpouring God.

Their God is no longer small, punitive, or tribal. They once worshipped their raft; now they love the shore where it has taken them. They once defended signposts; now they have arrived where the signs pointed. They now enjoy the moon itself instead of fighting over whose finger points to it most accurately, quickly, or definitively.

One's growing sense of infinity and spaciousness is no longer found just "out there" but, most especially, "in here." The inner and outer have become one. You can trust your inner experience now, because God has allowed it, used it, received it, and refined it.[5]

Gateway to Silence: "May what I do flow from me like a river, no forcing and no holding back." —Rainer Maria Rilke

DAY 5

A New Kind of Doing

In the second half of life, we do not have strong and final opinions about everything, every event, or most people, as much as we allow things and people to delight us, sadden us, and truly influence us. We no longer need to change or adjust other people to be happy ourselves. Ironically we are, more than ever before, in a position to change people—but we do not *need* to, and that makes all the difference.

We have moved from doing to being to an utterly new kind of doing that flows almost organically, quietly, and by osmosis. Our actions are less compulsive. We do what we are called to do, and then try to let go of the consequences. We usually cannot do that very well when we are young.

Now we aid and influence people simply by being who we are. Human integrity probably influences and moves people from potency to action more than anything else. An elder's deep and studied passion carries so much more power than superficial and loudly stated principles. Our peace is needed more than our anger.[6]

Gateway to Silence: "May what I do flow from me like a river, no forcing and no holding back." —Rainer Maria Rilke

DAY 6

Falling into God

The second half of life is a certain kind of weight to carry because you now hold the pain of the larger world, but no other way of being makes sense or gives you the deep satisfaction your soul now demands and enjoys. This new and deeper passion is what people mean when they say, "I must do this particular thing or my life will not make sense" or "It is no longer a choice." Your life and your delivery system are now one, whereas before, your life and your occupation seemed like two different things.

Your concern is not so much *to have what you love*, but *to love what you have*—right now. This is a monumental change from the first half of life, so much so that it is almost the litmus test of whether you are in the second half of life at all. Inner brightness, still holding life's sadness and joy, is its own reward, its own satisfaction, and your best and truest gift to the world.

Such wise elders are the "grand" parents of the world. Children and other adults feel so safe and loved around them, and they themselves feel so needed and helpful to children, teens, and midlife adults. And they are! They are in their natural flow.

Strangely, all of life's problems, dilemmas, and difficulties are now resolved, not by negativity, attack, criticism, force, or logical resolution, but always by falling into a larger brightness—by falling into the good, the true, and the beautiful, by falling into God. All you have to do is meet one such shining person and you know that he or she is surely the goal of humanity and the delight of God.[7]

Gateway to Silence: "May what I do flow from me like a river, no forcing and no holding back."—Rainer Maria Rilke

DAY 7

Sabbath Meditation

Remember: **The Second Half of Life**

In the second half of life, we can give our energy to making even the painful parts and the formerly excluded parts belong to the now-unified field. (Day 1)

In the second half, you try to influence events, work for change, quietly persuade, change your own attitude, pray, or forgive instead of attacking things head-on. (Day 2)

Life is more *participatory* than assertive, and there is no need for strong or further self-definition. (Day 3)

Because wise elders have built a good container, they are able to "contain" more and more truth, more and more neighbors, more and broader vision, more and more of a mysterious and outpouring God. (Day 4)

We have moved from doing to being to an utterly new kind of doing that flows almost organically, quietly, and by osmosis. (Day 5)

Your concern is not so much *to have what you love*, but *to love what you have*—right now. (Day 6)

Rest: **A Poem**

Read these words aloud as a prayer for this stage of your life—the fullness and generativity of your being.

I believe in all that has never yet been spoken.
I want to free what waits within me
so that what no one has dared to wish for
may for once spring clear
without my contriving.

If this is arrogant, God, forgive me,
but this is what I need to say.
May what I do flow from me like a river,
no forcing and no holding back,
the way it is with children.

Then in these swelling and ebbing currents,
these deepening tides moving out, returning,
I will sing you as no one ever has,
streaming through widening channels
into the open sea.[8]

Gateway to Silence: "May what I do flow from me like a river, no forcing and no holding back."—Rainer Maria Rilke

For further study:

Falling Upward: A Spirituality for the Two Halves of Life
Loving the Two Halves of Life: The Further Journey
A Spirituality for the Two Halves of Life
The Two Major Tasks of the Spiritual Life

THE ENNEAGRAM (PART ONE)

DAY 1
The Enneagram as a Tool for Transformation

The meditations during the next two weeks will be longer than usual to allow a thorough (though still brief!) overview of the Enneagram. To explore this theme in more depth, see the resources listed following each week.

The Enneagram is a very ancient tool (recognized by some members of all three monotheistic religions) whose Christian origins can be traced to the Desert Fathers and Mothers of the fourth century. I first learned the Enneagram in 1973 when it was taught to me by my spiritual director, Jesuit Fr. Jim O'Brien. The Enneagram has since been used by many spiritual directors to help us recognize our own compulsiveness in certain directions and our blind spots in other directions. The Enneagram probably emerged to help directors of souls to read the energies of people in an almost "shorthand" kind of way. In other words, you could be trained in it, and it was not just some airy, superstitious psychic ability enjoyed by a few.

Since the 1970s, many excellent teachers have emerged all over the world, and the Enneagram is now seen as a brilliant gift for the democratization of spirituality and a very effective "psychology of sin." By forcing us to face our own darkness and shadow in ways that are rather undeniable, it simultaneously opens us to our deepest gift. In fact, because it seems to show that shadow and gift are two sides of the same coin, it has brought many people to a very practical understanding of non-dual thinking and the endless paradox and mystery that human nature seems to be.

No one willingly does evil. Each of us has put together a construct by which we explain why what we do is necessary and good. That is why it is so important to "distinguish spirits" (see 1 Corinthians 12:10). We need support in unmasking our constructed self (seemingly a combination of nature, nurture, and free will) and viewing ourselves objectively. With the self-knowledge that the Enneagram gives us, we are not dealing only with the acknowledgement of "sin." (Note: In the Enneagram tradition, "sin" is simply that which doesn't work, i.e., self-defeating behavior, without the common Christian idea of culpability or "offending God.") It has a way of teaching us to let go of what only *seems* good in order to discover what in us is *really* good and is already within us. Surely this is what we mean by the soul.

So the Enneagram's amazing combination of centuries of astute psychological observation encourages a kind of spiritual transformation that is observable and even enjoyable. That is a remarkable feat, and it does it rather quickly and easily. The only people who reject the Enneagram in my experience are people who do not understand it or do not have the humility or readiness to recognize how true it is in their own case.

The Enneagram works by a life-changing insight. It helps us to see our own compulsive blindness and how we are acting at cross-purposes with our own intended self-interest. We finally see that *I am what I am*, good and bad put together into one self, and God's mercy is so great and God's love is so total that God uses even my mistakenness in my favor! God is using *all* of me to bring me to God. That is surely the best of Good News![1]

Gateway to Silence: I want to see all—my sin and my gift.

DAY 2

The Purpose of the Enneagram

The purpose of the Enneagram is not self-improvement as such, which would still be our ego's goal. Rather, it is the transformation of consciousness so that we can realize our essence, our True Self. Personality development and character building will happen as part of Enneagram work, but this is not its primary goal. The primary goal of any *spiritual* tool is simply union with God/Truth, and then we get united with ourselves in the process!

The Enneagram reveals that we are often *destroyed by our gift*! We naturally over-identify with our strengths in the first half of life, and eventually they become their own set of blinders. This allows real misperception, and allows our own "root sin" to remain mostly hidden from us. We cannot see the air we are breathing all the time. Our "sins" are the other side of our gift. Our compulsiveness/addictions emerge because they have become a seemingly effective way to get our energy and to survive in the press of life. We think they "work" for us. The Enneagram uncovers this false energy source for us and enables us to confront the compulsions and laws under which we live—usually without awareness. It invites us to go beyond them and take steps into a real domain of freedom—freedom from our foundational addiction to our self.

People who know the Enneagram in a superficial way, or who are just beginning to work with it, may think it puts people *into* boxes. But, in fact, one of the great graces is that people find themselves coming *out* of their own self-created boxes because they recognize their boxes are far too limiting. Also, as they continue to work with the Enneagram, they will see its brilliance and the way it reveals one level of discovery after another, which comes as a surprise, and usually a humiliation too. Such unveiling tells them they are in the realm of soul and mystery, if mystery means something that is *endlessly knowable* at ever-new levels. I have known the Enneagram for over forty years now, and it still unpacks new insight and healing for me.

The Enneagram, like the Spirit of Truth itself, can always set us free (see John 8:32), but first it will tend to make us miserable! Working with the Enneagram is intentionally humiliating. We need to feel, acknowledge, and see how exaggerated, excessive, and absurd our false energy source really is. If we own and take responsibility for our darkness, if we feel how it has wounded us and others—how *it has allowed us not to love and not to be loved*—if we do that, I promise that we will become alert to the other side, to our greater gifts, and even the actual depth of our gift. Our gift is amazingly our sin, sublimated and transformed by grace. What a surprise this is for most people![2]

Gateway to Silence: I want to see all—my sin and my gift.

DAY 3

Overview of Enneagram Triads and Types

The Enneagram defines its nine human types on the basis of nine "traps," "passions," or "sins." These strategies for survival can be understood as emergency solutions that were used in early childhood as a way of coming to terms with one's environment. But the older we get, the more clearly they reveal themselves as much of our problem too. We are addicted to one early set of glasses or blinders! *Too much of even a good thing becomes a bad thing.*

The nine sins of the Enneagram eventually were reduced by Pope Gregory the Great to the "seven deadly sins": pride, envy, anger, sloth, avarice, lust, and lack of moderation or gluttony— although he missed the two "sins" that most cultures need to thrive: deceit and fear. It is worth noting that we in the Western tradition have never unmasked and named these last two sins as such, even though the Bible says "Do not be afraid" *over and over again.* Jesus has many astute statements about honest self-perception and communication, but we just did not have the developed psychology to see how right he was about deceit as self-delusion. I would say that deceit and fear are indeed the foundation stones of all domination societies, which are all the more dangerous because we have agreed not to call them deceit and fear. Just observe any election cycle, and the patently absurd claims of most political rhetoric, which we do not just tolerate, but applaud!

The nine Enneagram types are arranged clockwise on the circumference of a circle for teaching purposes. They are then clustered together in three groups of three, or triads.

The Eight, Nine, and One are called the *gut people*, who each have a unique style of aggression. Their center of gravity lies in the belly, where the "raw material" of their existence is located. They usually experience daily life as altogether *too much*, somewhat like a full body blow to which they develop a characteristic defense: Eights hit back, Nines back off, and Ones try righteously to fix it (that's me!).

Two, Three, and Four are the *heart people,* or the social types. Although this is considered the feeling triad, they actually have no direct access to their own feelings. They experience themselves in reaction to the feelings of others. They unceasingly develop activities to secure the devotion or attention of others. Twos pose as lovable and helpful, Threes play whatever role "goes over" best publicly, and Fours put in an appearance as someone special and authentic (to themselves).

Five, Six, and Seven are the *head people*, or the self-preserving types. They are all plagued by fear and anxiety, with which they cope differently. Fives try to master it by gaining more and correct knowledge. Phobic Sixes link up with an authority or group for security. Counter-phobic Sixes may take foolish risks or make preemptive strikes to overcome their fears. Sevens deny and avoid pain and create fun and fantasy. All three are clever ways of largely living in your head.

While we do have a little of each type inside us, we all have one preferred stance, one Enneagram type, which we cannot change entirely, but which we can move toward redemption or transformation. The whole Enneagram diagram is called "the face of God." If you could look out at reality from nine pairs of eyes and honor all of them, you would look at reality through the eyes of God—eyes filled with compassion for yourself and everyone else![3]

Throughout the remainder of this week and all of next week, we will look at each of the nine types more closely. Although the best way to learn this oral tradition is by listening to an Enneagram teacher, spiritual director, or audio teaching—so you can pick up the precise "energy" of your type—I hope this brief introduction will inspire you to go further with the Enneagram.[4]

Gateway to Silence: I want to see all—my sin and my gift.

DAY 4

Type One: The Need to Be Perfect

Everything I am writing here, including the description of each Enneagram number, is a broad generalization using different common traits. The important thing is to get to the energy behind the traits. Not every trait will apply to each person, so forgive the generalizations you will read throughout this series.

I like to start by describing the One, because it is my Enneagram number; and if you'll allow me to first make fun of myself, then hopefully you'll allow me to do it with your number later.

The One is the reformist compulsion of the gut triad. Ones need to be perfect, and for a One this means feeling that they are right and good. Ones are idealists, motivated and driven by the longing for a true, just, and moral world. Somewhere in their childhood, they experienced the world as beautiful and perfect. And it's no wonder, because their "Soul Child" or original dream of life is the joyful Seven. I remember moments that were so wonderful, so serene, so whole, with no need to eliminate anything. God was in it and I was in it and life all made sense. Then, somewhere later on, I realized, "Darn it, it isn't a perfect world!" So I moved to the impossible conviction: "I'm going to find a way to make it perfect," and that became my entrapped Enneagram One position. It's the original, positive soul experience that all the types are trying to recreate, but their new agenda becomes a False Self and a finally unworkable agenda for life. In this case, they become overidentified with the critical mind.

Ones are often good teachers and reformers. They can spur others to work and mature and grow. The demanding, critical voices within them make it hard for Ones to live with imperfection—especially their own. "Anger" is their root sin, although they seldom get directly angry. It is more a low-level resentment because the world is not the way they know it should be. They repress their anger because they see it as something imperfect in themselves. At the same time, it energizes them to work really hard for their ideals and principles. Talk about an inner conflict! Ones are driven toward righteousness, arrogance, and perfectionism. They unfortunately believe in meritocracy: You get what you deserve, so you'd better be good and work hard. There is no free lunch! That is why the concept of grace is so foundationally important for me; it alone breaks down all this silly "there is a right way to do it" thinking.

In order to discover their gift, which is cheerful tranquility or serenity, Ones must first realize that they are *not* that good. They may have to "sin boldly" to see this, or at least recognize that every good thing they have ever done has been for mixed and even selfish motives. They are not as high-minded as they imagine themselves to be. Then alone can they allow themselves to experience totally *unearned grace*, which finally allows them to be at peace and happy—even with imperfection. Nothing else can deconstruct their world of meritocracy and overly harsh judgments.[5]

Gateway to Silence: I want to see all—my sin and my gift.

DAY 5

Type Two: The Need to Be Needed

The Two is the "obvious" compulsion of the heart triad. They appear to be very caring people. As children, they knew that they were beloved of the universe. Their Soul Child is the special and central Four. When they could not maintain this truth, they became needy of the love of others to "re-convince" themselves of the truth they already deeply knew. "Others must and will love me!" they demand, instead of resting in the love that they already are and have.

Twos need to be needed. "I will make you need me. I will ingratiate myself to you by loving service so that you cannot live without me." Perhaps the message they received as a child was, "I am loved when I am tender, understanding, ready to be helpful, and defer my own needs." But, in this way, the child also felt powerful, while grown-ups looked weak and needy. This provided fertile soil for the sort of false pride that is the root sin of Twos. They secretly look down on those they "serve," and they see themselves as wonderful because they can serve and love so well. Their pride is very subtle, but remember, all sin depends upon a good disguise.

Twos repress consciousness of their own needs and pretend they don't have any needs at all. "My only need is to meet your need." But be forewarned: Finally, one day, they realize, "No one's giving back to me the way I so generously give!" Then they get into the blame game and can become downright cruel. It's almost the flip side of what they want themselves to be, but it can also be the beginning of their conversion into who they really are without their games of manipulation for love and attention.

I have known Twos who cry for days as they realize their well-hidden self-interest—that, all along, they have been giving in order to get something back. Such humiliation leads to their emerging virtue, which is humility. I think we see it in Pope Francis.

A mature, healthy Enneagram Two returns to being the genuinely loving and beloved person that they once knew themselves to be. They have found their identity as the Love they already are, and they are now able to love themselves and others with God's love. They no longer need to be continually reinforced from the outside.[6]

Gateway to Silence: I want to see all—my sin and my gift.

DAY 6

Type Three: The Need to Succeed

The Three is the pure compulsion of the heart triad, because even their wings (Two and Four) are heart-based. Threes are the most disconnected from their own feelings and the most in tune to the feelings of a group or audience. The very young Three knew, like a healthy Six, that all things are passing and their only real security is in God. But gradually, through the encouragement of others for their many natural talents and good looks, and the praise of others for their accomplishments and wins, reliance on God was replaced by reliance on their own competence and effectiveness.

Threes have a strong need to succeed, and they often do. Their self-esteem comes from competence in the outer world. They thrive on praise, recognition, and admiration. They can play whatever role any group expects of them. Their root sin is "deceit" (embroidering the truth so it will sell), and first of all they deceive themselves about their own wonderfulness. They are so wrapped up with detecting the feelings of others in order to embody the expectations and values of whatever group they are in that they are very often completely out of touch with their own true motivations and needs for affirmation. This is exactly what allows them to be deceitful without seeing it as deceit.

Threes create a superficial image that looks good, can be sold, and will win. Most Threes seem optimistic, youthful, intelligent, dynamic, efficient, and highly productive. But often there is a terrible, deep fear in Threes that they would not be loved if they were not successful and productive.

Threes find their way to their virtue of truthfulness only when they take the painful path of self-knowledge and look their life-lies in the face. Their conversion is often precipitated by a major failure. Their "fall from grace" in others' eyes can be a letting go into God's grace and unconditional love. They return to their Soul Child and find their true identity and strength grounded solidly in God (see Isaiah 40:31) like a healthy Six would do. Mature Threes are able to use their tremendous gifts and energy to help other people competently and effectively, and to motivate them to discover their own potential. Much would not happen in the world if we did not have Threes.

America is an Enneagram Three country, and many of our recent presidents and nominees for the presidency are Threes. They fit into the American self-image of "can do," and they look good while doing it—to other Americans caught up in the same worldview. To outsiders, they can look too slick and superficial.[7]

Gateway to Silence: I want to see all—my sin and my gift.

DAY 7

Sabbath Meditation

Remember: **The Enneagram (Part One)**

The Enneagram helps us let go of what only *seems* good in order to discover what in us is *really* good and is already within us. (Day 1)

Our gift is amazingly our sin, sublimated and transformed by grace. (Day 2)

The whole Enneagram diagram is called "the face of God." If you could look out at reality from nine pairs of eyes and honor all of them, you would look at reality through the eyes of God. (Day 3)

In order to discover their gift, which is cheerful tranquility or serenity, Ones must first realize that they are *not* that good. (Day 4)

"Others must and will love me!" Twos demand, instead of resting in the love that they already are and have. (Day 5)

Threes find their way to their virtue of truthfulness only when they take the painful path of self-knowledge and look their life-lies in the face. (Day 6)

Rest: **Heart Attention**

The Syrian deacon, Evagrius Ponticus (345–399), who first wrote about eight of the sins that eventually became the Enneagram, saw them as ways in which our heart-presence is "suffocated." Enneagram teacher G. I. Gurdjieff (1866–1949) saw each type as a way of "self-forgetting": how we turn away from True Self. My fellow teacher in the Living School, Robert Sardello, offers a simple practice for attending to heart, which helps us remember True Self and return to full presence and authentic life.

First, we learn to enter the heart. It is best to initiate this learning when calmness rules. Then, with practice—sometimes taking years to develop, sometimes occurring right away—we can find our way into heart-presence even in the midst of greatest turbulence. It is simple. We enter the Silence by simply going to a quiet place and sitting, eyes closed, until we feel the embrace of the Silence. It is an "inner region," one to which we have to yield in order to experience. The practice of Silence is also ongoing, nothing to be mastered, for She is endless.

When we have, at least, entered the Silence, we place our attention at the center of the heart. Heart-attention differs, radically, from thinking about the heart. Try this: look at your foot and pay attention to your foot; it appears to be "over there"; you are really thinking about your foot. Then, instead, place your attention within your foot. Notice that this is suddenly something like, "Hmmm, the whole world now unfolds from this place of my foot." Wherever attention is, there you are.

What is heart interiority? Become a researcher into your own heart. Just observe, notice, sense the qualities. It is as if you are within a vast, spherical space. Within this space, you cannot find a boundary, an ending. The feeling is one of intimate infinity and infinite intimacy, both at once. There is warmth, all warmth. You feel encompassed, held, embraced; you find that you are within heart rather than heart being "inside" you. It is deep, and when there, you do not want to leave....

When we find, say, that we have fallen into anger, or any of the other transgressions, particularly when we struggle, over and over, with the recurring occurrence, we approach courage by going into Silence and then entering the heart. From within the center of the heart, the place of inviolability, the "not I but Christ in me" (see Galatians 2:20) feels the heart's ardor, that is the strong, strong, strong love of the heart. When that warmth is felt, we can let it resonate through the body until perfect calm comes. We feel the inherent, always-present, blessing return. It never went away; we went away from it.[8]

Gateway to Silence: I want to see all—my sin and my gift.

For further study:

The Enneagram: A Christian Perspective
The Enneagram and Grace: 9 Journeys to Divine Presence
The Enneagram as a Tool for Your Spiritual Journey
The Enneagram: The Discernment of Spirits

THE ENNEAGRAM (PART TWO)

DAY 1
Type Four: The Need to Be Special

Four is the conflicted number of the heart triad (Two, Three, and Four). Their Soul Child is the One. They try desperately to create an outer world of beauty and symmetry because they originally knew themselves to be an essential part of a perfect and whole world (Ones have the need to be perfect). Perhaps due to painful experiences of loss in childhood, the life of Fours is shaped by longing. They look forward to the day when the great love will come (back), and they are convinced this great love will redeem them. That love is especially experienced in *beauty*. That is why they tend *not* to be moralistic, which is the downfall of people who see love merely in seemingly objective truth or in moral goodness.

Fours may blame themselves for experiencing rejection or privation, and so they consider themselves "bad" or unworthy in that quite unique sense. Fours may repeatedly produce situations in which they are rejected or abandoned, almost as if to punish themselves. Fours have to be depressed or suffer from time to time in order to be creative. Really! The greater the pain, depression, and rejection, the more creative Fours can become. Go to any art colony, Hollywood, music or dance school, and you will be overwhelmed by the self-created dramas.

The root sin of Fours is envy. They immediately see who has more style, class, taste, or talent than they. Inside a Four is a child struggling with feelings of inferiority: "I don't deserve to be loved. I need to make an impression. Everything I do makes a 'statement' so that I cannot be overlooked and abandoned again." Fours strive to be aesthetically attractive, to be exceptional, to be creative, or to appear eccentric. *They long to be authentic*, but seldom allow themselves to fully enjoy it when it happens. "I will be special" is the mantra of the Four. Their whole life is a search for authenticity. Children, nature, and everything that radiates originality awakens in them the longing for simplicity and naturalness that they fear they lost at some point. Often they try so hard to be natural that they look anything but natural.

Fours have lived through all the emotional spaces and experiences, from agony to ecstasy. They know all the nuances of feeling and understand the human soul better than anyone else. A purified and mature Four can deal sensitively with real life—and not just with imaginary dramas. Working for peace and justice is good for Fours. In this they have to deal with the dirt of the world, which cannot be aesthetically transfigured. Such social commitment also helps them return to their One Soul Child.

Fours put their gifts to work to awaken a sense of beauty and harmony in their surroundings. They are emotionally very sensitive, for good and for ill, and almost always artistically gifted in at least one area. They are capable of transforming the negative and experiences of loss into something beautiful and universally valid, be it a poem, a song, a work of art, or an action of civil disobedience.

The gift of redeemed Fours is equanimity or emotional balance. If they can admit that they live in God and God in them, their soul will come to the deep authenticity and balance for which they have longed. They will finally know their Authentic Self.[1]

Gateway to Silence: I want to see all—my sin and my gift.

DAY 2

Type Five: The Need to Perceive

The Five appears to be the headiest of all the head types (Five, Six, and Seven). Their primal experience as an Eight Soul Child was of the absolute order of God and the genius of controlling all the parts in one working universe. Fives go inside the mind to find the power that they were denied, or denied themselves, in the external world.

The sin of the Five is avarice (or greed), and they are avaricious for knowledge, thoughts, ideas, silence, and space. To them, knowledge is power and they can never know enough to fill the emptiness they feel inside. Fives always need yet another course, another book, another silent retreat. They are always observing, often from a safe back corner or their private "man cave." Fives spend most of their lives behind a one-way mirror through which they can look out, but won't let you look back at them.

Fives try not to be drawn into the whirlpool of feelings and events, but instead develop their own kind of "objectivity." It's important to them to remain calm—at least externally—and to keep their emotions under control. In reality, most Fives have an intense emotional life. But, in any moment of even quasi-threat or need for vulnerability, something happens. It's as if their emotions are blocked and always come limping behind. Fives register things with eyes, ears, and brain, but less so with heart; they can stand alongside most events with seeming objectivity. As soon as they are alone, they begin to evaluate it, once again from the head space. That's how they can gradually get in touch with their emotions, if they do at all. But heart is never their first response.

Detachment can be seen as the virtue of the Five. Fives can be outstanding listeners and counselors. Their ability to withdraw themselves emotionally can help those seeking advice to appraise their own situation more clearly. But detachment can also be seen as the Five's greatest weakness. Among the life tasks of Fives is learning commitment, engagement, and action. Fives have to fall in love passionately, at least once, in order to be free. Learning to love is one of their great challenges because it crashes up against their wish for distance. Fives who won't allow themselves to "lose their heads" in love are incomplete. Without it, they remain emotionally stingy all of their lives.

Meditation and prayer are, for Fives, crucially important sources of power. Fives need to cultivate their inner world in order to find the courage to devote themselves to the outer world. The latter becomes possible only when the inner world is experienced as less threatening, when Fives have found repose and security in God and hence in themselves. Meditating on the Incarnation—that is, the commitment and passion of Christ, his readiness to get his hands dirty and heal human beings by touching them—can reconnect the Five with their Soul Child, the Eight. But, frankly, they are naturally attracted to metaphysics or Buddhism much more than the heart space of Jesus and Christianity.

Redeemed Fives link their knowledge to a search for wisdom and strive for a sympathetic knowledge of the heart. They have a quiet inner power and can be tenderly emotional, loving, polite, hospitable, and gentle—while still protecting strong personal boundaries. The stiff upper lip, and yet the sincere and studied politeness of the English gentleman, is perhaps the image here.[2]

Gateway to Silence: I want to see all—my sin and my gift.

Type Six: The Need for Security

Six is the central stress point of the head triad, because even their wings are "heady" in two different ways. Their Soul Child was the Nine. Their primal knowing was true and perfect presence, but, somehow, the world became a scary place for Sixes. They once held an image of an utterly reconciled and peaceful world, a benevolent universe; but instead of trusting that it comes from Another, they try to re-create it themselves by laws, authority, and structures of certitude. The root sin of the Six is fear, a sort of primal anxiety. Their core need is for security and self-preservation.

Today's ever-changing world seems to be producing more and more Sixes, as evidenced by the rise of fundamentalism in all three monotheistic religions. Growing up in a world where everything is in flux and there is little stability, the psyche needs something solid, authoritative, certain, and clear. Joining with seemingly infallible or fundamentalist groups can give Sixes the illusion of security.

There are two major types of Sixes: phobic and counter-phobic. Most Sixes are phobic. To overcome their fear, these Sixes align themselves with a strong leader, institution, church, or government. They need an outer authority to protect them and tell them what to do because they constantly doubt themselves. Phobic Sixes are naturally humble, teachable, reliable, and loyal. Once they decide to trust you, you've got a friend for life—even when others turn against you. Phobic Sixes are by nature careful, hesitant, and mistrustful. They have a hard time trusting themselves and their instincts. They continually sense danger. In their most immature forms, they are victims of paranoia. Every new situation is so threatening for them that the memory of earlier victories is useless.

Counter-phobic Sixes are a different breed altogether. They may seek out risky situations because they prefer taking the bull by the horns to continually torturing themselves with their anxieties. Their motto is "The best defense is a proactive offense." They disguise the fear that is the actual driving force of their actions and compensate for it by putting on a façade of hardness, strength, and daredevil behavior. The counter-phobic Six is a classic scapegoater. To control their constant anxiety, they focus the danger and evil on another particular race, nation, religion, or gender.

Phobic Sixes are also prone to scapegoating because their primary defense mechanism is projection. The pessimism and mistrust that they harbor against themselves leads them to imagine that others have similarly negative motives, so they project hostility, hatred, and negative thoughts onto other people. Instead of facing their own darkness, they see it, attack it, and kill it outside themselves. The Enneagram's teachings could have far-reaching political implications if it could expose the demonic power of fear projected elsewhere (and of the root sins of all the other types as well).

The quickest conversion experience for the Six is an authentic God experience. (Actually, the same is true for all nine Enneagram types.) The experience of unconditional love is the one thing that, in the long run, can be stronger than fear: "There is no fear in love, but perfect love casts out fear" (see 1 John 4:18). Perhaps the tragedy that Sixes have feared may be just what they need—so that they fall into the hands of the Living God and know very practically that God is always holding them, believing in them, and loving them—from within! The fearful gap is finally overcome.

Then the Six can move from relying on outer authority to knowing and trusting their Inner Authority. They move from needing certitude and answers to having *faith*, which demands not knowing and not being certain, but rather being able to hold some anxiety and ambiguity. They have returned to the Ground of their Being and to their primal knowing: It is all okay already! "If God is for us, who can be against us?" (see Romans 8:31). Hence, the virtue of the Six is both courage and loyalty to what really deserves loyalty. Redeemed Sixes know how to combine holding onto sound traditions with the readiness to take new paths.[3]

Gateway to Silence: I want to see all—my sin and my gift.

DAY 4

Type Seven: The Need to Avoid Pain

Sevens once lived in a world of "enoughness," an inner world of satisfaction and essence like that of the Fives. Sevens usually admit to an early kind of fantasy world where all was explained and had meaning and grounding. When this security was threatened, perhaps by traumatic childhood experiences, they decided on a one-sided response: "I will make it all positive and allow no negative." They once knew God as total foundation and reality as utterly satisfying, but now they insist on enjoying *it in an incomplete way*. They will not accept that God's character, and actually all of Reality, includes and incorporates the negative.

The need in the Seven is to avoid pain. They are masters of denial: "I will not admit, own, or participate in the dark side of anything. I will keep smiling, and I will make the best of it." Sevens radiate joy and optimism. The Seven is the "eternal child." But the merriment of the unredeemed Seven is the result of their fear of facing pain and a tool of their instinct for self-preservation. Sevens love infinite horizons and keeping their options open. They unconsciously avoid committing themselves too deeply to someone or something because, in depth, they always see pain lurking. Besides, in commitment, their own limits might become visible—and that too would be painful.

Sevens love adventures and travel, because here and now is always boring, painful, and insufficient. Unfortunately, when they get to wherever they're going, it's always a disappointment. So they have to up the ante and plan something even more exciting. But, down deep, none of it truly makes them happy, so they may move toward addiction. Their root sin is gluttony; their motto is "More is always better!"

The beginning of conversion for the Seven may be something dark or painful which they initially refuse to accept. Usually, it means the facing of pain that they cannot avoid, such as the death of a loved one, the loss of a job, or the failure of health. Then they may finally recognize that much of their life has been characterized by running from pain. At that point they begin to grow up. Like St. Francis, who was a Seven and known as the "Joyful Poor Man," they actually learn to dive right into pain instead of running from it.

The invitation to Sevens is full and positive cooperation with God. Unredeemed Sevens think that they are the fashioners of their own happiness, and so they continually plan new ways of optimizing their own lives. When they cooperate with God instead, they confront the reality of the world, which is always a combination of joy and pain, and they accept both sides of life. They then can step out from false idealism into a wide-awake realism. They go God's way, which always leads through death to resurrection—and not around it. They can bring joy and hope where grief reigns. Unhealthy Sevens wear you out by their ungrounded over-enthusiasm and their constant need for more of everything; healthy Sevens just energize you by their solid and sustainable positivity.

The gift of redeemed Seven is sober and deeply grounded joy in the face of, and despite, all the difficulties of life. Healthy Sevens find a deep self-acceptance when they discover they are accepted by God and by significant others, not only for their radiant side, but for their entire being. Now the very real negative is no longer able to cancel out the positive, as it did when they were younger.[4]

Gateway to Silence: I want to see all—my sin and my gift.

Type Eight: The Need to Be Against

The Eight belongs to the gut triad. Their Soul Child is needy and vulnerable—a little Two. The Eight's primal knowing was that God was warmth, food, protection, empathy, relationship, and total understanding of how needy we all are. Early on, they discovered that the strong rule and the weak are oppressed, so they decided to be strong and powerful, taking on God's work themselves and trying to protect the vulnerable and defenseless.

Immature Eights deny their own inner vulnerability. "I will never cry. I will make others cry," they say. They are perceived as the most negative type and can be cruel, rude, and unkind. But don't be put off by that; just remember there's a vulnerable, tender little child inside of all that bluster. Eights are so much softer and kinder than they appear! They have a passion for the poor, the weak, and the oppressed, and a mature Eight, like Mother Teresa, will take on the best qualities of their Soul Child, the Two.

The core need of the Eight is the need to be against. Eights oppose you and like it when you fight back. This is their indirect form of intimacy, strange as it seems to the rest of us. They think that because they like a good fight, you would too. The aggression of Eights comes from the gut and is directed against everything they perceive as hypocrisy and injustice. Revenge and retaliation are how immature Eights try to get the scales of justice back in balance. For them, "Whoever isn't for me is against me," and the world is naïvely divided into friend or foe. The worldwide phenomenon of terrorism comes out of the energy of retaliative justice or vengeance, which is often the way of the immature Eight.

It is very important for an Eight to look powerful and to be in control. They have a hard time admitting mistakes, because that could look like weakness. Because Eights know their own strengths and immediately see the weaknesses of others, they elevate themselves above other people. When you're really poor, helpless, and weak, the Eight's protective instinct is aroused, and they will do anything to assist you. But as soon as you express in any way that you have power, Eights will prove that they have more power than you. You will seldom win a dispute with an Eight.

The root sin of the Eight is lust, but it is closer to the German word *lust*, which implies passion or excess. Only the encounter with full and demanding truth about themselves can set them free. Eights, who demand honesty from the people around them and who immediately unmask dishonest behavior, must learn to demand this of themselves as well. They must recognize and acknowledge the innocent, vulnerable, and distressed child in their own soul.

A redeemed Eight, who has accepted his or her own weakness, will find that the positive side of lust is the gift of passion, passion in the double sense of a powerful love of life and the readiness to suffer for justice. Redeemed Eights, like Martin Luther King, Jr., can be larger than life and can protect others with their power and vitality instead of dominating them. More than any other type, well-developed Eights have the gift of leading other people to their real potential. They are "tiger mothers" and "tiger fathers" for those in need.[5]

Gateway to Silence: I want to see all—my sin and my gift.

DAY 6

Type Nine: The Need to Avoid

The Nines once knew that it was all about love and everything was connected, operative, and effective. Their Soul Child had the optimism and motivation of the Three—that all could be worked out and fixed because God is Love. It is an effective and workable universe for them. When it appears this isn't true, they give up; they stop trying to find any other pattern. "If love does not work, then it is basically an incoherent universe and I want out, or at least I will refuse to cooperate." They can be very passive aggressive or, in the positive sense, they just ignore or refuse to cooperate with stupid things instead of fighting them. Think of Gandhi's response to the English Empire.

Nines are in the center of the gut triad. Their response to the shock wave of perception is "Everything is just too much. I'm not going to feel it. I'm just checking out." Their sin is sloth or laziness, but it's a description of their lack of focused energy. They spend their life taking the path of least resistance. They love to procrastinate and constantly need a fire lit under them. Nines like to go with the flow, which usually makes them very easy to be with.

They often consider themselves simple and uncomplicated and present themselves accordingly. Nines are honest; they have no hidden motives. What you see is what you get. Nines are naturally humble. They like to stay in the background and cultivate the self-image of not being anything special. Because Nines don't take themselves so seriously or demand attention, they are often overlooked by others—which does hurt them, although they seldom admit it.

Almost everything that approaches Nines from the outside world is exhausting and draining. They spend their energy avoiding or deadening inner and outer conflicts and suppressing strong feelings. When they get to the point where they can no longer move at all, they absolutely need outside help in the form of love and attention. It works wonders for them, but it is only a start. The life task of Nines consists in discovering and developing their feelings of self-worth and their own inner drive in order to become independent of continual outside influences.

Nines are natural peacemakers. Precisely because they themselves often have no clear viewpoint, they are capable of shifting to and accepting other viewpoints. But the one or two issues upon which they are focused will define their whole life, and about those they can be quite stubborn. Normally they can understand both sides and bring them together under one umbrella. Nines somehow harmonize all the conflicting energies present at a meeting. Perhaps it's because their ego is not in the way as much as it is for the rest of us. Perhaps it's the peace of their body, refusing to be bothered by it all. Nonviolent resistance comes naturally to a Nine.

The conversion of the Nine comes when they are taken seriously and placed inside a structure where they can see they are able to get things done—and that others love them and believe in them, as does God. Their gift, as always, is the opposite of their sin. It is *decisive action*, like that of a healthy Three. Then they are quite willing to take their small and honest place in other peoples' plans.[6]

Gateway to Silence: I want to see all—my sin and my gift.

DAY 7

Sabbath Meditation

Remember: **The Enneagram (Part Two)**

The gift of redeemed Fours is equanimity or emotional balance. (Day 1)

Redeemed Fives link their knowledge to a search for wisdom and strive for a sympathetic knowledge of the heart. (Day 2)

Redeemed Sixes know how to combine holding onto sound traditions with the readiness to take new paths. (Day 3)

The gift of the redeemed Seven is sober and deeply grounded joy in the face of, and despite, all the difficulties of life. (Day 4)

More than any other type, well-developed Eights have the gift of leading other people to their real potential. (Day 5)

Nonviolent resistance comes naturally to a Nine. Their gift is decisive action. (Day 6)

Rest: **Child's Pose**

All conversion is turning around and knowing something that we deeply know (our True Self or, as the Enneagram calls it, our Soul Child) and yet deeply resist knowing. The mystery of God's revelation is hidden inside, and in each of us, in a different, unique way. Jesus became the Human One who believed the Divine Image in himself; who trusted it, followed it, and told us to do the same. "We do not recognize ourselves, just as we did not recognize him" (see 1 John 3:1). The Enneagram is given so that we might see, and, as T. S. Eliot said, "know the place for the first time," which is our truest and deepest Self, the Self that always was but seldom is.[7]

In yoga, child's pose is often used as a restful pause between more challenging poses. Perhaps something in the past two weeks of Enneagram study has challenged you—witnessing the difficult and humbling reality of your "sin" and neediness. I encourage you to go deeper in learning your Enneagram number. But, for now, take a pause and remember your Soul Child's innocence, security, joy, and vulnerability.

You might choose to literally kneel and bend forward into child's pose (for heart and head people, a body-prayer can be especially helpful in reconnecting with physical self). Or you might repeat a mantra that echoes your Soul Child's innate wisdom (words and ideas can ground feelings—both emotions and physical sensations—in truth). You could sit quietly in heart-to-heart communion with God and allow the feeling of original rootedness to flow from your heart to your head and through your whole body.

Rest in the gut-stirring, heart-throbbing, mind-bending reality of your True Self.

Gateway to Silence: I want to see all—my sin and my gift.

For further study:

The Enneagram: A Christian Perspective
The Enneagram and Grace: 9 Journeys to Divine Presence
The Enneagram as a Tool for Your Spiritual Journey
The Enneagram: The Discernment of Spirits

BECOMING WHO YOU ARE

DAY I
Your Inner Destiny

Now that we have run through our quick overview of the Enneagram these past two weeks, let's connect this tool with our foundational theme of the True Self and the False Self. Your Enneagram type is your concocted False Self (not your bad self), and yet the mercy of God uses it to bring you to a deep experience of your foundational/metaphysical/unlosable identity as an eternal child of God.

Your True Self is who you are in God and who God is in you; many would call it the soul. You can never really lose your soul; you can only fail to realize it, which is indeed the greatest of losses—to have it, but not have it (see Matthew 16:26). Your essence, your exact "thisness," will never appear again in another incarnation. As Oscar Wilde said, "Be yourself; everyone else is already taken." Your True Self and your soul come from the Manufacturer—"hidden inside the box," as the cereal commercials say.

In some ways, the soul and the True Self are interchangeable in the sense of revealing that eternal part of you, the part of you that knows the truth. However, I must add that the True Self is probably larger than the soul, because it includes Spirit and embodiment too. Both reveal to you the immortal diamond that God has planted within you, and they often operate as one.

You (and every other created thing) begin with a Divine DNA; an inner destiny, as it were; an absolute core that knows the truth about you; a blueprint tucked away in the cellar of your being; an *Imago Dei* that begs to be allowed, to be fulfilled, and to show itself. "It is the Holy Spirit poured into your heart, and it has been given to you" (see Romans 5:5). Your True Self is what makes you uniquely you, and that freedom is protected from the beginning by the perfect will and love of God (see Ephesians 1:3–6).[1]

Gateway to Silence: Love is the presence of God within me.

DAY 2

Divine DNA

The True Self is characterized by communion and contentment. It knows everything is okay. It's all right here, right now. The True Self is the self that is connected with Being itself. It is the realigned self. Christianity has used the word "saved" to describe this state, and Jesus spoke of the grain of wheat which has died to its small boundaries and grows to become the large self, the God Self, the Enlightened Self. It has to do with participating and resting in the Universal Being ("God") that is bigger than your own small being and yet includes it. You are inherently a part of it. *Your life is not about you; you are about life.*

The True Self needs only to uncover or discover itself. It's already there. We are all "temples" of God, as Paul says in several places. We've each been given the gift. And there are no degrees of givenness. The gift is equally given to all, but it is *received* in varying degrees of conscious realization, depending on the extent to which we now draw our life from that Source. You are the dwelling place of God. Your deepest DNA is Divine. God is not out there. Your deepest you is God, is good, is okay. The True Self cannot be hurt; it's invulnerable, it's indestructible. It's the Great I Am continued in your fully accepted and loveable "I am."

The True Self is inherently satisfied and overflowing. It lives an abundant life. "I have come that they may have life, and have it to the full" (see John 10:10). Spiritual gifts increase through use. If you love, you become more loving. As you learn to call upon the True Self, you draw life from that which is the Big Self, instead of the small ego. That's probably why Jesus commanded us to love one another. Love is something we have to do to be who we are, to reconnect, to be realigned, to be in full communion.[2]

Gateway to Silence: Love is the presence of God within me.

Divine Indwelling

Love is not really an action that you do. Love is what you are. Love is a place that already exists inside you. It is a place where you must learn to go, which is within you but bigger than you at the same time. That's the paradox: It's within you and yet beyond you. That's why the characteristic of the True Self is a sense of abundance, of enoughness. You know you've found the deep well, as St. Teresa of Ávila put it, or, as Jesus put it, a well that will never go dry (see John 7:38) and will never stop flowing. It will only increase by usage, as do all spiritual gifts (whereas material gifts decrease with use).

Love is not something you can buy, nor something you can attain or achieve, because you already have it; it is your deepest identity. It is quite simply the presence of God within you. Our word for that has been the Holy Spirit, uncreated grace, or the Divine Indwelling. God always loves and is forever united to this love within you. It is this that God sees in you, loves in you, and cannot reject.

When you pray, I think what happens is that you steadfastly refuse to abandon that inner place that knows and believes, loves and trusts. You go to this place, saying, "I'm staying here. I'm standing here. I'm going to believe this." That's daily prayer; that's eating the daily bread to again believe the Gospel, to again believe the Divine Indwelling, to again trust and draw upon who you most deeply are. You gradually learn how to live there, how to draw your strength and solace from there, how to draw your inherent and always-gifted dignity from this abundance.[3]

Gateway to Silence: Love is the presence of God within me.

DAY 4
Foundational Belonging

Your True Self is much larger than you! You are along for the ride. It is the same with consciousness. When you learn to live from your soul, you live with everyone and everything else too. Any language of exclusion or superiority no longer makes sense to you. Inside your True Self, you know you are not alone, and you foundationally belong to God and to the universe (see 1 Corinthians 3:23). You no longer have to work at feeling important. You are intrinsically important, and it has all been "done unto you" (see Luke 1:38), just as it was with Mary, who made no claims of worthiness or unworthiness.

And if God so gratuitously and graciously includes you here and now, in this world, why would such a God change God's mind in the next world? Love is the one eternal thing, and it takes away your foundational fear of death. As Paul says, "Love lasts forever" (see 1 Corinthians 13:13).

God has not been wasting your time here, and God will not be found ineffective, failing, or unfaithful toward what Divinity has created. Paul tells us, "We may be unfaithful, but God is always faithful, for God cannot disown God's own self" (see 2 Timothy 2:13). This is the only and full meaning of the victory of God. God does not lose.[4]

Gateway to Silence: Love is the presence of God within me.

DAY 5

A Riverbed of Mercy

There is something in you that is not touched by coming and going, by up and down, by for or against, by totally right or totally wrong. There is a part of you that is patient with both goodness and evil, exactly as God is. There is a part of you that does not rush to judgment or demand closure *now*. Rather, it stands vigilant and patient in the tragic gap that almost every moment offers.

God is a riverbed of mercy that underlies all the flotsam and jetsam that flows over it and soon passes away. It is vast, silent, restful, and resourceful, and it receives and also releases all the comings and goings. It is awareness itself (as opposed to judgment), and awareness is not the same as "thinking." It refuses to be pulled into the emotional and mental tugs-of-war that form most of human life. To look out from this untouchable silence is what we mean by contemplation.

In her book *The Interior Castle*, St. Teresa of Ávila says, "The soul is spacious, plentiful, and its amplitude is impossible to exaggerate...the sun here radiates to every part...and nothing can diminish its beauty."[5] This is your soul. It is God-in-you. This is your True Self.[6]

Gateway to Silence: Love is the presence of God within me.

DAY 6

Putting Together the Human and the Divine

In the tenth chapter of his Gospel, John says that the people were intent on killing Jesus because he was not content with merely breaking the Sabbath. He dared to speak of God as his own Father and made himself God's equal (see 10:30–39). Yet Jesus does not back down when confronted with such hostility. He declares (as all of us should), "The Father and I are one." At that point, the people fetch stones to kill him, saying, "You're only a man, but you claim to be God." Jesus responds by quoting Psalm 82, "Is it not written in your Law, 'I have said you are gods'? So the Law uses the word 'gods' of those to whom the word of God is addressed—and Scripture cannot be undone." This is an extraordinary breakthrough. He not only claims his full identity, but offers the same to "those to whom the word of God is addressed" (see 10:35), which is us! And, in both cases, this is still called "Blasphemy! You are only a man and you claim to be God" (see 10:33).

Whenever you try to take seriously what the Christ took seriously, the union of the human and the Divine, you will almost always be called a heretic. You will almost always be dangerous to religion. *The very thing that it's all about is the most threatening thing of all.* Our self-doubt and self-hatred resists such a total and undeserved gift. The autonomous ego will not have it! And the sad line from Paul can now be applied to us: "Since you do not think yourselves worthy of eternal life, we will now turn to the pagans" (see Acts 13:46). I find much of the secular world more excited about this announcement today than most bona fide Christians who are bored with it.

Nelson Mandela has been quoted as saying that human beings cannot bear the burden of their own inherent greatness. Perhaps that is because we think we can't live up to it. Maybe we know subliminally or unconsciously that, if we recognize our True Self, which is the Divine Indwelling, the Holy Spirit within, then we know we have to live with that kind of dignity, responsibility, and freedom. We are the tabernacles of God, and what happened in the Christ is what is happening in all of us. Allowing and exemplifying the exquisite combination of human and Divine *that you are* is clearly your greatest task and your supreme vocation.

"Remain in me" (see John 15:4). Make your home in me, as I have made mine in you.[7]

Gateway to Silence: Love is the presence of God within me.

DAY 7

Sabbath Meditation

Remember: **Becoming Who You Are**

Your True Self is who you are in God and who God is in you. (Day 1)
Your life is not about you; you are about life. (Day 2)
Love is what you are. (Day 3)

Inside your True Self, you know you are not alone, and you foundationally belong to God and to the universe. (Day 4)

There is a part of you that is awareness itself (as opposed to judgment). (Day 5)

Allowing and exemplifying the exquisite combination of human and Divine *that you are* is clearly your greatest task and your supreme vocation. (Day 6)

Rest: **River Flow**

Contemplative prayer requires a "yes" rather than a "no" energy. Resisting thoughts and sensations inevitably increases the strength of those distractions. However, simply observing them and letting them go allows contemplative prayer to be a practice in true surrender.

Visualizing being one with a river may help you move to a welcoming, "yes" approach to prayer. Imagine that you are lying in a river, supported by a firm bed of rock, looking up at the ripples and sky above. As floating leaves and debris come into view, notice them, then let them drift on by. There's no need to follow them downstream; you are rooted to the riverbed, firm and still. Welcome and release. The river flows over and around you, never disturbing the deep peace of Earth holding water.

Gateway to Silence: Love is the presence of God within me.

For further study:

Immortal Diamond: The Search for Our True Self
True Self/False Self

SPIRITUALITY AND THE TWELVE STEPS (PART ONE)

DAY 1
Powerlessness

We admitted we were powerless over alcohol—that our lives had become unmanageable.

—Step 1 of the Twelve Steps

I am convinced that the spirituality of Alcoholics Anonymous, as it was first called, is going to go down as the significant and authentic American contribution to the history of spirituality. With inspiration from the Holy Spirit, Bill Wilson and all the other founders rediscovered the core teachings of Jesus and formed them into a program that could really change lives. It is a spirituality of imperfection, in contrast to Western Christianity's emphasis on perfection, performance, and willpower. Like Jesus and the Spirit (both of whom "descended"), it tells us to go downward to find God and ourselves, whereas for centuries we have been told to fly upward toward a God who had reversed the direction.

I believe Jesus and the Twelve Steps of Alcoholics Anonymous are saying the same thing but with different vocabulary:

We suffer to get well.

We surrender to win.

We die to live.

We give it away to keep it.

This counterintuitive wisdom will forever be avoided, until it is forced upon us by some reality over which we are powerless—and, if we are honest, we are *all* powerless in the presence of full Reality.

Both the Gospel and the Twelve-Step Program insist that the experience of powerlessness is the absolutely necessary starting point for transformational healing. This is perennial wisdom. Jesus called it the Way of the Cross, and he told us to follow him on the downward journey into powerlessness. It is there where we will find what is real, what lasts, and what matters. Through the crucifixion, Jesus showed us that powerlessness is the way through. It is not the end, but truly the beginning.[1]

Gateway to Silence: God, grant me the serenity to accept the things I cannot change, the courage to change the things I can, and the wisdom to know the difference.

DAY 2

Present to Presence

We came to believe that a Power greater than ourselves could restore us to sanity.

—Step 2 of the Twelve Steps

If we are to believe that a Power greater than ourselves can restore us to sanity, then we will come to that belief by developing the capacity for a *simple, clear, and uncluttered presence.* Those who can be present with head, heart, and body, at the same time, will always encounter *The Presence,* whether they call it God or not. For the most part, those skills are learned by letting life come at us on its own terms, and not resisting the wonderful underlying Mystery that is everywhere, all the time, and offered to us too.

All we can do is keep out of the way, note and weep over our defensive behaviors, and keep our various centers from closing down—and the Presence that is surely the Highest Power is then obvious, all-embracing, and effective. The immediate embrace is from God's side; the ineffectiveness is whatever time it takes for us to "come to believe," which is the slow and gradual healing and reconnecting of head, heart, and body so they can operate as one.

Both movements are crucial: the healing of ourselves and the healing of our always-limited and even toxic image of God. This, of itself, will often reconnect all three parts of our humanity into a marvelous receiving station. A true God experience really does save us, because it is always better than we thought we could expect or earn.[2]

Gateway to Silence: God, grant me the serenity to accept the things I cannot change, the courage to change the things I can, and the wisdom to know the difference.

DAY 3

Sweet Surrender

We made a decision to turn our will and our lives over to the care of God as we understood God.

—Step 3 of the Twelve Steps

Jesus' version of Step 3 is, "If anyone wants to follow me, let him renounce himself [or herself]" (see Mark 8:34; Luke 9:23; Matthew 16:24). I am pretty sure that Jesus and Bill meant the same thing—a radical surrendering of our will to Another whom we trust more than ourselves.

The common way of renouncing the self, while not really renouncing the self at all, is being *sacrificial!* It looks so generous and loving, and sometimes it is. But usually it is still about me. You see, there is a love that sincerely seeks the spiritual good of others, and there is a kind of heroic love that is seeking superiority, admiration, and control for itself, even and most especially by doing "good" and admirable things.

The absolute genius of the Twelve Steps is that it refuses to bless and reward any moral worthiness game or heroic willpower. With Gospel brilliance and insight, Alcoholics Anonymous says that the starting point and, in fact, the continuing point, *is not any kind of worthiness at all but, in fact, unworthiness!* ("Hi! I'm Joe, and I'm an alcoholic.")

When the churches forget their own Gospel message, the Holy Spirit sneaks in through the ducts and the air vents. A.A. meetings have been very good ductwork, allowing fresh air both in and out of many musty and mildewed churches.

We have been graced for a truly sweet surrender, *if we can radically accept being radically accepted—for nothing!* "Or grace would not be grace at all" (see Romans 11:6). As my father, St. Francis, put it, when the heart is pure, "Love responds to Love alone" and has little to do with duty, obligation, requirement, or heroic anything. It is easy to surrender when you know that nothing but Love and Mercy are on the other side.[3]

Gateway to Silence: God, grant me the serenity to accept the things I cannot change, the courage to change the things I can, and the wisdom to know the difference.

A Good Lamp

We made a searching and fearless moral inventory of ourselves.
—Step 4 of the Twelve Steps

Jesus seems to have preceded modern depth psychology and Step 4 by two thousand years. He says, "Why do you observe the splinter in your brother's eye and never notice the plank in your own? How dare you say to your sister, 'Let me take the splinter out of your eye,' when all the time there is a log in your own? Take the log out of your own eye first, and then you will see clearly enough to take the splinter out of your brother's or sister's eye" (see Matthew 7:4–5).

Step 4 is about seeing your own log first, so you can stop blaming, accusing, and denying, and thus displacing the problem. It is about *seeing* truthfully and fully. Note that Jesus does not just praise good moral behavior or criticize immoral behavior, as you might expect from a lesser teacher, but instead he talks about *something caught in the eye.* He knows that if you *see* rightly, the actions and behavior will eventually take care of themselves.

Jesus also says, "The lamp of the body is the eye. If your eye is sound, your whole body will be filled with light" (see Matthew 6:22). Step 4 is about creating a good and trustworthy lamp inside of us that reveals what is really there, knowing that "anything exposed to the light will itself become light" (see Ephesians 5:13). God brings us—through failure—from unconsciousness to ever-deeper consciousness and conscience. Full consciousness always includes the dark side; it somehow allows it, forgives it, and thus makes use of it for good.[4]

Gateway to Silence: God, grant me the serenity to accept the things I cannot change, the courage to change the things I can, and the wisdom to know the difference.

Accountability IS Sustainability

We admitted to God, to ourselves and to another human being the exact nature of our wrongs.

—Step 5 of the Twelve Steps

As any good therapist will tell you, you cannot heal what you do not acknowledge, and what you do not consciously acknowledge will remain in control of you from within, festering and destroying you and those around you.

Step 5 fits the biblical notion of "restorative justice"—to restore relationships themselves, to restore integrity with oneself, and to restore a sense of communion with God. Humanity needs such an honest exposure of the truth, and true accountability and responsibility for what has happened. Only then can human beings move ahead with dignity.

Only mutual apology, healing, and forgiveness offer a sustainable future for humanity. Otherwise, we are controlled by the past, individually and corporately. We all need to apologize, and we all need to forgive or this human project will surely self-destruct. No wonder that almost two-thirds of Jesus' teaching is directly or indirectly about forgiveness. Otherwise, history winds down into the taking of sides, deep bitterness, and remembered hurts, plus the violence that inevitably follows. As others have said, "Forgiveness is to let go of our hope for a different past." *It is what it is*, and such acceptance leads to great freedom, as long as there is also accountability and healing in the process.[5]

Gateway to Silence: God, grant me the serenity to accept the things I cannot change, the courage to change the things I can, and the wisdom to know the difference.

DAY 6

Responsibility to Surrender

We were entirely ready to have God remove all of these defects of character.
—Step 6 of the Twelve Steps

Step 6, although not commonly followed, is thoroughly biblical. It struggles with—and resolves—the old paradox of which comes first, the chicken or the egg. It first recognizes that we have to work to see our many resistances, excuses, and blockages; but then we have to fully acknowledge that God alone can do the removing! Should grace or responsibility come first? The answer is that *both* come first.

All we can do is get out of the way and then the soul takes its natural course. Grace is inherent to creation from the beginning (see Genesis 1:2), just like springtime; but it is a lot of work to get out of the way and allow that grace to fully operate and liberate.

Step 6 paradoxically says that we must fully own and admit that we have "defects of character," but then, equally, we must step back and do nothing about it, as it were, *until we are "entirely ready" to let God do the job!* This really shows high-level spiritual consciousness. The waiting, the preparing of the mind for grace, the softening of the heart, the deepening of expectation and desire, the "readiness" to really let go, the recognition that I really do not want to let go, and the actual willingness to change *is the work of weeks, months, and years.*

But the recognition that it is finally "done unto me" is the supreme insight of the Gospels, which is taught practically in Step 6. It is the same prayer of Mary at the beginning of her journey (see Luke 1:38) and of Jesus at the end of his life (see Luke 22:42): "Let it be done unto me!"

We named our whole work after this dilemma: "The Center for Action and Contemplation." It seems we must *both* take responsibility (action) *and* surrender (contemplation).[6]

Gateway to Silence: God, grant me the serenity to accept the things I cannot change, the courage to change the things I can, and the wisdom to know the difference.

DAY 7

SABBATH MEDITATION

Remember: **Spirituality and the Twelve Steps (Part One)**
Both the Gospel and the Twelve-Step Program insist that the experience of powerlessness is the absolutely necessary starting point for transformational healing. (Day 1)

Those who can be present with head, heart, and body, at the same time, will always encounter *The Presence,* whether they call it God or not. (Day 2)

It is easy to surrender when you know that nothing but Love and Mercy are on the other side. (Day 3)

Jesus knows that if you *see* rightly, the actions and behavior will eventually take care of themselves. (Day 4)

Step 5 fits the biblical notion of "restorative justice"—to restore relationships themselves, to restore integrity with oneself, and to restore a sense of communion with God. (Day 5)

Step 6 paradoxically says that we must fully own and admit that we have "defects of character," but then, equally, we must step back and do nothing about it, as it were, *until we are entirely ready to let God do the job!* (Day 6)

Rest: **Welcoming Prayer**

Rather than resisting or fighting our addictions (to thoughts, things, behaviors, etc.), admitting powerlessness is the first step toward healing and freedom. A simple prayer brings this practice into the day-to-day circumstances of life when we are drawn into habitual reactions. While a set-aside time for meditation is truly valuable in rewiring our brains, Welcoming Prayer helps us find serenity through surrender in the midst of messy, ordinary moments.

When triggered or caught by something unpleasant, begin by simply *being present to your feeling*, experiencing it not just mentally but also emotionally and physically. Don't try to rationalize or explain the feeling, but witness and give attention to this sensation.

Welcome the feeling, speaking aloud, if you can: "Welcome, [anger, fear, hunger, longing, etc.]." Repeat this as many times as you need to truly sense yourself embracing and receiving the feeling.

Finally, *let go of the feeling*, perhaps speaking these words by Mary Mrozowski, the originator of Welcoming Prayer:

I let go of my desire for security and survival.
I let go of my desire for esteem and affection.
I let go of my desire for power and control.
I let go of my desire to change the situation.[7]

Gateway to Silence: God, grant me the serenity to accept the things I cannot change, the courage to change the things I can, and the wisdom to know the difference.

For further study:

Breathing Under Water: Spirituality and the Twelve Steps
Emotional Sobriety: Rewiring Our Programs for "Happiness"
How Do We Breathe Under Water? The Gospel and 12-Step Spirituality
The Little Way: A Spirituality of Imperfection

WEEK 26:

SPIRITUALITY AND THE TWELVE STEPS (PART TWO)

DAY 1

A God-Shaped Hole

We humbly asked [God] to remove our shortcomings
—Step 7 of the Twelve Steps

Gerald May, a dear and now-deceased friend of mine, wrote in his very wise book *Addiction and Grace* that *addiction uses up our spiritual desire.* It drains away our deepest and truest desire, that inner flow and life force which makes us "long and pant for running streams" (see Psalm 42:1). Spiritual desire is the drive that God put in us from the beginning for total satisfaction, for home, for heaven, for Divine Union. It has been a frequent experience of mine to find that many people in recovery have a unique and very acute spiritual sense, often more than others. It just got frustrated early and aimed in a wrong direction. Wild need, meaninglessness, and unfettered desire took off before boundaries, strong identity, impulse control, and deep God experience were in place.

The addict lives in a state of alienation, with a "God-shaped hole" inside that is always yearning to be filled. Addicts attempt to fill it with alcohol, drugs, food, non-intimate sex, shopping—anything they feel will give them a sense of control over their moods and relief from the sense of meaninglessness and emptiness. All of us, of course, have our own false programs for happiness, which we keep using more and more to try to fill that God-shaped hole. I suspect this is the real meaning of "sin."

God's positive and lasting way of removing our shortcomings is to fill the hole with something much better, more luminous, and more satisfying. God satisfies us at our deepest levels rather than punishing us at superficial levels, which so much of organized religion seems to teach. Then our old shortcomings are not driven away or pushed underground, as much as they are *exposed for the false programs for happiness that they are*. Our sins fall away as unneeded and unhelpful because we have found a new and much better vitality. This is the wondrous discovery of our True Self "hidden with Christ in God" (see Colossians 3:3), and the gradual deterioration of our false and constructed self.[1]

Gateway to Silence: God, grant me the serenity to accept the things I cannot change, the courage to change the things I can, and the wisdom to know the difference.

DAY 2

Wounded Healing

We made a list of all the persons we had harmed, and became willing to make amends to them all.

—Step 8 of the Twelve Steps

God fully forgives us, but the "karma" of our mistakes remains, and we must still go back and repair the bonds that we have broken. Otherwise, others will not be able to forgive us but will remain stuck, and they and we will both still be wounded. We usually must make amends to forgive even ourselves. "Amazing grace" is not a way to avoid honest human relationships, but to transform them—now gracefully—for the liberation of both sides. Nothing just goes away in the spiritual world; we must reconcile and account for it all.

All healers are "wounded healers," as Henri Nouwen said so well. In fact, you are often most gifted to heal others precisely where you yourself were wounded, or perhaps have wounded others. You learn to salve the wounds of others by knowing and remembering *how much it hurts to hurt*. Often this memory comes from the realization of your past smallness and immaturity, your selfishness, your false victimhood, and your cruel victimization of others. It is often painful to recall or admit, yet this is also the grace of lamenting and grieving over how we have hurt others. Fortunately, God reveals our sins to us gradually so we can absorb what we have done over time. "O God, little by little you correct those who have offended you, so that they can abstain from evil, and learn to trust in you," we learn in the Book of Wisdom (see 12:2).

It might take a long time, even years, to "become willing" to make amends. People working on Step 8 learn to make lists—but not of what others have done to them, which is the normal ego style, and a pattern, once practiced, that is very hard to stop. Instead, they have been given some new software, a program called *grace*, a totally new pattern, "a new mind" (see Ephesians 4:23; Colossians 3:10–11; 1 Corinthians 2:16). Rather than making lists of who hurt me, I now make lists of people *I* have perhaps hurt, failed, or mistreated. Making such lists will change your foundational consciousness from one of feeding resentments to a mind that is both grateful and humble.[2]

Gateway to Silence: God, grant me the serenity to accept the things I cannot change, the courage to change the things I can, and the wisdom to know the difference.

DAY 3

Wise Amends

We made direct amends to such people wherever possible, except when to do so would injure them or others.

—Step 9 of the Twelve Steps

Step 9 is an example of the wisdom implicit in the Twelve Steps. Eastern religions often called such wisdom "skillful means." Wisdom is not a mere motto or scripture quote in the head, but a practical and effective way to actually get the job done!

Jesus was a master of teaching skillful means, especially in his Sermon on the Mount and in many of his parables and one-liners. He was constantly teaching us and showing us how to be fully human, which somehow is to be Divine! To "follow him" is first of all to imitate him in his combining of humanity and divinity in his own person.

Step 9 is telling us how to use skillful means to both protect our own humanity and liberate the humanity of others. It says that our amends to others should be "direct," that is, specific, personal, and concrete. Jesus invariably physically touched people when he healed them. It is a face-to-face encounter, although usually difficult, that does the most good in the long run.

Insightfully, Step 9 includes "except when to do so would injure them or others." One often needs time, discernment, and good advice from others before one knows how to apologize or make amends in a proper way. If not done skillfully, an apology can actually make the problem and the hurt worse. You need to pray and discern about what the other needs to hear, has the right to hear, and can handle responsibly. Even sincere people can do a lot of damage if they are not prepared to handle the information they convey to others.

Thanks to the spirituality of the Twelve Steps, people are hopefully more prepared to handle an addict's efforts to make amends. Now we can see addiction as a spiritual illness, rather than a moral failure or lack of willpower. What we call addiction is what the New Testament called "possession." Following the example of Jesus the healer, the captive sufferer, or "demon-possessed" person, should be met with empathy and love (albeit sometimes "tough love"), rather than blame, shame, and punishment. Then they will feel safer to open to the only real cure for any kind of "demonic possession": *re-possession* by the Infinite Love who alone can meet our deepest desires![3]

Gateway to Silence: God, grant me the serenity to accept the things I cannot change, the courage to change the things I can, and the wisdom to know the difference.

DAY 4

Examination of Consciousness

We continued to take personal inventory and when we were wrong promptly admitted it.

—Step 10 of the Twelve Steps

I come from a religious-life practice where we learned from the Jesuits about a daily and personal "examination of *conscience*." But I found that people with a mature conscience did this naturally anyway, and some way too much. Now many of the Jesuits recommend instead an "examination of *consciousness*" which to me feels much more fruitful. That is what I would recommend if I were teaching Step 10.

You must step back from your compulsive identification and unquestioned attachment to yourself in order to be truly conscious. Pure consciousness cannot be "just me" but instead is able to watch "me" from a distance. It is *aware* of me seeing, knowing, and feeling. Most people do not understand this awareness, because they are totally identified with their own thoughts, feelings, and compulsive patterns of perception. They have no proper distance from themselves, which is what we mean by egocentricity.

You see why so many of our mystics and saints emphasized detachment. Without it, people could not move to any deep level of consciousness, much less to the level of soul. Meister Eckhart said detachment was almost the whole spiritual path, and the early Franciscans seemed to talk about nothing else, although they called it "poverty."

We do not live in a culture that much appreciates detachment or such poverty. We are consumers and capitalists by training and habit, which is exactly why we have such problems with addiction to begin with. We always think more is better, for some sad reason. For properly detached (that is, "non-addicted") persons, deeper consciousness comes rather naturally. *They discover their own soul, which is their deepest self, and thus have access to a Larger Knowing beyond themselves.*[4]

Gateway to Silence: God, grant me the serenity to accept the things I cannot change, the courage to change the things I can, and the wisdom to know the difference.

DAY 5

Prayer and Power

We sought through prayer and meditation to improve our conscious contact with God, as we understood [God], praying only for knowledge of [God's] will for us and the power to carry that out.
—Step 11 of the Twelve Steps

I have heard that Step 11 is the least taught and followed of the Twelve Steps. This is probably why the Twelve-Step Program often became a program for sustaining sobriety and never moved many toward the "vital spiritual experience" that Bill Wilson deemed absolutely foundational for full recovery. If we can speak of the traditional Christian stages of the spiritual journey as (1) purgation, (2) illumination, and (3) union, too many addicts never seem to get to the second stage—to any real spiritual illumination of the self—and even fewer get to the rich life of *experienced* union with God. In that, I am sad to say, they mirror many Christians.

The prayer of quiet and self-surrender ("contemplation") best allows us to follow Step 11, which Bill Wilson must have recognized by using the word *meditation* at a time when that word was not common in Christian circles. And he was right, because only contemplative prayer or meditation invades, touches, and heals the *unconscious*! This is where all the garbage lies—but also where God hides and reveals "in that secret place" (see Matthew 6:6). "Do you not know," Jesus says, "the kingdom of God is *within you!*" (see Luke 17:21). Contemplation opens us to the absolute union and love between God and the soul.

Prayer is not about changing God (to do what we want), but being willing to let God change us, or, as Step 11 states, "praying only for knowledge of [God's] will for us and for the power to carry it out" (that is, actual inner empowerment and new motivation from a deeper Source). People's willingness to find God in their own struggle with life—*and allow that struggle to change them*—is their deepest and truest obedience to God's eternal plan for them.

Remember, always remember, that *the heartfelt desire to do the will of God is, in fact, the truest will of God.* At that point, God has won, the ego has lost, and your prayer has already been answered.[5]

Gateway to Silence: God, grant me the serenity to accept the things I cannot change, the courage to change the things I can, and the wisdom to know the difference.

DAY 6

Flowing Out

Having had a spiritual awakening as a result of these steps, we tried to carry this message to alcoholics, and to practice these principles in all our affairs.

—Step 12 of the Twelve Steps

Step 12 found a way to expose and transform people's basic selfishness and egocentricity by telling us early on that we must serve others. We do not truly comprehend any spiritual gift until we give it away. What comes around must go around—or it is not around for very long. Spiritual gifts increase only with use.

Step 12 is a karmic law of in and out, and what Jesus really meant when he sent the disciples out "to cast out devils, and to cure all kinds of diseases and sickness" (see Matthew 10:1) or to "Go out to the world and proclaim the Gospel to all creation" (see Mark 16:15). He knew we had to hand the message on before we really understood it or could appreciate it ourselves.

Bill Wilson described his experience of working with alcoholics during the first six months of his own sobriety. None of the alcoholics responded, but his very work kept him sober. Bill realized the alcoholics couldn't meet his need for success or whatever it might be. Rather, his own stability came through giving, and not demanding that they receive. I think that is the necessary crossover point to maturity for any minister.

Like St. Francis, Bill taught us that it is better to give than to receive. Once you get in contact with the flow and the ultimate Source that is within you, then your stability comes from the only stable Source there is, whom most of us call God. Then you know that "you must do what is yours to do," as St. Francis said to the friars on his deathbed, and the flow outward is your security, not the dependence upon somebody else's response. In other words, *we stop depending on something outside of us to fill our inner needs. We reverse the flow and draw what we need from the inside, from the absolute union between God and our soul.* We let God's energy, God's Spirit, flow out from us to others, and then we know on a cellular level that God dwells within us.[6]

Gateway to Silence: God, grant me the serenity to accept the things I cannot change, the courage to change the things I can, and the wisdom to know the difference.

DAY 7

Sabbath Meditation

Remember: **Spirituality and the Twelve Steps (Part Two)**

Addiction uses up our spiritual desire—the drive that God put in us from the beginning for total satisfaction, for home, for heaven, for Divine Union. (Day 1)

God fully forgives us, but the "karma" of our mistakes remains, and we must still go back and repair the bonds that we have broken. (Day 2)

What we call addiction is what the New Testament called "possession." The only cure for possession is *re-possession* by the Infinite Love who alone can meet our deepest desires! (Day 3)

You must step back from your compulsive identification and unquestioned attachment to yourself in order to be truly conscious. (Day 4)

People's willingness to find God in their own struggle with life—*and allow that struggle to change them*—is their deepest and truest obedience to God's eternal plan for them. (Day 5)

We stop depending on something outside of us to fill our inner needs. We reverse the flow and draw what we need from the inside, from the absolute union between God and our soul. (Day 6)

Rest: **Breathing Out**

A person will suffocate if she just keeps breathing in! To breathe means to both breathe in and breathe out—to receive and to give. I'm afraid we are much more adept at receiving than giving. It takes some practice to come to know that infinite, abundant grace abides within, so there's no need to be stingy with our forgiveness, generosity, and compassion. Perhaps practicing lengthening the outbound breath might teach us to let go even further. Slowing the exhale also lowers stress and relaxes the mind and body.

You're already breathing as you read this, without thinking about it! Now turn your attention to observe your breath. Just notice the natural rhythm of breath for a few minutes, feeling the rise and fall of your abdomen and shoulders.

Count through your next natural inhalation. Pause, holding the fullness in your belly for just a moment. Then exhale slowly, counting twice as long as for your inhalation. (For example, inhale for 4 counts, pause for 2 counts, and exhale for 8 counts.) Continue breathing in this slowed, gradual way as long as you wish. Then rest again in the uncontrived beauty of your instinctual breathing.

Gateway to Silence: God, grant me the serenity to accept the things I cannot change, the courage to change the things I can, and the wisdom to know the difference.

For further study:

Breathing Under Water: Spirituality and the Twelve Steps
Emotional Sobriety: Rewiring Our Programs for "Happiness"
How Do We Breathe Under Water? The Gospel and 12-Step Spirituality
The Little Way: A Spirituality of Imperfection

WEEK 27:

COMPASSION

DAY 1
God-in-Me Loving God

In 2013 I had the honor of representing the Christian Tradition at the Festival of Faiths in Louisville, Kentucky. Leaders of many faiths, including the Dalai Lama, came together to talk about the role of compassion in our spiritual practice. The following is what I shared from the Christian perspective:

The Christian who has gone to his or her own depths—not all of us, I am afraid—uncovers an Indwelling Presence, what might even be experienced as an I-Thou relationship (to use the language of the Jewish philosopher Martin Buber). In Christian theology, this would be described as the Holy Spirit, which is precisely God as immanent, within, and even our deepest self. Some saints and mystics have described this Presence as "closer to me than I am to myself" or "more me than I am myself." Many of us would also describe this as our True Self. It must be awakened; it is never "created" by our actions or behavior, but is naturally "indwelling," that is, our inner being with God. It does not imply psychological wholeness or even moral perfection, but an ontological, untouchable foundation.

Much of culture and religion encourages us to cultivate our False Self or reputation, self-image, roles, and possessions. It is only as this fails us—and it eventually does—that the True Self stands revealed and ready to guide us. The True Self does not teach us compassion as much as it *is* compassion already, and, from this more spacious and grounded Self, we can naturally connect, empathize, forgive, and love all reality. In Christian language this is "God-in-me loving God" and even "God-in-me loving me" and, finally, "God-in-me loving everything."

The False Self does not know how to love in a very deep or broad way. It is too small and self-referential to be compassionate. The True Self also does not choose to love as much as it *is* love itself already. Loving from this spacious place is experienced as a river within you that flows of its own accord, as Jesus promises us so beautifully (see John 7:38).[1]

Gateway to Silence: May I see with eyes of compassion.

DAY 2

The First Gaze

I am just like you. My immediate response to most situations is with reactions of attachment, defensiveness, judgment, control, and analysis. I am better at calculating than contemplating.

Let's admit that we all start there. The False Self seems to have the "first gaze" at almost everything.

The first gaze is seldom compassionate. It is too busy weighing and feeling itself: "How will this affect me?" or "How can I get back in control of this situation?" This leads us to an implosion, a self-preoccupation that cannot enter into communion with the other or the moment. In other words, we first feel our own feelings, as limited as they might be, before we can relate to the situation and emotion of the other. We have to start somewhere. Only after God has taught us how to live "undefended" can we immediately stand with and for the other in each moment. It takes lots of practice and patience.

On my better days, when I am "open, undefended, and immediately present,"[2] as Gerald May says, I can sometimes begin with a contemplative mind and heart. Often I can get there later and even end there, but it is usually a second gaze. The True Self seems to always be ridden and blinded by the defensive needs of the False Self. It is an hour-by-hour battle, at least for me. I can see why all spiritual traditions insist on daily prayer—in fact, morning, midday, evening, and before we go to bed too! Otherwise, I can assume that I am back in the cruise control of small and personal self-interest, the pitiable and fragile "Little Richard self."[3]

Gateway to Silence: May I see with eyes of compassion.

The Second Gaze

It has taken me much of my life to begin to get to the second gaze. By nature I have a critical mind and a demanding heart, and I am so impatient. These are both my gifts and my curses, as you might expect. Yet I cannot have one without the other, it seems. I cannot risk losing touch with either my angels or my demons. They are both good teachers.

I am convinced that guilt and shame are never from God. They are merely the defenses of the False Self as it is shocked at its own poverty—the defenses of a little man who wants to be a big man. God leads by compassion toward the soul, never by condemnation. If God related to us by severity and punishment, God would only be giving us permission to do the same (which is, tragically, due to our mistaken images of God, exactly what has happened!). God offers us, instead, the grace to "weep" over our sins more than to ever perfectly overcome them, and to humbly recognize our littleness. (St. Thérèse of Lisieux brought this Gospel message home in our time.) The spiritual journey is a kind of weeping and a kind of wandering that keeps us both askew and thus awake at the same time. Thérèse called it her "little way."

So now, in my later life, contemplation and compassion are finally coming together. This is my second gaze. It is well worth the wait, because only the second gaze sees fully and truthfully. It sees itself, the other, and even God with God's own eyes, which are always eyes of compassion. It is from this place that true action must spring. Otherwise, most of our action is merely re-action, and does not bear fruit or "fruit that will last" (see John 15:16). It is all about me at that point, so I must hold out for the second gaze, when it becomes all about God, about the suffering of our world, and is filled with compassion for all of it. Some high-level mystics, notably the Jewish women Simone Weil and Etty Hillesum, actually "felt sorry" for God. Most Catholic mystics truly want to actively join God in suffering for the world (see Colossians 1:24). To the outsider it just looks like masochism when it is really very high-level mysticism—the classic desire to share everything with and for the Beloved.

The gaze of compassion, looking out at life from the place of Divine Intimacy, is really all I have, and all I have to give back to God and to the world.[4]

Gateway to Silence: May I see with eyes of compassion.

True Prayer Leads to Compassion

Although the common and universally available paths to Divine Union are great love and great suffering, conscious inner prayer will deepen and maintain what we momentarily learn in love and suffering. But the mere reciting of prayers can also be, as St. John Cassian (360–435) called it, a *pax perniciosa*, or a "dangerous peace." This early Christian monk, who brought the ideas and practices of Egyptian monasticism to the early medieval West, saw that even the way of prayer can be dangerous if it never leads you to great love and allows you to avoid necessary suffering in the name of religion. This is not uncommon, I am sorry to say.

Those who fall into the safety net of silence find that it is not at all a fall into individualism. True prayer or contemplation is instead a leap into commonality and community. You know that what you are experiencing is only held by the Whole and that you are not alone anymore. You are merely a part, and now also a very grateful and totally satisfied part. This is "the peace the world cannot give" (see John 14:27).

Real silence moves you from knowing things to perceiving a Presence that imbues all things. Could this be God? When you begin to experience a mutuality between you and all things, you have begun to understand the nature of Spirit. There begins an I-Thou relationship with the world instead of the extremely limited I-it relationship. Martin Buber said an I-it relationship is when we experience everything as commodity, useful, and utilitarian, with yourself always as the beneficiary. But the I-Thou relationship is when you can simply respect—and deeply love—everything, just as it is, without adjusting it, naming it, changing it, fixing it, controlling it, or trying to explain it. Is that the mind that can know God? I really think so. God refuses to be known as any kind of object, but only as a mutuality.[5]

Gateway to Silence: May I see with eyes of compassion.

Smelling Like the Sheep

The most obvious change that results from the holding and allowing that we learn in the practice of contemplative prayer is that we will naturally become much more compassionate and patient toward just about everything. Compassion and patience are the absolutely unique characteristics of true spiritual authority, and without any doubt are the way both SS. Francis and Clare led their communities. They led, not from above, and not even from below, but mostly from *within*, by walking *with* their brothers and sisters, or "smelling like the sheep," as Pope Francis puts it.

A spiritual leader who lacks basic human compassion has almost no power to change other people, because people intuitively know he or she does not represent the Whole and Holy One. Such leaders need to rely upon roles, laws, costume, and enforcement powers to effect any change in others. Such change does not go deep, nor does it last. In fact, it is not really change at all. It is mere conformity. Love waits and wants to become the Beloved, not merely to "obey" her. Not "servants but friends," as Jesus says (see John 15:15).

We see this movement toward a shared compassion in all true saints. For example, St. Francis was able to rightly distinguish between institutional evil and the individual who is victimized by it. He still felt compassion for the individual soldiers fighting in the crusades, although he objected to the war itself. He realized the folly and yet the sincerity of their patriotism, which led them, however, to be *un-patriotic* to the much larger kingdom of God, where he placed his first and final loyalty. What Jesus calls "the Reign of God" we could call the Great Compassion.

Only people at home in such a spacious place can take on the social illnesses of their time, and even the betrayal of friends, and not be destroyed by cynicism or bitterness.[6]

Gateway to Silence: May I see with eyes of compassion.

DAY 6

The Cross as Compassion

Every worldview has its own folly and usually its own form of wisdom, and Paul claims the cross has challenged all of them and come out with the best and most honest answer (see 1 Corinthians 1:17–2:16)—precisely *because it incorporates the tragic (the irrational, absurd, and sinful) and uses it for good purposes.* The Christian perspective can absorb and appreciate paradox— which is order within disorder, redemption through tragedy, resurrection through death, divinity through humanity. Most ideologies seek some kind of false purity or perfection. Communism, Fascism, idealized capitalism, justified genocide—note how dualistic each of these is. They resist all subtlety, sympathy, dialogue, and, therefore, compassion.

For Paul, therefore, *the cross and its transformative power* are his symbol for the depths of Divine Wisdom, which seems like mere "folly" to the "masters of every age" (see 1 Corinthians 2:6). The compassionate holding of essential meaninglessness or tragedy, as Jesus does on the cross, is the final and triumphant resolution of all the dualisms and dichotomies that we ourselves must face in our own lives. If we do not suffer their reconciliation, we end up bitter and angry. We are thus truly "saved by the cross"!

Paradox held and overcome is the beginning of non-dual thinking or contemplation, as opposed to paradox denied, which forces us to choose only one part of any and all mysterious truth. Such a choice will be false because we usually choose the one that serves our small purposes. Who would ever choose the cross? Yet life often demands it of us anyway. Would anyone will or wish their child to be born with a mental or physical disability? Yet how many such families rise to very high levels of love and compassion. Paul offers a new wisdom that challenges both "Jews and Greeks" (read religious conservatives and secular liberals) in 1 Corinthians 1:22–25.

Conversion, therefore, is not joining a different group, but seeing with the eyes of the crucified. The cross is Paul's philosopher's stone or "code breaker" for any lasting spiritual liberation. God can save sincere people of faith inside of any system or religion, if only they can be patient, trusting, and compassionate in the presence of human misery or failure, especially their own. This is life's essential journey. These trustful ones have surrendered to Christ, very often without needing to use the precise word "Christ" at all (see Matthew 7:21). It is the active doing and not the correct saying that matters.[7]

Gateway to Silence: May I see with eyes of compassion.

DAY 7
SABBATH MEDITATION

Remember: **Compassion**

The True Self does not teach us compassion as much as it *is* compassion already. (Day 1)

Only after God has taught us how to live "undefended" can we immediately stand with and for the other in each moment. (Day 2)

The gaze of compassion, looking out at life from the place of Divine Intimacy, is really all I have, and all I have to give back to God and to the world. (Day 3)

True prayer or contemplation is a leap into commonality and community. (Day 4)

Compassion and patience are the absolutely unique characteristics of true spiritual authority. (Day 5)

The compassionate holding of essential meaninglessness or tragedy, as Jesus does on the cross, is the final and triumphant resolution of all dualisms and dichotomies. (Day 6)

Rest: *Maitri*

In order to see with the eyes of the crucified, we must regularly practice smelling like the sheep. We can begin by recognizing our own need for mercy and compassion. Then, in contemplative prayer, we receive God's forgiveness as our failures are washed away with God's love. Then, as we move from silence into the world of relationships, we find ways of extending that mercy to others in practical ways.

Buddhists have a meditation that nurtures *maitri*, or loving kindness, which can teach us how to hold suffering and awaken compassion.

Begin by finding the place of loving kindness inside your heart (Christians might call this the indwelling Spirit).

Drawing upon this source of love, bring to mind someone you deeply care about, and send loving kindness toward them.

Now direct this love toward a casual friend or colleague, someone just beyond your inner circle.

Continue drawing from your inner source of loving kindness and let it flow toward someone about whom you feel neutral or indifferent, a stranger.

Remember someone who has hurt you or someone you struggle to like. Bless them. Send them your love.

Gather all these people and yourself into the stream of love and hold them here for a few moments.

Finally, let the flow of loving kindness widen to encompass all beings in the universe.

This practice can help you walk compassionately with your brothers and sisters. As God has showered you with loving kindness, you will naturally find yourself showering others with the same.

Gateway to Silence: May I see with eyes of compassion.

For further study:

Eager to Love: The Alternative Way of Francis of Assisi

"Gospel Call for Compassionate Action
(Bias from the Bottom)," *CAC Foundation Set*

Journey of Faith: Making One of Two

Silent Compassion: Finding God in Contemplation

IMAGE OF GOD

DAY 1
Do Not Be Afraid

For most of human history, God was not a likable, much less lovable, character. That's why almost every theophany in the Bible (an event where God breaks through into history) begins with the same words: "Do not be afraid!" Why? Because people have always been afraid of God—and afraid of themselves, as a result.

In general, humanity did not expect love from God, or to be invited to love God in return, before the biblical revelation. Even today, most humans feel that God's love and attention must be earned, and then we deeply resent that process, just as we do with our parents. In my experience, most people are still into fearing God and controlling God instead of loving God. They never really knew mutual love was possible, given the power equation. When one party has all the power—which is most people's very definition of God—all you can do is fear and try to control.

The only way fear can be dispelled is for God, from God's side, to change the power equation and invite us into a world of mutuality and vulnerability. Our living image of that power change is called Jesus. In him, God took the initiative to overcome our fear and our need to manipulate God and made honest Divine relationship possible. This unthinkable relationship is already planted in human consciousness with the Jewish idea of "covenant love." Walter Brueggemann lists a "credo of five adjectives" that continually recurs in the Hebrew Scriptures: This God that Israel—and Jesus—discovered is consistently seen to be *"merciful, gracious, faithful, forgiving, and steadfast in love."*[1] The people who really know this to be true for themselves are the same ones who continue to seek, pray, and, often, suffer—but now with meaning and in solidarity with the Divine suffering, which is what love always does.[2]

Gateway to Silence: I am a hole in a flute that the Christ's breath moves through—listen to this music. —Hafiz[3]

DAY 2

Let God Be Who God Is

It takes a long time for us to allow God to be who God really is. Our natural egocentricity wants to make God into who we want or need God to be. It's the role of the prophet to *keep people free for God*. But, at the same time, it's the responsibility of the prophet to *keep God free for people*. This is also the role of good theology, and why we still need good theology even though it sometimes gets heady. There are "pure of heart" people (see Matthew 5:8) who do not seem to really need theology; they come to "see God" somewhat naturally and easily. But most of us need lots of help.

If God is always Mystery, then God is always on some level the unfamiliar, beyond what we're used to, beyond our comfort zone, beyond what we can explain or understand. In the fourth century, St. Augustine said, if you comprehend it, it is not God.[4] Would you respect a God you could comprehend? And yet very often that's what we want: a God who reflects and even confirms our culture, our biases, our economic, political, and security systems.

The First Commandment says that we're not supposed to make any images of God or worship them. At first glance, we may think this deals only with handmade likenesses of God. But it mostly refers to images of God that we hold in our heads. God created human beings in God's own image, and we've returned the compliment, so to speak, by creating God in our image. In the end, we produced what was typically a tribal God. In America, God looks like Uncle Sam or Santa Claus or a calculating business man—in each case, a white, Anglo-Saxon male, even though it states (see Genesis 1:27) that "God created humankind in God's own image; male and female God created them." That already makes clear that God cannot be exclusively masculine, but I get hateful letters from people when I dare to say this. They have fallen in love with a metaphor, thereby breaking the first commandment.

Normally we find it very difficult to let God be a God who is greater than our culture, our immediate needs, and our projections. The human ego wants to keep things firmly in its grasp and so we've created a God who fits into our small systems and our understanding of God. Thus, we've produced a God who likes to go to war just as much as we do, and a domineering God because we like to dominate. We've almost completely forgotten and ignored what Jesus revealed about the nature of the God he knew. If Jesus is the "image of the invisible God" (see Colossians 1:15) then God is nothing like we expected. Jesus is in no sense a potentate or a patriarch, but the very opposite, one whom John the Baptist calls "a lamb of a God" (see John 1:29). In the doctrine of the Trinity, God is defined as relationship itself. Once we tried to define—or make use of—the Christ outside of the flow of the Trinity, we no longer had a Christian or relational understanding of God, which determines much of our history.[5]

Gateway to Silence: I am a hole in a flute that the Christ's breath moves through—listen to this music. —Hafiz

DAY 3

What Jesus Says about God

Jesus teaches about the God he knows. He offers a kind of "soul language" that makes sense to as many people as possible. Many of the citations he uses are from extra-biblical sources, aphorisms, legends, and stories. He takes wisdom from wherever it comes. When he does quote Scripture, the only Hebrew Scriptures that he quotes are those that move toward mercy, justice, and inclusivity. There *are* Scriptures that present God as punitive, imperialistic, or exclusionary, but Jesus never quotes them in his teaching. In fact, he speaks against them.

Jesus' longest single citation from his own Hebrew Scriptures is in Luke 4. He went into the synagogue and unrolled the scroll of the prophet Isaiah and "found the place where it was written, 'The Spirit of the Lord is upon me, because God has anointed me to preach good news to the poor. God has sent me to proclaim release to the captives and recovering of sight to the blind, to set at liberty those who are oppressed, to proclaim the acceptable year of the Lord.' And he closed the book, and gave it back to the attendant, and sat down" (see Luke 4:17–20). Wait a minute! Jesus stopped reading before he finished the text! Isaiah 61:2 actually says: "and to proclaim a *day of vengeance from our God.*" Jesus skips the last line because he isn't here to announce vengeance. He has a completely different message, and thus critiques his own Scriptures. This is quite telling. Not all Scriptures are created equal, it seems.

Jesus creates stories to communicate that God is good, faithful, and merciful (for example, the Good Samaritan, the Prodigal Son, and the Publican and the Pharisee). Jesus exemplifies biblical faith, which is not trust in ideas; it's trust in a *person*—God, his Father, whom he trusts so much he calls God Abba, Daddy, Papa. Jesus knows that God is always with him, and in a caring way.

The Christ did not become the incarnate Jesus to change the Father's mind about us (it did not need changing!); the incarnate Jesus was desperately *trying to change our mind about God*—and thus about one another. If God and Jesus are not hateful, violent, punitive, torturing, or vindictive, then our excuse for such behavior is forever taken away from us. Maybe we do not really want such a God? You can see why I often say that we are still in "early Christianity." The true and full God is always out ahead of us and beyond us and too much for us.[6]

Gateway to Silence: I am a hole in a flute that the Christ's breath moves through—listen to this music. —Hafiz

DAY 4

Is God a Person?

I consider the question of whether God is a "person" an important one for any serious understanding of mysticism and the experience of individual holy people. Yes, most Hindu, Sufi, Jewish, and Christian mystics, including SS. Francis and Clare, speak—in part—as if God is quite personal, friendly, and sitting in a chair next to them (a human writ large), which reveals the deep and personal character of mystical encounters.

Many rightly feel that humanity has moved far beyond any "old bearded man sitting on a throne" kind of God, who always ends up looking like our past authority figures and who must be "feared," yet can also be cajoled into doing our will. This view seems to cheapen any honest or profound notion of God, and it surely has been subject to misuse and manipulation by immature people and clergy. Critics of such traditional images of God are, of course, half correct (God is surely not male, nor a human writ large!), but I also believe their too-quick dismissal can keep us from wonderful possibilities and openings. Maybe God is *supremely* personal!

I would like to offer my "Yes, And" approach to help Christians and unbelievers alike know what is very good and deeply true about a personal notion of God, but then to move further too. Francis surely loved and related to God as "Jesus" in a personal and intimate way, and yet he also saw God in "Brother Wind and Air," as "Sister Water," "Brother Fire," and "Sister, Mother Earth."[7] When you get to the more mature levels of mystical union, everything becomes a metaphor for the Divine, and you grab for metaphors to concretize the Mystery that is now in everything and everywhere! Thus God is revealed as transpersonal ("Father"), personal ("Jesus"), and impersonal ("Holy Spirit") all at once! This is a good basis for profound mystical experience. The rediscovery of God as Trinity is essential to the foundational reform of Christianity.[8]

Gateway to Silence: I am a hole in a flute that the Christ's breath moves through—listen to this music. —Hafiz

DAY 5

Who Created Whom?

In Genesis, God says, "Let *us* make humanity in *our* own image, in the likeness of *ourselves*" (see 1:26). It's quite interesting that the plural form is used. It seems almost an intuition of what we will later call the Trinity. One could see this as an early capsulation of what finally becomes the revelation of God as community, God as relationship itself, a God who, for Christians, is seen as a mystery of perfect giving and perfect receiving, within and without. I personally take this pattern of God as the central template and pattern of all reality—which we now see in the atom, the ecosystem, and the planets and galaxies of the universe. *Everything lives in cycles and orbits and very creative balancing acts.*

God is both face and interface, with an infinite capacity for meaning, depth, mystery, and communication, and it is we who are created in this Divine design, not the other way around. This is, I sincerely believe, the absolute core of the Judeo-Christian revelation. So both Yahweh and Jesus are, indeed, the very essence of what we mean by being *"Personal"* (capable of mutual subjective interface).

This is not to deny that God is *Transpersonal* too—Energy, Life Itself, Formlessness, Consciousness, Ground of Being, Truth, Love, and so forth. This is surely what we mean by the metaphor of "Father." But God also needs to be known and mirrored in what we would call Impersonal ways too. Probably our metaphors for the Holy Spirit as a dynamic flow, fire, water, and descending dove were given to us to keep this dynamism and movement alive. The entire world of nature is a multivalent mirror of the endless impersonal images for the Divine. Poets and naturalists seem to know this best.

To be honest, most people probably begin with the personal. They need personal interface and mirroring to know their God. This is why Jesus indeed became "the gate" (see John 10:7) and "the way, the truth, and the life" (see John 14:6) for so many people. Our personhood makes it possible to understand and relate to the exact same personhood in God; we have a built-in capacity for the Divine *(capax Dei) since we are divinely constituted by the same love relations as the Trinity.* Remember: Let *us* create humanity in *our* image! We were created with an inherent capability and desire for essential relatedness, for communication, intimate love, connection, and mutuality. It is our "natural law," and actually our "first nature." I think any good psychologist would now back this up.[9]

Gateway to Silence: I am a hole in a flute that the Christ's breath moves through—listen to this music. —Hafiz

DAY 6

Personal and Transpersonal

Mature and mystical believers are eventually led toward a *transpersonal* notion of God as Pure Presence, consciousness itself, Naked Being, the very Ground of Being, God with us, and God in all things—and find God in impersonal things like flowers, the sun, and all beauty. Yet many of these very same people frequently find it helpful, if not necessary, to still relate to God through the intimate sharing of one trusting person to another. All three levels—transpersonal, personal, and impersonal—finally show themselves in a complete spiritual journey, and in most world religions.

As I said yesterday, most people—but not all—start with the personal. It takes two to love—a giver and a receiver. You really cannot fully give yourself to, fall in love with, or surrender to a concept, an energy, a force, or even to enlightenment as an idea. Persons love persons, and the brilliance of Judeo-Christianity is that it keeps the whole spiritual life intensely personal in this very rich sense, and yet also moves beyond it. (Ken Wilber's "transcend and include" is the brilliant principle here.)

The personal God revealed in both the Hebrew and Christian Scriptures, and very frequently in the mystical levels of the Perennial Tradition, makes known a Divine Nature that is seductive, self-disclosing, and immensely self-giving to those who are interested. This experience of "overflow" invites us into more freedom than most of us are even ready to experience, along with intimacy and real friendship. Such a face-to-face relationship deeply empowers anyone who engages with it.

For me, it really comes down to this: The individuals I know who are most genuinely happy and also fruitful for the world invariably relate to God in a way that is deeply personal, intimate, and almost conversational. Yet these same persons would be the first to admit and recognize that their personal God is also transpersonal and sometimes impersonal, "the one in whom we all live, and move, and have our being" (see Acts 17:28), and, finally, beyond all names for God. God is humbly recognized as beyond any of our attempts to domesticate, understand, or control the Mystery. All names for God are indeed "in vain."[10]

Gateway to Silence: I am a hole in a flute that the Christ's breath moves through—listen to this music. —Hafiz

DAY 7

Sabbath Meditation

Remember: **Image of God**

This God that Israel—and Jesus—discovered is consistently seen to be *"merciful, gracious, faithful, forgiving, and steadfast in love."* (Day 1)

If God is always Mystery, then God is always on some level the unfamiliar, beyond what we're used to, beyond our comfort zone, beyond what we can explain or understand. (Day 2)

Jesus was not changing the Father's mind about us; he was changing our mind about God—and thus about one another. (Day 3)

Francis surely loved and related to God as "Jesus" in a personal and intimate way, and yet he also saw God in "Brother Wind and Air," as "Sister Water," "Brother Fire," and "Sister, Mother Earth." (Day 4)

Trinity becomes the revelation of God as community, God as relationship itself, a God who, for Christians, is seen as a mystery of perfect giving and perfect receiving, within and without. (Day 5)

All three levels—transpersonal, personal, and impersonal—finally show themselves in a complete spiritual journey, and in most world religions. (Day 6)

Rest: **Imaginarium**

Each of our *imaginaria*—our unconscious but operative worldviews, constructed by our experience, including all the symbols, archetypes, and memories that inhabit it—are foundationally real and have very concrete effects on how we think and at what level we think. Jews, Catholics, Protestants, and Hindus all live in quite different *imaginaria*, and there is not much point in calling another "wrong."

Einstein said that "imagination is more important than knowledge."[11] Plato, later Neo-Platonists, and, in our time, Carl Jung, recognized that the shared imaginal world is where encounter and deep change really happen. Images have the power to transform us and even steer history. God can only come to any of us in images that we already trust and believe, and that open our hearts.

Draw to mind a symbol or metaphor from your *imaginarium* that reminds you of some aspect of God or Reality. Visualize it as fully and clearly as you can, imagining the shape, color, sound, texture, smell, taste. Let these details sink into your heart, deeper than head and rational thought. Feel them. Allow the image to move you beyond words to experience and encounter. Rest in the mystery of God's presence, within and infinitely more than your imagination can fathom.[12]

Gateway to Silence: I am a hole in a flute that the Christ's breath moves through—listen to this music. —Hafiz

For further study:

The Art of Letting Go: Living the Wisdom of Saint Francis
Eager to Love: The Alternative Way of Francis of Assisi
Hierarchy of Truths: Jesus' Use of Scripture
Simplicity: The Freedom of Letting Go
Things Hidden: Scripture as Spirituality

WEEK 29:

JESUS, THE CHRIST

DAY 1
Jesus: Transformative Icon of God

Jesus' entire journey told people two major things: that life could have a positive storyline, and that God was far different and far better than we ever thought. He did not just give us textbook answers from a distance, but personally walked through the process of being both rejected *and* forgiving, and then said, "Follow me."

The significance of Jesus' wounded body is his deliberate and conscious holding of the pain of the world and refusing to send it elsewhere. The wounds were not necessary to convince God that we were worth loving; the wounds are to *convince us of the path and the price of transformation.* They are what will happen to you too—if you learn from your own sinfulness and "the sin of the world" (see John 1:29) with compassion instead of projecting them on others with hatred.

- Jesus' wounded body is an icon for what we are all doing to one another, to ourselves, and to the world.
- Jesus' resurrected body is an icon of God's response to all of our crucifixions and is thus the final chapter of all history.
- These two images contain the whole message of the Gospel in shorthand form.

A naked, bleeding, wounded, crucified man is the most unlikely image for God, a most illogical image for Omnipotence (which is how most people see God). Apparently, we have got God all wrong! Jesus is revealing a very central problem for religion by coming into the world in this most unexpected and even unwanted way. The cross of Jesus was a mirror held up to history, so we could utterly change our normal image of God and of sin, and to give cosmic hope to all of history. Up to now, mainstream Christianity has not fully represented any of these very well. God is just too much for us.[1]

Gateway to Silence: In Christ all things hold together. (See Colossians 1:17.)

DAY 2

How Jesus "Takes Away the Sin of the World"

Humans make hard and impossible the very things they most want (see Romans 7:14–25). Such *contrariness* must be the meaning of any original wound or "sin." Mean-spiritedness and hate appear to be helpful to, needed, and even wanted by most people, believe it or not. Negativity unites most people far more quickly than love. The ego moves forward by contraction, self-protection, and refusal—by saying "no." The soul, however, does not proceed by contraction, but by expansion. It moves forward, not by exclusion, but by inclusion and by saying "yes."

Jesus came to reveal and resolve this central and essential problem. I consider it the very meaning of the Risen Christ, and why he is our Cosmic Hope. There is really no other way to save us from ourselves, and from each other, until we are saved from our need to fear and hate. God entered history in Jesus as the Forever-Forgiving Victim.

Conscious love is the totally enlightened, and often entirely nonsensical, way out of this universal pattern of negativity or "sin." Love has to be worked toward, received, and enjoyed, first of all, by facing our actual preference for fear and hate. But remember, we gather around the negative space quickly, while we "fall into" love rather slowly, and only with lots of practice at falling.

This is what Jesus did: He hung on the cross and did not return the negative energy directed at him. He held it inside and made it into something much better. That is how he "took away the sin of the world" (see John 1:29). He refused to pass it on! He absorbed evil until it became resurrection! And this is exactly what contemplative practice helps us to do. Meditation is refusing to project our anxieties elsewhere and learning to hold and face them within ourselves and within God.[2]

Gateway to Silence: In Christ all things hold together. (See Colossians 1:17.)

Following the Shape-Shifter

Jesus clearly taught the twelve disciples about surrender, the necessity of suffering, humility, servant leadership, and nonviolence. The men resisted him every time, and so he finally had to make the journey himself and tell them, "Follow me!" But we avoided his message too, by making it into something he never said: "Worship me." Worship of Jesus is rather harmless and risk-free; it is only actually following Jesus, in very practical ways, that will ever change the world. Candlesticks and incense will never do it.

Why does the Bible, and why does Jesus, tell us to care for the poor and the outsider? Because we need to stand in that position now and then—for our own conversion. We need to be in a position to actually need the mercy of God, the forgiveness of God, the grace of God. When we are too smug and content, then grace and mercy have almost no real meaning. They are just words. We do not even desire or think forgiveness is necessary (see Luke 7:47).

Jesus is always on the side of the crucified ones. He changes sides in the twinkling of an eye to go wherever the pain is to be found. He is not loyal to one religion, to this or that group, or to the worthy; *Jesus is only and always loyal to human suffering.* Jesus is what mythology calls a shape-shifter, and no one seeking power can use him for their private purposes. Those whose hearts are opened to human pain will see Jesus everywhere, and their old dualistic minds will serve them less and less, for the Shape-Shifter ends up shifting our very shape too.

The Gospel gives our suffering personal and cosmic meaning by connecting our pain to the pain of others and, finally, by connecting us to the very pain of God. Any form of contemplation is a gradual sinking into this fullness, or what I call the unified field, which always produces a deep, irrational, and yet very certain hope. And we never know exactly where it came from![3]

Gateway to Silence: In Christ all things hold together. (See Colossians 1:17.)

A Cosmic Christ Means Cosmic Hope

I am making the whole of creation new.... It will come true.... It is already done! I am the Alpha and the Omega, the Beginning and the End. (See Revelation 21:5–6.)

Is this Jesus of Nazareth speaking or Someone Else? Whoever's voice this is, is offering an entire and optimistic arc to all of history, and is not just the humble Galilean carpenter. This is much more than a mere "religious" message; it is also a historical and cosmic one. It declares a definite trajectory where there is a coherence between the beginning and the ending of all things. It offers humanity hope and vision.

This is the Cosmic Christ who is speaking here. Jesus of Nazareth did not talk this way. It was Christ who "rose from the dead," and even that is no leap of faith once you realize that *the Christ never died—or can die*—because he is the eternal mystery of matter and Spirit as one. Jesus willingly died—and Christ arose—yes, still Jesus, but now including and revealing everything else in its full purpose and glory (read Colossians 1:15–20).

When these verses were written, it was sixty to seventy years after Jesus' human body "ascended into heaven." The Christians have now met a fully available *presence* that defines, liberates, and sets a goal and direction for life. Largely following Paul, who wrote in the A.D. 50s, they have come to call this seemingly new and available presence a mystery that they address as "both Lord and Christ" more than just "Jesus" (see Acts 2:36).

Such Divine Presence had always been there, as we know from the experiences of "Abraham, Isaac, and Jacob" (see Luke 20:37–38). But, after Jesus, this eternal presence had *a precise, concrete, and personal referent*. Perhaps vague belief and spiritual intuition became specific—with a "face" that they could "see, hear, and touch" in Jesus (see 1 John 1:1).[4]

Gateway to Silence: In Christ all things hold together. (See Colossians 1:17.)

DAY 5

Jesus *and* Christ

Most Christians were never encouraged to combine the personal with the cosmic, or Jesus with Christ; nor were we told that we could honor and love both of them. Nor were we told that it is the same love but just in different frames. To love Jesus makes you an initial believer; to love Jesus Christ makes you a cosmic participant, finally at home in the embodiment of the world.

It is important to place ourselves in the largest possible frame, or we always revert back to a very non-catholic ("un-whole") place where both the Savior and the saved ones end up being far too small because Jesus of Nazareth has been separated from the Eternal Christ. Here Christianity becomes just another competing world religion, and salvation is far too privatized (and actually ineffective), because the social and historical message has been lost. We are back to a few private individuals "going" to a distant heaven, and leaving this world in apocalyptic ruin.

The full Gospel is so much bigger and more inclusive than that: Jesus is the historical figure, and Christ is the cosmic figure—and together they carry both the individual and history forward. Up to now, we have not been carrying history too well, because "there stood among us one we did not recognize" (see John 1:26), "one who comes after me, because he also existed before me," to quote John the Baptist (see John 1:30). We made Christ into Jesus' last name instead of realizing it was the description of his cosmic role in history and in all world religions.

Christ is eternal; Jesus is born in time. Jesus without Christ invariably becomes a time-bound and culturally bound religion that excludes much of humanity from Christ's embrace. On the other end, Christ without Jesus would easily become an abstract metaphysics or a mere ideology without much personal engagement. Love always needs a direct object. We need them both and thus we rightly believe in both, *Jesus* and *Christ*, just as most Christians would say.[5]

Gateway to Silence: In Christ all things hold together. (See Colossians 1:17.)

DAY 6

The One Face and the Everything

A cosmic notion of Christ takes mysticism beyond the mere individual level that has been seen as its weakness up to now. That perception is one of the major reasons that many people mistrust and even dislike "mysticism," because it feels all too private, pious, and mystified, and never gets to the transpersonal, social, and collective levels. False mysticism—and we have had a lot of it—often feels too much like "my little Jesus and my little me," and doesn't seem to make many social, historical, corporate, or justice connections. It is all too self-referential, as Pope Francis has said.

If authentic God-experience first makes you overcome the primary split between yourself and the Divine, then it should also overcome the split between yourself and the rest of creation. For some, the split is seemingly overcome in the person of Jesus; but for more and more people, union with the Divine is first experienced through the Christ: in nature; in moments of pure love, silence, inner or outer music; with animals, a sense of awe, or some kind of "Brother Sun and Sister Moon" experience.

If it is authentic mystical experience, it connects us and just keeps connecting at ever-newer levels, breadths, and depths, "until God can be all in all" (see 1 Corinthians 15:28). Or, as Paul also says, "The world, life and death, the present and the future are all your servants, for you belong to Christ and Christ belongs to God" (see 1 Corinthians 3:22–23). Full salvation is finally universal belonging and universal connecting. Our word for that is "heaven."

Irish novelist Elizabeth Bowen says, "To turn from everything to one face is to find oneself face to face with everything."[6] Jesus is the one face, we are the interface, and Christ is the Everything.[7]

Gateway to Silence: In Christ all things hold together. (See Colossians 1:17.)

DAY 7

Sabbath Meditation

Remember: **Jesus, the Christ**

The cross of Jesus was a mirror held up to history, so we could utterly change our normal image of God. (Day 1)

Jesus hung on the cross and did not return the negative energy directed at him. (Day 2)

The Gospel gives our suffering personal and cosmic meaning by connecting our pain to the pain of others and, finally, by connecting us to the very pain of God. (Day 3)

"I am the Alpha and the Omega, the Beginning and the End." (See Revelation 21:6.) (Day 4)

Jesus is the historical figure, and Christ is the cosmic figure—and together they carry both the individual and history forward. (Day 5)

Authentic mystical experience connects us and just keeps connecting at ever-newer levels, breadths, and depths, "until God can be all in all." (Day 6)

Rest: **The Jesus Prayer**

Let's look closely at the familiar Eastern Orthodox prayer, "Lord Jesus Christ, Son of God, have mercy on me, a sinner." Within the context of this week's study on Jesus, the Christ, these words can now hold rich meaning for you. Let's look at the words.

Lord – While the word can connote dominion and hierarchical authority (the Greek, *kurios*, means "master"), remember that the authority with which Jesus taught was an inner authority, born of his awareness that he was God's own child. And we have inherited this power!

Jesus Christ – He is both human and Divine, personal and infinite.

"Jesus" was a common name (Joshua in Hebrew); "Christ" means "anointed, chosen." We need both to ground us in the ordinary, suffering world and to draw us toward the "heaven" of union.

Sinner – Remember that "sin" is simply that which keeps us from knowing and living out of our True Self. We forget that we are inherently beloved. Don't think of sin as just individual "nastiness," which is largely shame-based thinking and, in itself, does not get you to a good place. We settle for moralism when we do not get to mysticism.

Mercy – We need the "salvation" of Love to overcome our fear-based disconnection, to return us to wholeness. Abundant, never withheld, restorative grace brings us back into intimacy with self, God, and others. Pope Francis says that mercy is the highest virtue in the hierarchy of Christian truths.

Using this prayer as a focal point, say the words repeatedly until the prayer moves from your head into your heart and you connect with the Presence already praying ceaselessly within.

"Lord Jesus Christ, Son of God, have mercy on me, a sinner."

For further study:

The Cosmic Christ
Culture, Scapegoating, and Jesus
Dancing Standing Still: Healing the World from a Place of Prayer
Eager to Love: The Alternative Way of Francis of Assisi

WEEK 30:

LETTING GO

DAY 1

The Spirituality of Subtraction

To paraphrase a frequent theme for Meister Eckhart, the spiritual life has much more to do with subtraction than it does with addition. *All great spirituality is about letting go.* But we have grown up with a capitalist world-view, and it has blinded our spiritual seeing. We tend to think at almost every level that more is better, even though, as the architect Ludwig Mies van der Rohe said, "Less is more." Zen has come to prominence in the West as we have now come to realize this. (Compare Zen architecture and design to Italian Catholic churches with elaborate art decorating every conceivable space, including floor and ceiling; French Provincial furniture and design that always needs one more flourish and a little more gold; American cities that are collapsing under the ugliness of their neon signs and video advertise-ments.) The Amish and the Shakers seem to be the only Christians who have chosen simplicity.

There is an alternative worldview. There is a worldview in which all of us can succeed. It isn't a win/lose capitalist worldview where only a few win and most lose. It's a win/win worldview—*if we're willing to let go* and recognize that this, right here, right now, is enough, and affirm, "This is all I need." But that can only be true if we move to the level of being and away from the levels of doing and acquiring.

Mystical religion is always pointing us toward the joy of naked being.

At that level, we experience enoughness, abundance, and even more-than-enoughness. If we've never been introduced to that world, we will of course try to satisfy ourselves with possessions, accomplishments, important initials after our names, fancy cars, beautiful homes—none of which are bad in themselves. They're only unable to satisfy, and that's exactly why we need more and more of them. As the Twelve-Steppers say, "We need more and more of what does not work." If it worked, we would not need more of it![1]

Gateway to Silence: Let go and let God.

The Three Big Demons

The spiritual journey is a journey into mystery, requiring us to enter the "cloud of unknowing" (a common metaphor for a necessary and acceptable ignorance, based on the fourteenth-century classic of the same name) where the left brain always fears to tread. Precisely because we're being led into mystery, we have to let go of our need to know and our need to keep everything under control. Most of us are shocked to discover how great this need is.

There are three primary things of which we have to let go, in my opinion. First is the compulsion to be successful and competent, and thus admired (see Matthew 4:3, where Jesus is asked to turn stones into bread). Second is the compulsion to be right—even, and especially, to be theologically right (see Matthew 4:5, where Jesus is standing on the parapet of the temple). Religion is often a well-disguised ego trip; nothing like having God totally on your side! Finally, we need to let go of the compulsion to be powerful, to have everything under your precise control (see Matthew 4:8–9: "I will give you all the kingdoms of the world").

I'm convinced these are the very three demons Jesus faced in the wilderness (see Matthew 4:1–11). I encourage you to read this text in this light, and see if it is indeed very helpful. Until we each look these three demons in their eyes, we should presume that they are still in charge of our lives. The demons have to be called by name, clearly, concretely, and practically, spelling out just how imperious, controlling, and self-righteous they make us. We could also see the three temptations as addressing the three common human agendas that appeal to heart (being liked), head (being correct), and gut (being secure). These demons must be recognized in each of us, and—even worse—we must understand that they never go away![2]

Gateway to Silence: Let go and let God.

Letting Go into God

To Western or comfortable people, surrender and letting go sound like losing, but they are actually about accessing a deeper, broader sense of the self, which is already whole, already content, already filled with abundant life. This is the part of you that has always loved God and has always said "yes" to God. It's the part of you that is Love, and all you have to do is *let go and fall into it.* It's already there. Once you move your identity to that level of deep inner contentment and compassion, you realize that you're drawing upon a Life that is larger than your own and from a deeper Abundance. Once you learn to do that, why would you ever again settle for some scarcity model for life?

But sadly, we continually do just that. The scarcity model is the way we're trained to think: "I am not enough. This is not enough. I do not have enough." So we try to attain more and more, and climb higher and higher. Thomas Merton said we may spend our whole life climbing the ladder of success, only to discover that, when we get to the top, our ladder is leaning against the wrong wall.

A daily practice of contemplative prayer can help you fall into the Big Truth that we all share, the Big Truth that is God, Grace itself, where you are overwhelmed by *more-than-enoughness*! The spiritual journey is about living more and more in that abundant place where you don't have to wrap yourself around your hurts, your defeats, your failures. You can get practiced in letting go and saying, "That's not me. I don't need that. I've met a better self, a truer self." Your True Self, more than anything else, is characterized by radical contentment.[3]

Gateway to Silence: Let go and let God.

Letting Go of Ego

We need forms of prayer that free us from fixating on our own conscious thoughts and feelings and from identifying with those thoughts and feelings, as if we are our thinking. Who are you before you have your thoughts and feelings? That is your naked being. We have to learn to be spiritually empty, or, as Jesus says in his first beatitude, "How blessed are the poor in spirit" (see Matthew 5:3). If we are filled with ourselves, there is no room for another, and certainly not for God. We need contemplative prayer, in which we simply let go of our constantly changing and ephemeral ego needs, so Something Eternal can take over.

This may sound simple, but it is not easy! Because we've lost the art of detachment, we've become almost fully identified with our stream of consciousness and our feelings. Don't misunderstand me; I'm not saying you should repress or deny your feelings. I'm challenging you to name them and observe them, but not to directly fight them, identify with them, or attach to them (which almost all people do before enlightenment). Unless we learn to let go of our feelings, we don't have our feelings; our feelings have us. (Is that the deepest meaning of "being possessed"?)

Now, you might ask: "What does this have to do with God? I thought prayer was supposed to be talking to God or searching for God. You seem to be saying that prayer is, first of all, about getting myself out of the way." As John the Baptist put it, "I must grow smaller so he can grow greater" (see John 3:30). That is exactly what I am saying.

God is already present. God's Spirit is dwelling within you. You cannot search for what you already have. You cannot talk God into "coming "into" you by longer and more urgent prayers. All you can do is become quieter, smaller, and less filled with your own self and your constant flurry of ideas and feelings. Then God will be obvious in the very now of things, and in the simplicity of things. To sum it all up, *you can never get there, you can only be there.*[4]

Gateway to Silence: Let go and let God.

DAY 5

Forgiveness Is Letting Go

Forgiveness is simply the religious word for letting go. To forgive reality is to let go of the negative storyline you created around something or someone that offended you, the storyline of victimhood that you've created to justify the humiliation that your False Self has suffered. Your True Self cannot be offended, or, as Paul puts it, "Love takes no offense" (see 1 Corinthians 13:5)! When that negative storyline, with you as its victim, becomes your identity, when you choose to live as an abused self (which is not who you are anyway), this strangely gives you a false kind of power and makes you feel morally superior to others. But let me tell you, it will also destroy you. It will make you smaller and smaller as you get older. You will find that you have fewer and fewer people you can trust, fewer and fewer people—if any—that you can love. Life itself becomes a threat. Your comfort zone becomes tinier and tinier.

Thankfully, God has given us a way to not let the disappointments, hurts, betrayals, and rejections of life destroy us. It is the art of letting go. If we can forgive and let go, if we don't hold onto our hurts against history and against one another, we will indeed be following Jesus. The wounds of the crucified Jesus symbolize sacred wounds, transformative wounds that did not turn him bitter. After the crucifixion, there's no record of Jesus wanting to blame anybody or accuse anybody. In fact, his dying words are breathing forgiveness: "Father, forgive them; they do not know what they are doing" (see Luke 23:34).

If we are to follow Jesus, he says we're simply to forgive one another as much as God has forgiven us, which seems to be infinitely. He says we should forgive one another not seven times, but "seventy times seven times" (see Matthew 18:22). What that implies, first of all, is that being all-merciful and all-forgiving are God's very nature—or, as Pope Francis says, "The name of God is mercy." But it also implies that Jesus knows we are going to make mistakes. He assumes even well-intended and good human beings are going to hurt one another and do it wrong—maybe even seventy times seven times. This should keep us all humble and ready to forgive.[5]

Gateway to Silence: Let go and let God.

DAY 6

Forgiving Ourselves

Perhaps the most difficult forgiveness, the greatest letting go, is to forgive ourselves, especially if the mistake carries a lot of guilt or shame. We need to realize that we are not perfect, and we are not innocent. "One always learns one's mystery at the price of one's innocence," says Robertson Davies' character, Magnus, in his book *Fifth Business*.[6] If I want to maintain an image of myself as innocent, superior, or righteous, I can only do so at the cost of truth. I would have to reject the mysterious side, the shadow side, the broken side, the unconscious side of almost everything. We have for too long confused holiness with innocence, whereas holiness is actually mistakes overcome and transformed, not necessarily mistakes avoided.

Letting go is different from denying or repressing. To let go of mistake or error, you have to admit it. You have to own it. Letting go is different from turning it against yourself. Letting go is different from projecting it onto others. Letting go means that the denied, repressed, rejected parts of yourself are seen for what they are. You see it and you hand it over to God. You hand it over to history. You refuse to let the negative storyline around which you've wrapped yourself define your life.

This is a very different way of living. It implies that you see your mistake, your dark side, and you don't split from it. You don't pretend it's not true. You allow what the saints called "the gift of tears." *Weeping* is a word to describe that inner attitude where I can't fix it, I can't explain it, I can't control it, I can't even understand it. I can only weep over it and let go of it. Grieving reality is different than hating it. Weeping is often a deep acceptance of one's powerlessness, and that is why it can be so cleansing.

Letting go of our cherished images of ourselves is really the way to heaven, because when you fall down to the bottom, you fall on solid ground, the Great Foundation, the bedrock of God. It looks like an abyss, but it's actually a foundation. On that foundation, you have nothing to prove, nothing to protect: "I am who I am who I am," and, for some unbelievable reason, that's what God has chosen to love.[7]

Gateway to Silence: Let go and let God.

DAY 7

Sabbath Meditation

Remember: **Letting Go**

All great spirituality is about letting go. (Day 1)

The spiritual journey is a journey into mystery, requiring us to enter the "cloud of unknowing" where the left brain always fears to tread. (Day 2)

A daily practice of contemplative prayer can help you fall into the Big Truth that we all share, the Big Truth that is God, Grace itself, where you are overwhelmed by *more-than-enoughness*! (Day 3)

Unless we learn to let go of our feelings, we don't have our feelings; our feelings have us. (Day 4)

If we can forgive and let go, if we don't hold onto our hurts against history and against one another, we will indeed be following Jesus. (Day 5)

Letting go of our cherished images of ourselves is really the way to heaven, because when you fall down to the bottom, you fall on solid ground, the Great Foundation, the bedrock of God. (Day 6)

Rest: *Lectio Divina*

Below are several passages in Scripture that encourage us to let go. Choose one (along with the surrounding text) that resonates with you and engage the passage with the simple practice of *lectio divina*.

Letting go of control (the faith theme throughout the Bible):
"The Lord will deliver you, and you have only to be still." (See Exodus 14:14)

Letting go of fear (the most frequent line in the Bible):
"Do not be afraid." (See John 6:20, Mark 6:50, Matthew 14:27, to name a few)

Letting go of the small self:
"Yahweh my Lord is my strength." (See Habakkuk 3:19)
"Cut off from me, you can do nothing." (See John 15:5)

Letting go of hurts (most of Jesus' teaching is about forgiveness):
"If you forgive others their failings, your heavenly Father will forgive you yours." (See Matthew 6:14)

Read your chosen passage slowly and aloud four times. With the first reading, *listen* with your heart's ear for a phrase or word that stands out for you. During the second reading, *reflect* on what touches you, perhaps speaking that response aloud or writing in a journal. Third, *respond* with a prayer or expression of what you have experienced and any action to which you are called. Fourth, *rest* in silence after the reading.[8]
Gateway to Silence: Let go and let God.

For further study:

The Art of Letting Go: Living the Wisdom of Saint Francis
Falling Upward: A Spirituality for the Two Halves of Life
Simplicity: The Freedom of Letting Go

PARADOX

DAY 1
The House That Wisdom Builds

"Paradox" comes from two Greek words, *para* + *doksos*, meaning beyond the teaching or beyond the opinion. A paradox emerges when you've started to reconcile seeming contradictions, consciously or unconsciously. Paradox is the ability to live with contradictions without making them mutually exclusive, realizing they can often be both/and instead of either/or. G. K. Chesterton stated that paradox has been defined as "Truth standing on her head to attract attention."[1]

"Dialectic" is the process of overcoming seeming opposites by uncovering a reconciling third. The third way is not simply a third opinion. It's a third space, a holding tank, where you hold the truth in both positions without dismissing either one of them. It often becomes the "house that wisdom builds" (see Proverbs 9:1–6). It's really the fruit of a contemplative mind.

Contemplation gives us a large inner capacity to live with paradoxes and contradictions. It is a quantum leap in our tolerance for ambiguity and mystery. More than anything else, this new way of processing the moment moves us from mere intelligence, or correct information, to what we normally mean by wisdom or non-dual thinking. The contemporary mind has almost no training in contemplative thought processes or how to think paradoxically. In fact, what it often means to be "smart" is the ability to make increasingly clever distinctions and to emphasize the differences! If you doubt this, just listen to almost any political debate. Unfortunately, we then never experience things in their wholeness, we never learn to be honest about the dark side of things, and we wrap our ego around a one-sided opinion. This does not bode well for the future of human communication. Volume and entertainment will try to substitute for the lack of any truth or substance.[2]

Gateway to Silence: Abide in the One who holds everything together.

DAY 2

Seeing with Wisdom

All that is hidden and all that is plain I have come to know through Wisdom. Within her is a spirit that is intelligent, unique, manifold, subtle, active, incisive, lucid, invulnerable, benevolent, dependable, unperturbed, all-seeing.... She pervades and permeates all things, she is the untarnished mirror of God's active power. She is one, and makes all things new, and in each generation passes into holy souls. (See Wisdom 7:21–27.)

The history of spirituality tells us that we must learn to accept paradoxes or we will never truly love anything, or see it correctly. (Normal dualistic thinking, for example, would say that you must be either human or Divine, but you really can't imagine being both at the same time—which means you are totally unprepared to deal with Jesus!) Seeming contradictions are not impediments to the spiritual life; they are an integral part of it. Struggling with seeming contradictions creates subtlety and humility in the mind and heart. Paradoxes don't encourage you to abandon your critical faculties, but actually to *sharpen* them. Please trust me on that.

The above passage, personifying Wisdom (*Sophia*), is an insightful description of how one sees things paradoxically and contemplatively. Interestingly enough, Scripture calls this subtle seeing "she," which in a patriarchal culture is a way of saying "alternative." Alan Watts says that the loss of paradoxical thinking is the great blindness of our civilization, which is what many of us believe happened when we repressed the feminine side of our lives as the inferior side. It was a loss of subtlety, discrimination, and capacity for complementarity.

Each of us must learn to *live with* paradox or we cannot live peacefully or happily even a single day of our lives, because everything on this earth is some mixture of positive and negative charges, just like the atom itself. In fact, we must even learn to *love* paradox, or we will never be wise, forgiving, or possess the patience of good relationships. "Untarnished mirrors," as Wisdom says, receive the whole picture, which is always the darkness, the light, and the subtle shadings of light that make shape, form, color, and texture beautiful. You cannot see in total light or total darkness. You must have variations of light to see at all.[3]

Gateway to Silence: Abide in the One who holds everything together.

Jesus as Paradox

In Christianity, the non-dual paradox and mystery was a living person, an icon upon which we could gaze and with whom we could fall in love. Jesus revealed the eternal Christ "in whom all things hold together" (see Colossians 1:17); he thus become "the Mediator" (one who goes between; see Hebrews 9:15), "very God and very human," as St. Anselm (1033–1109) put it. And he must be both at the same time.

Furthermore, he daringly says, "Follow me" in that same coming together of human and Divine. He is the living paradox, calling us to imitate him, as we realize that "[he] and the Father are one" (see John 10:30). In him, the great gaps are overcome; all cosmic opposites are reconciled in him, as the high-level mystical hymns in Colossians (1:15–20) and Ephesians (1:8–10) say so beautifully. Without these kinds of contemplative revelations, we have a lovely physical Jesus, but no universal Christ. Our message remains competitive with other visions of God instead of cosmic and metaphysical.

Jesus, as the icon of Christ consciousness (see 1 Corinthians 2:16), is the very template of total paradox: human yet Divine, heavenly yet earthly, physical yet spiritual, a male body yet a female soul, killed yet alive, powerless yet powerful, victim yet victor, failure yet redeemer, marginalized yet central, singular yet everyone, incarnate yet cosmic, nailed yet liberated. He resolves the major philosophical problem of "the one and the many." Jesus has no trouble with contraries. He is always holding contraries together (see Ephesians 2:14–22), which is the Divine Work of reconciliation.

I have often said that the job of religion is invariably to make one out of two: the healing of fractured relationships, the forgiveness of everything for being imperfect, marriage itself, the central process of divinization of the human person. Throughout most of our history, we could not, or were not told how to hold the opposites together. In most cases, people lacked either the inner spiritual experience or the intellectual tools, or both. We were largely unable to find the pattern that connected all the mysteries, even though it had been fully given to us in the very body of Jesus. We worshipped

WEEK 31: PARADOX 237

Jesus instead of following him on his same path. We made Jesus into a competing religion instead of a journey toward union with God and everything else. This shift made us into a religion of "belonging and believing" instead of a religion of transformation.

Open yourself to recognizing the great paradoxes within Jesus. Then you can begin to hold those same opposites together within yourself.[4]

Gateway to Silence: Abide in the One who holds everything together.

DAY 4
The Stable Witness

In the process of transformation, you need to find an objective position, detached from your egoic self and from the event or paradox that might be causing you conflict. Unless you find and learn to abide in the place of the Stable Witness, which is the Holy Spirit, who has been given to each of us (see Romans 8:16), you will remain trapped in the ever-changing ego, which could also be called the unobserved mind. From the place of the Stable Witness, you can observe both yourself and the conflicting circumstance with objective, calm, loving eyes. You can see yourself doing your compulsive little dance, but now you don't judge yourself and you don't hate yourself for it. Quite simply, you are not so identified with that small self because you are resting in the Big Self, in the God Self, in the One who knows all, loves all, and holds all things in their seeming imperfection.

Like the theological virtues of faith, hope, and love, picture the Holy Spirit as a "placeholder" within you. We were taught that these three virtues were an inner "participation in the very life of God" in even the oldest catechisms. You do not really "acquire" these virtues, you draw upon them—which does in fact increase their energy within you. It is the same with the Holy Spirit. The Stable Witness strengthens the more you rely upon it. All you can do is abide in God, and then God holds the tensions in you and through you and with you—and largely in spite of you! Such a way of living is a participation in the very life of God, which alone is spacious enough to hold all things in unity and compassion.

To hold questions *seriously* is much more a source of spiritual wisdom than to have quick and easy certitudes or answers. The ego and the mind want to rush to judgment. What the mystics and the true spiritual directors teach is how to negotiate that darkness, how to wait it out, how to hold on. Remember the oft-quoted aphorism: "It ain't what you don't know that gets you into trouble. It's what you know for sure that just ain't so."

I'm convinced that the only absolute the Bible offers us is God—not an institution, not an intellectual or moral belief system (which I believe we often try to substitute for authentic God-experience), and not even the written word; only the Living Word. We need to fall into the hands of the living God (see Hebrews 10:31), which implies growth, change, and development, as in any living relationship.[5]

Gateway to Silence: Abide in the One who holds everything together.

DAY 5

Understanding Spiritual Things Spiritually

Paul's exciting and paradoxical proclamation is that "God's folly is wiser than human wisdom, and God's weakness is stronger than human strength" (see 1 Corinthians 1:25). He says that only Spirit can hold and absorb the seeming contradictions and allow us to see and to know, from an utterly new and unitive vantage point, which is the deepening fruit of contemplation. Only Spirit-in-us can know non-dually or paradoxically and absorb contradictions—inside of and with God. Only God's Spirit-with-us can fully forgive, accept, and allow reality to be what it is. Neither logic nor law can fully achieve this, but participation with and in God can. (This does not make logic or law unnecessary; they are simply inadequate to the work of transformation.)

"Understanding spiritual things spiritually" (see 1 Corinthians 2:13–14) is Paul's summary statement about a different form of intuition that he calls "spiritual knowing" or "wisdom" and that he juxtaposes with "folly." As he so often does, Paul uses a paradoxical contrast to teach his major points. He does the same with other seeming opposites (flesh/spirit, Adam/Christ, death/life, Jew/Greek, and law/grace), in each case to bring us to a new synthesis on a higher level. Paul's use of the paradox of wisdom and foolishness teaches us how to think non-dually or "mystically" ourselves, as do each of these seeming polarities which he effectively collapses (except for flesh and spirit, which, in my opinion, he overdraws and then never fully reconciles).

The access point to deeper spiritual wisdom is consciously, trustfully, and lovingly remaining on "the Vine" (see John 15:1), which means being connected to our Source. We know by participation with and in God, which creates our very real co-identity with Christ: *We are also both human and Divine, as he came to reveal and model.* The foundational meaning of transformation is to surrender to this new identity and to consciously draw upon it. His common code word for this is *en Cristo*; to do something "in Christ" is to operate from this larger and different identity than "just me."[6]

Gateway to Silence: Abide in the One who holds everything together.

DAY 6

Abstract vs. Concrete

As long as you can deal with life in universal abstractions you can pretend that the usual binary way of thinking is true, but once you deal with a specific or concrete reality, it is always, without exception, a mixture of darkness and light, death and life, good and bad, attractive and unattractive. We who are trained in philosophy and theology have all kinds of trouble with that, because our preferred position is to deal with life in terms of abstractions and universals. We want it to be true "on paper"; whether it is true in concrete situations is less important or even denied.

This is what the dualistic mind does because it does not know how to hold creative tensions. It actually confuses rigid or black-and-white thinking with faith itself. In my opinion, faith is exactly the opposite—which is precisely why we call it "faith" and not knowledge or logic.

The universal Divine incarnation must always show itself in the specific, the concrete, the particular (as in Jesus), and it always refuses to be a mere abstraction. No one says this better than Christian Wiman: "But if nature abhors a vacuum, Christ abhors a vagueness. If God is love, Christ is love for this one person, this one place, this one time-bound and time-ravaged self."[7] When we start with big, universal ideas, at the level of concepts and -isms, we too often stay there—and forever argue about theory and making more "crucial distinctions." At that level, the mind is totally in charge. It is then easy to think that "I love people" (but not any individual people). We defend universal principles of justice much more easily than we can live fully just lives ourselves. *The universal gives us a way up and out. The concrete gives us a way down and in!* This is Christianity's foundational principle of Incarnation, which we have seldom fully appreciated.[8]

Gateway to Silence: Abide in the One who holds everything together.

Sabbath Meditation

Remember: **Paradox**

Paradox is the ability to live with contradictions without making them mutually exclusive, realizing they can often be both/and instead of either/or. (Day 1)

"Untarnished mirrors," as Wisdom says, receive the whole picture, which is always the darkness, the light, and the subtle shadings of light that make shape, form, color, and texture beautiful. (Day 2)

Open yourself to recognizing the great paradoxes within Jesus. Then you can begin to hold those same opposites together within yourself. (Day 3)

All you can do is abide in God, and then God holds the tensions in you and through you and with you—and largely in spite of you! (Day 4)

Paul says that only Spirit can hold and absorb the seeming contradictions and allow us to see and to know, from an utterly new and unitive vantage point, which is the deepening fruit of contemplation. (Day 5)

The universal Divine incarnation must always show itself in the specific, the concrete, the particular (as in Jesus), and it always refuses to be a mere abstraction. (Day 6)

Rest: **The Law of Three**

Cynthia Bourgeault has studied extensively the Law of Three, a metaphysical principle first articulated by G. I. Gurdjieff. She offers these insights in "Transgression," an issue of CAC's journal, *Oneing*:

> This principle states that in any new arising, anything that comes into being at any level, from the quantum to the cosmic, at whatever scale and in whatever domain—physical, physiological, or spiritual—is the result of the intertwining of three independent strands: affirming, denying, and reconciling. Note that reconciling is not the synthesis, but a mediating principle between the other two. This is a ternary, not a binary, system. Instead of paired opposites, we have the interplay of three energies that in turn creates a whole new realm of possibility.
>
> It is a great mistake to try to eliminate resistance. Rather, you have to work with it, weave it, honor its presence—because what is going to come into birth is not what you want or expect. It is going

to be completely new and surprising. The three forces working together dissolve gridlocks and move everything into a new playing field.[9]

How do we open ourselves to the third, reconciling energy that allows a new, fourth thing to arise? Cynthia says that most humans in our normal state of consciousness are "third-force blind." We are stuck in dualistic ways of thinking, unable to see a mediating possibility. While we can't of ourselves deal with paradox creatively, by practicing contemplation we can cultivate the awareness and spaciousness that allows new, unexpected insights to arise.

Call to mind a seeming contradiction in your life. Without analysis or critique, hold this paradox in the Mediator's presence and rest in Wisdom. Gradually you will begin to see with the eyes of the Stable Witness that knows and welcomes all.

Gateway to Silence: Abide in the One who holds everything together.

For further study:

A New Way of Seeing, a New Way of Being: Jesus and Paul
Breathing Under Water: Spirituality and the Twelve Steps
Eager to Love: The Alternative Way of Francis of Assisi
Holding the Tension: The Power of Paradox
The Naked Now: Learning to See as the Mystics See

OPEN HEART, OPEN MIND, OPEN BODY

DAY I
Mary, Model of Openness

The soul needs living models to grow and, quite precisely, we need exemplars with the expansive energies of love. In Scholastic philosophy, we called them "exemplary causes." *People who are eager to love change us at the deeper levels; they alone seem able to open the field of both mind and heart at the same time.* When our hearts and minds and bodies are open at the same time and we are eager to love, we find ourselves open to directions or possibilities we would never allow or imagine before or after. We are in a different force field.

When all three inner spaces (heart, mind, and body) are open and listening together, you are present. You know you are different. When you are fully present, a larger banquet will begin. *To be present is to know what you need to know in the moment.* To be present to something is to allow the moment, the person, the idea, or the situation to influence you and even to change you.

Jesus' mother, Mary, is a model of such presence. She is an Exemplary Cause for all who will allow her to be (usually Catholic and Orthodox Christians). Her kind of "yes" (see Luke 1:38) is an assent that comes from the deep self. It does not come easily to us. It always requires that we let down some of our boundaries, and none of us like to do that. Note that no preconditions or worthiness are required of Mary. Mary somehow is able to calmly, wonderfully trust that Someone Else is in charge. All she asks is one simple, clarifying question (see Luke 1:34)—not *if*, but *how*—and then she trusts the *how* even though it would seem quite unlikely.

Mary's "yes" is pure and simple in its motivation, open-ended in intent, and calm in confidence. Only grace and calm presence can achieve such perfect freedom in the body, heart, and mind at the same time. Some scholars are now of the opinion that there are many "Marys" in the New Testament, to make the point that they all exemplify this wonderful feminine quality in humanity. In a sense, they are all the same Mary! When you can allow such spaciousness, this Universal Mary has worked her magic in you.[1]

Gateway to Silence: Open me to Presence.

DAY 2

Being Present to Presence

By some wondrous coincidence, the mystical gaze happens whenever our heart space, our mind space, and our body awareness are all simultaneously open and nonresistant. I like to call it *pure presence*. It is experienced as a moment of deep inner connection, and it always pulls you, intensely satisfied, into the naked and undefended now, which can involve both profound joy and profound sadness, often at the same time. At that point, you want to write poetry, pray, or be utterly silent.

I call contemplation "full-access knowing"—not irrational, but prerational, rational, and trans-rational all at once. Contemplation cannot be reduced to any one thing. It is an exercise in *keeping your heart and mind spaces open long enough for the mind to see other hidden material.* It is a state where you are content with the naked now and wait for futures given by God and grace. As such, a certain amount of love for an object and for myself must precede any full knowing of it. A change of heart should normally lead to a change of mind. You could say the reverse as well—a change of mind is also a change of heart. Eventually they *both* must change for us to see properly.

Before receiving what we brilliantly call "communion," I always tell the people that there is no prerequisite of either *worthiness or understanding* to come to this table. (Who is worthy? Who understands?) The only prerequisite is a capacity for presence. The work of spirituality, which makes presence possible, is keeping the heart space open (which is the work of love), keeping the mind space in a "right mind" (which is the work of contemplation), and keeping the body present and positively accounted for (which is often the work of healing). Those who can keep all three open at the same time will know the Real Presence. That's the only prerequisite. Present people will know the Presence. *Adsum*, we friars said in Latin, before both our vows and our ordination; this might be translated, "My I is finally here!"[2]

Gateway to Silence: Open me to Presence.

DAY 3

Opening Through Love and Suffering

Great love has the potential to open the heart space and then the mind space. Great suffering has the potential to open the mind space and then the heart space. Eventually both spaces need to be opened and, for such people, this opening makes non-dual thinking easier.

People who have never loved or never suffered will normally try to control everything with an either-or attitude or all-or-nothing thinking. This closed system is the only thing for which they are prepared. The mentality that divides the world into "deserving and undeserving" has not yet experienced the absolute gratuity of grace or the undeserved character of mercy. This lack of in-depth God-experience can leave many of us judgmental, demanding, unforgiving, and weak in empathy and sympathy. Such people will remain inside the prison of meritocracy, where all has to be deserved. They are still counting when, in reality, God and grace exist outside of all accounting. Remember, however, to be patient with such people, even if you are the target of their judgment, because, on some level, that is how they treat themselves as well.

Non-dual people will see things in their wholeness and call forth the same unity in others simply by being who they are. Wholeness (head, heart, and body all present, positive, and accounted for!) can see and call forth wholeness in others. This is why it is so pleasant to be around whole and holy people.

Dualistic or divided people, however, live in a split and fragmented world. They cannot accept or forgive certain parts of themselves. They cannot accept that God objectively dwells within them, as it states in so many places in Scripture, including 1 Corinthians 3:16–17. This lack of forgiveness takes the forms of a tortured mind, a closed heart, or an inability to live calmly and proudly inside one's own body. The fragmented mind sees parts, not wholes, in itself and others, and invariably it creates antagonism, reaction, fear, and resistance—pushback from other people who themselves are longing for wholeness and holiness.[3]

Gateway to Silence: Open me to Presence.

DAY 4

Open to Healing

To finally surrender ourselves to healing, we have to have three spaces opened up within us—and all at the same time: our opinionated head, our closed-down heart, and our defensive and defended body. That is the summary work of spirituality—and it is indeed work. Yes, it is also the work of "a Power greater than ourselves," as the Recovery people say, and it will lead to a great *luminosity* and depth of seeing. That is why true faith is one of the most holistic and free actions a human can embrace. It leads to such broad and deep perception that most traditions would just call it "light."

Remember, Jesus said that *we also* are the light of the world (see Matthew 5:14), as well as saying it about himself (see John 8:12). Strange that we see light in him but do not imitate him in seeing the same light in ourselves. Such luminous seeing is the opposite of the closed-minded, dead-hearted, body-denying thing that much religion has been allowed to become. As you surely have heard before, religion is lived by people who are afraid of hell; spirituality is lived by people who have been through hell and come out enlightened.

The innocuous mental belief systems of much religion are probably the major cause of atheism in the world today, because people see that religion has not generally created people who are that different, more caring, or less prejudiced than other people. In fact, they are often worse because they think they have God on their small side. I wish I did not have to say this, but religion either produces the very best people or the very worst. Jesus makes this point in many settings and stories. Mere mental belief systems split people apart, whereas actual *faith* puts all our parts (body, heart, and head) on notice and on call. Honestly, it takes major surgery and much of one's life to get head, heart, and body to put down their defenses, their false programs for happiness, and their many forms of resistance to what is right in front of them. This is the meat and muscle of the whole conversion process.[4]

Gateway to Silence: Open me to Presence.

DAY 5

How to Stay Open: Mind and Heart

To keep the mind space open, we need some form of contemplative or meditative practice. This has been the most neglected in recent centuries, substituting the mere reciting, "offering," and "saying" of prayers, which is not the same as a contemplative mind and often merely confirms us in our superior or fear-based system. In fact, the mere recitation of prayers, if it does not lead to a different way of processing the moment (a change of consciousness), is actually counterproductive. Jesus daringly calls it "babbling on as the pagans do" (see Matthew 6:7), yet how many Christians have been content with forever chanting psalms, reciting rosaries, and even babbling in tongues! These are only entranceways, not ends in themselves. Even more shockingly, Jesus warns us against praying in public (see Matthew 6:5). Who of us has not done that?

One could say that authentic prayer is invariably a matter of *emptying the mind and filling the heart* at the same time, and to do that you normally have to move beyond recited, formulaic, and social prayers. The early Desert Fathers and Mothers just called it the "prayer of quiet," which, once learned, allows you to pray all the time, as Paul seems to believe is actually possible (see 1 Thessalonians 5:17, Ephesians 6:18, et al.).

To keep the heart space open, we almost all need some healing in regard to the hurts we have carried from the past. It also helps to be in right relationship with people, so that other people can love us and touch us at deeper levels, and so we can touch them. A healthy cell allows nutrients to flow in and toxins to flow out; a cancerous cell does not. In addition, I think the heart space is also opened by right-brain activities such as music, art, dance, nature, fasting, poetry, games, life-affirming sexuality, and, of course, the art of relationship itself. And, to be fully honest, I think your heart needs to be broken, and broken open, at least once to have a heart at all or to have a heart for others.[5]

Gateway to Silence: Open me to Presence.

DAY 6

How to Stay Open: Body

To keep our bodies less defended, to live in our body right now, to be present to others in a cellular way, is also the work of healing past hurts and the many memories that seem to lodge themselves in the body. It is very telling that Jesus often physically touched people when he healed them; he knew where the memory and hurt was held, and it was in the body itself. Eckhart Tolle rightly speaks of most people carrying a "pain body." Sometimes I fear that most of humanity has suffered from some form of Post-Traumatic Stress Disorder (PTSD), since war, torture, abandonment, and abuse have been the norm in most of history. No wonder that we needed to visually see God's solidarity with pain and suffering through the ghastly image of a crucified man. God knows and meets us in the physical, not just the spiritual.

It has always deeply disappointed me that the Christian religion was the only one that believed God became a human body, and yet we have had such deficient and frankly negative attitudes toward embodiment, the physical world, sexuality, emotions, animals, wonderful physical practices like yoga, and nature itself. We want to do spirituality all in the head. It often seems to me that Western Christianity has been much more formed by Plato (body and soul are at war) than by Jesus (body and soul are already one). For many of us, the body is more *repressed and denied* than even our mind or our heart. We punish it by diets, obesity, anorexia, bulimia, and all forms of addiction. It makes both presence and healing quite difficult, because our body, not just our mind, holds our memories very deeply.[6]

Gateway to Silence: Open me to Presence.

DAY 7

Sabbath Meditation

Remember: **Open Mind, Open Heart, Open Body**

When all three inner spaces (heart, mind, and body) are open and listening together, you are present. (Day 1)

The work of spirituality, which makes presence possible, is keeping the heart space open (which is the work of love), keeping the mind space in a "right mind" (which is the work of contemplation), and keeping the body present and positively accounted for (which is often the work of healing). (Day 2)

Wholeness (head, heart, and body all present, positive, and accounted for!) can see and call forth wholeness in others. (Day 3)

Honestly, it takes major surgery and much of one's life to get head, heart, and body to put down their defenses, their false programs for happiness, and their many forms of resistance to what is right in front of them. (Day 4)

To keep the mind space open, we need some form of contemplative or meditative practice. To keep the heart space open, we almost all need some healing. (Day 5)

It often seems to me that Western Christianity has been much more formed by Plato (body and soul are at war) than by Jesus (body and soul are already one). (Day 6)

Rest: **Body Prayer**

Julian of Norwich experienced severe bodily pain when she was thirty years old. It was during her illness that she received visions, which she later recorded in *Revelations of Divine Love*. Though I don't wish physical suffering on anyone, when we welcome and witness our body's sensations with openness, we are also open to Presence in a way that is less mediated by the mind (which is, for many of us, the primary conscious filter).

Julian wrote, "The fruit and the purpose of prayer is to be *oned* with and like God in all things."[7] Take a few minutes to let your heart and mind's attention sink deeper into your body, to remember your being's inherent oneness, through these simple words, postures, and intentions (the words are from the Order of Julian's motto):

AWAIT (hands at waist, cupped up to receive): Await God's presence, not as you expect, hope, or imagine, but just as it is in this moment.

ALLOW (reach up, hands open): Allow a sense of God's presence (or not) to come and be what it is, without meeting your expectations.

ACCEPT (hands at heart, cupped towards body): Accept as a gift whatever comes or does not come. Accept that you are not in charge. Accept the infinity of God's presence, which is present whether or not you are aware.

ATTEND (hands outstretched, ready to be responsive): Attend to those actions that God invites you to take from this stance of openness.

Gateway to Silence: Open me to Presence.

For further study:

Breathing Under Water: Spirituality and the Twelve Steps
Dancing Standing Still: Healing the World from a Place of Prayer
Eager to Love: The Alternative Way of Francis of Assisi
The Enneagram as a Tool for Your Spiritual Journey
The Naked Now: Learning to See as the Mystics See

WEEK 33:

INTIMACY

DAY 1
Mirroring

Your initial sense of connection with your mother, and hopefully with your father, is the beginning of the unitive consciousness to which we ultimately want to return. If, in the early months and years, you received wonderful gazes of love from your parents (or other caregivers), mirror neurons were formed that provide the physiological foundation for intimacy. They allow you to grow into an adult capable of intimate, close, tender I-Thou relationships with others and with God. (I suspect this means that psychopaths and sociopaths are people who never got such physical and soulful mirroring.) This is more than enough to make you forever "honor your father and mother"!

Intimate I-Thou relationships, experienced as adults, are the repetition of this initial ecstasy, so we dare not avoid them. By all means, you must find at least one loving, honest friend to ground you, which will allow you to trust the utterly accepting gaze of The Friend. Such a human mirror reveals your inner, deepest, and, yes, Divine image. At such a moment, that person is God for you—really! This is why intimate moments are often mirroring moments of beautiful mutual receptivity, and why such intimacy heals us so deeply. If they got this fix regularly, people could never be hateful or violent.

In our times of falling or failure, many of us finally allow the great Divine Gaze, the ultimate I-Thou relationship, because we need it to get through the next hour. Like any true mirror, the gaze of God receives us exactly as we are, without judgment or distortion, subtraction or addition. Such perfect receiving is what transforms us. Being totally received as we truly are is what we wait and long for all our lives.

All we can really do is receive and return the loving gaze of God every day. That would be more than enough religion. Such people can heal the world as they pass on this mirroring. The One who knows all has no trouble including, accepting, and forgiving all. Soon we who are gazed upon so perfectly can pass on the same accepting gaze to all others who need it.[1]

Gateway to Silence: The gaze of God receives me exactly as I am.

DAY 2
The Dance of Intimacy

A relationship demands at least two. So the first step in the dance of intimacy is an appropriate sense of self, a mirror that can receive the gaze. We cannot, as such, create the mirror; it has to be given to us by the loving gaze of another—and then the process can always deepen. We all know stories about teenagers, or even older people, who give themselves away to another person in the hope of finding themselves. It never works, of course. There has to be an "I" there to receive, trust, and enjoy the "Thou." The non-mirrored self thinks, "This handsome man or this beautiful woman is going to take care of me and give me my identity." Many people, who never got this mirroring from a human authority figure, go to the Divine Authority Figure and receive it from the Ultimate Source. What courage that must take! It is the courage of deep faith.

In the story of Moses and the burning bush (see Exodus 3), there is, first of all, an allurement, a seduction and attraction, a fascinating experience (the bush that is burning but not consumed). Moses is attracted to it. Then Yahweh says, "Take off your shoes. Come no nearer." God is not calling Moses to enmeshment or loss of his own self. Yahweh is telling Moses, "I know who I am, and you are about to enter into an experience of the sacred with me, but stand your ground. Come no nearer." God honors the other as distinct. So love is not absorption; love is not a martyr complex where you let other people use you. When you know your inherent Divine identity, you are truly ready to participate in the sacred dance of intimacy. And in the dance of love there must be at least two, who are no longer two, yet not absorbed entirely into one either. We see this in the definition and dance of the Trinity.[2]

Gateway to Silence: The gaze of God receives me exactly as I am.

DAY 3

Intimacy and Equality

The personal God, revealed in both the Scriptures and the Perennial Tradition, makes known a Divine Nature that is seductive, self-disclosing, and immensely self-giving to those who are interested. This experience of "overflow" invites us into a deep inner freedom, along with intimacy and the possibility of real friendship—unbelievably—with the Divine itself. Such a relationship deeply empowers anyone who engages with it.

Love in its mature form always creates some level of equality and mutuality between giver and receiver. That may seem totally impossible with God, but that gap is exactly what is overcome by God being "personal" and is why the Christian notion of God's great self-emptying (*kenosis*) in a personal Jesus is such a huge gift to our humanity. Jesus reveals that the give-and-take of human and Divine is utterly possible precisely because he became human and personal. (If any friendship does not somehow empower you, it is not true relationship or truly "personal.")

St. Bonaventure taught that we are each "loved by God in a particular and incomparable manner, as in the case of a bride and groom."[3] SS. Francis and Clare knew that the love God has for each soul is unique, which is why any "saved" person always feels beloved, chosen, and even "God's favorite," like so many in the Bible. Divine intimacy is always and precisely particular and made-to-order—and thus "intimate."[4]

Gateway to Silence: The gaze of God receives me exactly as I am.

DAY 4

Naked before God

God is giving you the broadest and deepest permission you can receive: to give back to God who you really are—warts and all. And your willingness to offer that, knowing it will be received, can bring you to tears on at least two levels. First, for your own incapacity: "I can't do it! Lord, have mercy on me." That's the only honest way to begin to pray: "I don't know how to pray!"

Then there's a second level of tears, which is total gratitude. I hope you've had that moment from one beloved partner or friend, maybe when you know you've just done a really stupid thing, but they don't judge you and they don't dismiss you. They just look at you with soft eyes and receive you.

Yours are the tears of immense release and joy and happiness—that there's a heart out there big enough to receive what you can't receive, to forgive what you can't forgive. That is what makes you fall in love with God. If you're on the spiritual journey, that will happen many times.

It's also the experience of a lover who sees you in your nakedness, when you don't have the perfect body you had when you were eighteen, when you're still not patient even though you've been praying for patience for years, and they love you anyway! They receive and embrace you anyway. That's the kind of love that we all want, for which we all wait, that we all need. Although we want it from one another and we get it occasionally, we find there is only One who can be relied upon to always receive us and mirror us perfectly as we are—without demanding that we change.

My great sadness is that so many humans don't know this. They're afraid to be naked before God, because what they expect from God is what they've learned to expect from other people, which is judgment and analysis. I'll take God's judgment any day over the judgment of other people. Really! Those who pray know that.

How could you not fall in love with Someone who always outdoes you in generosity and receptivity? The infallible sign that something is from God is the utter gratuity of it.[5]

Gateway to Silence: The gaze of God receives me exactly as I am.

DAY 5

Intimate with Otherness

It is an openness to the other—as other—that frees us for creativity and originality in our response. The other who is somehow outside my social system, or the Absolute Other who gives me a reference point that relativizes all my prior reference points, changes me. If I am not open to the beyond-me, I'm in trouble. Without the other, another, we are all trapped in a perpetual hall of mirrors that only validates and deepens our limited and already-existing worldviews.

When there is the encounter with the other, when there is mutuality, when there is presence, when there is giving and receiving, and both are changed in that encounter, that is when the process of transformation takes off. Maybe the word transformation scares you, but it means exactly the same as its Latin roots—to "change forms." When you allow other people or events to change you, you look at life with new and different eyes. That is the only real meaning of human growth.

One could say that the central theme of the biblical revelation is to call people to encounters with otherness: the alien, the sinner, the Samaritan, the Gentile, the hidden and denied self, all angels of which we are unaware (see Hebrews 13:2). And yet all of these are in preparation and training for hopeful meetings with the Absolute Other. We need practice in moving outside of our self-created comfort zones. It is never a natural or easy response.[6]

Gateway to Silence: The gaze of God receives me exactly as I am.

DAY 6

Saying "Yes"

The soul defines itself by expansion and inclusion—not by saying "no," but by offering a kind of courageous, risky "yes": "Yes, I am like everybody else, capable of the same good and the same bad. They are all my brothers and sisters." The soul knows that we are all equally naked underneath our clothes. When you allow the face of the other, the opinion of the other, the worldview of the other, to break through your barriers and boundaries, there is always a bit of pullback and push-forward, at the same time, as in the first moments of nakedness or intimacy.

I can see why Jesus said, "For the gate is narrow that leads to life, and there are few who find it" (see Matthew 7:14). He is talking, first, about life in this world—and not the way we interpret it, which is so often about "going to heaven." On the unconscious level, I know that true intimacy with anything is going to change me. Remember, the one thing that the ego hates, more than anything else, is change. I know that if I keep meditating, it is going to change my worldview, my priorities, and my preferences. It will be a new world, and I am comfortably hunkered down in this old one. It is a wonder that anyone continues the dangerous journey of prayer, step-by-step, into Divine and soul intimacy.[7]

Gateway to Silence: The gaze of God receives me exactly as I am.

DAY 7

SABBATH MEDITATION

Remember: **Intimacy**
Like any true mirror, the gaze of God receives us exactly as we are, without judgment or distortion, subtraction or addition. (Day 1)

God honors the other as distinct. So love is not absorption; love is not a martyr complex where you let other people use you. (Day 2)

The personal God, revealed in both the Scriptures and the Perennial Tradition, makes known a Divine Nature that is seductive, self-disclosing, and immensely self-giving to those who are interested. (Day 3)

How could you not fall in love with Someone who always outdoes you in generosity and receptivity? (Day 4)

When there is the encounter with the other, when there is mutuality, when there is presence, when there is giving and receiving, and both are changed in that encounter, that is when the process of transformation takes off. (Day 5)

When you allow the face of the other, the opinion of the other, the worldview of the other, to break through your barriers and boundaries, there is always a bit of pullback and push-forward, at the same time, as in the first moments of nakedness or intimacy. (Day 6)

Rest: **Council Circle**

In our hurried, busy days, it seems there are precious few interactions of deep sharing and listening, few intimate conversations. If you have the opportunity, I invite you to bring the practice of Council into your group interactions, perhaps in your family, faith group, or work place. This way of facilitating meaningful dialogue originated in several Native American traditions. We have applied variations within men's work, internships, and the Living School.

The process of Council is simple.[8] Someone is selected to prepare the conversational space and protect its boundaries. The group sits in a circle so all can see each other clearly. A "talking stick," some symbolic object, can be used to indicate the speaker. Only the individual holding the talking stick speaks. All others listen. The stick might be passed around the circle or placed in the center after speaking, for whomever is moved to take it next. Plenty of silence creates spaciousness for meaning—both spoken and unspoken—to be offered and received.

Begin by inviting each participant to set four intentions:
1. Speak from the heart (truthfully, including your feelings).
2. Listen from the heart (without judgment, with open mind).
3. Speak spontaneously (without preplanning your response).
4. Speak leanly (use only the necessary words; for many, this is the hardest discipline of all).

The facilitator might close the Council with a prayer or a few more moments of silence.

Gateway to Silence: The gaze of God receives me exactly as I am.

For further study:

A New Way of Seeing, a New Way of Being: Jesus and Paul
Dancing Standing Still: Healing the World from a Place of Prayer
Eager to Love: The Alternative Way of Francis of Assisi
Falling Upward: A Spirituality for the Two Halves of Life
Following the Mystics through the Narrow Gate
Intimacy: The Divine Ambush
Job and the Mystery of Suffering

WEEK 34:

TRINITY

DAY 1
Understanding the Trinity

The Blessed Trinity is the central and foundational doctrine of the Christian faith. But, as the Jesuit Karl Rahner observed, what is supposed to be the heart of the nature of God has, until recently, had few practical or pastoral implications in most people's lives. This is sort of unbelievable when you think of it; the foundation, shape, core, and energy for everything was allowed to become an arbitrary side issue! This alone tells me we are still in very "early Christianity."

For too many Christians, the doctrine of the Trinity was unfathomable, abstract, and boring theology because they tried to process it with their left brain, their dualistic mind. Remaining there, it was not much more than a speculative curiosity or a mathematical conundrum (yet surely never to be questioned by any orthodox Christian). However, the Trinity perfectly illustrates the dynamic and interactive principle of three and was made-to-order to demolish our dualistic thinking and to open us to the mystical level.

The Trinity can only be understood with the contemplative mind. It is only God in you that understands; your small mind cannot. That is participative knowledge. The Trinity can't be proved rationally. You must experience its flow in your life on different levels: transpersonal, personal, and impersonal. You must have moments where you know that a Big Life is happening in you (Holy Spirit), yet beyond you (Father), and also *as* you (Christ)!

Unfortunately, Christians mostly gave up even trying to understand the Trinity. But, if we're resolved that we want to go into the mystery—not to hold God in our pocket, but to allow God to *hold us in our deepest personhood*—then I think we must seek to understand the Trinity, experientially and contemplatively, which is not to understand at all, but to "stand under" a waterfall of infinite and loving Flow.[1]

Gateway to Silence: God for us, we call you Father. God alongside us, we call you Jesus. God within us, we call you Holy Spirit.

DAY 2

The Ultimate Paradigm Shift

Most of us began by thinking of God as One Being and then tried to make God into three (Father, Son, and Holy Spirit). However, what I want you to do—as the early Fathers of the Greek Church did in the fourth century—is start with the three, focus on the nature of the relationship between them, and recognize that such relationality creates the ONE.

Philippians 2:6–7 beautifully describes the Trinitarian style of relationship: "Jesus' state was Divine, yet he did not cling to equality with God, but he emptied himself." This is how the three persons of the Trinity relate. They all live in an eternal self-emptying (*kenosis*), which allows each of them to totally let go and give themselves to the other. They are simultaneously loving and totally loveable, one to another.

When we start with the three, we know that this God is perfect giving and perfect receiving, which makes communion, extravagant generosity, humble receptivity, and unhindered dialogue the very names of Being. Then we know God as the deepest flow of Life Itself, Relationship Itself. It is not that a static Divine Being decides to love; love is the very nature and shape of Divine Being.

This deep flow is then the pattern of the whole universe, and any idea of God's "wrath" or of God withholding what is now an infinitely outflowing love is theologically impossible. Love is the very pattern with which we start and move, and the goal toward which we move. It is the energy of the entire universe, from orbiting protons and neutrons to the social and sexual life of species, to the planets and stars. We were indeed created in communion, by communion, and for communion. Or, as Genesis 1:26 says, "created in the image and likeness of God."[2]

Gateway to Silence: God for us, we call you Father. God alongside us, we call you Jesus. God within us, we call you Holy Spirit.

Franciscan Trinitarian Mystics

SS. Francis and Clare and many later Franciscans (Giles, Juniper, Bonaventure, Anthony, Duns Scotus, Angela of Foligno, Catherine of Genoa, and many Poor Clares) appear to be literally living inside of a set of relationships that they quite traditionally name "Father, Son, and Holy Spirit." But these experiences of communion are real, active, and involved in their lives, as if they are living inside of a Love-Beyond-Them-Which-Yet-Includes-Them. They are drawn into an endless creativity of love in wonderful ways that reflect the infinite nature of God. You could say that they almost appear to be pan-erotic!

They seem to shout out gratitude and praise in several directions: from a deep inner satisfaction (the indwelling Holy Spirit), across to the other (the ubiquitous Christ), and beyond what they can name or ever fully know (the formless Father).

In the Trinity, love finally has a solid definition and description, and cannot be sentimentalized. If Trinity is the template for all creation, from atoms to galaxies, then a water wheel that is always outpouring in one direction is a very fine metaphor for God. Giving and surrendered receiving are the shape of reality, very similar to Indra's net or Krishna's dance in classic Hinduism. Now love is much bigger than mere emotions, feelings, infatuation, or passing romance. It is even the physical and metaphysical shape of the universe.

With Trinity as the first and final template for reality, love is the ontological "Ground of Being" itself (as Paul Tillich has said). It is the air that you breathe, as any true mystic discovers, consciously or unconsciously. You do not have to be able to describe this in words to experience it. In fact, you can't describe it. You can only live it and breathe it.[3]

Gateway to Silence: God for us, we call you Father. God alongside us, we call you Jesus. God within us, we call you Holy Spirit.

The Trinity as a Circle Dance

The fourth-century Cappadocian Fathers tried to communicate this notion of life as mutual participation by calling the Trinitarian flow a "circle dance" *(perichoresis)* among the three. They were saying that whatever is going on in God is a flow that's like a group dance. And God is not just the dancer; God is the dance itself! Then the Incarnation becomes a movement outward and downward (which is why we must never be afraid of these movements). Jesus comes forth from the Father and the Holy Spirit to take us back with him into this eternal embrace, from which we first came (see John 14:3). The circle dance broadens; we are invited to join in and even have participatory knowledge of God through the Trinity.

Trinity is the very nature of God, and this God is a centrifugal force, flowing outward and then centripetally drawing all things back into the dance (read 1 Corinthians 15:20–28 in this light). If this God names himself/herself in creation and in reality (see Genesis 1:26), then there must be a "family resemblance" between everything else and the nature of the heart of God.

Scientists are discovering this reality as they look through microscopes and telescopes. They are finding that the energy is actually in the space *between* the particles of the atom and *between* the planets and the stars—in the relationships more than the particles! This seems to mean that reality is relational at its core. When you really understand Trinity, however slightly, it's like you live in a different universe—and a very good and inviting one![4]

Gateway to Silence: God for us, we call you Father. God alongside us, we call you Jesus. God within us, we call you Holy Spirit.

DAY 5

God as Three Persons

The word "person," as we use it today, meaning a separate human individual, is not really found in the Hebrew Bible, but the idea of "face" is. Hebrew authors wanted to convey the effect of "interface" with their Yahweh God, who sought intimate communication with them: "May God let God's own face shine upon you, and may God's face give you peace" (see Numbers 6:25–26). This same usage is also found in several Psalms (see 42:2, 89:15–16, and 95:2), where it is often translated as "presence," meaning, more precisely, communicated presence—or a transference of selfhood from one to another.

In the Greek translations, the noun used for face was *prosopon*, which literally referred to the stage masks that Greek actors wore, which seemed to serve as both an enlarged identity and a megaphone. Teachers like Tertullian and the Cappadocian Fathers used similar language to show how God could be both one and three at the same time: ultimate autonomy of three persons, who are nevertheless in perfect communion by their total and generous *interface.*

Each member of the Trinity was considered a *persona,* or "face," of God. Each person of the Trinity fully communicated its face and glory to the other, while also maintaining its own "facial" identity fully within itself. Each person of the Trinity "sounded through" *(per sonare)* the other.

This theology about the shape of God became over time a way to psychologically understand how human beings operate too. We also are "soundings through"—of something much more, of others, and even of Someone Else, in whose "image and likeness" we are created. We are each a stage mask, a face, receiving and also revealing our shared DNA, our ancestors, and our past culture. It has become our very understanding of the ensouled human being, or what we now call an individual "person," turning the original usage around 180 degrees. In the Trinity there is a perfect overcoming, with no need for any individualism.[5]

Gateway to Silence: God for us, we call you Father. God alongside us, we call you Jesus. God within us, we call you Holy Spirit.

DAY 6

Living in the Flow

If the Trinitarian life flows between us, then every aspect of our lives is something that we can allow, enjoy, and steward. A Trinitarian theology gives you the understanding that you are being guided and you are participating in the Great Mystery. And it has very little to do with you except, like Mary, your "yes" seems to be crucial. It matters. God does not operate uninvited or undesired.

You are a part of the flow. The Father, Son, and Holy Spirit, and you too—to the degree you say "yes"—are also a giving and a receiving, constituted by the same relationships of love that are the Trinity. (Enjoy that for the rest of your life!) You dare not stop this flow without losing your essential self. Each person of the Trinity welcomes one hundred percent of what is offered, which is entire and unrestricted, and then pays it forward one hundred percent. This flow is the origin of our notions of Grace and an Abundant Universe. There is Divine Generosity at the center of everything.

You can live this Trinitarian mystery yourself. Trust love, trust communion, trust vulnerability, and trust mutuality. Always seek to be in relationship, finding little ways to serve others, to serve the sick, to serve the poor who cannot pay you back. Know that your heart is given to you and needs to be handed on, just like the Trinity. And you'll begin to know yourself inside this mystery called Love. There is actually nothing more to say. We could end the book right here.

Don't try to work this out too much with your head. Just trust the flow of the most natural, dynamic, and positive energy that's already flowing through you. It will always feel like Love, and even love that sometimes hurts.[6]

Gateway to Silence: God for us, we call you Father. God alongside us, we call you Jesus. God within us, we call you Holy Spirit.

DAY 7
SABBATH MEDITATION

Remember: **Trinity**

The Trinity can only be understood with the contemplative mind. It is only God in you that understands; your small mind cannot. (Day 1)

When we start with the three, we know that this God is perfect giving and perfect receiving, which makes communion, extravagant generosity, humble receptivity, and unhindered dialogue the very names of Being. (Day 2)

In the Trinity, love finally has a solid definition and description, and cannot be sentimentalized. (Day 3)

Trinity is the very nature of God, and this God is a centrifugal force, flowing outward and then centripetally drawing all things back into the dance. (Day 4)

We are "soundings through"—of something much more, of others, and even of Someone Else, in whose "image and likeness" we are created. (Day 5)

The Father, Son, and Holy Spirit, and you too—to the degree you say "yes"—are also a giving and a receiving, constituted by the same relationships of love that are the Trinity. (Day 6)

Rest: **Flow**

Recall a time when you experienced an ease of being and doing, where you felt focused, energized, and full of joy, where you were wholly present and yet more than yourself. Psychologists call this "flow." Perhaps these moments come while writing poetry, dancing, playing an instrument, painting, or even mundane tasks such as washing dishes or solving a mathematical equation.

Experiencing flow is like participating in the Divine dance of Trinity—a relationship of continuous giving and receiving between you and the task.

Seek out these times when you are actively one with the energy flowing through you. Listen within for hints of what may be your soul's calling and vocation, your unique way of participating in the life of the world.

Intentionally bring this same sense of flow to your interactions with others, to your day-to-day encounters. Say "yes" to the inflow and outflow of Love. Be receptive to and generous with this abundance. Rest in the Mystery flowing through you.

Gateway to Silence: God for us, we call you Father. God alongside us, we call you Jesus. God within us, we call you Holy Spirit.

For further study:

The Divine Dance: Exploring the Mystery of Trinity
Eager to Love: The Alternative Way of Francis of Assisi
The Shape of God: Deepening the Mystery of Trinity
What Difference Does Trinity Make?

THE EVOLVING JOURNEY

DAY 1
Looking Back and Looking Forward

Through these meditations, we've been following the trajectory of the spiritual journey. We began in innocence and simplicity, then explored the necessary development of ego and the Loyal Soldier. We looked at how failure, suffering, and death to False Self can bring us to resurrection, to a realization of our inherent True Self identity as God's beloved. Living from True Self is a continual evolution as we embrace shadow and integrate the broken pieces of ourselves.

Through the remainder of the year we will continue moving deeper and deeper into the practice and experience of union—with self, God, the world, and others.

The classic language of the stages of the spiritual journey is being validated by many developmental psychologists and integral studies in our time. However, not all (or perhaps not even most!) lives progress in a linear fashion. Many developmental models have generalized Western, white, male patterns of change to humanity as a whole. Some studies suggest that women in particular may not grow through "levels" or "stages" in a predictable sequence.[1]

For many years, I studied and taught masculine spirituality and developed rites of passage for men, as these seemed lacking in our culture and time. I cannot claim to know women's journeys as well as men's, but in the later stages of growth, I find the patterns and the pitfalls to be much the same for both men and women.

We do tend to start with different attractions, biases, preference, and fascinations. We have learned much in the last century about how to honor and support all of these diverse paths of growth and development. To illustrate this, I reference the insights of Kahlil Gibran's *The Prophet* when I teach, as follows:

> Say not, "I have found the path of the soul." Say rather, "I have met the soul walking upon my path."
> For the soul walks upon all paths.[2]

Gateway to Silence: Show me your ways; teach me your paths.

DAY 2
Circuitous Path

British theologian and poet Nicola Slee suggests that faith, "by its very nature must be changing and growing and in a state of perpetually shifting equilibrium rather than static and changeless."[3] It is really quite strange and unfortunate that we turned the Biblical genius of faith around to mean almost the exact opposite: people who love the status quo, are always certain, and absolutely know what is right and what is wrong. How did we get from Abraham and Sarah to that?

Life itself—and Scripture too—is always three steps forward and two steps backward. It gets the point and then loses it or doubts it. Our job is to see where the three steps forward are heading (invariably toward mercy, forgiveness, inclusion, nonviolence, and trust) which then gives us the ability both to recognize and to forgive the two steps backward (which are usually about vengeance, pettiness, law over grace, forms over substance, and requirements over relationship).

Isn't it a consolation to know that life is not a straight line? Many of us wish, and have been told, that it should be, but I haven't met a life yet that's a clear and straight line to truth, to self, or to God—and I even met Mother Teresa several times! It's always about getting the point and missing the point. It's God entering our lives and then our fighting, avoiding, running from that very possibility. Our times of intimacy with God seem too good to be true—for someone as little and seemingly unimportant as me! There is hopefully the moment of Divine communion or intimacy, and then the pullback that invariably says, "I am probably making this up. This is mere wishful thinking." Recently, I have begun to call this "negative capability" *the failure that often creates the positive momentum forward*. That is why I named one of my books *Falling Upward*.

Fortunately, God works with everything, both the forward and the backward, and that's what bases the whole journey in Divine Mercy, infinite forgiveness, and amazing grace. God uses the negative to create the positive, which is really good news for all of us.[4]

Gateway to Silence: Show me your ways; teach me your paths.

DAY 3

Evolving Consciousness

Many historians, philosophers, and spiritual teachers now agree that collective history itself has always been going through an evolution in consciousness. We can readily observe stages of consciousness or "growing up" in the world at large (e.g., today Christians do not believe that slavery is acceptable, but most did, at one time). The individual person, as he or show grows up (presuming they do), tends to mimic these historical stages, and they also seem to be sequential and cumulative.

You have to learn from each stage, and yet you can't completely throw out previous stages, as most people unfortunately do. In fact, a fully mature person appropriately draws upon all earlier stages. "Transcend and include" is Ken Wilber's clever aphorism here. Most people immensely overreact against their earlier stages of development, and earlier stages of history, instead of still honoring them and making use of them (e.g. liberal, educated Christians who would be humiliated to join in an enthusiastic "Jesus song" with their Evangelical brothers and sisters, even though they would intellectually claim to believe in Jesus; or adults who can no longer play; or rational people who completely dismiss the good in the non-rational).

C. S. Lewis believed it was undemocratic to give too much power to the present generation or one's own historical period. He called this "chronological snobbery," as if your own age was the superior age and the final result of evolution. I would say the same about one's present level of consciousness. Our narcissism always tends to think our own present stage of consciousness is the ultimate stage! People normally cannot understand anybody at higher stages (they seem heretical or dangerous) and look upon all in the earlier stages as superstitious, stupid, or naïve. We each think we are the proper reference point for all reality. G. K. Chesterton stated: "Tradition is only democracy extended through time."[5] And I would say that *enlightenment is the ability to include, honor, and make use of every level of consciousness—both in yourself and in others.* To be honest, such humility and patience is rather rare, yet it is at the heart of the mystery of forgiveness, inclusivity, and compassion.[6]

Gateway to Silence: Show me your ways; teach me your paths.

DAY 4

Stages of Consciousness

We clearly see the fluctuating nature of our journey in stages of consciousness. There is great wisdom within each stage, and also an inherent trap. Only as we trust and practice the task of each stage are we prepared to move forward.

There are different ways to name the stages of consciousness. Here is the rather simple form that I use: the archaic (infant), the magical (child), the powerful (heroic), absolute truth (and conformity to the group that has it), individual success (organized rational world), and pluralism (modern liberalism).

If we can get through these stages and are still ready to face the big death to our individualism and our superiority, we are poised to advance to what some call second-tier consciousness (really the mystical levels) where we finally see the importance and usefulness of *each* of these stages and yet also transcend all of them at the same time! This could be described as the necessary path toward any greater capacity for love, freedom, and enlightenment.

For me, contemplation—and all mystical religion—is a natural conveyor belt for moving us through each stage, learning from each stage, yet never stopping at mere conformity, rational thinking, or even pluralistic thinking as the final and full goal (what Jesus would call "the Reign of God"). Divine Love is bigger and more expansive than any of these. (It is highly ironic that the pluralistic and politically correct stage has the hardest time seeing this—people at that stage are quite happy and content with their advanced liberal thinking, but often know nothing of the mystical mind, nor would they even respect it.)

A regular practice of meditation will reinforce the neural pathways that bring us to wholeness, while also refusing to strengthen any toxic, self-destructive, or negative pathways. Without changing such "software," real and sustained change is almost impossible. We might have new information, but it will be the old self processing that new information—which will revert it back into the old, self-serving information. This represents much of the deeply entrenched ego of the successful and the academic, what I call information without transformation.[7]

Gateway to Silence: Show me your ways; teach me your paths.

The Dance of Action and Contemplation

I believe that human action from a contemplative center is the greatest art form. It underlies all those other, more visible art forms that we see in great sculpture, music, writing, painting, and, most especially, in the art form of human character development. When the external life and the inner life are working together, we always have beauty, symmetry, and actual transformation of persons—lives and actions that inherently sparkle and heal, in part because they can integrate the negativity of failure, sin, and rejection and also spot their own shadow games.

With most humans, the process begins on the action side; in fact, the entire first half of life for most of us, even introverts, is all about external action. We begin with crawling, walking, playing, speaking. We learn, we experiment, we try, we stumble, we fall. Gradually these enactments grow larger and more "mature," but we remain largely unaware of our inner and actual motivations or purpose.

Yes, there are feelings and imaginings during this time, maybe even sustained study, prayer, or disciplined thought, but it cannot be called contemplation. These reflections are necessarily and almost always self-referential, both for good and ill. At this point, life is still largely about "me" and finding my own preferred and proper viewing platform. It has to be. But it is not yet the great art form of the calm union between our inner and outer lives. We must go further.

We cannot grow in the integrative dance of action and contemplation without a strong tolerance for ambiguity, an ability to allow, forgive, and contain a certain degree of anxiety, and even a willingness to not know—and not even need to know. (When Western Christianity stopped teaching this, for five centuries now, its transformative power decreased markedly.) When we can balance action with contemplation and knowing with not needing to know, we have an ever wider and deeper perspective. This is how we allow and encounter any great mystery and move into the contemplative zone.[8]

Gateway to Silence: Show me your ways; teach me your paths.

DAY 6

The Great Turning

Contemplation is no fantasy, make-believe, or daydream, but the flowering of patience and steady perseverance. There is a deep relationship between the inner revolution of true prayer and the transformation of social structures and social consciousness. Our hope lies in the fact that meditation is going to change the consciousness of the society in which we live, just as it has changed us. It is that kind of long-term thinking in which God seems to be involved and kindly invites us into the same patient process. Only changed people can change other people at any depth.

I know the situation in the world can seem quite dark today. The negative forces are very strong, and the progressive development of consciousness and love sometimes feels very weak. But the Great Turning is indeed happening, as people like Joanna Macy, David Korten, Byron Katie, and Thomas Berry believe and describe, each in their own way.

In his Letter to the Romans, Paul has a marvelous line: "Where sin increases, grace abounds all the more" (see 5:20). In so many places, there are signs of the Holy Spirit working profoundly at all levels of society, almost in tandem with the emergence of unbelievable violence, fear, and hatred all over the world. Much of this is happening outside the boundaries of formal religion, but it is all the work of "one and the same Spirit" (see 1 Corinthians 12:11).

It seems to me that true progress, or the hope that we have, is not naïvely optimistic, a straight line, or without regression. Spiritual progress, ironically, develops through tragedy and through falling. To paraphrase Joseph Campbell, where we stumble and fall is where we find pure gold: the gold of the Gospels, the hidden gold of our own souls, and then the beautiful soul of the whole creation.[9]

Gateway to Silence: Show me your ways; teach me your paths.

DAY 7

Sabbath Meditation

Remember: **The Evolving Journey**

The classic language of the stages of the spiritual journey is being validated by many developmental psychologists and integral studies in our time. (Day 1)

Life itself—and Scripture too—is always three steps forward and two steps backward. (Day 2)

Many historians, philosophers, and spiritual teachers now agree that collective history itself has always been going through an evolution in consciousness. (Day 3)

A regular practice of meditation will reinforce the neural pathways that bring us to wholeness, while also refusing to strengthen any toxic, self-destructive, or negative pathways. Without changing such "software," real and sustained change is almost impossible. (Day 4)

When the external life and the inner life are working together, we always have beauty, symmetry, and actual transformation of persons—lives and actions that inherently sparkle and heal, in part because they can integrate the negativity of failure, sin, and rejection. (Day 5)

It seems to me that true progress, or the hope that we have, is not naïvely optimistic, a straight line, or without regression. Spiritual progress, ironically, develops through tragedy and through falling. (Day 6)

Rest: **Labyrinth**

Labyrinths are found in different forms on all continents, within many cultures and mythologies, carved or painted on ancient cave and church walls, and set in floors at sacred sites such as Gothic cathedrals. These circular paths are a way of learning and praying through movement instead of through thinking. Labyrinths seem to have emerged from the collective unconscious, representing a clear path to center, to the Divine. A classical labyrinth has seven cycles, each representing a stage of life, and seven U-turns as we learn to change course at least that many times in a normal life. A straight-line trajectory grows no one; it only makes you more and more rigid and inflexible.

Find a labyrinth (on the ground or printed on paper)[10] for your feet or fingers to traverse in the company of God's presence. Walk the labyrinth as if on pilgrimage, but without a goal beyond the experience of walking itself. Step consciously and slowly, allowing the Divine to guide and teach. Let the walk teach its own lessons. There is no one correct message. The turning circuits of a labyrinth remind us that life is change, transformation, and repentance (i.e., *metanoia* or turning around).

Gateway to Silence: Show me your ways; teach me your paths.

For further study:

Dancing Standing Still: Healing the World from a Place of Prayer
Things Hidden: Scripture as Spirituality

NON-DUAL CONSCIOUSNESS

DAY 1
Freedom in Not Knowing

It seems that God is asking humanity to live inside of a cosmic humility, as God also does. In that holding pattern, we bear the ambiguity, the inconsistencies, and the brokenness of all things (which might be called love), instead of insisting on dividing reality into the supposed good guys and the certain bad guys, as our dualistic mind loves to do. Such non-dual consciousness is our ultimate act of solidarity with humanity and even the doorway to wisdom. With this mind we realize, as Martin Luther wisely put it, we are *simul justus et peccator*, simultaneously both sinner and saint. Only the mind of God can hold these two together.

We read the story of humanity's original sin in Genesis. There Yahweh says, "Don't eat of the tree of the knowledge of good and evil" (see Genesis 2:17). Now why would that be a sin? It sounds like a good thing, doesn't it? We were actually trained to think that way. In the seminary we took four-year courses on "moral theology" to help us rightly discern who was good and who was bad, what actions pleased God and which did not. It was supposed to make it all very clear.

Unfortunately, this emboldened the very judgmental mind that Jesus warned us against (see Matthew 7:1–2). Some then thought that this was the whole meaning of Christianity—religion's purpose was to monitor and police society in regard to its morals. Religion became all about morality instead of being a result and corollary of Divine Encounter. As such, it ended up being much more a search for control or moral high ground than it was a search for truth, love, or God. It had to do with the ego's need for certitude, superiority, and order. Is that what Jesus came for?

Jesus never said, "You must be right," much less, "You must be sure you are right." Instead he said, "You must love one another" (see John 13:34). His agenda is about growing in faith, hope, and love ourselves, which often solidifies when we finally realize that "God alone is good" (see Mark 10:18), as he told the flattering young rich man who was also seeking his own secure future through moral concerns.

I guess God knew that dualistic thinking would be the direction religion would take. So the Bible says, right at the beginning, "Don't do it!" The word of God is trying to keep us from religion's constant temptation and failure: *a demand for certitude*, an undue need for perfect explanation, resolution, and answers. That is surely the basis for warning us against eating of "the tree of the knowledge of good and evil." This Divine prerogative, when it is assumed by mere mortals, carries a strong inherent punishment with it: "On the day you eat of this tree you will most surely die" (see Genesis 2:17). Really amazing that readers have not given this more serious reflection.

Such dualistic thinking (preferring a mental either/or to an always-complex real world) tends to create arrogant and smug people instead of humble and loving people. Too much "eating of the tree of the knowledge of good and evil" might just be the major sin of all religion—especially the three monotheistic "religions of the book": Judaism, Christianity, and Islam. Our very gift of one God and one Holy Book also led us to a kind of exclusivism and narrowness in our approach to truth. The Biblical notion of faith, or *not needing to know*, was supposed to balance this all out, but instead we even made faith into possessing knowledge that was absolutely certain instead of walking in trust.[1]

Gateway to Silence: It is what it is.

DAY 2

Balancing Knowing and Not Knowing

The great spiritual teachers always balance knowing with not knowing, light with darkness. In the Christian Tradition, the two great strains were called the *kataphatic* (according to the light) or "positive" way—relying on clear words, concepts, and ideas—and the *apophatic* (against the light) or "negative" way—moving beyond words and images into silence, darkness, and metaphor. Both ways are necessary, and together they create a magnificent form of higher non-dual consciousness called faith.

The *apophatic* way, however, has been underused, under-taught, and underdeveloped for most of the last five centuries. In fact, we became ashamed of our not-knowing and tried to fight our battles rationally. Much of Catholicism and most of Protestantism became highly cerebral. Protestantism's failure to teach the complementary "way of darkness" set them up for fundamentalism and endless verbal wrangling and dividing. God (who is really Mystery) became something you perfectly observed, a service you attended, words about which you argued, or worthiness for which you worked. God was never someone you had to *learn to trust*, or to whom you surrendered yourself (head, heart, will, and body).

In the capitalist West, the very word "surrender" is not to our liking. We are about winning, climbing, achieving, performing, and being the best. In that light, contemplation and non-dual thinking (I use the words almost interchangeably) are about as revolutionary and counter-cultural as you can get. Islam honors the word surrender, as that is what the very word Islam means; from a practical standpoint, however, they have to fight the same righteous ego that we all do.

When you don't balance knowing with not knowing, you get into the kind of religion and politics we have today—very arrogant, falsely self-assured, unable to admit wrong or to apologize because *"I know!"* According to the great spiritual teachers, ignorance does not result from what we *don't know*; ignorance results from what we think we *do know*—for certain! Anybody who really knows, also knows that they don't know (this is not just being clever!); this is especially true when we are talking about God! Medieval Catholic theology called this *docta ignorantia* or "learned ignorance."[2]

Gateway to Silence: It is what it is.

DAY 3

Reclaiming the Ancient Practice

The term "non-dual" will seem new to most Western Judeo-Christians, but for centuries (and even longer in the East), the mystics of all religions have tried to lead people to a higher, or non-dual, level of consciousness. We spoke of the "unitive way" in Catholic spirituality, which was the final stage. It is a much more subtle way of knowing, where we can see that things "are not totally one, but they are not two either." (You are supposed to be startled by that! Christians first learned this from the Trinity.) The radical union of things was honored, along with their appropriate distinctiveness—at the same time. This is called the first "philosophical problem of the one and the many."

Non-duality is at the core of the major Eastern religions of Hinduism, Buddhism, and Taoism. I am convinced that Jesus was the first non-dual teacher of the West; he lived in the Middle East and spoke Aramaic, which is actually more reflective of the Eastern mind than the Western mind. However, his words were first translated into Greek and then spread to the West, where thinking was influenced by Greek logic. We have mostly tried to understand Jesus' teaching with a dualistic mind, which probably explains many of our problems. The dualistic mind just does not get us very far in spiritual matters, although it is excellent for math, science, any form of engineering, and, most especially, daily practical life.

The Christian contemplative tradition was mostly assumed and implied in spiritual teaching, and sometimes systematically taught, for our first 1500 years. We find it in the Desert Fathers and Mothers, in the Celtic spirituality of Ireland, in many Eastern Fathers, and in some European monasteries. The Franciscan experience of the twelfth and thirteenth centuries was a flowering of very practical non-dual thinking. The teachings of the Dominican Meister Eckhart, Nicholas of Cusa (1401–1464), and Erasmus of Rotterdam (1466–1536) moved it all to high-level theology, but few appreciated them. Carmelites SS. Teresa of Ávila and John of the Cross in the sixteenth century were the last great supernovas of non-dual teaching. Yet few of us later knew what they were talking about; we just pretended we did. Even the Carmelites now recognize this.

With the Protestant Reformation and, even more, with the ironically named "Enlightenment," non-dual thinking largely went underground and has not been systematically taught for the last five hundred years. However, the two natural paths of non-dual consciousness—great love and great suffering—have nevertheless allowed individuals to break through to non-dual, contemplative consciousness, without always knowing that was what they were enjoying. It was Thomas Merton who almost singlehandedly brought back contemplation as a science and practice in the 1950s and 1960s. Now we finally have the language and skills to actually teach it again.[3]

Gateway to Silence: It is what it is.

DAY 4

What Is Non-dual Consciousness?

Non-dual or contemplative consciousness is not the same as being churchy or reflective or introverted. Unfortunately this is the way the word is often used, even by people who should know better. Contemplation is a panoramic, receptive awareness whereby you take in all that the situation, the moment, the event offers, without judging, eliminating, or labeling anything as up or down. It is pure and positive gazing at things and leaving them with all their power. That does not come naturally. You have to work at it and develop practices whereby you recognize your compulsive and repetitive patterns and allow yourself to be freed from them.

It seems we are addicted to our need to make distinctions and judgments, which we mistake for thinking. Most of us *think we are our thinking*, yet almost all thinking is compulsive, repetitive, and habitual. And here educated people are just as bad as the uneducated—sometimes even worse.

That is why all forms of meditation and contemplation are teaching you a way of quieting the dualistic, "thinking" mind. After a while, you see that this kind of thinking is not going to get you very far, simply because reality is not all about you and your preferences!

Non-dual consciousness is about receiving and being present to the moment and to the *now*, exactly as it is, without judgment, without analysis, without critique, without mental commentary, without your ego deciding whether you like it or not. It is a much more holistic knowing, where your mind, heart, soul, and senses are open and receptive to the moment *just as it is*, which allows you to love things in themselves, and as themselves. You learn not to divide the field of the moment (and eliminate anything that threatens your ego), but to hold everything together in one accepting gaze, attractive and non-attractive alike.

The non-dual, contemplative mind is a whole new mind! With it, you can stand back and simply observe the self and the event from the standpoint of the Stable Witness. Now you can laugh or weep over your little self-created dramas and dances, without being either attached to them or hating them. This is major freedom. You can eventually look at yourself and others calmly and compassionately because you are able to see things as *they* are in themselves and not from the viewpoint of how they affect you.[4]

Gateway to Silence: It is what it is.

The Change That Changes Everything

We are living in exciting times, where we are teaching people not *what* to see, but *how* to see! The broad rediscovery of non-dual, contemplative consciousness gives me hope for the change of religion and even for the change of politics. We are realizing that we have been trying to solve so many of our religious, social, political, and relational issues inside of the very mind that falsely framed the problems in the first place. And, as Einstein is purported to have said, no problem can be solved from the same level of consciousness that created it.

The contemplative mind can see things in a non-dualistic way, without being rebellious or enmeshed, without being reactionary nor hateful. Whenever you move to a higher level of consciousness, you always include the previous stages. That's what makes it a higher level of consciousness! You do not hate previous stages, you do not dismiss them, and you do not split and say that the previous group or stage was all wrong, as was done in almost all reforms and revolutions until very recently.

Only in the twentieth century did a few catch up with Jesus and rediscover the very possibility of nonviolent revolutions and reforms (Mahatma Gandhi [1869–1948] and Martin Luther King, Jr. [1929–1968] being the most visible examples). The very word nonviolence was not even in the vocabulary of major Western languages, because we didn't understand it (despite Jesus' clear teaching in his Sermon on the Mount), whereas the ancient Sanskrit word *ahimsa*, literally meaning "to do no harm," was already described and understood in early Hinduism as the appropriate response to the natural sacredness of all life.

When you finally come to maturity, you can nonviolently forgive even your own previous mistakes. You can let go of everyone who hurt you, even your former spouse. You don't even need to hate the church that hurt you. Wisdom is where you see it *all*, you eliminate none of it, and include all of it as important training. Finally, everything belongs. You are able to say, from some larger place that even surprises you, "*It is what it is*, and even the 'bad' was good." Probably forgiveness was the Christian form of nonviolence, but we never got real good at it because it was not an entire philosophy of life, as it was for some Eastern religions.

Such mature people are the only ones who will change the world or transform history. They literally live at a different level of consciousness; they process the moment differently than the rest of us. Non-dualistic people are able to be fully present to the now and trust God with the future and the past. God can use them because their small and petty self is finally out of the way.[5]

Gateway to Silence: It is what it is.

DAY 6

God Is Not "Out There"

When you move to non-dual thinking, God is no longer "out there," but not only "in here" either. That is universally true. In the great mystics of all religions, *God is always experienced in the soul* and, in seeming contradiction, *as totally transcendent and mysterious.* God is both intimate and ultimate. That is the full and utterly paradoxical realization. When you know that you are a living tabernacle and a living presence of the Great Transcendent One, the gap is forever overcome in your very existence. You gain a tremendous respect for yourself, while you also know you have received a total gift "from above." This is deep peace and contentment and ultimate *at-homeness.*

This realization levels the human playing field. The only solid and enduring foundation for recognizing human dignity and protecting human rights is not the American Bill of Rights or politically correct pluralistic thinking, but, frankly, God! Those who know that we all came forth from the same God and that God inhabits all creatures equally, are most prepared to overcome racism, sexism, classism, nationalism, and all forms of gender discrimination. And if God chooses to love me (and I know how silly and sinful I am), I am the best prepared to grant others the same gift and compliment!

Non-dual consciousness is about being present to the Presence of God in yourself and beyond yourself too. Presence is an *experience,* not just an idea in the mind. In fact, the mind, of itself, cannot be present (take my word for that!). The mind can only reprocess the past, judge the present, and worry about the future. The reason that practical atheism and common agnosticism have emerged as almost the norm is that we no longer teach people how to be present. And when you do not know how to be present, you cannot access the Presence, especially not *in here*—or anywhere else, for that matter.[6]

Gateway to Silence: It is what it is.

DAY 7

Sabbath Meditation

Remember: **Non-dual Consciousness**

It seems that God is asking humanity to live inside of a cosmic humility, as God also does. In that holding pattern, we bear the ambiguity, the inconsistencies, and the brokenness of all things (which might be called love). (Day 1)

According to the great spiritual teachers, ignorance does not result from what we *don't know*; ignorance results from what we think we *do know*. (Day 2)

For centuries, the mystics of all religions have tried to lead people to a higher, or non-dual, level of consciousness. (Day 3)

Non-dual consciousness is a much more holistic knowing, where your mind, heart, soul, and senses are open and receptive to the moment *just as it is*. (Day 4)

We have been trying to solve so many of our religious, social, political, and relational issues inside of the very mind that falsely framed the problems in the first place. (Day 5)

Non-dual consciousness is about being present to the Presence of God in yourself and beyond yourself too. (Day 6)

Rest: **Practicing Awareness**

With your *senses* (not so much your mind), focus on one single object until you stop fighting it or resisting it with other concerns. The concrete is the doorway to the universal. This should lead to an initial calmness in your body and mind.

You must choose not to judge the object in any way, attach to it, reject it as meaningless, like it or dislike it. This is merely the need of the ego to categorize, control, and define itself by preferences. You will thus learn to appreciate and respect things in and for themselves, and not because they benefit or threaten you. This should lead to a kind of subtle, simple joy in the object and within yourself.

"Listen" to the object and allow it to speak to you. Speak back to it with respect and curiosity. You thus learn to stop "objectifying" things as merely for your own consumption or use. You are learning to allow things to speak their truth to you as a receiver instead of the giver. This will lead to the beginnings of love for the object and a sense of loving kindness within yourself.

A kind of contented spaciousness and silence will normally ensue. This is a form of non-dual consciousness. The concrete, loving consciousness of one thing leads to pure consciousness or "objectless consciousness" of all things.[7]

Gateway to Silence: It is what it is.

For further study:

Beginner's Mind
Exploring and Experiencing the Naked Now
The Naked Now: Learning to See as the Mystics See

CONTEMPLATION

DAY 1
Being Conscious

The lower-level, *un*conscious mind is commonly dualistic, judgmental, and oppositional. It always takes sides. Whatever is unfamiliar, or whatever it does not already understand or agree with, it judges as *totally* wrong. In contemplative practice, you refuse to take sides. Contemplation goes beyond words (which naturally differentiate this from that) to pure, open-ended experience (which has the potential to unify seeming contradictions). This requires a higher level of consciousness that we are calling *non-dual* consciousness.

Consciousness is not the same as your brain. Neither is it a secretion of the brain, although it will usually feel like your head is processing whatever is coming through. The early Alexandrian Fathers knew this. They called consciousness *nous*, which is the Greek word for a combination of Spirit, God, and mind. It is a participative knowing, as if you are actually living and knowing inside of a larger mind.

The very word "consciousness" is from the Latin *con scire*, which means "to know *with*." When you really plug into consciousness, maybe it *feels* like it's coming through your brain, but it actually comes through a whole-hearted surrender to the moment—a surrender that encompasses everything and eliminates nothing. Some religious traditions would call that everything "God." When you're truly conscious, you have the feeling that you've been connected to something much bigger than yourself—and you are right. It is no longer just about "you"! Artists speak of the descent of a "muse" and others of being channeled by a spirit. These are all attempts to describe something real, and should not be so easily dismissed.

Emerson called non-dual consciousness the *over-soul*. Thomas Aquinas called it *connatural intelligence*; it is true to one's nature, but true to a larger nature at the same time. John Duns Scotus (1265–1308) called it *intuitive cognition* and distinguished it from rational cognition. The great thinkers took for granted that we had access to a different and larger mind. They recognized that a flow is already happening and that we can plug into it. In all cases, it is a participative kind of knowing. The most common and traditional word for that was, quite simply, "prayer."

You cannot know God with your conscious mind. That's why all teachers of contemplation are teaching you to let go of your workaday mind so you can plug into that deeper mind which we would call the "Mind of Christ" (see 1 Corinthians 2:16). It really is a different way of knowing, and you call tell it by its gratuity and non-assertiveness, while it is simultaneously being amazingly creative and energizing for those who are allowing the flow of the Holy Spirit to come through them.[1]

Gateway to Silence: Christ is in me, and I am in Christ.

DAY 2

Guarding Your Mind and Heart

Paul speaks beautifully of prayer in Philippians (see 4:6–7). An entire theology of prayer practice is summed up in very concise form in a couple of sentences. First he starts with, "Pray with gratitude, and the peace of Christ, which is bigger than knowledge or understanding [the making of distinctions], *will guard both your mind and your heart in Christ Jesus.*" Only a pre-existent *attitude of gratitude* (as opposed to any state of resentment or entitlement), a deliberate choice of love over fear, a desire to be positive instead of negative, will allow you to live in the spacious place we describe as "peace." Paul describes it as a "bigger" place or a "beyond" place.

To go there is, of itself, major work and sometimes requires surrender, yet without going there you cannot stand against the constant invitations and temptations to fear, resentments, and negativity. There must be a larger space that can contain, absorb, and finally undo your smaller self, which always wants to either take or give offense. As Paul says, it "guards" both "your mind and your heart"; we often say that it *stands witness* to protect you from the tyranny of passing thoughts and emotions. Once you can watch them from a bit of distance, you are no longer so fully identified with them. Trust me on that.

Emotions are given to us by God *so that we can fully experience our experiences.* The only problem is that we get addicted or attached to those emotions. We take them as final, lasting, or substantive. Emotions do have the ability to open you to consciousness, but then they tend to become the whole show. Most human thought is just obsessive, compulsive commentary. It's "repetitive and useless," as Eckhart Tolle says. I would say the same of emotions that we hold onto for too long.

Contemplation allows you to *simply see (contemplata* means "to see") what is happening in yourself from *a learned and practiced distance.* There is no freedom from the self without it. An oft-quoted aphorism describes the sequence well: "Watch your thoughts; they become words. Watch your words; they become actions. Watch your actions; they become habits. Watch your habits; they become your character. Watch your character; it becomes your destiny." Contemplation and detachment nip the ego and its negatives in the bud by teaching you how to watch and guard your thoughts and feelings the very moment they try to take hold, but from a "bigger" place of love and not judgment—which is always small. This is the beginning of both healing and presence.[2]

Gateway to Silence: Christ is in me, and I am in Christ.

DAY 3

Cleaning the Lens

True religion is always about love. *Love is the ultimate reality.* We can probably see this only through real prayer, for love can be hidden. We don't see it unless we learn how to see, unless we clean the lens. The Zen masters call it wiping the mirror. In a clean mirror, we can see exactly what's there without distortion—not that of which I'm afraid, nor what I need or want to be there, but what is *really* there.

Some have called Buddhism the religion of mirror-wiping. It is the inner discipline of constantly observing my own patterns—those things to which I pay attention and those I don't—in order to get my own ego out of the way. But lest you think this is only a Buddhist preoccupation, remember St. Teresa of Ávila's stark admonition: "For the most part, all our trials and disturbances come from our *not* understanding ourselves."[3] We must learn to observe our own stream of consciousness.

"What is my agenda? What is my predisposition? What are my prejudices? What are my angers?" The discernment process, asking such questions, is often called the development of our "third eye"—or maybe third ear. It refers to the ability to stand away from ourselves and listen and look with some kind of calm, nonjudgmental objectivity. This process is normally quite difficult at first (thus most people never go there), but it is absolutely necessary for truth and freedom. Otherwise the "I" that I am cannot separate from its identification with its own thoughts and feelings. Most people *become* their thoughts. They do not *have* thoughts and feelings; *the thoughts and feelings have them!* It's what the Scriptures rightly called "being possessed by a demon." In that sense, it seems to me most people are possessed by demons!

Prayer, however, is not finally self-observation, although it often needs to start there. Eventually it becomes a "falling into the hands of the living God," which is initially and indeed a "dreadful thing" (see Hebrews 10:31)—for one who has always tried, up to that point, to control everything himself or herself. So you see why another Zen master said, "Avoid spirituality at all costs. It is just one insult after another!" Every time you clean the mirror, you see more cosmetics and scars.[4]

Gateway to Silence: Christ is in me, and I am in Christ.

DAY 4

Unlocking Attachments

Contemplation is the key to unlocking the attachments and addictions of the mind so that we can see clearly. I think some form of contemplative practice is necessary to be able to detach from your own agenda, your own anger, your own ego, and your own fear.

I find most people operate, not out of "consciousness," but out of their level of learned and practiced brain function, which relies on early-life conditioning and has little to do with God-encounter, mercy, freedom, or love. We primarily operate from habituated patterns based on what "Mom told me," what went wrong when we were young, and the defense mechanisms we learned that helped us to be right and good, to be first and famous, or safe and secure. These are not all bad, but they are not all good either.

All of that old and practiced thinking has to be recognized and accounted for, which is the work of both healing and contemplation. Without this work, you just keep seeing everything through your own security needs, your own agenda, anger, and woundedness more than your giftedness. Isn't that the pattern for most people? Although they seldom know it, inner unconscious voices drive most people's lives. Few ever achieve much inner freedom. Contemplation helps you see your woundedness. That's why most people do not stay long with contemplative prayer, because it's not very glorious at the early stages.

As Mark's Gospel puts it, when you go into the "wilderness" of prayer, first you meet "the wild beasts" and only later do "the angels look after you" (see 1:13). But those angels are sure worth waiting for. The rule is common in all religions: Evil spirits must be replaced and overcome by good spirits. We might now call it "replacement therapy," but you normally cannot let go of things until and unless you have something better to take their place. Contemplation is asking for, waiting for, but also expecting, and thus finally creating—by grace—the better space and the larger place.

We need some form of contemplative practice that touches our unconscious conditioning, where all our wounds really lie hidden and denied, where all our defense mechanisms are secretly operative. Once these are not taken so seriously and definitively, there is immediately more than enough room for the inrushing of God and grace![5]

Gateway to Silence: Christ is in me, and I am in Christ.

DAY 5

Being in Love

For saints, mystics, and budding contemplatives, "words have become flesh," and experience leads beyond the limitations of words. Experience is always non-dual, an open field where both weeds and wheat are allowed (see Matthew 13:30). As St. Paul put it when speaking of praying in the Spirit, "My spirit is praying, but my mind is left barren" (see 1 Corinthians 14:14). You see that words are mere guideposts, and you recognize that most people have made them into hitching posts. Inside such broad and deep awareness, paradoxes are easily accepted and former mental contradictions seem to dissolve. That's why mystics can forgive, let go, show mercy, and love enemies, and why the rest of us can't!

Abstract concepts and verbal dogmas contain the air of mathematical or Divine Perfection, but mystics do not love concepts. They love the concrete and the particular. They have always had at least one significant encounter with the Divine, which is all it takes, and which they themselves cannot understand or describe as a clear concept. "There is only Christ; he is everything, and he is in everything" (see Colossians 3:11), they might say. That may sound like an overstatement or mere poetry, but the mystics are not rebels against anything except all attempts to block that very kind of encounter in themselves or in others, which unfortunately a lot of religion itself does. (That is why Jesus is so disapproving of so much of his own religion, almost more than anything else!)

Mystics—those who have experienced union with the Divine—are in love: in love with life and life for all. If they are not in love, they are not in union. Mystics usually look simplistic and even naïve to those who have not shared a similar experience, and that is a burden they must forever carry. Yet they have no time for being against; *there is now so much to be for!* Yes, Jesus was critical of religion, but that was only because he first recognized how right it could be.[6]

Gateway to Silence: Christ is in me, and I am in Christ.

DAY 6

Held by the Whole

I am convinced that most of the major beliefs and doctrines of the Christian churches (e.g., Jesus is "fully human and fully Divine," Mary is both virgin and mother, bread is both bread and the body of Jesus, etc.) can be understood, relished, and effectively lived only through non-dual consciousness, by people who know how to be *present* to the naked and broad now, without needing to eliminate "the problem" that is always there. As Karl Rahner is often quoted as saying, "The devout Christian of the future will either be a 'mystic'... or will cease to be anything at all."[7]

I think we are on the very edge of history—and about to be edged over—by the depth of the need for wider consciousness and by the depths of our own desire. We live in an amazing time, where quantum physics, biocentrism, and neural science often support our mystical intuitions! It seems God has wired us for love, for intimacy, for empathy, for compassion, and for union—beginning with the gaze between a mother and her newborn, which some say creates the mirror neurons necessary for healthy relationship.

To practice contemplative prayer is to practice being in loving relationship with everything and even with oneself. Those who fall into *the safety net of Divine Silence* find that it is not at all a fall into individualism, but just the opposite. True prayer or contemplation is a leap into commonality, community, and connection. You know that what you are experiencing is also enjoyed by the Whole and that you are not alone anymore. You are a part, and a forever-grateful part. As a part, you are participating in the whole and you no longer have any need to stand out, emphasize your specialness, or assert your importance or dignity. That has now been taken care of at a deep and final level.[8]

Gateway to Silence: Christ is in me, and I am in Christ.

DAY 7

SABBATH MEDITATION

Remember: **Contemplation**

When you really plug into consciousness, maybe it *feels* like it's coming through your brain, but it actually comes through a whole-hearted surrender to the moment—a surrender that encompasses everything and eliminates nothing. (Day 1)

Contemplation and detachment nip the ego and its negatives in the bud by teaching you how to watch and guard your thoughts and feelings, but from a "bigger" place of love and not judgment. (Day 2)

Contemplation is the inner discipline of constantly observing my own patterns—those things to which I pay attention and those I don't—in order to get my own ego out of the way. (Day 3)

We need some form of contemplative practice that touches our unconscious conditioning, where all our wounds really lie hidden and denied, where all our defense mechanisms are secretly operative. (Day 4)

Mystics—those who have experienced union with the Divine—are in love: in love with life and life for all. If they are not in love, they are not in union. (Day 5)

Those who fall into *the safety net of Divine Silence* find that it is not at all a fall into individualism, but just the opposite. True prayer or contemplation is a leap into commonality, community, and connection. (Day 6)

Rest: **Boats Floating Downstream**

In Centering Prayer, the contemplative practice taught by Thomas Keating, we choose a sacred word to help us return to our intention of awareness of God's presence. The word might be "Peace" or "Be" or "Love"—something simple. Don't spend too much time analyzing the word. Hold it lightly and let it go when it is no longer needed, but come back to it any time your thoughts interrupt the stillness.

Keating uses the imagery of a river in Centering Prayer to help compartmentalize our thinking mind. He says our ordinary thoughts are like boats on a river, so closely packed together that we cannot experience the river that flows underneath them. The river is the Presence of God holding us up. When we find ourselves getting distracted or hooked by a thought or feeling, we are to return ever-so-gently to our sacred word, letting the boat (thought or feeling) float on downstream. Gradually, the mind is quieted, with fewer thoughts/feelings and more space between "boats."

Be patient with this practice. We all have ingrained patterns. Sometimes the same thought or feeling will circle by, again and again, saying "Think me! Think me! Feel me! Feel me!" as it tries harder to be noticed. Just keep returning to the sacred word and letting the boats float downstream.

Gateway to Silence: Christ is in me, and I am in Christ.

For further study:

Contemplative Prayer
The Naked Now: Learning to See as the Mystics See
Silent Compassion: Finding God in Contemplation
Transforming the World through Contemplative Prayer

WEEK 38:

LIFE AS PARTICIPATION

DAY I
Your Life Is Not about You

In his letter to the Ephesians (see 4:1–7), Paul says,

I, a prisoner in the Lord, implore you to lead a life worthy of your call. Bear with one another in love, in complete selflessness, gentleness, and patience. Do all you can to preserve the unity of the Spirit by the peace that binds you together. There is one body, there is one Spirit, just as you were called into the one and same hope. There is one Lord, one faith, one baptism, one God who is Father of all, over all, through all, and within all. And each one of us has been given God's own share of this grace.

Once you assert there is *one* God, eventually what you come to is that there's one pattern, one center, one source, and basically *one* reality—and then it's a coherent world. You would think the three monotheistic religions would have been the first to come to this realization, but to see this you must at least be at the early mystical level. Most religion up to now has been at the magical, tribal, or rational levels. My conviction is that Paul's mystical knowing is telling us that we are participating in something much bigger than we are. Spirit, as Paul uses the term, is this realm of shared consciousness (*con-scire* = to know with). Our life is first, last, and foremost a participation in this *one* Bigger Reality.

Your life is not about you; you are about life. You are an instance in this world of the one universal pattern that, for Paul, was uncovered, made clear, validated, and made available to all in the microcosmic life of Jesus. That's why Jesus is called the Christ, the Messiah, the Anointed One, who reveals the cosmic, universal pattern in which we all participate, from Divine conception, through human life, to Divine return. "In him all things hold together and he is the [consciousness] of the whole body [expressed in his one body person]" (my interpretation of Colossians 1:17).

We now have the physics to support such a possible metaphysics. And we always had the theology that *all creation is constituted in the infinite relations of the Trinity* ("Let us create in our own image," as it says in Genesis 1:26). But everything is coming together in our lifetime as the sciences parallel one another's discoveries. Now we know that we actually are physically more a "we" than we are any autonomous "I." All light in the universe is actually one connected light, and consciousness connects all things.[1]

Gateway to Silence: I am hidden with Christ in God. (See Colossians 3:3.)

DAY 2

You Are about Life

Before a unitive encounter with God or creation, almost all people will substitute the part for the whole and take their little part far too seriously—both in its greatness and in its badness. But after any true God-experience, you know that you are a part of a much bigger Whole. *Life is not about you; you are about life.* You are an instance of a universal, and even eternal, pattern. Life is living itself in you. This realization is an earthquake in the brain, a hurricane in the heart, a Copernican revolution in the mind, and a monumental shift in consciousness. Yet most do not seem interested in it.

Understanding that your life is not about you is the connection point with everything else. It lowers the mountains and fills in the valleys that we have created, as we gradually recognize that the myriad forms of life in the universe, including ourselves, are operative parts of the One Life that most of us call God. After such a discovery, I am grateful to be a part—and quite satisfied to be only a part! I do not have to figure it all out, straighten it all out, or even do it perfectly by myself. I do not have to be God.

It is an enormous weight off my back. All I have to do is *participate!* My holiness is, first of all—and really only—God's, and that's why it is certain and secure, and always holy. It is a participation, a mutual indwelling, not an achievement or performance on my part.

After this epiphany, things like praise, gratitude, and compassion come naturally—like breath and air. True spirituality is not *taught*; it is *caught* once our sails have been unfurled to the Spirit. Henceforth, our very motivation and momentum for the journey toward holiness and wholeness is just immense gratitude—for already having it![2]

Gateway to Silence: I am hidden with Christ in God. (See Colossians 3:3.)

DAY 3

Getting the *Who* Right

When we are introduced to the One Life, our smaller life becomes a matter of lesser importance. We are less concerned about who, how, where, why, and whether. A new, larger Self takes over, which answers the big "who" and "why" questions on the soul level. It's all about getting your True Self right. "Who are you?" is the soul's urgent question. Who I am, and the power that comes with the response, answers all my deepest questions. Life becomes a joyful participation in Being! Basically, you are enlightened every time you awaken to your True Self. I do not believe it just happens once, although the first time is a whopper, as we see in the enlightenment of the Buddha or even in the baptism of Jesus at the age of thirty.

Every time you are tempted to hate yourself, just think, *"Who am I?"* The answer will be: "I am hidden with Christ in God" (see Colossians 3:3) in every part of my life. In Christ, I am bearing the mystery of the suffering of humanity, its sad woundedness; but I am also bearing the very glory of God, and even "sharing in the Divine Nature" (see 2 Peter 1:4). I am a living paradox of Divine and human, just as Jesus was and that Jesus fully accepted, enjoyed, and drew upon.

It seems that God insists on looking at what is good in me, what is God in me, and of course always finds it entirely lovable. God fixes God's gaze intently where I refuse and where I fear to look—on my shared, Divine Nature as God's daughter or son (see 1 John 3:2). And one day my gaze meets God's gaze (that is what we mean by both conversion and prayer). At those times I will find God fully lovable and myself fully lovable at the same time. Why? Because it is the same gaze, but they have become symbiotic and look out at life together.[3]

Gateway to Silence: I am hidden with Christ in God. (See Colossians 3:3.)

DAY 4

In the One Flow

It seems to me that contemplation makes it almost inevitable that your politics is going to change, the way you spend your time is going to be called into question, and any smug or inferior social and economic perspective will be slowly taken away from you. When anyone meditates consistently, the things that we think of as our necessary ego boundaries—giving us a sense of our independence, autonomy, and private self-importance—fall away, little by little, as unnecessary and even unhelpful. This imperial "I," the self that most people think of as the only self, is not substantial or lasting at all. It is largely a creation of our own minds. Through contemplation, protecting this relative identity, this persona, eventually becomes of less and less concern. "Why would I bother with that?" the True Self asks.

If your prayer goes deep, invading your unconscious, your whole view of the world will change from fear to connection, because you don't live inside your fragile and encapsulated self anymore. In meditation, you are moving from ego consciousness to soul awareness, from being driven to being drawn. Of course, you can only do this if Someone Else is holding onto you in the gradual dying of the False Self, taking away your fear, doing the knowing, satisfying your desire for a Great Lover. If you can allow that Someone Else to have their way with you in contemplation, you will go back to your life of action with new vitality, but it will now be smooth, a much more natural Flow. It will be "no longer you" who acts or contemplates, but the Life of One who lives in you (see Galatians 2:20), now acting *for* you (Father) and *with* you (Holy Spirit) and *as* you (Christ)!

Henceforth, it does not even matter whether you first act and then contemplate, or contemplate and then act, because both will be inside the One Flow, which is still and forever loving and healing the world. (Did you know that Krishna tells Arjuna the same thing in many ways in the ancient Hindu text, the *Bhagavad Gita?*) Christians would call this the one flow of full life that is the Trinity. Here alone do we all "live and move and have our being" (see Acts 17:28). Truth really is one.[4]

Gateway to Silence: I am hidden with Christ in God. (See Colossians 3:3.)

DAY 5

In Christ

Most of us were not raised to understand that we are participating in something that is already happening. Rather, we were given private tasks to accomplish individually and on our own. This placed the entire burden on the single, isolated person. That's not participation; that's perfectionism—thinking I have to do it all or that I can do it all (the American myth). I'm convinced that's why we have so much of what we call negative self-image in the West—because of this impossible spiritual burden put on the separate individual. *The Good News is that it's not about being correct. It's about being connected.* When the Spirit within you connects with God's Spirit, given from without, you are finally home. Now you know that *your deepest you is God,* and Christ is living his life in you and through you and with you and as you.

In most of his teachings, the Apostle Paul does not talk about individuals. He describes something much larger, in which we are participating. His most common phrase is "in Christ." Paul uses it 164 times. We participate in this reality that is larger than our individual lives by trusting and allowing that we are already *in Christ* (Ephesians 1:4–14 says from all eternity!). We are saved by standing consciously inside the universal force field that is Christ—not by getting things right within our private selves. Remember, consciousness is the ultimate reality, which even science is beginning to recognize.

In 1 Corinthians we find Paul's foundational metaphor of the Body of Christ: "For just as the body is one and has many members, and all the members of the body, though many, are one body, so it is with Christ. For by one Spirit we were all baptized into one body—Jews or Greeks, slaves or free—and all were made to drink of one Spirit" (see 12:12–13). Paul is not talking here about water baptism. He's talking about a universal initiation experience of death and resurrection, through which all human beings must go, willingly or unwillingly. It is the only way to know what is finally Real. Many do not go, I am afraid, and so they never become conscious. You must surrender to the death of the small self to discover the Big Self in God. That is the price; that is the baptism in the Spirit.[5]

Gateway to Silence: I am hidden with Christ in God. (See Colossians 3:3.)

DAY 6

Falling into Life

We are not seeking uniformity, but rather unity, which implies differences. Unity created by the Spirit can only be had among people who are different! We are not talking about conformity, which is low-level religion. Paul says, "Now there are varieties of gifts, but the same Spirit; and there are varieties of service, but the same Lord; and there are varieties of working, but it is the same God who inspires them all in every one. To each is given the manifestation of the Spirit for the *common good*" (see 1 Corinthians 12:4–7). Our word for this is a "charism," a gift that is given to you, not for your own self, but to build up the community, to build up the whole Body of Christ.

In 1 Corinthians 12:27–30, Paul explains that you, in your togetherness, are Christ's Body, but each of you is a different part of it, with different gifts. Then, in chapter 13, he says that *love* is the greatest gift. When you live in love, in that "vibrational state," if you will—when you live at that level of communion where you allow the Larger Life within you and let the same life flow out of you—you are living a transformed life in your own unique way. Up to then, it is all play, and largely conformity. This alone is what it means to be "in Christ" and, with great irony, it is the birth of the true and unique individual; it is the birth of authentic inner freedom.

What we're doing in contemplation is consciously choosing to let go of our ego, to let go of our mind and our identification with what is merely our *life situation* (with which most people self-identify) so that we can fall into the *One True Life*, which is "hidden with Christ in God" (see Colossians 3:3).[6]

Gateway to Silence: I am hidden with Christ in God. (See Colossians 3:3.)

DAY 7

SABBATH MEDITATION

Remember: **Life as Participation**

Your life is not about you; you are about life. (Day 1)

After any true God-experience, you know that you are a part of a much bigger Whole. You are an instance of a universal, and even eternal, pattern. (Day 2)

In Christ, I am bearing the mystery of the suffering of humanity, its sad woundedness; but I am also bearing the very glory of God, and even "sharing in the Divine Nature" (see 2 Peter 1:4). (Day 3)

Contemplation makes it almost inevitable that your politics is going to change, the way you spend your time is going to be called into question, and any smug or inferior social and economic perspective will be slowly taken away from you. (Day 4)

The Good News is that it's not about being correct. It's about being connected. (Day 5)

What we're doing in contemplation is consciously choosing to let go of our ego, to let go of our mind and our identification with what is merely our *life situation* (with which most people self-identify) so that we can fall into the *One True Life*, which is "hidden with Christ in God." (Day 6)

Rest: **Community**

Our Western culture leans toward self-sufficiency and independence, and we often need to be reminded that we are part of a greater whole and that we are not alone in our longings and efforts for peace, justice, and healing. This is one of the great gifts of what we usually mean by "church"— a gathering of people in solidarity of purpose, praying and seeking God's presence together.

Find some way in which you can join in the life that is greater than your own. Participate in a vigil, sharing the grief and hope of your neighborhood or world. March with others to bring visibility and voice to an important issue. Make a pilgrimage to a sacred or violated site to connect your small place in time with a history and a broader meaning.

Rest in the knowledge that God's Spirit weaves your participation as a single thread within a life-renewing pattern. You are connected to the source of Life!

Gateway to Silence: I am hidden with Christ in God. (See Colossians 3:3.)

For further study:

Adam's Return: The Five Promises of Male Initiation
Dancing Standing Still: Healing the World from a Place of Prayer
Great Themes of Paul: Life as Participation
Things Hidden: Scripture as Spirituality

EUCHARIST

DAY 1
Take, Thank, Break, Give

At his Last Supper, which was really the Jewish Passover meal, Jesus gave us an action, a mime, a sacred ritual of the Eucharist for a community that would summarize his core and lasting message for the world—one to keep repeating until his return. This deep message was to slowly sink in until "the bride" (the church, those who follow Jesus the Christ) is fully ready to meet "the bridegroom" (Jesus the Christ) and drink at the eternal wedding feast. I want you to note how the meal and the metaphor are based in physicality; *the incarnation continued in the elements of the universe.* Good stuff, and yet it has always been a scandal to overly spiritual people, starting at the very beginning (see John 6:60): "This is intolerable language. How could anyone accept it?"

The Eucharist, which means "thanksgiving," has four main aspects:

First, you take your whole life in your hands, as Jesus did. In very physical and scandalously incarnational language, table bread is daringly called "my body" and alcoholic wine is called "my blood." We are saying a radical "yes" to both the physical universe itself and the bloody suffering of our own lives and all the world.

Second, you then thank God (*eucharisteo* in Greek), who is the origin of all that life and who allows and uses that death. You are making a choice for gratitude, abundance, and appreciation for Another, which has the power to radically de-center you. Your life and death are pure gift, and must be given away in trust, just as they were given to you as gift—in an attitude of gratitude.

Third, you break it. You let your life be broken, give it away, and don't protect it. The sharing of the small self will be the discovery of the True Self in God. "Unless the single grain of wheat dies, it remains just a grain of wheat" (see John 12:24). The crushed grain becomes the broken bread, the whole and newly connected "Body of Christ."

Finally, you chew on this mystery! This truth is known by participation and practice, not by more thinking or discussing. "Take this," "eat and drink this"—not alone, but together, "until I return," and you will have the heart of the message, a "new covenant" of indwelling love that is not grounded in worthiness in any form, but merely in a willingness to participate and trust. Your drinking and eating is your agreement to "do what I can to make up in my own body all that still has to be undergone by Christ for the sake of his body the church" (see Colossians 1:24). *We should hold ourselves apart from this meal only if we are not at least willing to try this.* (That might mean that many of us should not participate!) Eucharist is a risky and demanding act of radical *solidarity and responsibility with the work of God*—much more than a reward for good behavior or any "prize for the perfect," as Pope Francis says.[1]

Gateway to Silence: I am present to Presence.

DAY 2

The Living Body of Christ

Jesus' last supper was a Passover meal of deep table fellowship—with his closest followers—that evolved into the formatted, highly ritualized meal of bread and wine that many of us enjoy today. The first disciples soon came to understand it as a way of gathering, as the way to define their reality and their relationship, with one another and with Jesus.

Eucharist became, already in the first centuries after Jesus' death and resurrection, a powerful symbol of unity, of giving and sharing, of allowing the breaking of self and the giving over of self for the world. It was originally somewhat of a secret ritual by which the community defined itself and held itself together in its essential message. Frankly, most people have never been ready for its radically demanding message of solidarity with both suffering *and* resurrection. So we made it into a worthiness contest and something that you could understand with your mind—both a terrible waste of time, in my opinion.

Yes, we are to recognize Jesus himself in the Eucharist, but we are also to recognize the present-day Body of Christ (see 1 Corinthians 11:29). There is no true Eucharist without a living assembly; yet, in the pre-Vatican II Catholic Church, priests often said "private" Masses, which shows how much we needed radical reform! The Eucharist was meant to be a "sacrificial meal" in the sense that the Body had to die to its smallness to enter into such Greatness, and called us to live in a new world order of true sisterhood and brotherhood, and of redemptive suffering and solidarity with the pain of the world. It is not just Jesus' own sacrifice that we are recalling, but also our agreement to participate in the same! It is not just the human incarnation in Jesus that we are remembering, but that this mystery of incarnation is continued in space, time, and the physical universe itself (e.g., ordinary "worldly" elements of bread and wine).

Paul deeply understood the entire force field of the Body of Christ because of his astounding conversion experience, where he heard a voice saying, "Saul, Saul, why do you persecute *me*?" He finally realized that Jesus was fully identifying the people Paul was killing with himself! They were one and the same! This deep identity between human beings and the body and soul of the earthly Christ became absolute, and then practical, truth for Paul. This was then communicated and experienced by sharing in the ritual meal of Eucharist: "We eat who we are!" as St. Augustine so boldly put it, and we become what we eat.[2]

Gateway to Silence: I am present to Presence.

DAY 3

Jesus in Me and I in Jesus

At the end of the Eucharistic Prayer, the priest holds up the bread and the cup and speaks three prepositions: "through him, with him, and in him." Once, when I was holding up Jesus as bread and wine, I had an astounding realization:

I don't know how to talk to you, God. I don't know who you are. I don't know how to look for your face. But don't look at me. Just look at your Son. I'm with him. He is my badge of honor. He is my defense. He is my identity. This is my solidarity. This is my communion. This is my participation. He is praying through me, with me, in me, and as me!

The Father only and forever loves the Cosmic Christ, and it is *Jesus in you* upon whom God eternally looks with respect and desire. The Father cannot *not* love the Son, just as the Father loves us. But we defined the Son of God in an exclusive way, whereas the whole point was that Jesus came *to include* all of us in the same deal! To the degree that you can trust and allow this radical inclusivity, you become an "adopted daughter" or an "adopted son," to use Paul's clever language (see Ephesians 1:5 and Romans 8:30). You are even physically grafted to the vine, it seems, which is why the Eucharist must be physical and not just mental, leading to our Pauline and eventually Creedal belief in "the resurrection of the body" (see 1 Corinthians 15).

When Jesus says he's giving himself to you as the Bread of Life and, if you eat this bread, you will live forever, he's saying, "Find yourself in me." Be reflected truthfully before the mirror of perfect freedom (see James 1:23–25) that is the Divine Gaze, and you will be free from the revolving hall of mirrors that is the people and culture around you. Don't let other people's responses and expectations determine who you are and how you feel about yourself. If you eat this food as your primary nutrition, you are psychologically and spiritually indestructible.

And who you are in God is who you are! Everything else is changing or passing away. The Eucharist becomes our ongoing touchstone for the Christian journey, a place to which we must repeatedly return in order to find our face, our name, our absolute identity, who we are in Christ, and thus who we are forever. It is indeed the defining Christian ritual.[3]

Gateway to Silence: I am present to Presence.

DAY 4

Being Present to Presence

All my life as a Catholic, I have believed that the "Real Presence" of Christ is in the Eucharist. Now I also recognize that the very concept of presence is inherently and necessarily relational. We Catholics can defend the doctrine of the Real Presence all we want (and I do), but if we don't teach the children of God how to be *present to Presence*, there is no Real Presence for them!

We spent much of our history arguing about the "how" and the "if" and who could do what we called "transsubstantiation" of the bread, instead of simply learning how to *be present* ourselves (which is contemplation). We made it into a magic to be believed instead of transformation to be experienced. We emphasized the priest as the "transformer" instead of the people as the transformed. (Yet even Canon Law has always stated that the Sacraments are always and first *"pro populo,"* for the sake of the people—and not an end in themselves.)

The Eucharist is an encounter of the heart, knowing Presence through our available presence. In the Eucharist, we move beyond mere words or rational thought and go to that place where we don't talk about the Mystery anymore; we begin to chew on it. Jesus did not say, "Think about this" or "Stare at this" or even "Worship this." Instead he said, "Eat this!" It was to be a bodily action and a social action with the group.

We must move our knowing to the bodily, cellular, participative, unitive level. Then we keep eating and drinking the Mystery, until one day it dawns on us, in an undefended moment, "My God, I really am what I eat!" Then we can henceforth trust and allow what has been true since the first moment of our existence: We are the very Body of Christ. We have dignity and power flowing through us in our very naked existence—and everybody else does too—even though most do not know it. This is enough to steer and empower your entire faith life.[4]

Gateway to Silence: I am present to Presence.

DAY 5

God Is Present

The Incarnation Mystery is repeated and represented in the Eucharist. In it we have material reality in the form of these universal foods of bread and wine, as the hiding place and the revelation place for God. We are reminded that God is always perfectly hidden and perfectly revealed in this very concrete and material world. This is the Cosmic Christ experience. If we deny that the spiritual can enter the material world, then we are in trouble, since that is exactly what we are—fully spiritual and fully material human beings. We had best encounter Incarnation in one focused, dramatic moment, and then the *particular* truth has a chance of becoming a *universal* truth, and even *your* truth. You are *supposed* to struggle with this, just as his disciples first did (see John 6:59–60)! Otherwise you are not sincerely engaged with it. But the final goal is universal presence and encounter, so all your day is lived in communion.

The sixteenth question in the old Baltimore Catechism was "Where is God?" and it was answered straightforwardly: "God is everywhere." The summit of Christian prayer is accomplished when you can trust that you are constantly in the presence of God. You cannot *not* be in the presence of God!

Where would you go? As the psalmist says (see Psalm 139:7–10), if you go up to the heavens or underneath the earth, you still can't get away from God. God is either in all things, or God is in nothing.

In the Eucharist, we slowly learn how to surrender to the Presence in one place, in one thing, in one focused moment. The priest holds up the Host and says, "See it here, believe it here, get it here, trust it here." Many people say they believe in that Presence in the Eucharist, but they don't get that it is everywhere—which is the whole point! They don't seem to know how to recognize the Presence when they leave the church, when they meet strangers or people who are of a different religion or race. They cannot also trust that every person is created in the image of God. Jesus spent a great deal of his ministry trying to break down the false distinctions between "God's here" and "God's not there." He dared to see God everywhere, even in sin, in enemies, in failures, and in outsiders. Usually, early stage religion is not yet capable of that, but fortunately God is patient.[5]

Gateway to Silence: I am present to Presence.

DAY 6

Death *and* Resurrection

While the Eucharist has always been a consoling mystery with an ecstatic, mystical language surrounding it (such as "Happy are those who are called to the wedding feast of the lamb" in Revelation 19:7–9), it has also been clothed in the language of suffering, blood, and death. It makes what the mystics always confirm: There is an inherent link between love and suffering. I think the tradition is correct in saying that somehow this mystery of the Eucharist is both a festive meal and an experience of the inevitability of suffering for what we love (a "sacrifice"). The wedding banquet table is decorated with a cross, as it were.

The Eucharist embraces both the great love *and* the great suffering that are the only things strong enough to take away our pretentiousness and our illusions. They are our avenues to the Real. Contact with reality is what redeems you, and Jesus is, for us, the Really Real. In the Eucharist, the Real is brought to a focus and to a moment. I believe we are transformed when we eat every part of the Real: the good and the bad, the dark and the light, the suffering and the ecstasy both.

We say, therefore, that the Eucharist is the ongoing celebration of the cross *and* the resurrection. Not the cross *or* the resurrection, but precisely *both*, and even the connection between the two. I am not sure which is harder. With Jesus, we find the power to hold the pain of life until it transforms into happiness.

The Eucharist is all about changing: changing bread and wine into the body and blood of Jesus, which then changes us into the death and resurrection of Jesus. It is too much to think or understand with the mind alone; we can only eat it until its very nutrition changes us. I have often said, when celebrating the Mass, that *it is much easier to convince bread and wine that they are Christ than it is to convince most people!* The bread and wine "believe" immediately, as soon as they are told. We hedge our bets and slowly wait to be convinced, or deny it altogether.[6]

Gateway to Silence: I am present to Presence.

DAY 7

Sabbath Meditation

Remember: Eucharist

At his Last Supper, Jesus gave us the Eucharistic meal as an action, a mime, a sacred ritual for community that would summarize his core and lasting message for the world. (Day 1)

The Eucharist was meant to be a "sacrificial meal" in the sense that the Body had to die to its smallness to enter into such Greatness, and called us to live in a new world order of true sisterhood and brotherhood, and of redemptive suffering and solidarity with the pain of the world. (Day 2)

The Eucharist becomes our ongoing touchstone for the Christian journey, a place to which we must repeatedly return in order to find our face, our name, our absolute identity, who we are in Christ, and thus who we are forever. (Day 3)

We keep eating and drinking the Mystery, until one day it dawns on us, in an undefended moment, "My God, I really am what I eat!" (Day 4)

You are constantly in the presence of God. You cannot *not* be! (Day 5)

I believe we are transformed when we eat every part of the Real. It is too much to think or understand with the mind alone; we can only eat it until its very nutrition changes us. (Day 6)

Rest: The Mass on the World

In the spirit of *lectio divina*, sacred reading, meditate on these words by the Jesuit philosopher Pierre Teilhard de Chardin:

Since once again, Lord—though this time not in the forests of the

Aisne but in the steppes of Asia—I have neither bread, nor wine, nor altar, I will raise myself beyond these symbols, up to the pure majesty of the Real itself; I, your priest, will make the whole earth my altar and on it will offer you all the labours and sufferings of the world.

Over there, on the horizon, the sun has just touched with light the outermost fringe of the eastern sky. Once again, beneath this moving sheet of fire, the living surface of the earth wakes and trembles, and once again begins its fearful travail. I will place on my paten, O God, the harvest to be won by this renewal of labour. Into my chalice I shall pour all the sap which is to be pressed out this day from the earth's fruits.

My paten and my chalice are the depths of a soul laid widely open to all the forces which in a moment will rise up from every corner of the earth and converge upon the Spirit. Grant me the remembrance and the mystic presence of all those whom the light is now awakening to the new day. . . .

Over every living thing which is to spring up, to grow, to flower, to ripen during this day say again the words: "This is my Body." And over every death-force which waits in readiness to corrode, to wither, to cut down, speak again your commanding words which express the supreme mystery of faith: "This is my Blood."[7]

Gateway to Silence: I am present to Presence.

For further study:

Dancing Standing Still: Healing the World from a Place of Prayer
Eucharist as Touchstone
Great Themes of Paul: Life as Participation
Jesus' Plan for a New World
Things Hidden: Scripture as Spirituality

WEEK 40:

MUTUAL INDWELLING

DAY 1

Perfection as Union

You must therefore be perfect just as your heavenly Father is perfect.

Live generously and graciously toward others, the way God has lived toward you.

(Two translations of Matthew 5:48.[1])

The oft-retranslated passage above is an excellent indicator of the two minds that have tried to understand the Bible. The first mind reads the passage in terms of Platonic idealism and purity-based moralism. It uses a mathematical or Divine concept ("perfection") and mandates it for the human person. This leads readers to impossible, head-based abstractions that only result in denial, splitting, and pretending. Yet, it appeals to the binary ("yes/no") system of the ordinary mind, where all actually lose since none of us is perfect and never will be. This was the Gospel read and preached when I, as a fervent nineteen-year-old, took my first vows as a Franciscan in 1962. Most of my fellow novices left when they honestly realized such perfection was beyond them. Only pretenders and optimists stayed on! I was one of them.

The second translation still sets the ideal very high, but now the goal has become Divine Union instead of any kind of private perfection. This translation is believable to everyone who has already experienced Divine Union at some level—and they know they were chosen and loved precisely in their *imperfection*! As Ken Wilber so brilliantly teaches, "It is not what a person says, but the level from which they say it, that determines the truth of a spiritual statement."[2] A spiritually mature person could use the word *perfection* and know they are talking about God's perfect abiding in us. An immature and still-egocentric person will think of it as a moral achievement that they can personally attain by trying harder. SS. Thérèse of Lisieux and Francis of Assisi are my favorite saints precisely because they so clearly saw through this disguise and pretense.

The higher-level approach is illustrated by a rather prescient statement from Paul: "I no longer seek any perfection from my own efforts...but only the perfection that comes from faith and is from God.... We who are called perfect must all think in this way" (see Philippians 3:9, 15). Paul rightly redefines perfection as the result of Divine Union with the only One who is perfect, rather than any kind of achievement or performance on our own. All we can do is agree and cooperate with—and fully enjoy—what God is already doing.[3]

Gateway to Silence: Remain in me.

DAY 2

A Coherent Pattern

The full biblical revelation has given us the history within the history, the coherence inside of the seeming incoherence. The clear goal and direction is mutual indwelling, where "the mystery is Christ within you, your hope of glory" (see Colossians 1:27). In this mutual indwelling, you no longer live as just you, but you live in a larger force field called the body of Christ (see Galatians 2:20). As British writer (and fellow Inkling with C.S. Lewis and J.R.R. Tolkien) Charles Williams said, the "master idea" of Christianity is *co-inherence*, that everything exists in essential relationship with one another. But it takes a long time to allow, believe, trust, and enjoy such wonder. Only in the final chapter of the Bible can Scripture say, "Now God lives among humans; they have become God's people, and God has become their God" (see Revelation 21:3).

Remember the story of the four-year-old who spoke to his newborn brother: "Quick, tell me who made you! Where'd you come from? I'm beginning to forget." In the complexity of life's journeys, we all begin to forget. As we get older, the patterns become too complex for most people if they try to totally fit them into human logic and, eventually, they don't even expect any patterns. As a result, we are facing today a deep crisis of meaning, which has become a crisis of hope, and an empty, frenetic scramble for external power, perks, and possessions. It will never work. Meaning always comes from *within*.

In a sense, the Christ is always too much for us. He's always "going ahead of us into Galilee" (see Matthew 28:7). The Risen Christ is leading us into a future for which we're never ready or can barely imagine. Only little by little do we become capable of mutuality, of communion, of pure presence. Start with stones, move to plants and trees, return the humble gaze of animals, love your neighbor as yourself; then you will be ready to "entertain angels" (see Hebrews 13:2) and, finally, you will be ready for God—but probably not before.[4]

Gateway to Silence: Remain in me.

Universal Restoration

The whole movement of the Bible is toward ever-greater incarnation and embodiment, until the mystery of mutual indwelling is finally experienced and enjoyed here in this world and this life. The end is not Armageddon or *Apocalypse Now* or Hal Lindsey's *Late Great Planet Earth*, which have all situated history inside of futility and hopelessness. Our history ends in Resurrection, intimated by Jesus' common metaphor of a wedding banquet, when the bride and the bridegroom are finally one. For Christians, the Risen Christ is the ultimate symbol of this Divine goal, pattern, and final embodiment: "When Christ is revealed, and he is your life, you will be revealed in all your glory with him" (see Colossians 3:4).

Paul's notion of the body of Christ has a material and cosmic character to it, and begins in this world but somehow continues beyond it (note that we believe in the resurrection of the body and not just the soul). Yes, there is "a new heaven," but there is also "a new earth" (see Revelation 21:1). What more fitting meaning could the Second Coming of Christ have than that collective humanity becomes "a beautiful bride all dressed for her husband" (see Revelation 21:2)? That is likely the meaning of "The Second Coming of Christ" in my opinion. Union is finally enjoyed as a total gift to all of us—no exceptions—and God's win-win storyline has achieved its full purpose. What a hopeful end to history! What an *apokatastasis*, or "universal restoration" (see Acts 3:21), as Peter promises in his very first recorded sermon. What a

WEEK 40: MUTUAL INDWELLING   305

total victory for God—and thus also for humanity! God does not lose. So, once and for all, let's believe the Gospel and move from Apocalypse Now to Universal Restoration.[5]

Gateway to Silence: Remain in me.

DAY 4

Quantum Entanglement

God is creating Real Presence all the time, and inviting us into Mutual Presence, which is probably why the images of an intimate bride and bridegroom are used throughout the Bible. Mutual presence, even intimacy, is clearly the ultimate goal. Bride and bridegroom are together just for the sake of being together! The rather universal image of a wedding feast celebrates the pure language of union, of being lost and found in the face of the other, or, as with Jesus, in the very breath of the Other (see John 20:22). If that is the core meaning of eternal life, then why wouldn't we practice it now, enjoy it now, choose it now? *How you get there determines where you will arrive.*

Why has so much of Christian history settled for a courtroom instead of a bridal chamber? For a threatening torture chamber instead of a joyous invitation? It is really quite disturbing how this has corrupted the whole Gospel.

You don't have to figure it all out or get it all right ahead of time. You just have to stay on the journey. All you can do is stay connected to the Source, which connects you to everything else. We don't know how to be perfect, but we can stay in union. "If you remain in me and I remain in you," says Jesus, "you can ask for whatever you want and you're going to get it" (see John 15:7). When you're connected, there are no coincidences or accidents anymore.

Union realigns you with everything, and synchronicities, coincidences, and "providences" just keep happening. What spirituality called mutual presence, science sometimes now calls "quantum entanglement" (especially when we connect "center to center")! I myself cannot explain the physics of it all. All I know from my side is that "the branch cut off from the vine is useless" (see John 15:5), but, connected to the vine, it bears much fruit (see 15:5, 7). The False Self is fragile, needy, and insecure; the True Self is endlessly generative, in touch with its Source, and inside the Big Flow. If you want to read of someone who really lived this, treat yourself to St. Thérèse of Lisieux's memorable biography, *The Story of a Soul.* She has "entangled" many a life, for God and for good, as all true saints do.[6]

Gateway to Silence: Remain in me.

Remaining on the Vine

Consciously, trustfully, lovingly remaining on the vine (see John 15:1), which is to be connected to our Source, is precisely our access point to deeper spiritual wisdom. We know by participation with and in God, which creates our very real co-identity with Christ: *We are also both human and Divine, as he came to reveal and model.* The foundational meaning of Divine Transformation is to surrender to this new identity and to consciously draw upon it every day.

This realization that Someone is living in us and through us is exactly how we plug into a much larger mind and heart beyond our own. Afterward, we know in a different way, although we have to keep relearning this truth over and over again (which is probably the point of daily prayer). This demands a major surrendering of our small self, our little ego boundaries. This "foundational holiness" or ontological union with God is actually our *first nature.* In fact, God has always—and only—been in union with our obviously imperfect humanity. That is the essential and eternal character of Divine Mercy and the perfect and infinite love of God.

Living and thinking autonomously, separately, or cut off from such a Source is what Paul means by being "foolish" or "unspiritual," whereas surrendering to our identity in God is the beginning of all wisdom and an unending power Source. Surrender to Another, participation with Another, and Divine Union are finally the same thing. Once we rest in this union, we look out at the world from a much fuller Reality with eyes beyond and bigger than our own. This is precisely what it means to "live in Christ" (*en Cristo*), to begin our many prayers with "in the name of" and to end them "through Christ our Lord. Amen!" We are praying with a transformed sense of our self; we stand in a different "name."[7]

Gateway to Silence: Remain in me.

Awakening as the Beloved

Symeon the New Theologian (949–1022) pointed to the new force field that we call the Body of Christ in his *Hymns of Divine Love.* Hymn 15 beautifully names the Divine Union toward which God is forever inviting and edging us:

We awaken in Christ's body
as Christ awakens our bodies,
and my poor hand is Christ, He enters
my foot, and is infinitely me.

I move my hand, and wonderfully
my hand becomes Christ, becomes all of Him
(for God is indivisibly
Whole, seamless in His Godhood).

I move my foot, and at once
He appears like a flash of lightning.
Do my words seem blasphemous? —Then
open your heart to Him

and let yourself receive the one
who is opening to you so deeply.
For if we genuinely love Him,
we wake up inside Christ's body

where all our body, all over,
every most hidden part of it,
is realized in joy as Him,
and He makes us, utterly, real,

and everything that is hurt, everything
that seemed to us dark, harsh, shameful,
maimed, ugly, irreparably
damaged, is in Him transformed

and recognized as whole, as lovely,
and radiant in His light
we awaken as the Beloved
in every last part of our body.[8]

Gateway to Silence: Remain in me.

SABBATH MEDITATION

Remember: **Mutual Indwelling**

A spiritually mature person could use the word *perfection* and know they are talking about God's perfect abiding in us. (Day 1)

The full biblical revelation has given us the history within the history, the coherence inside of the seeming incoherence. The clear goal and direction is mutual indwelling, where "the mystery is Christ within you, your hope of glory" (see Colossians 1:27). (Day 2)

The whole movement of the Bible is toward ever-greater incarnation and embodiment. (Day 3)

You don't have to figure it all out or get it all right ahead of time. All you can do is stay connected to the Source, which connects you to everything else. (Day 4)

Surrender to Another, participation with Another, and Divine Union are finally the same thing. (Day 5)

"We awaken in Christ's body, as Christ awakens our bodies." —Symeon the New Theologian (Day 6)

Rest: **Bodily Knowing**

St. Francis was a human being who objectively experienced mutual indwelling, with Jesus and with all of God's creatures, so much so that, late in his life, the cruciform shape of reality became the very shape of St. Francis' body after he received the marks of the five wounds of Christ in his own body (this is historically documented from many sources[9]). St. Francis learned the message, price, and glory of love in the very cells of his body. Full knowing is always *psychosomatic* knowing, and St. Francis seems to exemplify someone who fully absorbed the Gospel with his entire being, not just with his head. This is kinesthetic knowing and full-body believing.

Take a few minutes to quietly observe and be present to your body. Sitting upright with legs uncrossed and eyes closed, bring your attention to your left knee. Lightly scratch the knee with your fingernails. Focus on the tingling sensation that lingers. Forget about the rest of your body and focus entirely on your knee, feeling it move, touching its outline. Acknowledge distracting thoughts as they arise and then let them go, returning to awareness of your knee.

Repeat this practice with other parts of your body, wordlessly witnessing your body's sensations and contours. Gradually let the tingling flow without controlling it; simply follow your awareness at its own pace and wherever it leads, trusting God's presence within.[10]

Gateway to Silence: Remain in me.

For further study:

Eager to Love: The Alternative Way of Francis of Assisi
New Great Themes of Scripture
Things Hidden: Scripture as Spirituality

WEEK 41:

THE GATE OF HEAVEN
IS EVERYWHERE

DAY I

At the Center of Our Being

One of my favorite quotes from Thomas Merton is from his book *Conjectures of a Guilty Bystander* (emphasis and words in brackets are mine):

At the center of our being is a point of nothingness, which is untouched by sin and by illusion, a point of pure truth, a point or spark which belongs entirely to God, [We would call it, of course, the Holy Spirit, the divine indwelling; the soul, if you will.] which is never at our disposal, from which God disposes of our lives, which is inaccessible to the fantasies of our own mind or the brutalities of our own will. This little point of nothingness [and that's what it always feels like, which is why it's so hard to describe or sell—how do you sell nothing?] and *of absolute poverty* is the pure glory of God in us. It is, so to speak, God's name written in us, as our poverty, as our indigence, as our dependence, as our sonship [and daughterhood]. It is like a pure diamond, blazing with the invisible light of heaven. It is in everybody, and if we could see it we would see these billions of points of light coming together in the face and blaze of a sun that would make all the darkness and cruelty of life vanish completely. I have no program for this seeing. It is only given. But *the gate of heaven is everywhere.*[1]

It's true—the gate of heaven is everywhere. This is what I mean by the great democratization of God and the total accessibility and availability of God. It has always been my disappointment that we've tried to make God so hard to get to, as if you have to perform or work to earn access to God. The problem is almost the simplicity of it.[2]

Gateway to Silence: The kingdom of heaven is at hand. (See Matthew 3:2.)

DAY 2

Breathing Yahweh

I cannot emphasize enough the importance of the Jewish revelation of the name of God. As we Christians spell and pronounce it, the word is *Yahweh*. In Hebrew, it is the sacred Tetragrammaton YHVH (*yod, he, vav,* and *he*). I am told that those are the only consonants in the Hebrew alphabet that are not articulated with lips and tongue. Rather, they are *breathed* with the tongue relaxed and lips apart. YHVH was considered a literally unspeakable word for Jews, and any attempt to know what they were talking about was "in vain." As the commandment said: "Do not utter the name of God in vain" (see Exodus 20:7). All attempts to fully think God are in vain. From God's side, the Divine Identity was kept mysterious and unavailable to the mind. When Moses asked for the divinity's name, he received only the phrase that translates "I AM WHO I AM" (see Exodus 3:14).

This unspeakability has long been recognized, but now we know it goes even deeper: Formally, the name of God was not, could not, be spoken at all—only *breathed*. Many are convinced that its correct pronunciation is an attempt to replicate and imitate the very sound of inhalation and exhalation. Therefore, the one thing we do every moment of our lives is to speak the name of God. This makes the name of God our first and last word as we enter and leave the world.

I have taught this to people in many countries, and it often changes their faith and prayer lives in substantial ways. I remind people that there is no Islamic, Christian, or Jewish way of breathing. There is no American, African, or Asian way of breathing. There is no rich or poor, gay or straight way of breathing. The playing field is utterly leveled. It is all one and the same air, and this Divine Wind "blows where it will" (see John 3:8). No one can control this Spirit.

When considered in this way, *God is suddenly as available and accessible as the very thing we all do constantly—breathe.* Exactly as some teachers of prayer say, "Stay with the breath, attend to your breath"—the same breath that was breathed into Adam's nostrils by this Yahweh (see Genesis 2:7); the very breath "spirit" that Jesus handed over with trust on the cross (see John 19:30) and then breathed on us as *shalom*, forgiveness, and the Holy Spirit, all at once (see John 20:21–23). And isn't it wonderful that breath, wind, spirit, and air are precisely *nothing*—and yet everything?[3]

Gateway to Silence: The kingdom of heaven is at hand. (See Matthew 3:2.)

DAY 3

Passing Through the Narrow Gate

James Finley describes the gate to life that is within us as follows:

Jesus said, "Narrow is the gate that leads to life and few there are who enter it" (see Matthew 7:14). What a great metaphor for the spiritual journey! We can think of the path along which we are awakened to oneness as a process of passing through a narrow gate into this realization. It is only narrow, I think, because it is so simple and does not demand our attention! There is in the depths of every moment a gate that grants access to the depths of God. And it is through this same simple gate that God accesses the depths of us.

We understand life as God and ourselves taking turns passing through this gate into each other until there is one common Being. With each passage through the gate, union deepens, until we are fully at home on the other side of the gate.

Finally, we realize that all of our faults and ego possessions are just heavy and burdensome luggage that keep us from walking through this always-open gate—or even seeing it in the first place.[4]

Gateway to Silence: The kingdom of heaven is at hand. (See Matthew 3:2.)

DAY 4

The Infinite in the Finite

St. Francis of Assisi knew that if you can accept that the finite manifests the infinite, and that the physical is the doorway to the spiritual (which is the foundational principle we call "incarnation"), then all you need is right here and right now—in this world. *This* is the way to *that!* Heaven includes earth. Earth reveals heaven. Time opens you up to the timeless, space opens you up to spacelessness, if you only recognize them as the clear doorways that they are.

There are not sacred and profane things, places, and moments. There are only sacred and *desecrated* things, places, and moments—and it is *we alone* who desecrate them by our blindness and lack of reverence. It is one sacred universe, and we are all a part of it.

The Christ Mystery refuses to be vague or abstract, and it is always concrete and specific. When we stay with these daily apparitions, we see that everything is a revelation of the Divine—from rocks to rocket ships. Our only blindness is our own lack of fascination, humility, curiosity, awe. The only thing needed is a willingness to surrender to the naked now, which God always inhabits, where the Incarnation is always taking place and always mysterious, where God, in every moment, is perfectly hidden and, at the same time, perfectly revealed. Hold that paradox. Those who have eyes to see can allow both to be true.[5]

Gateway to Silence: The kingdom of heaven is at hand. (See Matthew 3:2.)

DAY 5

The Eternal Now

Jesus' primary metaphors for the Eternal Now are "the kingdom of God" and "the kingdom of heaven." He is trying to tell you that there is a place where you can live connected to the Real and to the Eternal. That place is simply *the here-and-now*, which always feels like nothing, like nowhere (now-here), and is where everything always happens! So be sure to be here—and not somewhere else!

The reason we can trust the Now so much is because of the Incarnation and because of the Divine Indwelling. The Word has become flesh, God has entered into the human, God is here and everywhere! The early Fathers saw this as occurring, not just in one human being, but as a "yes," even a metaphysical union, with human nature itself, human nature as a whole. Unfortunately, most Christians limit the incarnation just to Jesus, which misses out on its precise, transformative message and function for the rest of creation.

John Duns Scotus, one of the great Franciscan teachers, said that God did not create genus and species; God only created what Scotus called "this-ness," in Latin *haecceity*. He said that until you can experience each thing in its specific "thisness," you will not easily experience the joy and freedom of Divine Presence. In other words, I can't be present to all women in general. I've got to be present to this woman, right here, right now, in her specificity and particularity, and maybe even her eccentricity. Might that be what love means?

In that way, the here-and-now has the power to become the gateway and the breakthrough point to the universal. The concrete, the specific, the physical, the here-and-now—when you can be present to it in all of its ordinariness—becomes the gateway to the Eternal. I call this the very foundational Christian principle of Incarnation. It is the great and unique insight that we offer to all world religions, yet we ourselves have often not celebrated this immense breakthrough.[6]

Gateway to Silence: The kingdom of heaven is at hand. (See Matthew 3:2.)

DAY 6

Heaven Is Both Now and Later

They call me the mailman at the CAC because almost every day I take the mail to, and pick up the mail from, the post office. At the end of our street, which is called Five Points Road, five streets come together, and I have to go this way to get the mail. The stoplight at this intersection seems interminably long. One day, as I was impatiently waiting and waiting for the light to turn green, I felt God asking me, "Richard, are you really going to be any happier on the other side of Bridge Boulevard?"

Now it has become my daily meditation place, where I get to practice living right here, right now. If I can't experience God and love and happiness, and everything that matters, in this impatient moment, I probably won't experience it on the other side of Bridge Boulevard either. As Catherine of Siena is reputed to have said, the path to heaven lies through heaven and "all the way to heaven is heaven."

Maybe one day we will all say, like Jacob at the foot of his dreamy ladder, where angels ascend and descend between heaven and earth, "You were here all the time, and I never knew it! This is nothing less than the house of God; this is the very gate of heaven" (see Genesis 28:16–17). And Jacob was sleeping on a hard stone pillow![7]

Gateway to Silence: The kingdom of heaven is at hand. (See Matthew 3:2.)

DAY 7

Sabbath Meditation

Remember: **The Gate of Heaven Is Everywhere**
The gate of heaven is everywhere. This is what I mean by the great democratization of God and the total accessibility and availability of God. (Day 1)

God is suddenly as available and accessible as the very thing we all do constantly—breathe. (Day 2)

All of our faults and ego possessions are just heavy and burdensome luggage that keep us from walking through this always-open gate—or even seeing it in the first place. (Day 3)

It is one sacred universe, and we are all a part of it. (Day 4)

The here-and-now has the power to become the gateway and the breakthrough point to the universal. (Day 5)

"You were here all the time, and I never knew it! This is nothing less than the house of God; this is the very gate of heaven" (see Genesis 28:16–17). (Day 6)

Rest: **Fourth and Walnut**

Thomas Merton described a transformative, perhaps unitive, experience in *Conjectures of a Guilty Bystander:*

> In Louisville, at the corner of Fourth and Walnut, in the center of the shopping district, I was suddenly overwhelmed with the realization that I loved all these people, that they were mine and I theirs, that we could not be alien to one another even though we were total strangers. It was like waking from a dream of separateness, of spurious self-isolation in a special world. . . . This sense of liberation from an illusory difference was such a relief and such a joy to me that I almost laughed out loud. . . . I have the immense joy of being man, a member of a race in which God Himself became incarnate. As if the sorrows and stupidities of the human condition could overwhelm me, now that I realize what we all are. And if only everybody could realize this! But it cannot be explained. There is no way of telling people that they are all walking around shining like the sun.
>
> Then it was as if I suddenly saw the secret beauty of their hearts, the depths of their hearts where neither sin nor desire nor self-knowledge can reach, the core of their reality, the person that each one is in God's eyes. If only they could all see themselves as they really are. If only we could see each other that way all the time. There would be no more war, no more hatred, no more cruelty, no more greed. . . . But this cannot be seen, only believed and "understood" by a peculiar gift.[8]

Watch for your own "Fourth and Walnut" corner wherever you find yourself today. Allow the gates of heaven to open, showing you that God is here, now, in all. Let one person or creature or stone remind you of their, and your, own identity, indwelled by God's presence.

Gateway to Silence: The kingdom of heaven is at hand. (See Matthew 3:2.)

For further study:

Eager to Love: The Alternative Way of Francis of Assisi
How Do We Get Everything to Belong?
Living the Eternal Now
The Naked Now: Learning to See as the Mystics See

WEEK 42:

THE PRINCIPLE OF LIKENESS

DAY I

Be the Change

"Be *the change you wish to see in the world.*"
—Mohandas Gandhi

To have a spiritual life is to recognize early on that there is always a similarity and coherence between the seer and the seen, the seekers and what they are capable of finding. You will seek only what you have already partially discovered and therefore desire. Spiritual cognition is invariably *re*-cognition. God plants the desires in us for what God already wants to give us, but, like all true love, Divine Love is never forced on us. We must be included in the process.

Call this reality of recognition the Principle of Likeness, if you will. When you honor and accept the Divine Image within yourself, you henceforth cannot help but see it in everybody else too—and you know it is just as undeserved and unmerited in them as it is in you. That is almost the only way you can stop judging, and that is how you start loving unconditionally and without asking whether someone is worthy or not. The breakthrough often occurs like a momentary thunderbolt, although the living realization deepens and takes on more conviction only over many years.

Spirituality is always about you changing *your own* way of seeing and your own way of hearing (not changing other people!). It's about opening your heart space every day and keeping it open with some form of prayer, every few minutes if need be, so that the hurts and disappointments of life won't close you down. You have to find some practice, some ritual, some silence, or whatever it is that helps you recognize how God is trying to get in, as well as how you may be closing down. What you seek is what you will surely get. Jesus states this directly in Matthew 7:7–8, but I have often thought that most people just hear this line as pious poetry.[1]

Gateway to Silence: The silence in me will love the Divine Silence.

DAY 2
Your Response Is Your Reality

What you see is what you get. What you seek is also what you get.
(See Matthew 7:7–8.)

We mend and renew the world by strengthening inside ourselves what we seek outside ourselves, and not by demanding it of others or trying to force it on others.

This truth may sound like the Law of Attraction that is so widely discussed today, and often called "the Secret," but there is one major difference. Drawing good things toward yourself, such as love, a successful relationship, some kind of reward, is fine and good—as far as it goes. But it is still all about you! The true contemplative mind does not deny the utter "facticity" of the outer world, but allows outer reality to be its guide and teacher. The Secret seems to be saying that your mind fully creates reality, which is only partly true. *You do create your response to reality, and that response, for all practical purposes, is your reality.* But do not imagine you can think away typhoons and very real tragedies. Instead, you must deal with them in the Spirit, which is a very different way of dealing with them.

Some Eastern religions have called the correspondence between who you are and what you can make happen, or what will happen, *karma*. Jesus said it this way (see Luke 6:37–38):

Do not judge, and you will not be judged,
Do not condemn, and you will not be condemned,
Grant pardon, and you will be pardoned,
Give, and there will be gifts for you. . . .
The amount you measure out is the amount you will be given back.

If you want others to be more loving, choose to love first. If you want a reconciled outer world, reconcile your own inner world. If you are working for peace out there, create it inside as well. If you wish to find some outer stillness, find it within yourself. If you want to find God, then honor God within you and you also will always see God far beyond you. For it is only God in you who knows where and how to look for God. By ourselves, we are fairly blind.[2]

Gateway to Silence: The silence in me will love the Divine Silence.

DAY 3

You Become the God You Worship

The Principle of Likeness means that like knows like, love-in-me knows love—and hate-in-me will see hate everywhere else. If there's no love in you, if you are filled with fear and hatred, you cannot know God. You actually can't. There's no abiding place for an infinite God in you, because your field is too small and safe. The infinite cannot abide inside of the finite unless the finite is somehow released from its small boundaries and attracted to a Larger Field outside itself. To be fully at home in a much larger field is surely what we mean by "salvation" or the Kingdom of God.

The commandments, you know, are not requirements to get God to love you. God has forever and already taken care of that. Moral mandates are requirements for *your own* self-expansion and transformation, allowing you to begin to see in a broad, calm, clear, and non-self-referential way. Morals put up necessary barriers to your natural egocentricity and allow you to encounter and reverence *the other precisely as other* (and not you!), and, frankly, so you can recognize your own stingy spirit. How can you possibly be prepared to know the Ultimate Other, which some of us call God, if you cannot stretch yourself to meet the little everyday needs of others that are often an irritant, a demand, a stretch?

Each daily encounter is your chance for training and concrete practice in mercy, forgiveness, and compassion. As this *love place* grows within you, you will be increasingly capable of knowing and loving God too. Although, to be honest, I am not sure which comes first. Do loving people meet God or do people who have met God know how to love? All I know is that there is eventually a major equivalence between you and the God you worship. If you are a merciful, forgiving person, then I know you've met the real God. If you are narrow, stingy, and fearful, then you are worshiping something that is not God, and probably some form of yourself.[3]

Gateway to Silence: The silence in me will love the Divine Silence.

Smiling at Tide Boxes

To repeat, because it is so important: There is a natural affinity between the knower and the known, between the seer and what we see. How you get there determines where you arrive. For example, you've got to start with some level of love or you cannot know the love of God—or the love that is your own deepest soul. Jesus makes this pattern very clear. Only the merciful will receive mercy. Only the generous will receive generosity.

And yes, fearful people will create more fear; hateful hearts will see hate everywhere else. We know reality by affinity, by likeness, by an inner resonance. We see who we are everywhere else because we see *through who we are* at any one moment. Nothing else is really possible. It is early stage contemplation that helps you to see these humiliating and rewarding patterns within yourself. Jesus rightly said, "Be careful how you see" and "Be careful how you hear" (see Luke 8:16–18). How you do anything is how you do everything.

Eckhart Tolle teaches in many ways that the silence within us will always love the Divine silence. I hope you've had such a divine moment, when you just want to stop, taste, and enjoy—when an ordinary moment is totally satisfying and more than enough. One day I experienced this in a local Kmart! I "came to" and found myself happily standing in an aisle, just looking at boxes of Tide. I don't know how long I stood there, but there I was, just smiling at the Tide boxes! Life was all utterly okay. I was okay and all was right with the world (and this was after a day of emotional trials). Just buying detergent had the effect that church was supposed to have! Some fellow shoppers probably thought I was on drugs.

The precise object of your affection is not really important at all. What is important is that the love finds an object, any object, and pays it forward. The power is in the relationship itself. In other words, we might be able to love a tree or a frog with the full flow of divine love, and we might love other humans just because they are somehow an advantage to us. The first love can and will "mend the world"; the second is just passing show and hardly love at all. The power is always in the authenticity of the relationship itself and not in the supposed worthiness of the object loved. Think about that.[4]

Gateway to Silence: The silence in me will love the Divine Silence.

Seek and You Will Find

In Matthew 13:11–13, the disciples ask Jesus why he speaks to the people with parables.

And he answered them, "To you it has been given to know the secrets of the kingdom of heaven, but to them it has not been given. For to the one who has, more will be given, and he will have abundance; but from the one who has not, even what he has will be taken away. This is why I speak to them in parables, because seeing [with their normal mind] they do not see, and hearing they do not hear, nor do they understand."[5]

This is how I read this enigmatic passage:

You disciples have already made the breakthrough, so I can talk to you straightforwardly and you get it. But for those who are still enclosed and over-defended, I've got to tell little riddles and stories to undermine their usual and comfortable way of thinking, so that they'll reframe both the question and the answer.

Jesus' parables, like Zen koans and many riddles, are almost always counterintuitive and resist your commonsense intellect. You have to "change heads" to understand. That is their whole point.

I'd say that is still pretty much the way it is today when preaching the gospel. There are those who get it, and they get it largely because they've already learned how to be loving people. When you preach the gospel of love to loving people, they get even more loving. When people are invested in fear, hate, anger, or distress, you can say all kinds of wise words to them and it will go right over their heads or they will even push back. To them, wisdom seems like gibberish or nonsense, or of no interest.

There's a correspondence between the seer and the seen. If you're not ready, you don't get it. You don't even pay attention to it. I recognize this in the vestibule of the church after some of my Sunday sermons. Sometimes what I thought were my best lines go nowhere, while a quick throw-away line ends up changing someone's life trajectory. Sometimes I even ask myself, "Did I say that?" It is all about the receiver—his humble readiness and her deep desire—which fill in the blanks that I only helped create! People who are ready hear me say very good things and, frankly, people who are not ready do not care one way or the other, or they hear it entirely inside their own agenda and fear.

Jesus was describing this when he said, "Seek and you will find" (see Matthew 7:7). What you seek is what you are going to get. What you expect is what you will call forth and recognize. What you allow and what you're ready for is what can come toward you. But it has to be in you first, at least in the form of desire (Is this how we intuit the Indwelling Spirit?), or you won't see it or recognize it when it is right in front of you. What a mystery this is.[6]

Gateway to Silence: The silence in me will love the Divine Silence.

DAY 6

My Mystery Opens Me to God's Mystery

Only love can know love, only mercy can know mercy, only the endless mystery I am to myself is ready for God's Infinite Mystery. When I can stand *in mystery* (not knowing and not needing to know—and being dazzled by such freedom); when I don't need to split, to hate, to dismiss, to compartmentalize what I cannot explain or understand; when I can radically accept that "I am what I am what I am," then I am beginning to stand inside the Divine Freedom (see Galatians 5:1 or James 1:25).

We do not know how to stand there on our own. Someone Else needs to sustain us in such a deep and spacious place. This is what the saints mean by our emptiness, our poverty, and our nothingness. They are not being negative or self-effacing, but just utterly honest about their inner experience. God alone can sustain me in knowing and accepting that I am not a saint, not at all perfect, not very loving at all—and in that very recognition I can fall into the perfect love of God. Remember Jesus' first beatitude: "How happy are the poor in spirit; theirs is the kingdom of God" (see Matthew 5:3). How amazing is that? I think this might just be the description of salvation and perfect freedom. They are the same, you know.

I used to pray at the tomb of Fr. Karl Rahner when I was studying one summer in Innsbruck, Austria. He is the German Jesuit who so influenced the Second Vatican Council. Rahner taught me this (in his long German sentences, even worse when translated into English): The infinite mystery that you are to yourself is alone able to accept and love the Infinite Mystery that God will always be. It is, finally, two infinite mysteries, humbly bowing and deferring to one another. He taught me how to be patient and merciful toward *both* of these uncanny mysteries. Thank you, Karl! [7]

Gateway to Silence: The silence in me will love the Divine Silence.

DAY 7

Sabbath Meditation

Remember: **The Principle of Likeness**

"Be the change you wish to see in the world." —Mohandas Gandhi (Day 1)

If you want others to be more loving, choose to love first. If you want a reconciled outer world, reconcile your own inner world. (Day 2)

If you are a merciful, forgiving person, then I know you've met the real God. If you are narrow, stingy, and fearful, then you are worshiping something that is not God, and probably some form of yourself. (Day 3)

You've got to start with some level of love or you cannot know the love of God—or the love that is your own deepest soul. (Day 4)

What you seek is what you are going to get. What you expect is what you will call forth and recognize. (Day 5)

Only love can know love, only mercy can know mercy, only the endless mystery I am to myself is ready for God's Infinite Mystery. (Day 6)

Rest: **Resting in Love**

How do we come to know love so that we can live from its depths? Love cannot be understood by the mind. And if God is love, God will never be subject to the mind as we know it. God and love can only be experienced. This simple practice is an invitation to encounter love in its very physical, connective reality.

Place the palm of one of your hands on your heart. Feel your heart beating, letting its rhythm bring you into the present moment and into the awareness of God's blessing on your life, beat after beat after beat.

Bring to your conscious mind a loved one, a favorite place or animal, or anything that makes you smile with undeniable, spontaneous, unconditional love and joy.

Bring that particular beloved being or thing down from your mind and place it right under your palm, in your heart space. Relax your mind and let your heart relax at the same time, feeling the sensation of blood vessels, muscles, and chest cavity opening in warmth and love for that particular loved thing. Smile.

Now humbly place a challenging person, issue, or problem directly under your palm, within your wide-open heart space. Silently continue to smile and hold this challenging thing in the warmth of your heart.

With closed eyes, look at the thing that causes you pain, visualizing the detail that bothers you the most, all the while smiling. Consider that there may be reasons why this thing brings hurt. Smile at the fragility, suffering, or misunderstanding that makes it this way.

Finally, give the person or problem to your heart and ask that your heart's wisdom and love take over. Rest in the Love that loves both you and the other and wants to transform all into its loving image.

Gateway to Silence: The silence in me will love the Divine Silence.

For further study:

The Enneagram as a Tool for Your Spiritual Journey
Franciscan Mysticism: I AM That Which I Am Seeking
Holding the Tension: The Power of Paradox
The Naked Now: Learning to See as the Mystics See

WEEK 43:

LUMINOUS DARKNESS

DAY I
Dark Night of the Soul

There comes to many seekers, at some time or a few times in their lives, a "dark night," a period of seeming distance from God, and from the ways in which we've experienced and understood God. The previous comforts have fallen away and we can no longer conceptualize God.

St. John of the Cross (Juan de la Cruz) gave us a map of sorts to guide us through these necessary and important "dark nights." He distinguished between the dark night of sense (in which all *perceptions* of God vanish) and the dark night of the spirit (in which we no longer grasp *ideas* about God). The goal of these times is to draw the self beyond ego into full transfiguration and union in God. St. John went through such a dark period during a time when he was imprisoned, tortured, and starved. He felt as if his Beloved had abandoned him.

After St. John miraculously escaped from prison, he composed his mystical poem, "The Dark Night of the Soul." Almost a year later, he wrote the commentary to the poem, which he also titled *The Dark Night of the Soul.* In her translation, my friend and fellow New Mexican, Mirabai Starr, writes:

> In the dark night, says John, the secret essence of the soul knows the truth, and is calling out to God: Beloved, you pray, please remind me again and again that I am nothing. Strip me of the consolations

of my complacent spirituality. Plunge me into the darkness where I cannot rely on any of my old tricks for maintaining my separation. Let me give up on trying to convince myself that my own spiritual deeds are bound to be pleasing to you. Take all my juicy spiritual feelings, Beloved, and dry them up, and then please light them on fire. Take my lofty spiritual concepts and plunge them into darkness, and then burn them. Let me love you, Beloved. Let me quietly and with unutterable simplicity just love you.[1]

Like few other teachers, it was Juan de la Cruz who firmly planted the absolute need for an illuminating darkness, and *not knowing*, back into Christian spirituality, almost as if to warn us against both the excesses of the Reformation and the false light of the Enlightenment that were soon to be upon us. Alas, few got the message.

Gateway to Silence: O, night that joined Beloved with lover. —St. John of the Cross

DAY 2

Inexplicable Darkness

St. John of the Cross writes, in his prologue to *The Ascent of Mount Carmel:*

A deeper enlightenment and wider experience than mine is necessary to explain the dark night through which a soul journeys toward that divine light of perfect union with God that is achieved, insofar as possible in this life, through love. The darknesses and trials, spiritual and temporal, that fortunate souls ordinarily undergo on their way to the high state of perfection are so numerous and profound that human science cannot understand them adequately. Nor does experience of them equip one to explain them. Only those who suffer them will know what this experience is like, but they won't be able to describe it.[2]

You can't go forward by "knowing" in the usual way, but only by a different kind of *experiencing*. At some time in your life, I hope you are so ambushed by God that God catches you by surprise. If you try to go by what you already know—St. John of the Cross makes this very clear—you will pull God back into your preexistent categories, and you won't get very far.

That is why most people stay with their childish faith and we have too few mystics and non-dual thinkers in Christianity.

When God leads you into a dark night, it is to deepen and mature your faith—which, by its very definition, "is the substance of things hoped for, the evidence of things not seen" (see Hebrews 11:1). The gift of darkness draws you to know God's presence beyond what thought, imagination, or sensory feeling can comprehend. During the dark night, the tried-and-true rituals and creeds of religion no longer satisfy or bring assurances of God's love. (You might get bored with church services for very good reasons, but that is not the same as mere spiritual laziness or a lack of faith.)

God is calling you into deeper and closer intimacy, beyond anything you could achieve with your most sincere attempts; closer than you could even dream. But you must learn to proceed without any guarantees from your feelings or your intellect. The only real way to grow in faith and Divine Love is to hand over the steering wheel to Someone Else.[3]

Gateway to Silence: O, night that joined Beloved with lover. —St. John of the Cross

DAY 3

Surrendering in Stillness

Mirabai Starr writes of the dark night as one who has gone through it herself, like St. John of the Cross. Her description is so valuable, I will quote it at length:

The dark night descends on a soul only when everything else has failed. When you are no longer the best meditator in the class because your meditation produces absolutely nothing. When prayer evaporates on your tongue and you have nothing left to say to God. When you are not even tempted to return to a life of worldly pleasures because the world has proven empty and yet taking another step through the void of the spiritual life feels futile because you are no good at it and it seems that God has given up on you, anyway.

This, says John, is the beginning of blessedness! This is the choiceless choice when the soul can do nothing but surrender. Because even if you cannot sense a shred of the Beloved's love for you, even if you can scarcely conjure up your old passion, it has become perfectly clear that you are incapable of doing anything on your own to remedy your spiritual brokenness. All efforts to purge your unspiritual inclinations have only honed the laser of attention on the false self. Unwilling to keep struggling, the soul finds itself surrendering to its deepest inner wound and breathing in the stillness there.

The only action left to the soul, ultimately, is to put down its self-importance and cultivate a simple loving attention toward the Beloved. That's when the Beloved takes over and all our holy intentions vaporize. That's when the soul, says John, is infused passively with his love. Though his radiance is imperceptible to the faculty of the senses and invisible to the faculty of the intellect, the soul that has allowed itself to be empty can at last be filled and overflow with him.[4]

Gateway to Silence: O, night that joined Beloved with lover. —St. John of the Cross

DAY 4

Ambushed by Love

I wonder if the only way that conversion, enlightenment, and transformation ever happen is by a kind of Divine ambush. We have to be caught off guard. As long as you are in control, you are going to keep trying to steer the ship using your previous experience of being in charge. The only way you will let yourself be ambushed is by trusting the Ambusher and learning to trust that the darkness of intimacy will lead to depth, safety, freedom, and love.

Any use of fear techniques or trying to shame people into the spiritual journey is inherently counterproductive. Either one simply makes you more defensive and protective of your boundaries, but now at an unconscious level. (I am afraid this is true of a high percentage of Christians, who were largely raised on fear of "hell" and intense social pressure.) We need spiritual teachers like St. John of the Cross to help us see the patterns of the spiritual journey that actually work, so we can be a bit less defended, a bit less boundaried, with ourselves and with God. Only then can God do the soul-forming work of seduction and union.

God needs to catch us by surprise because our very limited preexisting notions keep us and our understanding of God small. We are still trying to remain in control and we still want to "look good"! God tries to bring us into a bigger world where, by definition, we are not in control and no longer need to look good. A terrible lust for certitude and social order has characterized the last five hundred years of Western Christianity, and it has simply not served the soul well at all. Once we lost a spirituality of darkness as its own kind of light, there just wasn't much room for growth in faith, hope, and love.

So God has to come indirectly, catching us off guard and out of control, when we are empty instead of full of ourselves. That is why the saints talk about suffering so much. They are not masochistic, sadistic, negative, morbid, or oppositional. The mystics have seen the pattern and, as St. Teresa of Ávila says, it is not that you are happy for the suffering—who would be, who could be?—*you are happy for the new level of intimacy to which the suffering brought you.* You only know this after the fact, perhaps days or weeks, or even years, later. One day you realize, "God is so real to me now. How did I get here?" All you know is that you did not engineer or even imagine this. You were taken there when you were off guard. St. John's word for that is *darkness.*[5]

Gateway to Silence: O, night that joined Beloved with lover. —St. John of the Cross

DAY 5

Holding the Darkness

When we try to live in solidarity with the pain of the world—and do not spend our lives running from necessary suffering—we will surely encounter various forms of "crucifixion." Many say pain is merely physical discomfort, but suffering comes from our resistance to, denial of, and our sense of injustice or wrongness about that pain. This is the core meaning of suffering, on one level or another, and we all learn it the hard way.

As others have said, pain is the rent we pay for being human, but suffering is, to some degree, optional. *The cross was Jesus' voluntary acceptance of undeserved suffering as an act of total solidarity with all the pain of the world.* Deep reflection on this mystery can change your whole life. It seems there is an inherent negative energy or resistance from all of us, whenever we are invited to a more generous response. Yet this is the necessary dying through which the soul must walk to go higher, further, deeper, or longer. The saints called these deaths "nights," darkness, unknowing, doubt. This is when you grow—but "in secret," which is an amazingly common word, in the teachings of both Jesus and many of the mystics.

Our secular world has almost no spiritual skills to deal with these "nights" now, so we resort to addictions and other distractions to get us through our pain and sufferings. This does not bode well for the future of humanity. Only truly inspired souls choose to fully jump on board this ship of life and death. The rest of us waste our time blaming or playing the victim to our own advantage.

Without the inner discipline of faith ("positive holding instead of projecting"), most lives end in negativity, blaming others, or deep cynicism—without being aware of it. Jesus hung in the crucified middle and paid the price for all such reconciliation (see Ephesians 2:13–18); he then invited us to do the same, and showed us the outcome—resurrection![6]

Gateway to Silence: O, night that joined Beloved with lover. —St. John of the Cross

DAY 6

A Bright Sadness

"Because I die by brightness and the Holy Spirit."
—Thomas Merton

There is a gravitas in the second half of life, held up by a much deeper lightness, or "okayness." Our mature years are characterized by a kind of bright sadness and a sober happiness, if that makes any sense. There is still darkness in the second half of life—in fact, maybe even more. But there is now a changed capacity to hold it creatively and with less anxiety. It is what St. John of the Cross called "luminous darkness," and it explains the simultaneous coexistence of deep suffering and intense joy that we see in the saints, which is almost impossible for most of us to imagine.

Life becomes much more spacious, the boundaries of the container having been enlarged by the constant addition of new experiences and relationships. You are like an expandable suitcase, and you became so almost without your noticing. Now you are just *here*, and here holds more than enough. Such "hereness," however, has its own heft, authority, and influence.

One's growing sense of infinity and spaciousness is no longer found just "out there" but, most especially, "in here." The inner and the outer have become one. You can trust your inner experience, because even God has allowed it, used it, received it, and refined it.[7] As St. Augustine dramatically wrote in his *Confessions*:

> You were within, but I was without. You were with me, but I was not with you. So you called, you shouted, you broke through my deafness, you flared, blazed, and banished my blindness, you lavished your fragrance, and I gasped.[8]

Gateway to Silence: O, night that joined Beloved with lover. —St. John of the Cross

DAY 7

Sabbath Meditation

Remember: **Luminous Darkness**

The goal of the dark night of the soul is to draw the self beyond ego into full transfiguration and union in God. (Day 1)

The gift of darkness draws you to know God's presence beyond what thought, imagination, or sensory feeling can comprehend. (Day 2)

"The only action left to the soul, ultimately, is to put down its self-importance and cultivate a simple loving attention toward the Beloved." —Mirabai Starr (Day 3)

God needs to catch us by surprise because our very limited preexisting notions keep us and our understanding of God small. (Day 4)

Without the inner discipline of faith ("positive holding instead of projecting"), most lives end in negativity, blaming others, or deep cynicism. (Day 5)

"You called, you shouted, you broke through my deafness, you flared, blazed, and banished my blindness, you lavished your fragrance, and I gasped." —St. Augustine (Day 6)

Rest: **Keep Praying**

I came out of seminary in 1970 thinking that my job was to have an answer for every question. What I've learned since then is that not-knowing and, often, not even needing to know is a deeper way of knowing and a deeper form of compassion. Maybe that is why Jesus praised faith even more than love; maybe that is why St. John of the Cross called faith "luminous darkness."

That's why all great traditions teach some form of contemplation, because it is actually a different form of knowledge that emerges inside of the "cloud of unknowing." It is a refusal to eat of the tree of the knowledge of good and evil; instead, you find freedom, grace, and comfort in not needing to know, which ironically opens us up to a much deeper consciousness that we would call the mind of God. That's because our small mind and lesser self are finally out of the way.

My contemplative sit every morning is an exercise in assured failure. It's often only in the last thirty seconds that I begin to get a glimpse of freedom but, for the most part, my prayer is a continual practice of surrender, *kenosis*. I often turn to the words, "Lord, have mercy; Christ, have mercy; Lord, have mercy." It is simply a confession of my incompetence and inadequacy. This confession leaves inside me an emptiness that becomes readiness. I realize I need help, I need more, I need love. I, in my I-ness, my Richard-ness, don't know how to do this by myself, and that's really okay. In fact, it is good because it realigns me with the truth of Divine Union.

The only people who pray well are those who keep praying. In the dark night, when all other practices and beliefs about God lose their meaning, keep returning to silent, contemplative prayer. It will keep you empty and ready for God's ongoing revelation of an ever-deeper love.[9]

Gateway to Silence: O, night that joined Beloved with lover. —St. John of the Cross

For further study:

Eager to Love: The Alternative Way of Francis of Assisi
Falling Upward: A Spirituality for the Two Halves of Life
Intimacy: The Divine Ambush
Things Hidden: Scripture as Spirituality

WEEK 44:

TRUST

DAY I
You Are Being Guided

The full life of faith becomes a life of deep joy and rest. Once you are "grafted to the Vine," to use Jesus' words (see John 15:4–5), you don't have to be anxious about many things (see Luke 10:40). You don't have to be worried about the next moment or about tomorrow (see Matthew 6:34). You can trust that you are being guided; in fact, almost everything is seen as guidance. Your ability to trust that there is guidance available allows it to *become* guidance! You realize that God is letting this happen to you now to teach you something, to show you something, or to love you in a new way. Basically you switch from the fixing, fully understanding, and controlling mode to the trusting, listening, and allowing mode. Then you start allowing the Divine Flow instead of stopping it with a "no" or a question mark.

The Spirit in you allows you to trust that there's a reason for everything: "God is even in this!" That does not mean you can't finally work to change things or to improve them; in fact, quite the contrary. But when your first heart and soul response is a "yes" and not a "no," then you can see God in the moment and see guidance in this event being given to you by the provident hand of God. You can trust that nothing is wasted. If there are changes and fixes that have to be made, you can now take care of them in an appropriate, calm, and positive way. That is what characterizes a mature believer in any religion.

Faith, as we see in the Hebrew Scriptures and Jesus' usage of the same, is much closer to our words "trust" or "confidence" than it is about *believing doctrines to be true* (which demands almost no ego-surrender or real change of the small self). We have wasted too many centuries now defending such an intellectual notion of biblical faith, whereas holding confidence that *God is good, God can be trusted, and God is actively involved in my life* is a much more powerful and effective practice. This is the practical power of biblical faith. Faith-filled people are, quite simply, usable for larger purposes because they live in and listen to a much Larger Self.[1]

Gateway to Silence: Lord, let your mercy be on us, as we place our trust in you.

DAY 2
All Shall Be Well

"All shall be well, all shall be well, and all manner of thing shall be well." It is amazing that Julian of Norwich could say such a thing after her visions of the crucified Christ. A God who could take the worst thing in the world (the killing of the God-Man) and turn it into the best thing (the redemption of the world) is surely a God we can trust to "work all things together for good" (see Romans 8:28). Only after a person has once seen the worst turn into the best does their understanding of spiritual reality begin to mature.

Paul speaks of "the folly of the cross" in several places. He seems to see that *the mystery of the cross allowed people to incorporate the tragic (the irrational, absurd, and sinful) and even use it for very good purposes.* In his thinking, only the Christ perspective can absorb and appreciate paradox—which is order within disorder, redemption through tragedy, resurrection through death, divinity through humanity. For Paul, therefore, *the cross and its transformative power* is his summary symbol for the depths of Divine Wisdom, which seems like mere "folly" to the "masters of every age" (see 1 Corinthians 2:6). The compassionate holding of essential meaninglessness or tragedy, as Jesus does in hanging on the cross, is the final and triumphant resolution of all the dualisms and dichotomies that we ourselves must face in our own lives. We are thus "saved by the cross"!

Christian conversion is not joining a different group, but seeing with the eyes of the crucified. The cross is Paul's philosopher's stone or "code breaker" for any lasting spiritual liberation. God can save sincere people of faith inside any system or religion, if only they can be patient, God-trusting, and compassionate in the presence of misery, failure, or imperfection—especially their own. This is life's essential journey. These trusting ones have surrendered to the Eternal Christ Mystery, very often without needing to use the exact word "Christ" at all (see Matthew 7:21). It is the doing, not the saying, that matters (see Matthew 21:28–32). God is not so insecure that you must pronounce the right name for God. After this many millennia, God must be used to responding to many, many names.[2]

Gateway to Silence: Lord, let your mercy be on us, as we place our trust in you.

DAY 3
Trust Your Own Experience

The most unfortunate thing about the concept of mysticism is that the word itself has become *mystified*—and relegated to a "misty" and distant realm that implies it is only available to a very few. For me, the word simply means *experiential knowledge of spiritual things*, as opposed to book knowledge, secondhand knowledge, or even church knowledge.

Most of organized religion, without meaning to, has actually discouraged us from taking the mystical path by telling us almost exclusively to trust outer authority, Scripture, Tradition, or various kinds of experts (what I call the "containers")—instead of telling us the value and importance of inner experience (which is the actual "content" the containers were made to hold). In fact, most of us were strongly warned against *ever* trusting ourselves. Roman Catholics were told to trust the church hierarchy first and last, while some mainline Protestants were often warned that inner experience was dangerous, unscriptural, or even unnecessary.

Both Catholic and Protestant prohibitions on trusting our inner authority were ways of discouraging actual experience of God, which often created passive (and passive-aggressive) people and, more sadly, a lot of people who concluded that there was no God to be experienced. We were taught to mistrust our own souls—and thus the Holy Spirit! Contrast that with Jesus' common phrase, "Go in peace, your faith has made you whole!" (For example, see Luke 8:48.) He said this to people who had made no dogmatic affirmations, did not think he was God, did not pass any moral checklist, and often did not belong to the "correct" group! *They were simply people who trustfully affirmed, with open hearts, the grace of their own hungry experience—in that moment—and that God could or would even care about them!*[3]

Gateway to Silence: Lord, let your mercy be on us, as we place our trust in you.

DAY 4
Trust Your Inner Authority

Paul trusts his experience of God and of Christ over his own upbringing, over the Twelve Apostles, over Peter, and over the Jewish Christians. Paul doesn't follow the expected sources of outer authority in his life, neither his own Jewish religion nor the new Christian leaders in Jerusalem. He dares to listen to—and trust—his own inner experience, which trumps both of them. It's amazing, really, that institutional religion makes him the hero that it does, and almost half of the New Testament is attributed to him, because in many ways he's a rebel. He's not, by any definition, a "company man"—anybody's company, in fact! In terms of human biographies, he is almost in a category all his own.

It is ironic that the ability to trust one's own experience to that degree has not been affirmed by the later church, even though both Jesus and Paul did exactly that. They trusted their experience of God in spite of the dominant tradition. And the church came along and domesticated both Jesus and Paul. We were never told to trust our own experience. In fact, we were probably told not to have any experience. It was considered unnecessary! (Yet the church still produced people like Augustine, Francis, Teresa of Ávila, Thérèse of Lisieux, and Teresa of Calcutta—who trusted their own soul experiences, against the prevailing attitudes.)

Once you know something, you can't deny that you know it. You don't need to dismiss outer authority—its intuitions are often correct—but you're not on bended knee before it either. The church's fear of inner authority has not served the Gospel well and has not served history well either. I am afraid this has to do with those in charge wanting to keep you codependent. I don't think Paul wants to keep you dependent upon him at all. He is the great apostle of freedom—a scary freedom with which much of Tradition, and most clergy, have not been comfortable at all (see Galatians 5:1–12, Romans 8:20–23).[4]

Gateway to Silence: Lord, let your mercy be on us, as we place our trust in you.

Peace of Mind?

To be trapped inside of your own small ego is always to be afraid, seeking some kind of control to settle the dust. To *not* have Someone that you can trust deeply is necessarily to become a control freak. Thus, great religion tries to free individuals from the tyranny of their small and fragile selves and introduce them to Someone-They-Can-Trust. Only if you trust such a Someone will you eventually know that you do not have to create all the patterns, nor do you have to solve all the problems. (You realize that your own seeing is invariably the problem.) You know you are, in fact, being guided.

Also, you do not have to explain the failures or take responsibility for fixing things. You know you are part of "the general dance," as Merton calls it. What else would be the beginnings of peace? As long as you think you've got to fix everything, control everything, explain everything, and understand everything, you will never be a peaceful person. Your fixation on your own ego keeps your mind preoccupied with endless rumination and commentaries, which are usually negative.

The Enneagram taught many of us that "fearful" people are actually "head people," which was a great surprise to most folks, as we would have located the fear in the gut. The common phrase "peace of mind" is a complete misnomer. *When you are in your mind, you are never at peace, and when you are at peace, you are never in your mind,* but in a much larger, unified field that includes body, mind, soul, and others, all at once! Some of the Christian denominations call it the "communion of saints."[5]

Gateway to Silence: Lord, let your mercy be on us, as we place our trust in you.

Don't Push the River

All of us are much larger than the good or bad stories we tell about ourselves: our hurts, our agendas. They're so small. They are not the whole you, not the Great You. They're not the Great River, nor are they where Life is really going to happen. No wonder the Spirit is described as "flowing water" and as "a spring inside you" (see John 4:10–14) or, as it states at the end of the Bible, as a "river of life" (see Revelation 22:1–2). Your life is not really about you; it is part of a much larger stream called God. The separate self is finally an illusion for those who stay on the journey of inner prayer.

I believe that faith might be the ability to trust the river, to trust the flow and the Lover. It is a process that we don't have to create, coerce, or improve. We simply need to allow it to flow. That takes immense confidence in God, especially when we're hurting. Usually, I can feel myself get panicky. I want to make things right, and right now! I lose my ability to be present, and I go up into my head and start obsessing. I try to push or even create the river—but the river is already flowing through me.

Faith does not need to push the river precisely because it is able to trust that *there is a river*. The river is flowing; we are in it. The river is God's providential love—so do not be afraid. We have been given the Spirit (see Luke 11:13). Without this awareness of the always-flowing river, without a sense that we are supported, we will all succumb to fear and control mechanisms. Why wouldn't we? To stay in God's holding means that I have to let go of myself, at least to some degree. I have to be able to hold a certain degree of uncertainty, ambiguity, and tension. Paradoxically, this leads to a much calmer and more content way of "being in control"! All the frenzy and fear disappear.[6]

Gateway to Silence: Lord, let your mercy be on us, as we place our trust in you.

DAY 7

Sabbath Meditation

Remember: **Trust**

Your ability to trust that there is guidance available allows it to *become* guidance. (Day 1)

A God who could take the worst thing in the world (the killing of the God-Man) and turn it into the best thing (the redemption of the world) is surely a God we can trust to "work all things together for good" (see Romans 8:28). (Day 2)

Jesus healed people who trustfully affirmed, with open hearts, the grace of their own hungry experience—and that God could or would even care about them. (Day 3)

Paul trusts his experience of God and of Christ over his own upbringing, over the Twelve Apostles, over Peter, and over the Jewish Christians. (Day 4)

The common phrase "peace of mind" is a complete misnomer. When you are in your mind, you are never at peace, and when you are at peace, you are never in your mind, but in a much larger, unified field. (Day 5)

The river is flowing; we are in it. The river is God's providential love—so do not be afraid. (Day 6)

Rest: **Be Well**

It's one thing to believe intellectually that your life is headed toward a hopeful end—which is really just a new form of more life—but until your heart and body trust Reality, no number of Scripture passages or my well-intended ramblings can assuage your anxiety. Chanting is a powerful contemplative practice that helps quiet the mind and allows truth to sink into deeper-than-rational consciousness. To experience this week's meditations more fully, I invite you to chant this affirmation from Julian of Norwich: "All shall be well, and all manner of thing shall be well."

You don't need any skill or experience to begin chanting. Chant is simply the combination of breath and tone, both of which you've been doing since you were born. You could chant on a single note or to a simple melody. As with any contemplative practice, begin by becoming aware of your desire to be open to God's presence and setting an intention. While you chant, if thoughts, emotions, or sensations arise, simply return your focus to the words and tune. Finally, when you return to silence, rest in God's love, trusting, as Julian came to do, that "all shall be well."

Gateway to Silence: Lord, let your mercy be on us, as we place our trust in you.

For further study:

Dancing Standing Still: Healing the World from a Place of Prayer
Eager to Love: The Alternative Way of Francis of Assisi
Everything Belongs: The Gift of Contemplative Prayer
St. Paul: The Misunderstood Mystic

WEEK 45:

RIPENING

DAY 1
A Clear Trajectory

Beginning with Jesus' four kinds of soil and receptivity (see Matthew 13:4–9), continuing to St. John of the Cross' "nights" and St. Teresa of Ávila's "mansions," through the modern schemas of Jean Piaget, James Fowler, Lawrence Kohlberg, Erik Erikson, Abraham Maslow, Carol Gilligan, and Bill Plotkin, we see there is a clear direction and staging to maturity and, therefore, to human life. We live inside of some kind of coherence and purpose, a believer might say.

Unless we can somehow chart this trajectory, we have no way to discern growth or maturity, and no ability to discern what might be a full, fuller, or fullest human response. Neither do we have any criteria for discerning an immature, regressive, or even sick response. Throughout this book of meditations, I have explored where this thing we call "life" is headed. Now, as we near the end of the book, I want to talk about ripening and eldership—which most often come near the end of life, but not always.

There must be a direction to ripening, but we must also recognize that *any steps toward maturity are by necessity immature*. Thank God, Pope Francis is introducing an old and commonsense word to Catholic moral thinking— "gradualism." An understanding of ripening basically teaches us the wisdom of timing, love, and patience, and allows us to be wise instead of judgmental. No one "gets it" one hundred percent right away; it is the work of a lifetime.

Why do we reject people because they are not totally there yet? I am not totally there yet myself.

Having said that, if I am to believe the novels, myths, poems, and people that I have studied in my life, old age is almost never described as an apex of achievement, hardly ever seen as sitting atop a summit with the raised arms of a victorious athlete. It is something else—usually something other than what was initially imagined, or even desired. Let's call it a slow ripening.[1]

Gateway to Silence: Ripen me into fullness.

DAY 2

You Are Being Led

"The life and death of a human being is so exquisitely calibrated as to automatically produce union with Spirit."

—Kathleen Dowling Singh

Ripening reveals much bigger or very different horizons than we realize. The refusal to ripen leads to what T. S. Eliot spoke of in "The Hollow Men": lives that "end not with a bang but a whimper."[2] I hope that you are one of those people who will move toward your own endless horizons and not waste time in whimpering. Why else would you even read this? Perhaps these meditations may help you trust that you are, in fact, being led. Life—your life, all life—is going somewhere, and somewhere good.

Ripening, at its best, is a slow, patient learning, and sometimes even a happy letting-go—a seeming emptying-out to create readiness for a new kind of fullness, about which we are never totally sure. If we do not allow our own ripening, and I do believe it is a somewhat-natural process, an ever-increasing resistance and denial sets in, an ever-increasing circling of the wagons around an over-defended self. At our very best, we learn how to hope as we ripen, to move outside and beyond self-created circles, which is something quite different from the hope of the young. Youthful hopes have concrete goals, whereas the hope of older years is usually aimless hope, hope without goals, even naked hope—perhaps real hope. Such stretching is the agony and the joy of our later years.

Old age, as such, is almost a complete changing of gears and engines from the first half of our lives and does not happen without slow realization, inner calming, inner resistance, denial, and eventual surrender, by God's grace, working with our ever-deepening sense of what we really desire and who we really are. This process seems to operate largely unconsciously, although we jolt into consciousness now and then, and the awareness that you have been led, usually despite yourself, is experienced as a deep gratitude that most would call happiness. Religious people might even call it mercy.[3]

Gateway to Silence: Ripen me into fullness.

DAY 3

The Shape of the Journey

The movement toward gratitude, authenticity, and union is the natural and organic inner work of the second half of our lives, especially if we are granted the full "seventy years, or eighty if we are strong" (see Psalm 90:10). Of course, for many, the whole process of ripening, and the deepening of desire, is cut short by tragic, untimely death. I have seen the entire process accelerate in some young people through an early, perhaps fatal, illness. If the dying process occurs consciously, it is an extremely accelerated ripening, as in a hothouse. Why would any of us ripen until it is demanded of us? For some, the demand comes early. Maybe God knows that most of us are slow learners and need more time to ripen.

Reality, fate, destiny, providence, and tragedy are slow but insistent teachers. The horizon of old age seems to be a plan that God has prepared as inevitable and part of the necessary school of life. What is gratuitously given is also gratuitously taken away, just as Job slowly came to accept. Remember that Job's final, pained response to this was, "Blessed be the name of the Lord!" (See Job 1:21.)

We all live in the same cycle of unrequested birth and unrequested death. Someone else is clearly in control, yet most of our lives are spent accepting and surrendering to this truth, trusting that this "Someone" is good, and trustworthy besides. It is the very shape and journey of faith.[4]

Gateway to Silence: Ripen me into fullness.

DAY 4

Floating in Love

If we are to speak of a *spirituality of ripening*, we need to recognize that it is always (and I do mean *always*) characterized by an increasing tolerance for ambiguity, a growing sense of subtlety, an ever-larger ability to include and allow, and a capacity to live with contradictions and even to love them! I cannot imagine any other way of coming to such broad horizons except through many trials, unsolvable paradoxes, and errors in trying to resolve them.

Without such a gradually renewed mind and heart, we almost certainly will end with a whimper—not just our own, but also the whimpering of those disappointed souls gathered around our sickbed or gravestone. Too many lives have indeed been lives of quiet desperation, and God must surely rush to console and comfort all humans before, during, and after their passing. Many put off enlightenment as long as they can—and some, it seems, until the last five minutes of life! Perhaps some never do reach enlightenment, which is why most religions have some metaphor similar to hell.

Maybe this whole phenomenon of late-stage growth is what Catholics actually mean by purgatory. Without such after-death hope, I would go crazy with sadness at all the lives which appear to end so *unripened*. The All-Merciful One is surely free to show mercy even after we die. Why would God be all-loving before death but not after death? Isn't it the same God? I've not seen anyone die perfectly "whole." We are all saved by mercy, "wound round and round," as Gerard Manley Hopkins said.[5] Some do appear to float into pure love in their very final days among us. Heaven is an endless continuum of growth and realization.[6]

Gateway to Silence: Ripen me into fullness.

DAY 5

Eldering

We live in a society with elderly people, but very few elders. That's not because they're bad people, but there haven't been guides to walk them from the first half to the second half of life, so most of them stay innocently in the first half. True second-half-of-life people are wonderful mirrors. They no longer need to be mirrored themselves, so they can do it for others (see 2 Corinthians 3:18). They are not crying, "Notice me! I'm important." Real elders are masters at granting their attention and awareness to other people. They are now the mirrors, and the truthful mirrors when hard truth needs to be told (see James 1:23–25), but also gentle mirrors that can affirm, praise, and not distort the moment, and enjoy it for exactly what it offers.

The great elders I've met in my life reveal both a brightness and a sadness at the same time. They're bright, they're here, they're clear, their eyes are open, they're present. They mirror you, rather than asking you to mirror them. It's like they're listening and seeing at a deeper level.

They usually don't talk much. They need very few words to make their point. Too many words (the use of which I am surely guilty) are not needed by true elders. The second simplicity toward which we are moving has its own kind of brightness and clarity, but much of it is expressed in nonverbal terms, and only when really needed. Elders just keep taking it all in, rather than giving a knee-jerk response, joke, or clever comeback intended to entertain or impress everybody.

Elders have a wider, long-distance lens. They are patient with first-half-of-life folks who are still ego-driven, because they know they were once there too. Healthy cultures have been guided by such wise seniors who naturally live a generative existence in service of the common good. They "live simply so others may simply live."[7]

Gateway to Silence: Ripen me into fullness.

DAY 6

Practicing the Ripening

A ripening mind and heart might simply be described as a capacity for non-dual consciousness and contemplation. Many might just call it growth in compassion, but surely no growth in compassion is likely unless one learns how to forgive as a very way of life, and to let go of almost everything as we first imagined it *had to be*. This is possible as we grow in the Jewish, Islamic, and Christian notion of faith, where not knowing (the *apophatic* way) must be carefully paired with knowing (the *kataphatic* way).

The Judeo-Christian Tradition balances our so-called knowing with trust, patience, allowing, waiting, humility, love, and forgiveness, which comprise very nearly the entire message, and surely the core message, necessary for any possibility of actual ripening. Otherwise, we all close down, and history freezes up with all of its hurts, memories, and resentments intact. A non-dual way of knowing in the moment gives us a *life process* and not simply momentary, dualistic answers, which always grow old because they are never totally true.

My guidance is a simple reminder of what we will be forced to learn by necessity and under pressure anyway—the *open-ended way of allowing* and the *deep meaning* that some of us call faith. To live in trustful faith is to ripen; it is almost that simple. We can all start practicing now, at any age, so we do not have to take a crash course in the final years, weeks, days, and minutes of our lives. The best ripening happens over time, lots of time.[8]

Gateway to Silence: Ripen me into fullness.

Sabbath Meditation

Remember: **Ripening**

An understanding of ripening basically teaches us the wisdom of timing, love, and patience, and allows us to be wise instead of judgmental. (Day 1)

The refusal to ripen leads to what T. S. Eliot spoke of in "The Hollow Men": lives that "end not with a bang but a whimper." (Day 2)

The movement toward gratitude, authenticity, and union is the natural and organic inner work of the second half of our lives. (Day 3)

If we are to speak of a *spirituality of ripening*, we need to recognize that it is always characterized by an increasing tolerance for ambiguity, a growing sense of subtlety, an ever-larger ability to include and allow, and a capacity to live with contradictions and even to love them! (Day 4)

Real elders are the truthful mirrors when hard truth needs to be told, but also gentle mirrors that can affirm, praise, and not distort the moment, and enjoy it for exactly what it offers. (Day 5)

A ripening mind and heart might simply be described as a capacity for non-dual consciousness and contemplation. (Day 6)

Rest: **Sitting in the Sun**

When James Finley was a young monk at the monastery of Gethsemane, he shared with Thomas Merton, his spiritual director, his frustration at his seemingly inept efforts to experience God's presence. Merton responded: "How does an apple ripen? It just sits in the sun."[9] Not that we don't need to continue to seek God, but by our own efforts alone we cannot achieve spiritual maturity. We must bring ourselves to the Light, where God's grace seasons us into juicy, sweet, flavorful ripeness.

During autumn, we in the northern hemisphere have fewer and fewer hours of daylight. We may have to seek out the sun's rays more intentionally. In moderation, sunlight strengthens the immune system, enhances emotional health, and synchronizes biorhythms. Find some time where you can simply bask in sunshine, exposing your skin and soul to the light freely given, only waiting to be received.

Gateway to Silence: Ripen me into fullness.

For further study:

Falling Upward: A Spirituality for the Two Halves of Life
Loving the Two Halves of Life: The Further Journey
"Ripening," *Oneing,* Vol. 1 No. 2

WEEK 46:

WHOLENESS

DAY 1

A Flicker of a Larger Flame

Holiness is revealed in our capacity for positive connection. The more we can connect, and the more we can connect with, the "holier" we are. God is precisely the One who connects all things, one to another. Before enlightenment, you rank things up or down; afterward you connect things horizontally—almost automatically!

Many have said that most of our problems today tend to be psychological, but the solution is always spiritual. Only healthy, great religion is prepared to realign, re-heal, and reconnect all things, and reposition us inside the whole universe of things. Thomas Merton said the True Self should not be thought of as anything different than life itself—not my little life, but the Big Life.

I'm not going to call the True Self just "life" or "being." More basically, I'm going to call it "love." We were made for love and love is who we are, as *I believe we are metaphysically created out of the infinite love relationships that are the Trinity* (see Genesis 1:26–27). There is increasing evidence that love is the very physical structure of the universe, as revealed in all things existing in orbital, contextual, magnetic, and sexual ways. The Song of Songs (see 8:6) says that love is as strong as death, and the flash of love is like a flash of fire, a flame of Yahweh. Everything can be seen as a little experience of the Big Flame. We are just a little tiny flicker of a much-larger flame that is Life itself, Consciousness itself, Being itself, Love itself, God's very self. Once we say it, it seems obvious. What else would it be?[1]

Gateway to Silence: Wholeness holds you.

DAY 2

Holons and Holiness

John Duns Scotus' philosophical concept of "the univocity of being" holds that our being is not just analogous to the being of trees, animals, and even God, but we may speak of our supposedly different beings with "one voice." Scotus was laying the philosophical foundation for what Michael Talbot (1953–1992) and Ken Wilber in our time are speaking of as a holographic universe, where everything is a holon, or a part of a larger whole. We know that the part invariably contains the whole or replicates the whole, and yet each part still has a wholeness within itself. This feels like an ultimate connectivity. Benoit Mandelbrot's (1924–2010) discovery of fractals has also revealed that repetitive and imitative patterns are found in all of nature, mathematics, and art.

We now believe such wholeness is true physically, biologically, and spiritually, and can even be seen as a basis for any understanding of mystical union. It implies that there is an inherent sympathy between God and all created things. Each of us replicates the Wholeness of God and has a certain wholeness within ourselves—but we are never entirely whole, apart from our connection with the larger Whole and the other parts.

Holons create a very fine language for what I call the mystery of participation, for understanding how holiness transmits and how God's life is an utterly shared phenomenon. *If you are "holy" alone, you are not holy at all.* Salvation is not a Divine transaction that takes place because you are morally perfect, but much more: It is an organic unfolding, a becoming who you already are, an inborn sympathy with and capacity for the very One who created you, and with everything else too. You can then recognize that same deep sympathy or resonance in all others—even in its rejected or denied forms (which is why you can still love and honor, for example, a drug addict or a murderer).[2]

Gateway to Silence: Wholeness holds you.

Reconnecting

On one level, soul, consciousness, love, and the Holy Spirit can all be thought of as one and the same. Each of these point to something that is larger than the self, shared with God, and even eternal. That's what Jesus means when he speaks of "giving" us the Spirit or *sharing his consciousness with us.* One whose soul is thus awakened actually has "the mind of Christ" (see 1 Corinthians 2:10–16). That does not mean the person is psychologically or morally perfect, but such a transformed person does see things in a much more expanded and compassionate way. Ephesians calls it "a spiritual revolution of the mind" (see 4:23)—and it is!

Jesus calls this implanted Spirit the "Advocate" (see John 14:16) who is "with you and in you" (see 14:17), makes you live with the same life that he lives (see 14:19), and unites you to everything else (see 14:18, 20). He goes on to say that this "spirit of truth" will "teach you everything" and "remind you of all things" (see 14:26) as if you already knew this somehow. Talk about being well-equipped from a Secret Inner Source. It really is too good to believe—so we didn't believe it!

Consciousness, the soul, love, the Holy Spirit, on both the individual and shared levels, has sadly become largely *unconscious*! No wonder some call the Holy Spirit the "missing person of the Blessed Trinity." No wonder we try to fill this *radical disconnectedness* through various addictions. There is much evidence that so-called "primitive" people were more in touch with this inner Spirit than many of us are. British philosopher and critic Owen Barfield (1898–1997) called it "original participation," and many ancient peoples seemed to have lived in daily connection with the soulful level of everything—trees, air, the elements, animals, the earth itself, along with the sun, the moon, and the stars. They were at home in this world, whereas many Christians have largely tried to deny or exit from it, leaving it in a disenchanted and unholy state.

Most of us no longer enjoy a sacred consciousness in our world, and Sunday services do not appear to overcome this. We really are disconnected from one another and the Divine, and are thereby unconscious. Religion's main and final goal is to reconnect us (*re-ligio*) to the Whole, to ourselves, and to one another—and thus heal us. When you just keep telling people how unworthy they are, it seems to become a self-fulfilling sermon.[3]

Gateway to Silence: Wholeness holds you.

DAY 4

Participating in Divinity

Creation itself is the Body of God, and the Christ is the mystery of matter and spirit operating as one. Well then, you ask, what makes the church special? What makes believers different?

In the first thousand years of the church's formation, a great deal of ink was spilled trying to unpack one verse in the first chapter of Genesis, where it states that we are "created in the image and likeness of God" (see 1:26). This was the consensus they came to: "Image" is the objective identification with God that is given to all of creation. Everything bears the Divine DNA. Therefore, everything is objectively the Body of God. Everything came forth from the Creator and reveals the Creator in some unique way.

"Likeness" is your *subjective* appropriation of this reality, your subjective actualization of God's image. Something can be absolutely true, but until you bring the unconscious truth into conscious choice and realization, it isn't true *for you*.

We are all equal on the first level, the level of image. On the second level, we are clearly at different levels of maturity—same image, but different *likeness*. Most of the church's work has been focused at the second level, trying to make people more like Christ. We got so preoccupied with growing in likeness that we underplayed or even denied the absolutely essential foundation of *image* or core identity. The Eastern Church held onto the objective image and taught this much better. But both Roman Catholics and Protestants are profoundly Western Christians, largely without honoring the other hemisphere of the church (nor does the East honor the West very much!). The point is that we both lost out on the full glory of the immense Christ Mystery.

One of my favorite Eastern Fathers, Symeon the New Theologian, said, "What I have seen is the totality recapitulated as One, received not in essence but by participation. It is just as if you lit a flame from a live flame: It is the entire flame you receive."[4] We're not saying "I am God." No one can, or wants to, live up to that! What we are saying is that we *participate,* really and objectively, in the Divinity. That's the whole point of religion: to let you know that what you're drawing upon is already planted within you! You don't manufacture it by good moral behavior or by going to church on Sunday. You do *awaken it,* however, by participating in a community of faith, eating the Eucharist, living in an entirely sacramental universe, and fully enjoying

God's image in nature, animals, and other human beings.[5]

Gateway to Silence: Wholeness holds you.

DAY 5

Being-in-God

The biblical revelation is about awakening, not accomplishing. *You cannot get there, you can only be there*, but the foundational Being-in-God, for some reason, is too hard to believe and too good to be true for most people. Only the humble usually believe it and receive it, because it affirms more about God than it does about us. Proud people are not attracted to such explanations.

St. Bonaventure tells us that "by God's power, presence, and essence, God exists uncircumscribed in all things."[6] In other words, it's all sacred. You can find God everywhere. You don't have to go to monasteries. As St. Francis of Assisi said, the whole world is our cloister.[7]

St. Bonaventure goes on to say, although this is my own paraphrase:

God is, therefore, all-inclusive. God is the essence of everything. God is most perfect and immense: within all things, but not enclosed; outside all things, but not excluded; above all things, but not aloof; below all things, but not debased. Finally, therefore, this God is all in all.... Consequently, from God, through God, and in God, all things exist.[8]

That is not simplistic pantheism (everything is God), but it is a much more profound pan-*en*-theism (everything is in God and God can be found in everything). This is Christianity's great message, which it has, in large part, found too good to be true and too hard to believe!

Our outer world and its full inner significance must come together for there to be any wholeness—and holiness—in our world. The result in the soul and in society is both deep joy and a resounding sense of coherent beauty.[9]

Gateway to Silence: Wholeness holds you.

DAY 6

Wholeness Holds You

Psychological wholeness and spiritual holiness never exclude the problem from the solution. Wholeness doesn't really overcome the problem, but holds it and transforms it as Jesus did on the cross. As Carl Jung said, most of the great problems of life are never resolved; they're just outgrown.

Wholeness holds you. You can't figure this out ahead of time or fully choose this wholeness; *you fall into it when you stop excluding.* And you are changed in the process. Everything belongs, even the "bad" and dark parts of yourself. Nothing needs to be rejected or denied. No one needs to be hated. No one needs to be excommunicated, shunned, or eliminated. You don't have time for that anymore. You've entered into the soul of the serene disciple where, because the Holy One has become one in you, you are able to see that oneness everywhere else—almost like magic![10]

In Thomas Merton's words, "A door opens in the center of our being, and we seem to fall through it into immense depths which, although they are infinite, are all accessible to us; all eternity seems to have become ours in this one placid and breathless contact."[11]

Gateway to Silence: Wholeness holds you.

DAY 7

Sabbath Meditation

Remember: **Wholeness**

We are just a little tiny flicker of a much-larger flame that is Life itself, Consciousness itself, Being itself, Love itself, God's very self. (Day 1)

Each of us replicates the Wholeness of God and has a certain wholeness within ourselves—but we are never entirely whole, apart from our connection with the larger Whole and the other parts. (Day 2)

Religion's main and final goal is to reconnect us (*re-ligio*) to the Whole, to ourselves, and to one another—and thus heal us. (Day 3)

Creation itself is the Body of God, and the Christ is the mystery of matter and spirit operating as one. (Day 4)

"By God's power, presence, and essence, God exists uncircumscribed in all things." —St. Bonaventure (Day 5)

Wholeness holds you. You fall into it when you stop excluding. And you are changed in the process. (Day 6)

Rest: **Making a Mandala**

Mandala, the Sanskrit word for circle, is a Hindu and Buddhist symbol for the universe. It represents the Whole of which we are a part. In Carl Jung's words, a mandala is "a safe refuge of inner reconciliation and wholeness."[12]

There are many ways to make your own mandala; the following is just one idea. Begin by gathering a large sheet of blank paper, extra paper, scissors, pencil, compass, coloring pencils, markers, paints, etc. Find a quiet place where you won't be disturbed.

You might start with silence or by journaling, setting an intention for this time and practice. Bring to heart and mind four areas in your life or the world for which you desire healing. Record them on a spare piece of paper using words, symbols, or colors.

Cut the large piece of paper into a square. Mark the center of the page with a small dot and use a compass to draw a circle a couple of inches from the edge of the paper (if you don't have a compass, trace a small plate or bowl). Within the circle, draw a square and divide it into four quadrants. In each section, draw an image or design that represents each desire. Beginning at the corners of the squares, create concentric circles with repeating shapes or curving lines. Work meditatively, gradually moving toward the edge of the circle and beyond. Add color if you wish, filling in the design methodically and slowly.

When you have finished creating your mandala, consecrate the time, energy, and focus you've given to the healing and "wholing" of self and world. Spend some time simply gazing with nonjudgmental eyes at the mandala and surrendering your desires and expectations.

Tibetan and Navajo rituals involve ceremonially destroying their intricate sand mandalas after completion. When your mandala has served its purpose, you might choose to intentionally burn, bury, or otherwise somehow let go of it.

Gateway to Silence: Wholeness holds you.

For further study:

Breathing Under Water: Spirituality and the Twelve Steps
Loving the Two Halves of Life: The Further Journey
Things Hidden: Scripture as Spirituality
True Self/False Self

WEEK 47:

ONEING

DAY I

Whole-Making

We don't know the real name of Julian of Norwich. She is simply named after the church in Norwich, England—St. Julian's—where she had her little residence. One window of her small room looked into the sanctuary for mass and another opened to the street, where the people would come by for her counsel and prayer. Julian experienced her "showings," as she called them, on the night of May 8, 1373, then she lived in the anchor-hold for another twenty years, trying to process and communicate what she had experienced on that one night. Julian wrote about these showings in her book *Revelations of Divine Love*, the first book published in English by a woman.

Julian experienced and wrote of a compassionate, relational, and joyful God. She writes:

For before God made us, God loved us; and when we were made, we loved God. And this is our substantial goodness, the substantial goodness in us of the Holy Spirit. It is nothing we create; it is our substance. God revealed to me that there may, and there will be, nothing at all between God and the soul. And in this endless love, the human soul is kept whole as all the matter of creation is kept whole.[1]

As I have mentioned before, Julian uses the Middle English word "oneing" to describe this whole-making work of God. God is always oneing everything: making twos and threes and fours, divisions and dichotomies and dualisms, into one. As she explains,

> God wants us to know that this beloved soul [that we are] was preciously knitted to him in its making, by a knot so subtle and so mighty that it is oned with God. In this oneing it is made endlessly holy. Furthermore, he wants us to know that all the souls which will be saved in heaven without end are knit in this knot, and united in this union, and made holy in this [one identical] holiness.[2]
> Gateway to Silence: We are one in God.

DAY 2
Interbeing

The Christian mystics always go to the Trinitarian level, because here God is a verb more than a noun. God is a flow more than a substance. God is an experience more than an old man sitting on a throne. And we are inside that flow. We are indeed products and images of God's outflowing. This is what all the language in John's Gospel means when Jesus says in several places, "I have come forth to take you back with me" (see John 14:3, also 17:24). We end where we began.

Julian of Norwich says, "Greatly ought we to rejoice that God dwells in our soul; and more greatly ought we to rejoice that our soul dwells in God. Our soul is created to be God's dwelling place, and the dwelling of our soul is God."[3] This we might now call *interbeing*, or *life as participation*. Julian continues: "It is a great understanding to see and know inwardly that God, who is our Creator, dwells in our soul...and our soul, which is uncreated, dwells in God in substance, of which substance, through God, we are what we are."[4] We share in the same substantial unity as God, she seems to say. This is not pantheism (I am God), but it is orthodox *panentheism* (God is in me and I am in God). We would call that ontological union or metaphysical union between two distinguishable beings, although God is not *a* being as much as *Being Itself*.

In the end, Julian is quite careful to preserve the mystery of twoness within the dance and flow of Divine Oneness. We cannot bear the impossible burden of being God, but we can and should enjoy the privilege and dignity of being with and in God. Here we accept being fully and freely accepted which, for some sad reason, is very hard for the ego to do.[5]

Gateway to Silence: We are one in God.

Reuniting Our Split Self

I mentioned earlier this year that there are four splits through which we humans go in the process of creating our mental ego, our False Self. We split our individual self from other selves, and over-identify with this separate self. We split life from death and try to avoid death. We split mind from body and soul, and we give mind pre-eminence. Finally, we split our acceptable self from our unacceptable self and identify with an idealized, acceptable self-image.

In the experience of suffering and death, those four splits are overcome, often in reverse order. It is probably another description of enlightenment. Many of us put this off until our deathbed. But the mystics overcome the splits early and are able to live as truly whole people (not necessarily always psychologically whole) ahead of time, and do not wait until their deathbed.

St. Francis of Assisi is a wonderful example of this realization.

Embracing the shadow: After his major conversion, in which he embraced a leper whom he had previously avoided as nauseating, St. Francis identified with the poor, the marginalized, and those on the bottom, which you normally cannot do until you embrace the wounded leper within yourself.

Putting the mind in its place: St. Francis was a bit of an anti-intellectual and in no way idealized the mind. He was all about *living* his faith, not conceptualizing it with words, and he did confess and repent near the end of his life that he had rejected "Brother Ass," his physical body.

Dying before you die: Rather than avoiding death, he dove into it when he chose poverty and powerlessness. St. Francis knew that life and death were not two, but one. You can't have one without the other. That's *the* mystery of Christian faith.

What you do to another, you do to yourself: St. Francis overcame the first split of self from non-self by truly following Jesus' commands to love his enemies and to love his neighbor. What you do to your neighbor, you do to Christ. And you must love your neighbor as you love yourself. In the end, it all becomes one, single love, and how you do anything is how you do everything.[6]

Gateway to Silence: We are one in God.

Unitive Consciousness: Beyond Gender

Julian of Norwich sometimes refers to God as Father and sometimes refers to Jesus as Mother. Gender means almost nothing to her because she is beyond that. There's something deeper than gender. As alluring and as important as gender is—it is our metaphor, held in our body—it is not our ontological identity. It is not our foundational, essential truth. Your gender is not the True Self; it's part of the False Self. That's what Jesus is referring to when he says, "In heaven, they neither marry nor are given in marriage" (see Mark 12:25). But, because gender is embedded so deeply in our early conditioning, many of us cling to it until the very end.

Male and female are most different at their most immature levels and most alike at their most mature levels. When you have matured to the point where you are beyond the dualisms that our dualistic minds have imposed on reality, then you know you are children of the resurrection. You are children of light and there is no male or female, as both Paul and the Gospel of Thomas say. People who already begin to experience such unity in this world will usually find it very easy to be compassionate toward lesbian, gay, and transgendered people, because they know that the True Self, who we objectively are in God, is prior and superior to any issues of gender, culture, or sexuality. Gender is important, but it is still an "accidental" part of the human person and not its substance.

The object and goal of all spirituality is finally the same for all genders: union, Divine Love, inner aliveness, soul abundance, forgiveness of offenses, and generous service to the neighbor and the world. Here "there is no distinction... between male and female" (see Galatians 3:28). Mature Christian spirituality leads us toward such universals and essentials, yet people invariably divide and argue about nonessentials!

Fortunately, Christ "holds all things in unity... the fullness is found in him, and all things are reconciled through him and for him, everything in heaven and on earth" (Colossians 1:17, 19–20)—including everything sexual that seems to always be un-whole or split in halves (*sectare* = to cut or divide).[7]

Gateway to Silence: We are one in God.

DAY 5

Surrendering to Union

We must fully recognize that mystics like SS. Francis and Clare were speaking from this place of conscious, chosen, and loving union with God, and such union was realized by *surrendering* to it and not by achieving it! Surrender to Another, participation with another, and Divine Union will be experienced as the same thing. Once we are in this union, we can look *out from* a much fuller Reality with eyes beyond and larger than our own. This is precisely what it means to "live in Christ" (*en Christo*), to pray "through Christ," or to do anything "in the name of God."

Such a letting go of our own small vantage point is the core of what we mean by conversion, but also what we mean by Franciscan "poverty." Poverty is not just a life of simplicity, humility, restraint, or even lack. Poverty is when we recognize that myself—*by itself*—is largely powerless and ineffective. John's Gospel puts it quite strongly when it says that a branch that does not abide in Jesus "is withered and useless" (see John 15:6). The transformed self, living in union, no longer lives in shame or denial of its weakness, but even rejoices because it does not need to pretend that it is any more than it actually is—which is now more than enough![8]

Cynthia Bourgeault, who masterfully teaches *kenosis* and "non-clinging," says, "There comes a point where each of us must step outside even those places of our most intense wounding and our most intense identification to just return to our virgin soul," which is to live in full contentment and peace in this place of non-self-definition or self-assertion. What freedom![9]

Gateway to Silence: We are one in God.

DAY 6

God Is in Our Deepest Self

Little by little, we overcome the splits from everything, so in the end there's just One. God is in all things and all things are in God. The goal of Christianity (and any mature religion) is for you to be able to experience your unity with yourself, with creation, with neighbor, with enemy, and with God in this world. God is never far away. God is not as transcendent as we first imagine. God is humble, with us, indwelling, on our side, and for us more than we are for ourselves. God is not found in distant glory, but in humility, where we are all living our oh-so-humble lives. This awareness totally repositions the spiritual journey. Now the goal is poverty, not affluence. Now the goal is God's full cosmos and not tribal churchiness. Now the goal is the bottom, not the top. We stop ranking vertically and we start connecting horizontally.

In the Incarnation, God "emptied Godself" (see Philippians 2:7), came to the bottom, and henceforth it was to be apparent that God is found at the bottom of things and on the hidden inside of things. Surprise of surprises— that is the last place most of us would look for God: inside of things and, even less, inside of ourselves! True Transcendence is no longer transcendent in the way we feared and suspected, but within! Dignity was inherent to creation from the beginning. That was supposed to be the "Eureka!" discovery of the Christian religion.

As James Finley puts it in his book *Merton's Palace of Nowhere*, "If we draw close to the roots of our existence, to the naked being of our self, we will find ourselves at that point where God and ourselves unite in ontological communion."[10] His famous novice master, Thomas Merton, called it *le point vierge* (the virginal point) where the soul is untouched and untouchable by anyone except the perfect love of God. Wow! That is enough to comfort and convert anyone.[11]

Gateway to Silence: We are one in God.

DAY 7

SABBATH MEDITATION

Remember: **Oneing**

God is always oneing everything: making twos and threes and fours, divisions and dichotomies and dualisms, into one. (Day 1)

God is a flow more than a substance. And we are inside that flow. (Day 2)

Mystics overcome the splits early and are able to live as truly whole people (not necessarily always psychologically whole) ahead of time, and do not wait until their deathbed. (Day 3)

The object and goal of all spirituality is finally the same for all genders: union, Divine Love, inner aliveness, soul abundance, forgiveness of offenses, and generous service to the neighbor and the world. (Day 4)

We must fully recognize that mystics like SS. Francis and Clare were speaking from this place of conscious, chosen, and loving union with God, and such union was realized by *surrendering* to it and not by achieving it! (Day 5)

The goal of Christianity (and any mature religion) is for you to be able to experience your unity with yourself, with creation, with neighbor, with enemy, and with God in this world. (Day 6)

Rest: **The Broken Truth**

A wonderful children's book, *Old Turtle and the Broken Truth*,[12] tells a story of how the world came to be so fragmented when it is meant to be whole and how we might put it back together again.

One night, in a far-away land that "is somehow not so far away," a truth falls from the stars. As it falls, it breaks into two pieces; one piece blazes off through the sky and the other falls straight to the ground. One day, a man stumbles upon the gravity-drawn truth and finds carved on it the words, "You are loved." It makes him feel good, so he keeps it and shares it with the people in his tribe. The thing sparkles and makes the people who have it feel warm and happy. It becomes their most prized possession, and they call it "The Truth." Those who have the truth grow afraid of those who don't have it, who are different. And those who don't have it covet it. Soon people are fighting wars over the small truth, trying to capture it for themselves.

A little girl who is troubled by the growing violence, greed, and destruction in her once-peaceful world goes on a journey—through the Mountains of Imagining, the River of Wondering Why, and the Forest of Finding Out—to speak with Old Turtle, the wise counselor. Old Turtle tells her that the Truth is broken and missing a piece, a piece that shot off in the night sky so long ago. Together they search for it and, when they find it, the little girl puts the jagged piece in her pocket and returns to her people. She tries to explain, but no one will listen or understand. Finally, a raven flies the broken truth to the top of a tower, where the other piece has been ensconced for safety, and the rejoined pieces shine their full message: "You are loved / and so are they." And the people begin to comprehend. And the earth begins to heal.

Gateway to Silence: We are one in God.

For further study:

God As Us! The Sacred Feminine and the Sacred Masculine
Eager to Love: The Alternative Way of Francis of Assisi
Intimacy: The Divine Ambush

LOVE

DAY I
Love Is What Is

The core belief of all the great world religions is that *the* underlying reality is love. Teilhard de Chardin says that "love is the very physical structure of the universe." Everything is desiring union with everything in one sense or another. I actually believe that *to know and trust God is to trust that Love is the source, heart, engine, and goal of life.* Our primal and deepest act of faith is our willingness to somehow say, "It's okay," because, at its core, all of reality is good and of God. (Ironically and sadly, many religious people say they love God but they do not trust the goodness at the heart of all reality, so their religiosity tends to be quite ineffective and unimpressive.)

The Christian belief in the Trinity makes it clear that God is an event of communion. God is not a noun nearly as much as a verb. We've traditionally thought of God as an autonomous Supreme Being, rather than as Being itself, as an energy that moves within itself ("Father"), beyond itself ("Christ"), and draws us into itself ("Holy Spirit"). When Christianity begins to take this pivotal and central doctrine of the Trinity with practical seriousness, it will be renewed on every level.

All of creation is a perfect giving and a perfect receiving between the Father and the Son and the Holy Spirit, with no withholding and no rejecting. St. Bonaventure called God "A Fountain Fullness." Once we begin with outpouring love as the foundational pattern of reality and love as the very shape of God, then everything somehow has to fall into that *same family resemblance*. If this is the Creator, then somehow this must be the DNA of all of the creatures.

We come from love and we will return to love. When we live in love, we will not be afraid to die. We have built a bridge between worlds. As Paul says, "Love does not come to an end" and "Love never fails" (see 1 Corinthians 13:8, 13).[1]

Gateway to Silence: Love is What Is.

DAY 2

The Meaning of Spiritual Love

When you regarded me
Your eyes imprinted your grace in me,
In this, you loved me again,
And thus my eyes merited
To also love what you see in me....
Let us go forth together to see ourselves in Your beauty.
　　　　　　　　　　　　　　　　—St. John of the Cross[2]

When we read poetry as beautiful and profound as these verses, we can see why St. John of the Cross was far ahead of his time in the spiritual and psychological understanding of how love works and how *true love changes us at a deep level*. He consistently speaks of Divine Love as the template and model for all human love, and human love as the necessary school and preparation for any transcendent encounter. If you have never experienced human love, it will be very hard for you to access God as Love. If you have never let God love you, you will not know how to love humanly in the deepest way. Of course, grace can overcome both of these limitations.

In the inspired passage above, St. John describes the very process of love at its best, and here is my paraphrased attempt to say the same:

You give a piece of yourself *to* the other.
You see a piece of yourself *in* the other (usually unconsciously).
This allows the other to do the same in return.
You do not need or demand anything back from them, because
you know you are both participating in a single Bigger Gazing
and Loving—one that fully satisfies and creates an immense Inner
Aliveness.

Simply to love is its own reward.
You accept being accepted—for no reason and by no criteria whatsoever!

This is the key that unlocks everything in you, for others, and toward God—so much so that we call it "salvation"![3]
Gateway to Silence: Love is What Is.

DAY 3

Love Is the Only Goal

Jesus said the whole law (and there were about 897 individual laws at that point) and the words of the prophets too, are summed up in the two great commandments: "to love God with your whole heart and your whole soul and to love your neighbor as you love yourself" (see Matthew 22:37–40). It's almost too simple, and yet, as you well know, it's almost too hard. It's sadly easier to simply obey laws and to live inside of an always-defeating reward/punishment system. Somehow a win/win worldview, where God wins and the soul wins too, is largely unbelievable...until you experience and allow God's grace.

True spiritual encounter changes you at a deep and unconscious level. Henceforth, the most important thing is to grow deeper and deeper in love. What spurs you on in that journey into love is actually the constant experience of your own lack of love: your impatience, irritation, or self-centeredness. Paul called these the "thorns in the flesh to keep me from becoming too proud" (see 2 Corinthians 12:7). You will have them until the end of your life. They allow you to love God and others by reason of a Larger Love flowing through you, not because "you" are doing it right or even know how to love!

St. Francis of Assisi granted all of reality, even elements and animals, an intimate I-Thou relationship. He called all things "sister" and "brother." This could be a definition of what it means to be a contemplative, which is to look at reality with much wider eyes than mere usability, functionality, or self-interest, but with *inherent enjoyment for a thing in itself, as itself.* Remember, as soon as your "love" needs or wants a reward in return, you have backed away from Divine Love, which is why even our common notion of a "reward in heaven" can keep us from the actual love of God or neighbor! A pure act of love is its own reward, and needs nothing in return. Love is shown precisely *in an eagerness to love.*

St. Francis moved beyond the world that most of us inhabit. He rebuilt the spiritual life on "love alone" and let go of the lower-level needs of social esteem, security, self-image, and manufacturing of persona. Remember, when your only goal is love, especially love of God, you really cannot fail.[4]

Gateway to Silence: Love is What Is.

DAY 4

You Are Love Becoming More Love

Your True Self is who you are, and always have been, in God; at its core, it is love itself. Love is both who you are and who you are still becoming, like a sunflower seed that becomes its own sunflower. Most of human history has called the True Self your "soul" or "your participation in the eternal life of God." The great surprise and irony is that "you," or who you think you are, has nothing to do with its original creation or its demise. It's sort of disempowering and utterly empowering at the same time! All you can do is nurture it, which is saying quite a lot. It is love becoming love in this unique form called "me."

It seems to be a fully cooperative effort, according to Paul (see Romans 8:28) and according to my own limited experience too. God never forces Godself on us or coerces us toward life or love by any threats whatsoever. God seduces us to respond with "yes"; God does not coerce us (see Jeremiah 20:7; Matthew 11:28–30). Whoever this God is, he or she is utterly free and utterly respects our own human freedom. Love cannot happen in any other way. Love flourishes inside freedom and then increases freedom even more. "For freedom Christ has set us free!" shouts Paul in his critique of all legalistic religion (see Galatians 5:1).

We are allowed to ride life and love's wonderful mystery for a few years—until life and love reveal themselves as the same thing, which is the final and full message of the risen Christ: life morphing into a love that is beyond space and time. He literally breathes *shalom* and forgiveness into the universal air (see John 20:22–23). You get to add your own finishing touches of love, your own life-breath to the Great Breath, and then return the completed package to its maker in a brand-new, but also the same, form. It is indeed the same "I," but now it is in willing union with the great "I AM" (see Exodus 3:14). We are no longer absolutely one, but we are not two either![5]

Gateway to Silence: Love is What Is.

DAY 5

You Are What You Are Seeking

I believe the meaning of the resurrection of Jesus is totally summed up in the climactic line from the Song of Songs (see 8:6) that I translate as *"love is stronger than death."* Love will win! Love is all that remains. Love and life are finally the same thing, and you know that for yourself once you have walked through any real death (there are many forms).

Love has you. Love *is* you. Love alone, and your deep need for love, recognizes Love itself. Remember that you already are what you are seeking. As Paul, the master teacher, says, any fear "that your lack of fidelity could cancel God's fidelity, is absurd" (see Romans 3:3–4).

Love has finally overcome fear, and your house is being rebuilt on a new and solid foundation. This foundation was always there, but it took us a long time to find it, for "It is love alone that lasts" (see 1 Corinthians 13:13). All you have loved in your life, and all that has loved you, is eternal and true, and is the very shape of whatever we mean by heaven. Two of the primary biblical images of final salvation are Noah's ark (see Genesis 6:19) and "the Peaceable Kingdom" (see Isaiah 11:6), and, interestingly enough, both are filled with images of *animals*—apparently also worth saving as givers and receivers of love. How stingy we are to think that an infinite love would or could be limited to humans.[6]

Gateway to Silence: Love is What Is.

DAY 6

Love Everything

To be fully conscious would be *to love everything* on some level and in some way—even our mistakes. To love is to fall into full consciousness, which is contemplative, non-dualistic, and includes everything—even "the last enemy to be destroyed, which is death itself" (see 1 Corinthians 15:26). That is why we must, absolutely must, *love!* And why we must not be afraid of death.

Didn't Jesus tell us that we must love even our enemies? When we can, on some level, even love our sins and imperfections, which are our "enemies," we are fully conscious and fully liberated. God, who is Universal Consciousness itself, knows all things, absorbs all things, and forgives all things—for being what they are. *If Jesus commands us to love our enemies, then we know that God must and will do the same.* What hope and joy that gives us all! It takes away all fear of admitting our mistakes, and allows us to forgive our primary enemy, which is often our self.[7]

Let's end this wonderful week with one of my favorite quotes from the Catholic Bible (Wisdom 11:24–12:1):

> Yes, you love all that exists, you hold nothing of what you have made in abhorrence, for had you hated anything, you would not have formed it. And how, had you not willed it, would a thing persist in being? How could it be conserved if not called forth by you? You spare all things, because all things are yours, Lord, lover of life, you whose imperishable spirit is in all.

Gateway to Silence: Love is What Is.

DAY 7

Sabbath Meditation

Remember: **Love**

The core belief of all the great world religions is that *the* underlying reality of everything is love. (Day 1)

Love does not need or demand anything back, because you know you are participating in a single Bigger Gazing and Loving—one that fully satisfies and creates an immense Inner Aliveness. (Day 2)

When your only goal is love, especially love of God, you really cannot fail. (Day 3)

Love is both who you are and who you are still becoming, like a sunflower seed that becomes its own sunflower. (Day 4)

Love has you. Love *is* you. You already are what you are seeking. (Day 5)

To be fully conscious would be to love everything on some level and in some way—even our mistakes. (Day 6)

Rest: **Welling Up**

Jesus said, "Love your neighbor *as* you love yourself," not "*as much as* you love yourself." We are to love our neighbor *in the same way* we love ourselves. "We love because God has first loved us" (see 1 John 4:19). When we accept the unconditional love and undeserved mercy that God offers us—knowing that we are not worthy of it—then we can allow God to love others through us in the same way. It's God in you loving you, warts and all, and God in you loving others as they are. This is why the love you have available to give away is limitless. As Jesus told the Samaritan woman, "The water that I shall give you will turn into a spring inside of you, welling up into limitless life" (see John 4:14).

The following exercise is based on a teaching from Francisco de Osuna, OFM (1492–1542), whose book *The Third Spiritual Alphabet* deeply inspired St. Teresa of Ávila. Here is what he taught his students:

1. Dam up the fountain of your soul, where love is always springing forth.
2. It will be forced to rise.
3. Yet it will remain quiet and at rest within you; wait for that quiet.
4. You will see the image of God reflected in your own clear waters, more resplendent than in any other thing—provided the disturbing turmoil of thoughts dies down.

What follows is a commentary and aid on that teaching, so that you can experience it for yourself. It is really quite similar to what the Hindus discovered in *tantra*, where you hold the powerful gift so that it can be deepened and refined before being expressed.

Try to stay *beneath* your thoughts, neither fighting them nor thinking them. Hold yourself at a deeper level, perhaps in your chest, solar plexus, or breath; stay in your *body self* somehow, and do not rise to the mind. Resist any desire to repress or express, just allow animal contentment. It will feel like "nothing" or darkness. Stay "crouched" there at the cellular level without shame, long enough for Another Source to begin to flow and *well up* as light or sight or joy.

This is the "super-essential life." From this place you *become seeing,* and the love flows through you from the Source, as an energy more than as an idea. You cannot "think" God. God is never an object of consciousness like any other thing, person, or event that you know. God is always and forever the subject, the doer, the initiator, the Prevenient Grace. *You have then become what you hope to see.* Subject and object are one. God in you and through you sees and loves God—in yourself and in others too.[8]

Gateway to Silence: Love is What Is.

For further study:

The Art of Letting Go: Living the Wisdom of Saint Francis
Breathing Under Water: Spirituality and the Twelve Steps
Eager to Love: The Alternative Way of Francis of Assisi
Emotional Sobriety: Rewiring Our Programs for "Happiness"
Gate of the Temple: Spirituality and Sexuality

WEEK 49:

DEATH AND HEAVEN

DAY 1

Love Never Fails

In last week's meditations, I wrote:

Love is where we came from, and love is where we are going. When we live in love, we will not be afraid to die. We have built a bridge between worlds. As Paul says, "Love does not come to an end" and "Love never fails" (see 1 Corinthians 13:8, 13).

I am saying it again because it's so important.

You must die into your one-and-only Life, the Life that you must learn to love. It will show itself to be one continuous movement, first learning to love your life and then allowing yourself to fully *die into it*—and never to die away from it.

Once you practice such dying, you find that on the other side is a new empowerment, a new freedom, a new greatness, a new identity in God. Then you are not so afraid of the final handing-over; you can see death as the final gift: "God, I give myself to you one more time. *You are not taking away my life. I am giving you mine.*"

Once death is joyfully incorporated into life, you are already in heaven, and there is no possibility or fear of hell. That is the Franciscan way. *The Gospel is not a fire insurance policy for the next world, but a life assurance policy for this world.* SS. Francis and Clare and many of the mystics somehow came to see through the common disguises of heaven and hell. My hope and desire is that you can know heaven too, and *now!*[1]

Gateway to Silence: Falling forever into the deathless depths of God

Eternity Is the Shape of Everything

Scientists tell us that everything was created in the Big Bang. There are the same number of atoms now as there were then. Nothing has died. Everything has simply existed through fourteen billion years of change—changing forms, but not substance. The risen Jesus reveals a different form, but is still Jesus, the Christ. Nothing goes away. When you die, you don't leave. There is no place to which you go; this is it! You leave the encapsulation of this finite body, which you and I take far too seriously because it's the only one we have known.

Julian of Norwich writes: "In this endless love, we are led and protected by God and we never shall be lost for God wants us to know that the soul is a life which life is joined to God's goodness and grace and will last in heaven without end."[2] We are treasured and hidden in God, without end, despite our sinfulness. Julian is all cosmic optimism and hope, precisely because of her firm belief and personal experience of the cosmic meaning of Jesus' resurrection.

If Jesus is the map for the entire human journey, then Julian sees in the suffering, death, resurrection, and ascension of Christ the map and trajectory for all of creation. Paul taught that the final chapter of history will be resurrection (see 1 Corinthians 15), but we made it into a worthiness contest at which very few seem to win the prize. Fortunately, we still say in the Eucharistic Preface of the funeral liturgy, "Life is not ended. It is merely changed." Eternity seems to be the shape of everything.

Christianity should have been the most optimistic religion of all. What a shame that we denied such hope and vision to so many centuries of Christians and chose to live in fear instead. The true Gospel has always been too good to be believed and trusted, and so we decided not to believe or trust! All we know for sure is that God is not stingy, as all of creation proudly proclaims.[3]

Gateway to Silence: Falling forever into the deathless depths of God

WEEK 49: DEATH AND HEAVEN   371

Do Not Be Afraid

Kathleen Dowling Singh, an inspired author and hospice worker (I think *The Grace in Dying* is a must-read), says that many times those who, in the last hours of life, fight death the most are very religious people. Fear of God and fear of death are the same thing. When it's all a matter of counting, earning, meriting, and achieving by various performance principles, you're afraid of death and also afraid of God. Why wouldn't you be? Until we clear away the idea of hell, the universe is not benevolent, but hostile and dangerous, where an angry god does not follow his own commandment about love of enemies.

In his book, *Inventing Hell*, Jon Sweeney blames the modern Christian view of hell on Dante. The imagery that has influenced the Western psyche for eight hundred years is not the imagery of the Bible, but of Dante's *Divine Comedy*. It's great Italian poetry, but not always excellent theology. It portrays a threatening God, not an inviting, alluring, or revealing God. We've been preconditioned by an unbiblical storyline. The word "hell" is not mentioned in the Pentateuch or any of the Hebrew Scriptures (Sheol, Hades, and Gehenna are all quite different notions). Paul and John never once use the word "hell." It is not a part of their theology.

This has created a schizophrenic religion in which we have two different gods—one before we die, and another one after we die. The god before we die tells us to love our neighbor as our self, but apparently God doesn't. Jesus teaches us to forgive seventy-times-seven times (see Matthew 18:22), but apparently God has a cut-off point. This is theologically unworkable and untenable.

You can't be more loving than God; it's not possible! If you understand God as Trinity—the fountain full of outflowing love, relationship itself—there is no possibility of any hatred in God. Finally, God—who is Love—wins. And we're all saved by mercy. Knowing this ahead of time gives us courage, so we don't need to live out of fear, but from love. *To the degree you have experienced intimacy with God, you won't be afraid of death because you're experiencing the first tastes and promises of heaven in this world.*[4]

Gateway to Silence: Falling forever into the deathless depths of God

Day 4

Practicing Heaven Now

Hope, it seems to me, is the fruit of a learned capacity to suffer wisely and generously. The ego needs success to thrive; the soul needs only meaning. The Gospel gives our suffering personal and cosmic meaning by connecting our pain to the pain of others and, finally, by connecting us to the very pain of God. Any form of contemplation is a gradual sinking into this Divine fullness. This is precisely to live in a *unified field* which produces in people a deep, irrational, and yet calmly certain hope.

People of deep prayer are doing themselves a great favor, or, as Jesus says, they get a hundred times more already in this life, which then bubbles forth later into a limitless life (see Mark 10:30). If we have life now, we will have it then. Why would God not give Divine Union to us later, while giving it so freely, gratuitously, and undeservedly now? Why would God change the general policy? A life of inner union, a contemplative life, is simply practicing for heaven now. God allows us to bring "on earth what is in heaven" (see Matthew 6:10) every time we allow, receive, and forgive the conflicts of the moment and sit in peace and freedom. God holds together all the seeming opposites and contradictions within us.

Authentic mystical experience connects us, and just keeps connecting at ever-newer levels, breadths, and depths, "until God can be all in all" (see 1 Corinthians 15:28). Or, as Paul also writes, earlier in the same letter, "The world, life and death, the present, and the future are all your servants, for you belong to Christ and Christ belongs to God" (see 1 Corinthians 3:22–23). Full salvation is finally universal belonging and universal connecting. The biblical word for that was "heaven," and some notion of it is found in all religions.[5]

Gateway to Silence: Falling forever into the deathless depths of God

DAY 5

Falling Forever

James Finley writes in "Ripening," an issue of CAC's journal, *Oneing*:

The lifelong process of ripening brings about a corresponding ripening of our ability to understand the fundamentals in a wiser, peace-giving manner. For example, when people who believe in God go through painful experiences, they are naturally troubled. They often feel, "If God watches over me, how could God let this happen to me?" This is such an understandable response to suffering in the life of those who trust and believe in God's providential care. However, as a person ripens in unsayable intimacies in God, they ripen in a paradoxical wisdom. They come to understand God as a presence that protects us from nothing, even as God unexplainably sustains us in all things. This is the mystery of the cross that reveals whatever it means that God watches over us; it does not mean that God prevents the tragic thing, the cruel thing, the unfair thing, from happening. Rather, it means that God is intimately hidden as a kind of profound, tender sweetness that flows and carries us along in the intimate depths of the tragic thing itself—and will continue to do so in every moment of our lives, up to and through death, and beyond....

St. John of the Cross talks about a windfall of delight. When fruit becomes very ripe, the slightest wind can cause it to fall to the ground. The windfall of delight first pertains to those little promises along the way, but also to our last breath, which we know and trust will send us falling forever into the deathless depths of God.[6]

Gateway to Silence: Falling forever into the deathless depths of God

DAY 6

The Eternal Home of Love

We are saved by simply remaining in the one circle of life and love, and not by standing separate or superior. *This is the One Great Love that will lead and carry you across when you die.* If you are already at home with Love here, you will quite readily move into the eternal home of Love, which most of us call heaven.

Death is not a changing of worlds, as most imagine, as much as it is *the walls of this world infinitely expanding.* If you get love here, you have found the eternal home base, and you will easily and naturally live forever. Life is never about being correct, but only and always about being connected. *Just stay connected!* At all costs, stay connected. Our only holiness comes through participation and surrender to the Body of Love, and not through any private performance. This is the joining of hands from generation to generation that can still change the world—and will, *because Love is One, and this Love is either shared and passed on or it is not the Great Love at all.*

The One Love is always *eager*, and, in fact, such eagerness is precisely the giveaway that we are dealing with something Divine and eternal. In this eternal home of love, the growth never stops and the wonder never ceases. (If life is always change and growth, eternal life must be infinite possibility and growth!) So, by all means, every day, and in every way, we must *choose* to live in love—it is mostly a decision—and even *be eager to learn the ever-deeper ways of love*, which is the unearned grace that follows from the decision![7]

Gateway to Silence: Falling forever into the deathless depths of God

DAY 7

Sabbath Meditation

Remember: **Death and Heaven**

You must die into your one-and-only Life, the Life that you must learn to love. It will show itself to be one continuous movement, first learning to love your life and then allowing yourself to fully *die into it*—and never to die away from it. (Day 1)

If Jesus is the map for the entire human journey, then we see in the suffering, death, resurrection, and ascension of Christ the map and trajectory for all of creation. (Day 2)

To the degree you have experienced intimacy with God, you won't be afraid of death because you're experiencing the first tastes and promises of heaven in this world. (Day 3)

Full salvation is finally universal belonging and universal connecting. The biblical word for that was "heaven." (Day 4)

"The windfall of delight...pertains...to our last breath, which we know and trust will send us falling forever into the deathless depths of God." —James Finley (Day 5)

Death is not a changing of worlds, as most imagine, as much as it is *the walls of this world infinitely expanding.* (Day 6)

Rest: **Practicing Dying**

Elizabeth Lesser, author and co-founder of Omega Institute, offers ways of practicing death:

+ **Become an "I don't know it all."**
  Whenever you find yourself getting anxious about the big and small deaths of daily life—being out of control, not getting what you want,

endings and partings—take a few minutes to allow in the possibility that you do not see the full picture. Often what looks terrible today will, in retrospect, have been a blessing. Just allow that possibility in. You do not have to understand or figure everything out. You can relax into the mystery of not knowing.

+ **Disengage from the ego.**
Develop a simple meditation practice. Every day, spend some time sitting in silence.... Sit with a straight back and relaxed body. Feel the nobility, patience, and strength of the posture. Allow your identification to broaden out beyond the ego with its constant thoughts and its shifting likes and dislikes. Just observe everything.... This is the practice of meditation.

+ **Take birth and death back from the experts.**
Because we are more frightened of what is not known to us, it makes sense to become familiar with the two bookends of life: birth and death. If you can, be at the births and deaths of family members and friends; sit with sick people; help others who are suffering. Do not shy away from what makes you uncomfortable. Learn about death— study its biological and spiritual stages.[8]

Gateway to Silence: Falling forever into the deathless depths of God

For further study:

Dancing Standing Still: Healing the World from a Place of Prayer
Eager to Love: The Alternative Way of Francis of Assisi
Intimacy: The Divine Ambush
A New Way of Seeing, A New Way of Being: Jesus and Paul
"Ripening," Oneing, Vol. 1 No. 2

WEEK 50:

PRESENCE

DAY 1

The Duty of the Present Moment

A book that for many years has been voted a must-read by spiritual directors is Jean-Pierre de Caussade's *Abandonment to Divine Providence*. De Caussade (1675–1751) was a French Jesuit. I'd like to share some of my favorite quotes from this book.

"Every moment we live through is like an ambassador that declares the will of God to us."[1] There is no more infallible way to seek the will of God than, moment by moment, to see that what this moment offers me *is* the grace of God. If we did nothing more than that, de Caussade says, we would attain the highest levels of transformation. Everything in life is to be welcomed as somehow the expression of the will of God. Your reaction to whatever happens has to be "as if" it were the will of God, or you can't respond to it graciously. De Caussade writes, "We must accept what we very often cannot avoid, and endure with love and resignation things which could cause us weariness and disgust. This is what it means to be holy."[2] I think all of us shrink from his challenge because we know we can't do it on our own. We only succeed by God's grace, now and then.

De Caussade says true mystics "seek reality; we seek the ephemeral. They want God as God is; we want God as we imagine or would like God to be."[3] The greatest ally of God is *what is*. God can always work with what is. That is why there can be no real obstacle to union with God except our own resistance. God can and will use everything, absolutely everything, even the worst things—which is the meaning of Jesus' crucifixion and resurrection.

De Caussade continues, "We can find all that is necessary in the present moment."[4] Perhaps a summary sentence in his teaching is this: "If we have abandoned ourselves to God, there is only one rule for us: the duty of the present moment."[5] "What does this moment ask of me?" is always the right question.[6]

Gateway to Silence: What this moment offers is the grace of God.

DAY 2

Right Here, Right Now

St. Augustine said, "And thus the end will be the one Christ, loving himself."[7] This means that the whole of Creation is the Christ Mystery. The Eternal One has come forth and has taken on form and manifestation: us; the whole planet; the animals, plants, and elements; the galaxies; and all the endless forms and faces that have come forth from God. Our job as conscious humans is to bring the beauty and goodness of *everything* to full consciousness, to full delight, to full awareness. When you understand that, you can understand what Paul means when he says that, in the end, "God will be all in all" (see 1 Corinthians 15:28), which is surely where St. Augustine got the courage to say the same.

When Paul says to "pray always" (see 1 Thessalonians 5:17), he can't mean to walk around saying the Our Father and Hail Mary all day, or even chanting psalms, although those might be good ways to start. Prayer is basically a total-life stance. It is way of being present in the world in which we are present to the Presence and present to the Presence in all things.

Being fully present to the moment and to God would be total conversion, but we're all still learners on that path. I hope we've learned how to appreciate at least one or two moments, how to rest and abide in one or two special moments, and to learn to say, "This is good. This is enough. In fact, this is everything." Once you recognize that it's all right here, right now, then you'll carry that awareness everywhere else. How you do anything is how you do everything. This is what Julian of Norwich meant when she looked at one little hazelnut in the palm of her hand and said, "This is everything that is."[8]

Once we can learn to be present to the Presence, the things that used to bother us don't bother us quite as much. The things that used to defeat us no longer defeat us. The things to which we thought we could never surrender, we now can. Even to accept that we are not ready to accept something is still a form of this utterly grounding and accepting Presence.[9]

Gateway to Silence: What this moment offers is the grace of God.

The Always-Coming Christ

Jesus said to his disciples, "Be awake. Be alert. You do not know when the time will come. It is like a man travelling abroad. He leaves home and places his servants in charge, each with his own work. And he orders the gatekeeper to be on watch. So I tell you, watch. You do not know when the Lord of the house is coming, whether in the evening, or at midnight, or at cock crow, or in the morning. May he not come suddenly and find you asleep. What I say to you, I say to all: stay awake." (See Mark 13:33–37)

Sadly, we're almost programmed (perhaps by childhood conditioning) to hear the Gospel in a threatening or punitive way, as if Jesus is saying, "You'd better do it right, or I'm going to get you." With that outlook, we are likely to largely miss the point in this—and many other—passages. This is the bad fruit of using religion and Scripture to threaten people into love, which is actually a total impossibility. Most people who start with fear stay with fear and never get to the higher motivations.

Let's try to hear it in a much more exciting and positive way. Jesus is not talking about the second coming of Christ. He's not talking about your death, either. What he's talking about here is the *forever* coming of Christ, the *always* coming of Christ, the *eternal* coming of Christ…*now*…and *now*…and *now*. In the passage from Mark above, Jesus says this clearly: "in the evening, at midnight, at cock crow, [and] in the morning."

You see, Christ is *always* coming; God is *always* present. *It's we who aren't!* We're always somewhere else—at least, I often am. Jesus tells us to be conscious, to be awake, to be alert, to be alive. It's the key to all spirituality, because that is the one thing we aren't. Be honest; most of us live on cruise control. We just go through the motions of our daily routines. We wake up and we repeat what we did the day before, and we're upset if there are any interruptions.

But, in fact, when God has the best chance of getting at us is in the gaps, in the discontinuities, in the exceptions, in the surprises. This is what it means to be awake: to be constantly willing to say that God could even be coming to me in anything and everything! I have begun a new verbal practice. I say "Just this!" even amidst the things I don't want, I don't expect,

379

and sometimes don't like—in the evening, at midnight, at cock crow, or in the morning.[10]

Gateway to Silence: What this moment offers is *the grace of God.*

DAY 4

The Eternal Now

Thomas Merton entered the monastery in Kentucky when he was twenty-seven years old, on December 10, 1942. He was accidentally electrocuted in Bangkok exactly twenty-seven years later, on December 10, 1968, at the age of fifty-four; a perfect two halves of life. Perhaps more than any other single person, Merton reacquainted Christianity with its contemplative roots. He pulled back the veil. His writings inspired many, including myself, to return to *le point vierge*, "the virgin point," instead of trying to make ourselves "virginal" by any purity code whatsoever. *The virgin point is the soul, the True Self, the "delightful windfall" into the eternal now.*

If you watch your mind, you will see you live most of your life in the past or in the future—against both of which Jesus warns us. That's just the way the mind works. If you are to experience the ever-present and ever-coming Christ, the one place you have to be is the one place you are usually not: *now here* or "nowhere." Everything that happens to you happens right now; if you can't be present right now, nothing new is ever going to happen to you. You will not experience your experiences; they will not go to any depth in your soul. You really won't grow unless you're willing to be present, to live right here, right now.

How are you present? Jesus describes it rather profoundly: "You must love the Lord your God with your whole heart, with your whole soul, with your whole mind, and with your whole strength" (see Luke 10:27). Whenever all of these parts are working together at the same time, you are present. He finishes by saying, "Do this and life is yours!" (See 10:28.) I like to say that prayer happens whenever *all* of you is present—body, mind, soul, spirit, emotions—all together. That's hard work. This is the core and constant meaning of all spiritual practice, no matter what religion: *how to be here now!* Then you will know what you need to know to go forward.

Usually we have to be shocked into it, I'm sorry to say. Great love does it. When you are deeply in love—with anything—you tend to be present to the now. Someone has said, "To be a saint is to have loved many things"—*many things*—the tree, the dog, the sky, the flowers, even the color of someone's clothing. You see, when you love, *you love,* and love extends to everything, all the time and everywhere. When you love, you're much more likely to be present.

Another time when all of you is present is when you suffer or when someone dies. For some reason, all the forms of death pull us into the now. In the presence of dying, for some reason, we discover our deepest life. Someone said there are only two themes in all of literature: love and death. I can understand why.[11]

Gateway to Silence: What this moment offers is the grace of God.

DAY 5

God Is Here and Thus Everywhere

The last words Jesus spoke to his apostles in the Garden of Gethsemane were "Stay awake." In fact, he says it twice (see Matthew 26:38–41). I believe the work of religion is, more than anything else, to keep you awake, alert, alive, conscious. Consciousness comes from a wholehearted surrender to the moment. If you're conscious, you *will* experience God. I can't prove God to you, but people who are present will experience the Presence. It's largely a matter of letting go of our resistance to what the moment offers us.

To *be here now* is the simplest thing in the world and the hardest thing to teach. In many ways, it is the very foundation of all religion and all spirituality. You cannot get there by any kind of worthiness contest whatsoever. You cannot *get there;* you can only *be there.* I am convinced that the purest form of spirituality is the ability to accept the "sacrament of the present moment" (as Jean-Pierre de Caussade called it) and to find God in what is right in front of me. At that level, there is almost nothing about which to argue. In fact, argumentative religion proceeds from *not* being present.

It seems we all start out thinking of God as "out there." Yet we also need to believe, even spatially, that God is "in here." We must *know* that deeply before we can take the now seriously. The reason we can trust the now so much is because of the Incarnation and because of the Divine Indwelling of the Holy Spirit. Christians have been given the promise that the Word has become flesh, that God has entered into *human nature itself* (as the early Eastern Fathers dared to put it), and that the human soul is the temple of God. This is Paul's discovery too (see 1 Corinthians 3:16–17), and it is repeated through various metaphors by every Christian mystic, yet it was seldom taught in the local Christian church. This is the heart of our problem.[12]

Gateway to Silence: What this moment offers is the grace of God.

DAY 6

Love Is the Presence of the Sacred

You've all met, I hope, at least one or two older people who are still working to improve the world. They continue to do their little piece, and they don't get cynical and discouraged when they don't see immediate results. Often they do not even use God talk! Yet, if that's not the Presence of God, I don't know what the Presence of God might be. It's a hope from nowhere. It's a love beyond me. It's a faith *in* me from Someone Else. Someone is believing in me and through me and for me and with me and often, it seems, in spite of me. Such people are rather indestructible. They are the hope of the world, often much more so than ostensibly religious people.[13]

As Kathleen Dowling Singh puts it,

Relying upon only our senses and conceptual mind, we have cre-ated an experience of existence marked by separation: separation from others, from our own essential nature, and from the Sacred.... Love [is] the very presence of the Sacred.... We spend much of our lives ignorant of the love in which we live and move and have our being.... We do not, in our ordinary, everyday minds, recognize love as our ever-present ground, our hallowed Reality. It is only through the eye of contemplation that we can realize and come to know our essential nature and the essential, holy nature of all things.... With that revelation of Presence, we surrender what was always only an illusory ego and, no longer obstructed, enter the open arms of formless awareness.

We come, gradually, with love's intention, to see that this form, this self we mistook for the final statement on our being, is here as function. Once we change the nature of our relationship with each moment to that of an awakened stance, formlessness can function through form and spirit can shine through our transformed, utterly unique self.[14]

Gateway to Silence: What this moment offers is *the grace of God.*

Sabbath Meditation

Remember: **Presence**

A summary sentence in Jean-Pierre de Caussade's teaching is this: "If we have abandoned ourselves to God, there is only one rule for us: the duty of the present moment." (Day 1)

To "pray always" is a stance, a way of being present in the world in which we are present to the Presence and present to the Presence in all things. (Day 2)

This is what it means to be awake: to be constantly willing to say that God could even be coming to me in anything and everything! "Just this!" (Day 3)

If you are to experience the ever-present and ever-coming Christ, the one place you have to be is the one place you are usually not: *now here* or "nowhere." (Day 4)

I am convinced that the purest form of spirituality is the ability to accept the "sacrament of the present moment" and to find God in what is right in front of me. (Day 5)

"Once we change the nature of our relationship with each moment to that of an awakened stance, formlessness can function through form and spirit can shine through our transformed, utterly unique self." —Kathleen Dowling Singh (Day 6)

Rest: **If You Want**

Read aloud the following (an interpretation by Daniel Ladinsky of a poem by St. John of the Cross) slowly, meditatively, resting in the awareness of Presence within your own soul's womb.

If
you want
the Virgin will come walking down the road
pregnant with the holy
and say,

"I need shelter for the night, please take me inside your heart,
my time is so close."

Then, under the roof of your soul, you will witness the sublime
intimacy, the divine, the Christ
taking birth
forever,

as she grasps your hand for help, for each of us
is the midwife of God, each of us.

Yes there, under the dome of your being does creation
come into existence externally, through your womb, dear pilgrim—
the sacred womb of your soul,

as God grasps our arms for help; for each of us is
His beloved servant
never
far.

If you want, the Virgin will come walking
down the street pregnant
with Light and
sing. . . .[15]

Gateway to Silence: What this moment offers is the grace of God.

For further study:

Collection of Homilies 2008
The Enneagram: The Discernment of Spirits
Living the Eternal Now

WEEK 51:

I AM WHO I AM

DAY 1

The Spiritual Journey in a Nutshell

Throughout this year of Daily Meditations, we have basically been following the stages of spiritual development. We begin with the original blessing of being created in the image and likeness of God (see Genesis 1:26), who is Love (see 1 John 4:8). But early in life, we seem to forget our origin and who we really are. We leave our original innocence and the proverbial Garden to begin the task of the first half of life, which involves building a container, a necessary but still False Self, and an independent ego.

Dualistic thinking dominates after childhood, especially in the Western world, as education emphasizes the left side of the brain, competition, and success. Boundaries, group-think, and exclusion thrive. The shadow self hides whatever is considered unacceptable. Even our True Self becomes hidden beneath the False Self we have constructed to meet our needs for security, control, and esteem. The goal is personal individuation, and the emphasis is on the individual and his or her positive self-image. This is fine, as far as it goes, which is not very far, I am afraid; but it is all that a secular culture knows.

God's goal is always union. And the great surprise, which should also be hopeful, is that "God comes disguised as our life," as Paula D'Arcy so cleverly proclaimed the first time we taught together. Life lived fully and honestly inevitably involves both joy and suffering, a path of descent, doubt, lots of little deaths that teach us to let go of our artificially created self and to live in the simple joy of Divine Union—and *voila*, the True Self stands revealed—present and accounted for! Our carefully constructed ego container must gradually crack open, as we realize that we are not separate from God, from others, or from our true selves. Now the ego is seen for the partial, but limiting, gift that it always is. It slowly learns to become the servant of the soul, and is even willing to "die" for the sake of the Spirit. Our big mistake is that we let the servant become the master.

We now know that God is in us and we are in God. Through grace, necessary suffering, and experiencing our experiences in depth, our consciousness is gradually transformed. We overcome the splits created in the first half of life. Now we are capable of non-dual thinking and we can forgive and accept our imperfections and those of others. We no longer have anything to prove or protect, so we can let go and surrender to Reality/God, which are now experienced as the same thing. As St. Francis said, "What a person is in God's eyes, that he is and nothing more."[1]

We may appear foolish, or even naïve, to those at earlier levels of development, but we are finally free and alive, living in quiet union with God, which is all of reality. This is often called a second *naïveté*, our return to an almost-childlike simplicity and serenity. It is where you should naturally find yourself if you have stayed on the full journey. You don't have to try to be anything because you have become one with everything.

Gateway to Silence: I am who I am in the eyes of God, nothing more and nothing less.

DAY 2

Finding Your Soul

In the final stage of life, what I call the "I Am Who I Am" goal, you know your body is not you by itself; you have found your soul and have been contacted by Spirit. You do not need to protect your external self, roles, money, or status symbols. You do not need to promote them or prove them to anyone. You can even let go of your image of being superior in any way: a holy person, more moral than others, smarter, or more advanced or enlightened in any sense. You know that whatever has happened to you is all God's work and you have merely been the lucky recipient. You did not do it; it was done to you.

You do not waste time admiring yourself; it takes most of your time to admire the God who has done this *to* you and *for* you and *as* you—and for no good reason! God creates exquisite wildflowers in hidden valleys that no human eye will ever see—just for the inherent joy and beauty of it! Goodness is always diffuse, always outpouring, by its very nature. In fact, that is what makes goodness so beautiful.

At this later and more mature stage, it's enough to be simply human. I can now let God take care of whatever it means to be spiritual, because I am not even sure what "spiritual" means anymore. Everything seems to be both material and spiritual at the same time. Finally I have met my worst enemy, and that enemy is me—not the other, whose very enmity has often turned out to be friendship and intimacy at the soul level. By now, I have faced much of my shadow and found out that God loves me best in and through my mistakes, so I do not need to posture any more.

St. Francis said he wore a patched robe because he wanted to appear to others exactly as he was on the inside—wounded and weak—as we all are, if we are honest. He had faced his broken self, and it was precisely there that he met the most unconditional of loves. God uses everything, you see, even and especially our mistakes. There is a wonderful quote, often attributed to St. Augustine but much more expected from SS. Francis or Thérèse of Lisieux, which says: "In my deepest wound I found you, Lord, and it dazzled me." I have this quote hanging in my hermitage; it somehow expresses the deepest counter-intuitive wisdom of the Gospels.

At this point, you are not tied to believing that your religion is the only one that gets people to God. You can see God in all things, everywhere, and easily in people outside your own religion. Others did not change, your doctrines did not change, but you did! You have met the Formless One, so the forms of religion are not so important now. Still, you do not throw out any of the previous stages; you now know that people need to go through all of them. You do not waste time opposing the rituals, the doctrines, the hierarchies, the scriptures, or the belief systems that got you on this path—but now you know they are all just fingers pointing to the moon; they are not the moon itself. This is total non-dual thinking, a different mind and a different experience. This is the mind of the mystic.[2]

Gateway to Silence: I am who I am in the eyes of God, nothing more and nothing less.

Becoming Like Children

Some years ago, I visited an old Franciscan who lived in Gallup, New Mexico. He spent most of his life working with the native people, and he loved them deeply. When I knew him, he was probably in his late eighties. He was bent over and he would walk the streets of downtown Gallup in his Franciscan robe and sandals, carrying a cane. He would lift his bent head and greet everybody with the greeting of St. Francis: "Good morning, good people!" Our job is to remind people of their inherent goodness, and this is what this dear man did.

On his cane he had strung a string of battery-powered, blinking Christmas lights. Now, to anyone who was a tourist in town, they must think him quite the old fool—bent over, in a brown robe and sandals, with blinking Christmas lights on his cane—especially when it was not even Christmas time!

One day I asked him, "Father, why do you put those blinking Christmas lights on your cane?"

He cocked his head toward me, looked up grinning, and said, "Richard, it makes for good conversation. See, you are talking to me now. Everybody asks about them, and I am able to talk to everybody because of my Christmas lights."

Now, was he a fool in most people's eyes? Was he a naïve innocent? Yes, I guess he was, but he also touched many lives. The Holy Fool is the final stage of the full human journey. Maybe this is what Jesus meant when he said, "It is those who become like little children who will enter the Kingdom of God" (see Matthew 18:3). Jesus, in his frequent allusions to children, was in his own way describing this final stage of life. We return to that early childhood, as it were, running naked and exposed into the great room of life and death. "I am who I am who I am" now. God has accepted me in my most naked being, and I can now give it all back to God, exactly as it is, with conscious, loving trust that it will be received, just as a parent loves the scribblings of a six-year-old and places them on the refrigerator door. What else could God want or be?[3]

Gateway to Silence: I am who I am in the eyes of God, nothing more and nothing less.

Holy Fools

St. Francis illustrates the Holy Fool stage in many memorable ways. When he hears one day that the people of Assisi are calling him a saint, he invites Br. Juniper to join him in a walk through his old hometown. Br. Juniper was the first simpleton (that is a compliment!), the Holy Fool of the original friars. St. Francis knew he could always trust him to understand what he was saying. St. Francis once said, "I wish I had a whole forest of such Junipers!"

St. Francis told Br. Juniper, "Let's take off these robes, get down to our underwear, and just walk back and forth through Assisi. Then all these people who are thinking we are saints will know who we really are!" Now that's a true saint: someone who doesn't need to be considered a saint at all.

A few years later, when people were again calling St. Francis a saint, he said, "Juniper, we've got to do it again." This time they carried a plank into the piazza. They put it over some kind of a stone, or maybe the fountain, and there they seesawed all day. They had no need to promote or protect any reputation or positive self-image whatsoever.

The spiritual tradition of the Holy Fool was a constant in the Eastern Church and in the Desert Fathers and Mothers, but it pretty much got lost after the thirteenth-century Franciscans. We became more and more serious about our role in others' salvation, or, you might say, we took *ourselves* far too seriously. Moralism replaced mysticism, and this only increased after the in-house fighting of the sixteenth-century reformations. We all needed to prove we were right. Have you noticed that people who need to prove they are right cannot laugh or smile?

When you are a Holy Fool, you've stopped trying to look like something more than you really are. That's when you know, as you eventually have to know, that we are all naked underneath our clothes, and we don't need to pretend to be better than we are. "I am who I am, who I am, who I am," and that unique creation, for some unbelievable reason, is who God loves, precisely in its uniqueness. My true identity and my deepest freedom come from God's infinite love for me. If we seek a "horizontal" source of identity, we will be constantly insecure (see John 5:44). Both the people who praise me and those who hate me are usually doing it for the wrong reasons anyway.[4]

Gateway to Silence: I am who I am in the eyes of God, nothing more and nothing less.

Incarnation

Jesus said, "You must lose yourself to find yourself" (see Matthew 16:25). For some sad reason, most people have presumed that the self that had to die, the self we had to lose, was the physical self, when actually Jesus meant the ego self, the separate self, the self created by our own mind and adventures. This is what passes away, and it is very fragile and fractured for most of our lives.

There seems to be some deep bias against embodiment, materiality, and physicality. That is where we harbor our inferiority feelings. You'd think, if there would be any religion in the world that would *not* think that way, it would be Christianity, because Christianity is the only religion that believes that God became a body, became a human being: Jesus. That's why we get so excited about Christmas! We call it the Feast of the Incarnation or "enfleshment." But I find most mainstream Christians to be quite "excarnational," moving opposite to the path of Jesus and trying to be "spiritual," whatever that means.

The eternal Christ Mystery began with the Big Bang, where God decided to materialize as the universe. Henceforth, the material and the spiritual have always coexisted, just as Genesis 1:1–2 seems to be saying. Although this Christ existed long before Jesus, and is coterminous with creation itself, Christians seem to think Christ is Jesus' last name.

What Jesus allows us to imagine—because we see it in him—is that the Divine and the human are forever one. God did not just take on one human nature, although that is where we could first risk imagining it: in the body of Jesus. *God took on all human nature, as both genus and species—and said "yes" to it forever! In varying degrees and with infinite qualities, God took on everything physical, material, and natural as Godself. That is the full meaning of the Incarnation.* To allow such a momentous truth, to fully believe it, to enjoy it in practical ways, to suffer it with and for others—this is what it means to be a Christian! Nothing less will do now. Nothing less will save the world.

For most Christians, though, Jesus is totally Divine, but not totally human. We deny his humanity and overly assert his divinity—instead of the very synthesis that he came to exemplify, announce, and share! We've paid a big price for such dualistic thinking because, when we can't put it together in him, we can't put it together in ourselves either. And that's the whole point! *You and I are simultaneously children of heaven and children of earth, Divine and human, coexisting in a well-hidden disguise.* We are a living paradox, just as Jesus was.

We also are a seeming contradiction that is not a contradiction at all. Most Christians were simply never told the truly good news that flesh and spirit, Divine and human, coexist. That was not made clear in Jesus and surely not in ourselves. The consequences have been disastrous at all levels. Matter always reveals Spirit, and Spirit lies hidden in all that is physical, material, earthly, human, flawed, and failing. *Everything is a sacrament!* Nothing else could be called utter and final good news except this message. It is indeed a benevolent universe.[5]

Gateway to Silence: I am who I am in the eyes of God, nothing more and nothing less.

DAY 6

Surrendering to the Great I AM

The first definition or name that God gives of God's self in the Bible is "I am who am" (see Exodus 3:14). There it is: "I am existence itself. I am pure being. I am the deepest selfhood of all that exists." I'm convinced that, when we can surrender to the Great I AM, the Great Universal Being, the great shared consciousness that we all are, God gives us courage to accept our own *I am,* in all of its eccentricity and in all of its brokenness. Your participation in the Universal Being or *I am-ness* of God gives you the courage to hand back to God the only life you'll ever have. That will be the most humbling and the most courageous act of faith you'll ever live, because what you hand back will always seem so tawdry and insignificant. But it isn't; it is precisely the handing back that makes it momentous.

I'm just this little Richard creature, this little moment of time that's going to be gone in a few years. I'm so aware of what I'm *not,* of how phony I am, and of how I say it so much better than I live it. I have a thousand reasons to reject myself and hate myself, and you do too. It's really not enjoyable to grow in self-knowledge, because the more you know about yourself, the more you are *not* impressed! But, as long as you're being held and received by the Great I AM, all shame and unworthiness is taken away. We realize that this little *I am* that I am is what God has always loved anyway, even with all of its imperfections and silliness.

We participate in a universal, cosmic forgiveness for being who we are and for all of reality being what it is: so utterly ordinary and so chosen as beloved! "How can this be?" the ego shouts! That's the entrance into what the Buddhists call the Great Compassion. Once you find this compassion toward your own little *I am,* tiny and broken and poor as it is, then you're able to share compassion with everyone and everything. The important thing is the *willingness to give back the gift that is you, not the perfection of the gift itself.* Can you feel the difference?[6]

Gateway to Silence: *I am who I am in the eyes of God, nothing more and nothing less.*

DAY 7

Sabbath Meditation

Remember: **I Am Who I Am**

We no longer have anything to prove or protect, so we can let go and surrender to Reality/God, which are now experienced as the same thing. (Day 1)

St. Francis faced his broken self, and it was precisely there that he met the most unconditional of loves. (Day 2)

God has accepted me in my most naked being, and I can now give it all back to God, exactly as it is, with conscious, loving trust that it will be received. (Day 3)

My true identity and my deepest freedom come from God's infinite love for me. (Day 4)

God took on all human nature, as both genus and species—and said "yes" to it forever! In varying degrees and with infinite qualities, God took on everything physical, material, and natural as Godself. That is the full meaning of the Incarnation. (Day 5)

Once you find this compassion toward your own little *I am,* tiny and broken and poor as it is, then you're able to share compassion with everyone and everything. (Day 6)

Rest: **Training for the "Third Eye"**

The lamp of the body is the eye. (See Matthew 6:22.)

The ego self is the unobserved self. If you do not find an objective standing point from which to look back at yourself, you will almost always be egocentric—identified with yourself instead of in relationship with yourself. Ego is not bad; it is just what takes over when you do not see truthfully and completely.

Much of the early work of contemplation is discovering a way to observe yourself from a distance and learning how to return there in moments of emotional turmoil (positive as much as negative), until you can eventually live more and more of your life from this awareness. You will find yourself smiling, sighing, and "weeping" at yourself, more than either hating or congratulating yourself (both of which are ego needs).

This knowing of self must be compassionate and calmly objective. It names the moment for what it is, without need to praise or blame your reaction to it. This takes away your reaction's addictive and self-serving character so that it no longer possesses you. Now you have a feeling instead of a feeling having you. It gives you a strong sense of "I," because there is now no need to eliminate or deny the negative. (Your full self is accepted.) Ironically, the truly destructive part of the negative is exposed and falls away now as unnecessary. To see the negative is to defeat it, for evil relies upon denial and disguise.

The Christian name for this Stable Witness is the Holy Spirit. You only need to connect with the deepest level of desiring where "the Spirit bears common witness with our spirit that we are indeed children of God" (see Romans 8:16). It is a common knowing, a participative event, and it feels like you are being "known through" with total acceptance and forgiveness. This will change your life! You will then "know as fully as you are known" (see 1 Corinthians 13:12).[7]

Gateway to Silence: I am who I am in the eyes of God, nothing more and nothing less.

For further study:

The Art of Letting Go: Living the Wisdom of Saint Francis
Francis: Turning the World on Its Head: Subverting the Honor/Shame System
Immortal Diamond: The Search for Our True Self
In the Footsteps of Francis: Awakening to Creation
The Naked Now: Learning to See as the Mystics See
True Self/False Self

WEEK 52:

SILENCE

DAY I

Silence as the Foundation of Reality

People who are interested in issues of peace and justice surely recognize how communication, vocabulary, and conversation have reached a very low point in our society, both in our politics and in our churches. It feels like the only way through this is a re-appreciation for this wonderful, but seemingly harmless, thing called *silence*.

Blaise Pascal, the French philosopher and mystic, is supposed to have said centuries ago that our unhappiness springs from one thing alone: our incapacity to sit quietly. (If you think this is an exaggeration, a study[1] at the University of Virginia said that 67 percent of men and 25 percent of women would sooner endure an unpleasant electric shock rather than be alone in silence for even 15 minutes!) Perhaps you see why I have given so much time and energy to male initiation rites and retreats in general. Very few, including priests and bishops, know how to be silent, even during a retreat.

Silence is not just something that wraps around words and underneath images and events. It has a life of its own. It's a phenomenon with an almost-physical identity. It is almost like a being in itself, to which you can relate. Philosophically, we would say *being* is that foundational quality which precedes all other attributes. When you relate to the naked being of a thing, you learn to know it at its core. Silence is at the very foundation of all reality. It is that out of which all being comes and to which all things return. (If the word "silence" does not grab you, you can interchange it with nothingness, emptiness, vastness, formlessness, open space, or any undefined reality.)

All things are in fact a *creatio ex nihilo* (Latin for "creation from nothing"); every something, by God's plan, it seems, first comes from nothing! If you can first rest in the nothing, you will then be prepared for the something. When nothing creates something, we call that *grace*!

Such silence is described in the first two verses of Genesis. The first reality is described in the Bible as a "formless void," and the Spirit is expectantly "hovering" over this "trackless waste and emptiness" (*tohu bohu* in the Hebrew of Genesis 1:2), *as if to impregnate creation with God, a silent mystery I would call the original birth of "Christ"!* The Spirit is silent, secret, invisible, but totally powerful and always effective, humble, and quite willing to give the credit to others for all the further millennia of unfolding (that is, to evolution). The coming together of these Two Great Silences—the silence of matter and the silence of the Spirit—is the primal conception and the beginning of everything![2]

Gateway to Silence: Just be.

DAY 2

Finding God in the Depths of Silence

Silence precedes, undergirds, and grounds everything else. Unless we learn how to live there, go there, and abide in this different phenomenon, everything—words, events, relationships, identities—becomes rather superficial, without depth or context. We are left to search for meaning in a life of events and situations that need to contain ever-greater stimulation, more excitement, and more color, in an attempt to add vital signs to our inherently bored and boring existence.

This need for stimulation is the character of America and most Western countries. We are in danger of becoming just a shell, with less and less inside, and less contact with the depth and reality of things—where all the lasting vitality is found. This is what Jesus calls "a spring inside us—welling up unto eternal life" (see John 4:14). God is always found at the depths of things, even the depths of our sin and brokenness. And in the depths, it is always silent. Thinking, and especially dualistic thinking, is useless to unpack the moment and take us into this deeper reality.

As I said previously, it seems we, as a culture, are deeply afraid of silence. The running from silence is undoubtedly running from God, from our soul, from our selves, from the truth, and from freedom. One of the beginnings of freedom is to stop thinking and "just look" (*contemplata* in Latin), or just be. That's when God can meet us exactly where we are, in this embodied spirit that we are.

Give yourself permission to get out of your head, to let go of your explanations and certitudes that too often make us believe we don't need personal listening, waiting, seeking, and praying! My single biggest disappointment in serving as a priest for over forty years is the lack of spiritual curiosity among the vast majority of Catholics. (I can only pick on them, as those are the ones I've served!) They too often settle for glib answers that make silent awe and pregnant questioning unnecessary—which is the very birth of the authentic religious spirit. This means we meet things "surface to surface" instead of "center to center."

In silence and solitude, we can finally get our selves (our feelings, our needs, our compulsions, our reactions) out of the way and return to "the face we had before we were born," as the Zen masters put it. Maybe that face sees things most clearly? Who am I before I was a priest or a teacher, a male or an American, or whatever I am? And before that, and before that? That free and deeply desirous position of nothingness, nakedness, and emptiness is where God can most powerfully meet us and teach us.[3]

Gateway to Silence: Just be.

DAY 3
Silence as an Alternative Consciousness

For me, the two correctives of all spirituality are silence and service. If either of those is missing, it is not true, healthy spirituality for the long run. Without silence, we do not really experience our experiences. We may serve others and have many experiences, but without silence, nothing has the power to change us, to awaken us, to give us that joy "that the world cannot give," as Jesus says (see John 14:27). And without clear acts of voluntary service (needing no payback of any sort, even "heaven"), a person's spiritual authenticity can and should be called into question. Divine Love *always* needs to, and must, overflow! What you do for free is who you are. What you do beyond your occupation—how you pay your bills—is probably your true vocation and calling.

To live in this primordial, foundational being itself, which I am calling silence, creates a kind of sympathetic resonance with what is right in front of us. Without it, we just react instead of respond. Without some degree of silence, we are never living, never tasting, as there is not much capacity to enjoy, appreciate, or taste the moment as it purely is. *The opposite of contemplation is not action, it is reaction.* We must wait for pure action, which always proceeds from a contemplative silence, in which we are able to listen anew to truth and to what is really happening. Such spiritual silence demands a deep presence to oneself in the moment, which will probably have the same practical effect as being present to God.

You do not hear silence (precisely!), but *it is that by which you do hear.* You cannot capture silence; it captures you. Silence is a kind of thinking that is not thinking. It's a kind of thinking which mostly *sees (contemplata).* Silence, then, is an alternative consciousness. It is a form of intelligence, a form of knowing beyond bodily reaction or emotion. It is a form of knowing beyond mental analysis, which is what we usually call thinking. All of the great world religions at the higher (mystical) levels discovered that our tyrannical mode of everyday thinking (which is largely compulsive, brain-driven, and based on early patterning and conditioning) has to be relativized and limited, or it takes over, to the loss of our primal being and identity, in God and in ourselves. I used to think that mysticism was the eventual fruit of years of contemplation; now I think it all begins with one clear moment of pure and uncluttered consciousness, which then becomes a constant "spring inside us, welling up unto infinite life" (see John 4:14).[4]

Gateway to Silence: Just be.

DAY 4

Is It an Uprush or a Downrush?

My best writings and teachings have not come from thinking but, as Malcolm Gladwell writes in *Blink,* much more from *not* thinking. Only then does an idea clarify and deepen for me. Yes, I need to think and study beforehand, and afterward try to formulate my thoughts. But my best teachings by far have come in and through moments of interior silence—and in the "non-thinking" that underlies a sermon, or interaction, or a moment of counsel.

For me, Aldous Huxley described it perfectly in a lecture he gave in 1955, titled "Who Are We?" He said, "I think we have to prepare the mind in one way or another to accept the great uprush or downrush, whichever you like to call it, of *the greater non-self.*"[5] That precise language might be off-putting to some, but it is a quite-accurate way to describe the very common experience of inspiration and guidance.

All grace comes precisely from nowhere—from silence and emptiness, if you prefer—which is what makes it grace. It is both you and yet so much greater than you, at the same time, which is probably why believers chose both uprushing water (see John 7:38) and downrushing doves (see Matthew 3:16) as metaphors for this universal and grounding experience of spiritual encounter. Sometimes it is an uprush and sometimes it is a downrush, but it is always from a silence that is larger than you, surrounds you, and finally names the deeper truth of the full moment that is you. I call such a way of knowing the *contemplative* way of knowing, as did much of the older Tradition. (The word "prayer" has been so consistently trivialized to refer to something *you do*, instead of something that is done to you, with you, in you, and *as* you.) Then, like Mary, you are ready to give birth. You are ready to give birth to another "Christ."[6]

Gateway to Silence: Just be.

DAY 5

Silence as the Heart of Prayer

When peaceful silence lay over all, and when night had run half way her swift course, down from the heavens, from the royal throne, leapt your all-powerful Word. (See Book of Wisdom 18:14–15.)

Words are necessarily dualistic. That is their function. They distinguish this from that, and that's good. But silence has the wonderful ability to *not* need to distinguish this from that! As in the magnificent quote above from the Catholic Bible, the Divine Word itself can only enter the world in silence and at nighttime. Silence can hold impossibilities together in a quiet, tantric embrace. Silence, especially loving silence, is always non-dual, and that is much of its secret power. It stays with mystery, holds tensions, absorbs contradictions, and smiles at paradoxes—leaving them unresolved, and happily so. Any good poet knows this, as do many master composers and musicians. Politicians, engineers, accountants, and most seminary-trained clergy have a much harder time.

In his classic book, *The World of Silence,* Max Picard tells us that our spirits need silence as much as our bodies need food and oxygen. As a general spiritual rule, you can trust this: *The ego gets what it wants with words. The soul finds what it needs in silence.* The ego prefers full solar light—immediate answers, full clarity, absolute certitude, moral perfection, and undeniable conclusions. The soul, however, prefers the subtle world of shadow, the lunar world that mixes darkness and light together, or, as the Book of Wisdom more poetically puts it above, "When night had run *half way* her swift course"!

Robert Sardello, in his magnificent, demanding book *Silence: The Mystery of Wholeness,* writes: "Silence knows how to hide. It gives a little and sees what we do with it."[7] Only then will it, or can it, give more. Rushed, manipulative, or opportunistic people thus find silence impossible, even a torture. They never get to the "more." Sardello goes on to say, "But in Silence everything displays its depth, and we find that we are a part of the depth of everything around us."[8] This is so good and so true!

When our interior silence can actually feel and value the silence that surrounds everything else, we have entered the house of wisdom. This is the very heart of prayer. When the two silences connect and bow to one another, we have a third dimension of knowing, which many have called spiritual intelligence or even "the mind of Christ" (see 1 Corinthians 2:10–16). No wonder that silence is probably *the* foundational spiritual discipline in all the world's religions, although it is only appreciated as such at the more mature and mystical levels. Maybe the absence of silence and the abundance of chatter is the primary reason that so much personal incarnation does not happen. Christmas remains a single day instead of a full year of ever-deepening realizations.[9]

Gateway to Silence: Just be.

DAY 6

What Sustains Me: Contemplation

As the name of our center probably makes clear (Center for Action and Contemplation), my daily and primary practice is contemplation. I try in every way and every day to see the events, people, and issues in my world through a much wider lens that I hope is "Christ Consciousness." I have to practice, hour by hour, letting go of my own agenda, my own anger, fear, and judgments, in very concrete ways. In that empty space, often made emptier by my very failure, God is always able to speak to me, and sometimes I am able to hear. In that space, I find joy.

I have worked for most of my life, with the help of my Franciscan tradition and other spiritual teachers, to spend a good chunk of every day in silence, solitude, and surrender to what God and the moment are offering. I fail at it far more than I succeed, but grace grants me just enough "wide-lens experience" to know that it is my home base, my deepest seeing, and by far the best gift I can also offer to the world, and to you.

Without a daily contemplative stance, I would have given up on the church, America, politics, many people, and surely myself, a long time ago.

Without a daily contemplative practice, I would likely be a cynical and even negative person by now, but, by Somebody's kindness, I do not think that I am. I hope not. With contemplative eyes, I can live with a certain *non-dual consciousness* that often allows me to be merciful to the moment, patient with human failure, and generous toward the maddening issues of our time. For me, it is the very shape of Christian salvation, or any salvation. My sadness is that so few have been taught this older and wiser tradition, although many still come to it by great love and great suffering. We taught people *what* to see instead of *how* to see. Really!

How good to end this book on the note of silence, so you will not take any of these words as the final word, the only word, or the best word. Surround my too many words with the holy silence of God, and allow me my many overstatements, understatements, and misstatements. Only God is true. I do not want to get in the way of you and the Great Mystery.[10]

Gateway to Silence: Just be.

DAY 7

SABBATH MEDITATION

Remember: **Silence**

Silence is at the very foundation of all reality. It is that out of which all being comes and to which all things return. (Day 1)

The running from silence is undoubtedly running from God, from our soul, from our selves, from the truth, and from freedom. (Day 2)

The two correctives of all spirituality are silence and service. (Day 3)

Sometimes grace is an uprush and sometimes it is a downrush, but it is always from a silence that is larger than you, surrounds you, and finally names the deeper truth of the full moment that is you. (Day 4)

As a general spiritual rule, you can trust this: *The ego gets what it wants with words. The soul finds what it needs in silence.* (Day 5)

With contemplative eyes, I can live with a certain non-dual consciousness that often allows me to be merciful to the moment, patient with human failure, and generous toward the maddening issues of our time. (Day 6)

Rest: **Centering Silence**

Choose a word or phrase (such as this week's Gateway to Silence—*Just be*—or Grace, Rest, etc.) as an expression of your intent and desire. Sit comfortably and upright, eyes closed, breathing naturally, and begin to silently repeat this sacred word. As your attention is focused on the desire behind the word, gradually let the word slip away. Rest in silence. When thoughts, images or sensations arise, gently return to the word, a symbol of your consent to God's presence and action within you.

For further study:

Are You Eager to Love?
The Art of Letting Go: Living the Wisdom of Saint Francis
Sic et Non: Yes, And
Silent Compassion: Finding God in Contemplation

AFTERWORD

I am pleased to have been invited to write an afterword to these meditations by my friend Richard Rohr. In wondering what to say, I am inclined
to invite you to join me in reflecting on the graces we have received in
reading these meditations day by day.

One likely place to begin is to recall the graces we received in those
moments we were actually engaged in reading each meditation in a sincere and prayerful manner. We can recall with gratitude that graced shift
of awareness that occurred within us each time the meditation became a
rendezvous with God's loving presence in our life.

We can also recall the intimate and mysterious manner in which the
renewed awareness of God's loving presence did not vanish when our time
with God in meditation ended and we stood to go about our day. For we
were able to discern the ever-so-subtle ways our renewed awareness of God's
loving presence continued to linger within us after our prayerful encounter
with God came to an end.

It is true that this lingering afterglow tends to dissipate as we turn to
the details and demands of the day. But if we have been faithful to the daily
rendezvous with God embodied in each meditation, we have perhaps begun
to realize the lingering afterglow of our renewed awareness of God's loving
presence is becoming a habitual, underlying, felt sense of God, sustaining
and guiding us as we go through our day.

As we learn to live in this way, we realize we are learning the gentle art
of contemplative living. We see within ourselves an emerging readiness to

turn within, to reground ourselves in God's presence, hidden in the midst of whatever it is we are experiencing at the moment. We can take delight in our heightened sensitivity to those moments when God does not wait for us to turn within, but rather comes welling up into our minds and hearts, prompting us to be more loving, more compassionate, more patient with ourselves and with each person we meet as we go through our day.

I know Richard would be pleased to know that God has used these meditations to touch and access your mind and heart in this life-changing way. We can be grateful to Richard for his fidelity to God, who inspires and guides him to share these meditations with us.

—James Finley

NOTES

FOREWORD

1. T. S. Eliot, "Four Quartets," http://www.davidgorman.com/4Quartets/.

ACKNOWLEDGMENTS

1. T. S. Eliot, "Four Quartets."

WEEK 1: INTRODUCTION

1. See Richard Rohr, *The Naked Now: Learning to See as the Mystics See* (New York: Crossroad, 2009), Appendix V.

2. Paragraph adapted from Richard Rohr, *Silent Compassion: Finding God in Contemplation* (Cincinnati: Franciscan Media, 2014), 67.

3. Paragraph from Richard Rohr, *The Divine Dance: The Trinity and Your Transformation* (New Kensington, PA: Whitaker House, forthcoming).

WEEK 2: YES, AND

1. Adapted from Richard Rohr, *Sic et Non; Yes, And . . .* (Albuquerque, NM: Center for Action and Contemplation, 2013), MP3.

2. Adapted from Rohr, *Sic et Non; Yes, And . . . .*

3. Ibid.

4. Adapted from Rohr, *Naked Now*, 46–47.

5. Adapted from Rohr, *Sic et Non; Yes, And . . . .*

6. Richard Rohr, *Eager to Love: The Alternative Way of Francis of Assisi* (Cincinnati: Franciscan Media, 2014), chapter 5 better develops this important theme and shows how mature religion actually has a different epistemology, or way of knowing.

7. Adapted from Rohr, *Naked Now*, 114–115.

8. Adapted from Rohr, *Sic et Non; Yes, And . . . .*

9. Adapted from Richard Rohr, *Yes, And . . . : Daily Meditations* (Cincinnati: Franciscan Media, 2013), x.

10. Adapted from Rohr, *Yes, And . . . : Daily Meditations*, x–xi.

11. Learn more about *Lectio Divina*, sacred reading, at http://www.contemplativeoutreach.org/category/category/lectio-divina.

12. Adapted from Rohr, *Naked Now*, 180–181.

WEEK 3: MYSTICISM: INNER EXPERIENCE

1. Adapted from Richard Rohr, *Things Hidden: Scripture as Spirituality* (Cincinnati: St. Anthony Messenger Press, 2007), 80–81.

2. Adapted from Rohr, *Naked Now,* 29–30.

3. Heard by the author on a retreat led by Fr. Donovan.

4. Adapted from Richard Rohr, *Franciscan Mysticism: I AM That Which I Am Seeking* (Albuquerque, NM: Center for Action and Contemplation, 2012), Disc 1.

5. Adapted from Rohr, *Silent Compassion*, 49.

6. Adapted from Rohr, *Franciscan Mysticism*, Disc 2.

7. Adapted from Rohr, *Franciscan Mysticism*, Disc 4.

8. Ibid.

WEEK 4: THE PERENNIAL TRADITION

1. Adapted from Vanessa Guerin, "Editor's Note" and Richard Rohr, "Introduction," *Oneing* 1 no. 1 (2013): 5, 11.

2. Julian of Norwich, *Showings, The Classics of Western Spirituality*, trans. Colledge, Edmund, et al. (Mahwah, NJ: Paulist Press, 1978), 9.

3. Ibid, 65.

4. Ibid, 51.

5. Adapted from Rohr, "Introduction," *Oneing* 1 no. 1: 12, 14.

6. Adapted from Rohr, "Introduction," *Oneing* 1 no. 1: 13.

7. Sentence adapted from Rohr, *The Divine Dance: The Trinity and Your Transformation*.

8. Ibid.

9. Adapted from James Finley, "Epilogue," *Oneing* 1 no. 1: 81–82.

10. To learn more about Centering Prayer, visit http://www.contemplativeoutreach.org/category/category/centering-prayer.

WEEK 5: LEVELS OF SPIRITUAL DEVELOPMENT (PART ONE)

1. Thomas Aquinas, *Summae Theologica*, First Part, Question 75, Answer 5.

2. Adapted from Richard Rohr, *The Art of Letting Go: Living the Wisdom of Saint Francis* (Louisville, CO: Sounds True, 2010), Disc 5; Richard Rohr, *Where You Are Is Where I'll Meet You* (Albuquerque, NM: Center for Action and Contemplation, 2009), Disc 1; and Rohr, *Naked Now*, 163–164.

3. Ibid.

4. Ibid.

5. Ibid.

6. Adapted from Rohr, *Art of Letting Go*, Disc 5.

7. Ibid.

WEEK 6: LEVELS OF SPIRITUAL DEVELOPMENT (PART TWO)

1. Adapted from Rohr, *Where You Are,* Disc 1.
2. Adapted from Rohr, *Art of Letting Go,* Disc 5.
3. Adapted from Rohr, *Where You Are,* Disc 1 and Rohr, *Art of Letting Go,* Disc 5.
4. Adapted from Rohr, *Art of Letting Go,* Disc 5.
5. Adapted from Rohr, *Where You Are,* Disc 2 and Rohr, *Art of Letting Go,* Disc 5.
6. Ibid.

WEEK 7: IN THE BEGINNING

1. Adapted from Richard Rohr and Bill Plotkin, *Soul Centering through Nature* (Albuquerque, NM: Center for Action and Contemplation, 2011), Disc 2.
2. Ibid.
3. Ibid.
4. Adapted from Richard Rohr, *A New Cosmology: Nature as the First Bible* (Albuquerque, NM: Center for Action and Contemplation, 2009), insert.
5. Adapted from Richard Rohr, *The Soul, the Natural World, and What Is* (Albuquerque, NM: Center for Action and Contemplation, 2009) and Richard Rohr, *The Cosmic Christ* (Albuquerque, NM: Center for Action and Contemplation, 2009), Disc 1.
6. If you want to learn from some who are making an art, discipline, and contemplative experience out of walking, visit http://walk2connect.com/.

WEEK 8: THE TRUE SELF

1. Adapted from Richard Rohr, *Falling Upward: A Spirituality for the Two Halves of Life* (San Francisco: Jossey-Bass, 2011), 86.
2. Adapted from Richard Rohr, *True Self/False Self* (Cincinnati: Franciscan Media, 2013), Disc 2.
3. Ibid.
4. Adapted from Richard Rohr, *Immortal Diamond: The Search for Our True Self* (San Francisco: Jossey-Bass, 2013), 10–11.
5. Adapted from Rohr, *True Self/False Self,* Disc 3.
6. Thomas Merton, *New Seeds of Contemplation* (New York: New Directions, 1961), 34.
7. Adapted from Rohr, *True Self/False Self,* Disc 2 and insert. For more on this topic, see *Oneing* 3, no. 2 (2015) on Innocence.
8. Adapted from Rohr, *True Self/False Self,* Disc 2 and Rohr, *The Divine Dance: The Trinity and Your Transformation.*
9. Adapted from Rohr, *True Self/False Self,* Disc 2.

WEEK 9: LEAVING THE GARDEN

1. Adapted from Rohr, *Things Hidden,* 210.
2. William Wordsworth, "Ode: Intimations of Immortality from Recollections of Early Childhood," *The Oxford Book of English Verse: 1250–1900,* ed. Arthur Quiller-Couch, http://www.bartleby.com/101/536.html.
3. T. S. Eliot, "Four Quartets."

4. Adapted from Rohr, *Things Hidden*, 210–211. Julian of Norwich quotation from *Revelations of Divine Love*, chap. 61.
5. Adapted from Richard Rohr, *Everything Belongs: The Gift of Contemplative Prayer* (New York: Crossroad, 2003), 68 and Rohr, *Franciscan Mysticism*, Disc 4.
6. Adapted from Rohr, *Franciscan Mysticism*, Disc 4.
7. Adapted from Rohr, *Immortal Diamond*, 29 and Rohr, *Franciscan Mysticism*, Disc 4.
8. Adapted from Rohr, *Franciscan Mysticism*, Disc 4; Rohr, *Immortal Diamond*, 29; and Rohr, *Falling Upward*, 127–128. Rumi quote from Coleman Barks, *Essential Rumi* (San Francisco: HarperOne, 2004).

WEEK 10: THE FIRST HALF OF LIFE
1. Adapted from Ronald Rolheiser and Richard Rohr, *Adult Christianity and How to Get There* (Albuquerque, NM: Center for Action and Contemplation, 2004), Disc 4.
2. Adapted from Rohr, *Falling Upward*, 1–3.
3. Adapted from Rohr, *Falling Upward*, 4–5 and Richard Rohr, *The Two Major Tasks of the Spiritual Life* (Albuquerque, NM: Center for Action and Contemplation, 2005).
4. "The Visionary," *Rainer Maria Rilke: Selected Poems*, trans. Albert Ernest Flemming (New York: Routledge, 2011), 72.
5. Adapted from Rohr, *Falling Upward*, 25–26.
6. Adapted from Rohr, *Falling Upward*, 26–27.
7. Adapted from Richard Rohr, Ron Rolheiser, and Edwina Gateley, *Loving the Two Halves of Life: The Further Journey* (Albuquerque, NM: Center for Action and Contemplation, 2011), Disc 1.

WEEK 11: THE FALSE SELF
1. Adapted from Rohr, *Immortal Diamond*, 27, 64–65.
2. Adapted from Rohr, *Immortal Diamond*, 28–29.
3. Adapted from Rohr, *Immortal Diamond*, 36–37.
4. Adapted from Rohr, *Immortal Diamond*, 38–39.
5. St. Augustine, *Ten Homilies on the Epistle of John to the Parthians*, Tract VII, 8.
6. Adapted from Rohr, *Immortal Diamond*, 48–49.
7. Adapted from Rohr, *Immortal Diamond*, 59–60, 65–66.

WEEK 12: DUALISTIC THINKING
1. Adapted from Rohr, *Falling Upward*, 146–147.
2. Adapted from Richard Rohr, *A New Way of Seeing, a New Way of Being: Jesus and Paul* (Albuquerque, NM: Center for Action and Contemplation, 2007), Disc 2.
3. Adapted from Rohr, *New Way of Seeing*, Disc 1.
4. Adapted from Rohr, *Naked Now*, 160.
5. Adapted from Rohr, *New Way of Seeing*, Disc 2.
6. Adapted from Rohr, *Naked Now*, 74.

7. Adapted from Rohr, *Falling Upward,* 15.

8. Adapted from Rohr, *Naked Now,* 94.

9. Adapted from Rohr, *Falling Upward,* 151.

10. Learn more about Examen of Consciousness at http://www.ignatianspirituality.com/ignatian-prayer/the-examen.

WEEK 13: SUBVERTING THE HONOR/SHAME SYSTEM

1. Adapted from Richard Rohr, *Francis: Turning the World on Its Head: Subverting the Honor/Shame System* (Albuquerque, NM: Center for Action and Contemplation, 2009).

2. Ibid.

3. Ibid.

4. Ibid.

5. Adapted from Rohr, *Francis: Turning the World* and Richard Rohr, *The Path of Descent* (Albuquerque, NM: Center for Action and Contemplation, 2003), Disc 1.

6. Adapted from Richard Rohr, *Dancing Standing Still: Healing the World from a Place of Prayer* (Mahwah, NJ: Paulist Press, 2014), 42–43.

WEEK 14: THE PATH OF DESCENT

1. Adapted from Rohr, *Path of Descent,* Disc 1.

2. Adapted from Rohr, *Things Hidden,* 89–90.

3. *Reflections on the Art of Living: A Joseph Campbell Companion,* ed. Diane K. Osbon (New York: Harper Perennial, 1995), 24.

4. Adapted from Rohr, *Falling Upward,* 58, 65–68. Original Julian of Norwich quotation from *Revelations of Divine Love,* chap. 61.

5. Adapted from Rohr, *Path of Descent,* Disc 1; Rohr, *Things Hidden,* 136; and Rohr, *Falling Upward,* 59.

6. Adapted from Richard Rohr, *Great Themes of Paul: Life as Participation* (Cincinnati: Franciscan Media, 2012), Disc 3.

7. Adapted from Rohr, *Things Hidden,* 100, 62.

8. Julian of Norwich, *Revelations of Divine Love,* chap. 78.

9. Adapted from Richard Rohr, untitled talk on contemplative practice (talk given to staff at contemplative sit, Center for Action and Contemplation, Albuquerque, NM, September 19, 2011).

WEEK 15: TRANSFORMATIVE SUFFERING

1. Adapted from Rohr, *Things Hidden,* 25–26 and Richard Rohr, *Job and the Mystery of Suffering* (New York: Crossroad, 1998), 90–91.

2. Adapted from Richard Rohr, *Breathing Under Water: Spirituality and the Twelve Steps* (Cincinnati: St. Anthony Messenger Press, 2011), 120–122 and Rohr, *Job,* 18.

3. Adapted from Richard Rohr, *The Authority of Those Who Have Suffered* (Albuquerque, NM: Center for Action and Contemplation, 2005).

4. Adapted from Rohr, *Authority* and Rohr, *New Way of Seeing,* Disc 2.

5. Adapted from Rohr, *Job,* 178–179.

6. Adapted from Rohr, *Breathing Under Water*, 123 and Rohr, *Authority*.

WEEK 16: TRANSFORMATIVE DYING

1. Adapted from Richard Rohr, "Dying: We Need It for Life," *Richard Rohr on Transformation: Collected Talks, Volume One* (Cincinnati: St. Anthony Messenger Press, 2005), Talk Four and Rohr, *Things Hidden*, 193.
2. Adapted from Rohr, "Dying."
3. Adapted from Rohr, *Falling Upward*, 85, 95–96, 100–101.
4. Adapted from Rohr, "Dying" and Richard Rohr, "The Spirituality of Imperfection," *Richard Rohr on Transformation: Collected Talks, Volume One* (Cincinnati: St. Anthony Messenger Press, 2005), Talk Two.
5. Kathleen Dowling Singh, "Living in the Light of Death," *Oneing* 1 no. 2 (2013): 42–44.
6. Adapted from Rohr, *Everything Belongs*, 179–182.
7. Adapted from Singh, "Living in the Light of Death," 44–46.

WEEK 17: THE COMMON WONDERFUL

1. Adapted from Richard Rohr, *Adam's Return: The Five Promises of Male Initiation* (New York: Crossroad, 2004), 2–3, 9–10, 32–33, 152–153.
2. Adapted from Rohr, *Adam's Return*, 152–155.
3. Adapted from Rohr, *Adam's Return*, 155–157.
4. Adapted from Rohr, *Adam's Return*, 157–161.
5. Adapted from Rohr, *Adam's Return*, 161–163.
6. Adapted from Rohr, *Adam's Return*, 163–166.

WEEK 18: DISCHARGING YOUR LOYAL SOLDIER

1. Adapted from Rohr, *Falling Upward*, 43–44.
2. Adapted from Rohr, *Falling Upward*, 45.
3. Adapted from Rohr, *Falling Upward*, 47–49.
4. Adapted from Rohr, "Imperfection"; Richard Rohr, *Discharging Your "Loyal Soldier"* (Albuquerque, NM: Center for Action and Contemplation, 2009); Richard Rohr and Russ Hudson, *The Enneagram as a Tool for Your Spiritual Journey* (Albuquerque, NM: Center for Action and Contemplation, 2009), Disc 6; and Rohr, *Falling Upward*, 4.
5. Adapted from Rohr, *Falling Upward*, 49–50.
6. Adapted from Rohr, *Discharging Your "Loyal Soldier"*; Rohr, *Things Hidden*, 162; and Richard Rohr and Laurence Freeman, *Transforming the World through Contemplative Prayer* (Albuquerque, NM: Center for Action and Contemplation, 2013), Disc 5.

WEEK 19: GROWING IN GRACE

1. *The Baltimore Catechism*, rev. ed. (1941), Part One, Lesson 9, Question 101.
2. Adapted from Rohr, *Things Hidden*, 155–157.
3. Adapted from Rohr, *Things Hidden*, 158–159.
4. Adapted from Richard Rohr, "Forever Young," *Sojourners* (December 2007),

https://sojo.net/magazine/december-2007/forever-young.

5. Adapted from Rohr, *Immortal Diamond*, xix–xx and Richard Rohr and Russ Hudson, *The Enneagram and Grace: 9 Journeys to Divine Presence* (Albuquerque, NM: Center for Action and Contemplation, 2012), Disc 1.

6. Adapted from Rohr, *Immortal Diamond*, xx–xxii.

7. Adapted from Rohr, *Job*, 57 and Rohr and Hudson, *Enneagram and Grace*, Disc 1.

8. http://www.worldprayers.org/archive/prayers/celebrations/this_ritual_is_one.html.

WEEK 20: SHADOWBOXING

1. Adapted from Rohr, *Discharging Your "Loyal Soldier"* and Richard Rohr, *Near Occasions of Grace* (Maryknoll, NY: Orbis, 1993), 96. Eckhart quotation from "Sermon 52," *Meister Eckhart: The Essential Sermons, Commentaries, Treatises, and Defense, The Classics of Western Spirituality*, trans. Edmund Colledge and Bernard McGinn (Mahwah, NJ: Paulist Press, 1981), 202.

2. Adapted from Rohr, *Falling Upward*, 127–129.

3. Osbon, *Reflections*, 24.

4. Adapted from Rohr, *Falling Upward*, 131.

5. Adapted from Rohr, *Falling Upward*, 131–132 and Rohr, *Things Hidden*, 166.

6. Robertson Davies, *Fifth Business* (Toronto: Macmillan of Canada, 1970), 259.

7. Adapted from Rohr, *Falling Upward*, 132–133.

8. Adapted from Rohr, *Dancing Standing Still*, 19–20 and Rohr, *Great Themes of Paul*, Disc 2.

9. Visit http://thework.com/en/do-work for a free worksheet and resources.

WEEK 21: THE SECOND HALF OF LIFE

1. Eliot, "Four Quartets."

2. Adapted from Rohr, *Falling Upward*, 87, 114–115.

3. Adapted from Rohr, *Falling Upward*, 118–119.

4. Adapted from Rohr, *Falling Upward*, 119–120.

5. Adapted from Rohr, *Falling Upward*, 121–122.

6. Adapted from Rohr, *Falling Upward*, 122–123.

7. Adapted from Rohr, *Falling Upward*, 124–125.

8. Rainer Maria Rilke, *Rilke's Book of Hours: Love Poems to God*, trans. Anita Barrows and Joanna Macy (New York: Riverhead Books, 2005), 65.

WEEK 22: THE ENNEAGRAM (PART ONE)

1. Adapted from Richard Rohr and Andreas Ebert, *The Enneagram: A Christian Perspective* (New York: Crossroad, 2001), xvi–xxi, 28–29, 32; and Richard Rohr, *The Enneagram: The Discernment of Spirits* (Albuquerque, NM: Center for Action and Contemplation, 2004), Disc 1.

2. Adapted from Rohr and Ebert, *Enneagram: A Christian Perspective*, 4–5, 25–27; Rohr, *Enneagram: Discernment of Spirits*, Disc 1; and Rohr and Hudson, *Enneagram and Grace*, Disc 1.

3. Adapted from Rohr and Ebert, *Enneagram: A Christian Perspective*, 32, 35–36,

45, 85, 88; Rohr, *Enneagram: Discernment of Spirits*, Discs 1, 2, and 4; and Rohr and Hudson, *Enneagram and Grace*, Disc 1.

4. Additional resources, including a list of tests, are available from the International Enneagram Association: http://www.internationalenneagram.org/enneagram/index.html.

5. Adapted from Rohr and Ebert, *Enneagram: A Christian Perspective*, 49, 52–55 and Rohr, *Enneagram: Discernment of Spirits*, Disc 2.

6. Adapted from Rohr and Ebert, *Enneagram: A Christian Perspective*, 45, 63–65, 72 and Rohr, *Enneagram: Discernment of Spirits*, Disc 2.

7. Adapted from Rohr and Ebert, *Enneagram: A Christian Perspective*, 46, 81–89 and Rohr, *Enneagram: Discernment of Spirits*, Disc 2.

8. Robert Sardello, "Transgression and the Return of the Mystical Heart," *Oneing* 2 no. 1 (2014): 80–81.

WEEK 23: THE ENNEAGRAM (PART TWO)

1. Adapted from Rohr and Ebert, *Enneagram: A Christian Perspective*, 46, 98–103, 107–108, 111 and Rohr, *Enneagram: Discernment of Spirits*, Disc 2.

2. Adapted from Rohr and Ebert, *Enneagram: A Christian Perspective*, 46, 115, 116, 121, 124, 127 and Rohr, *Enneagram: Discernment of Spirits*, Disc 3.

3. Adapted from Rohr and Ebert, *Enneagram: A Christian Perspective*, 46–47, 131–138, 141, 143 and Rohr, *Enneagram: Discernment of Spirits*, Disc 3.

4. Adapted from Rohr and Ebert, *Enneagram: A Christian Perspective*, 47, 146, 147, 150, 151, 155, 159–160 and Rohr, *Enneagram: Discernment of Spirits*, Disc 3.

5. Adapted from Rohr and Ebert, *Enneagram: A Christian Perspective*, 47, 162, 163–164, 166, 167, 168–169, 170, 173, 176 and Rohr, *Enneagram: Discernment of Spirits*, Disc 3.

6. Adapted from Rohr and Ebert, *Enneagram: A Christian Perspective*, 47–48, 180, 181–182, 184, 187–188, 192 and Rohr, *Enneagram: Discernment of Spirits*, Disc 3.

7. Adapted from Rohr and Ebert, *Enneagram: A Christian Perspective*, 48.

WEEK 24: BECOMING WHO YOU ARE

1. Adapted from Rohr, *Immortal Diamond*, 16–17.

2. Adapted from Rohr, *True Self/False Self*, Disc 1.

3. Adapted from Rohr, *True Self/False Self*, Disc 2.

4. Adapted from Rohr, *Immortal Diamond*, 23–25.

5. Teresa of Ávila, *The Interior Castle*, I, 2.

6. Adapted from Rohr, *Immortal Diamond*, 23.

7. Adapted from Rohr, *True Self/False Self*, Disc 1.

WEEK 25: SPIRITUALITY AND THE TWELVE STEPS, PART ONE

1. Adapted from Rohr, *Breathing Under Water*, xvii, xxiv, 1; Richard Rohr, *How Do We Breathe Under Water? The Gospel and 12-Step Spirituality* (Albuquerque, NM: Center for Action and Contemplation, 2005), Disc 1; and Richard Rohr, *The Little Way: A Spirituality of Imperfection* (Albuquerque, NM: Center for Action and Contemplation, 2007).

2. Adapted from Rohr, *Breathing Under Water*, 7, 14–15.
3. Adapted from Rohr, *Breathing Under Water*, 17, 24–25, 27.
4. Adapted from Rohr, *Breathing Under Water*, 29, 34–35.
5. Adapted from Rohr, *Breathing Under Water*, 37, 39, 47–49.
6. Adapted from Rohr, *Breathing Under Water*, 52, 54–56.
7. Cynthia Bourgeault, *The Wisdom Jesus* (Boston: Shambhala, 2008), 180.

WEEK 26: SPIRITUALITY AND THE TWELVE STEPS, PART TWO
1. Adapted from Rohr, *Breathing Under Water*, 59, 64–65; Rohr, *Little Way*; and Richard Rohr, *Emotional Sobriety: Rewiring Our Programs for "Happiness"* (Albuquerque, NM: Center for Action and Contemplation, 2011).
2. Adapted from Rohr, *Breathing Under Water*, 67–69, 73–74.
3. Adapted from Rohr, *Breathing Under Water*, 75–81 and Rohr, *Emotional Sobriety*.
4. Adapted from Rohr, *Breathing Under Water*, 83–86.
5. Adapted from Rohr, *Breathing Under Water*, 93, 96, 99, 102, 103; Rohr, *How Do We Breathe*, Disc 2; Rohr, *Little Way*; and Rohr, *Emotional Sobriety*.
6. Adapted from Rohr, *Breathing Under Water*, 105, 107, 109 and Rohr, *Emotional Sobriety*.

WEEK 27: COMPASSION
1. Adapted from Rohr, *Silent Compassion*, 46–48.
2. Gerald G. May, *The Awakened Heart: Opening Yourself to the Love You Need* (New York: HarperOne, 1993), 193.
3. Adapted from Richard Rohr, "Contemplation and Compassion: The Second Gaze," *Radical Grace* 18, no. 6 (2005).
4. Ibid.
5. Adapted from Rohr, *Silent Compassion*, 15, 26–27.
6. Adapted from Rohr, *Eager to Love*, 28, 157–158.
7. Adapted from Rohr, *Eager to Love*, 75–76.

WEEK 28: IMAGE OF GOD
1. Walter Brueggemann, *Theology of the Old Testament: Testimony, Dispute, Advocacy* (Minneapolis: Fortress, 2009), 215 ff.
2. Adapted from Rohr, *Things Hidden*, 9–10.
3. Daniel Ladinsky, *A Year With Hafiz* (New York: Penguin, 2011), 3.
4. Augustine of Hippo, *Sermon 52*, 16.
5. Adapted from Richard Rohr, *Simplicity: The Freedom of Letting Go* (New York: Crossroad, 1991), 21–22.
6. Adapted from Richard Rohr, *Hierarchy of Truths: Jesus' Use of Scripture* (Albuquerque, NM: Center for Action and Contemplation, 2014) and Rohr, *Dancing Standing Still*, 72.
7. Bernard McGinn, ed., *The Essential Writings of Christian Mysticism* (New York: Modern Library, 2006), 291.
8. Adapted from Rohr, *Eager to Love*, 229, 230–231.
9. Adapted from Rohr, *Eager to Love*, 230, 235–237, and Rohr, *Things Hidden*, 35.

10. Adapted from Rohr, *Eager to Love,* 237–238, 239, 245–246.

11. George Sylvester Viereck, "What Life Means to Einstein: An Interview by George Sylvester Viereck," *The Saturday Evening Post,* October 26, 1929, 17, col. 1, as cited in http://quoteinvestigator.com/2013/01/01/einstein-imagination/.

12. Adapted from Rohr, *Eager to Love,* 256, 258.

WEEK 29: JESUS, THE CHRIST

1. Adapted from Rohr, *Dancing Standing Still,* 73, 76–78.

2. Adapted from Rohr, *Dancing Standing Still,* 66–70, 77–80.

3. Adapted from Rohr, *Dancing Standing Still,* 89, 95–97, 99.

4. Adapted from Rohr, *Eager to Love,* 209–210.

5. Adapted from Rohr, *Eager to Love,* 211–213.

6. Christian Wiman, *My Bright Abyss: Meditation of a Modern Believer* (New York: Farrar, Straus and Giroux, 2013), 67.

7. Adapted from Rohr, *Eager to Love,* 223–224, 226, 228.

WEEK 30: LETTING GO

1. Adapted from Rohr, *Art of Letting Go,* Disc 1.

2. Adapted from Rohr, *Simplicity,* 42–43.

3. Adapted from Rohr, *Art of Letting Go,* Disc 6 and Rohr, *Falling Upward,* xvii.

4. Adapted from Rohr, *Simplicity,* 40, 44–45 and Rohr, *Art of Letting Go,* Disc 6.

5. Adapted from Rohr, *Art of Letting Go,* Disc 6.

6. Robertson Davies, *Fifth Business* (New York: Penguin, 2001), 245.

7. Adapted from Rohr, *Art of Letting Go,* Disc 6.

8. Adapted from Richard Rohr and John Feister, *Jesus' Plan for a New World: The Sermon on the Mount* (Cincinnati: St. Anthony Messenger Press, 1996), 124.

WEEK 31: PARADOX

1. G. K. Chesterton, *The Paradoxes of Mr. Pond* (Thirsk, UK: House of Stratus, 2008), 41.

2. Adapted from Rohr, *Breathing Under Water,* 53; Richard Rohr and Mary Beth Ingham, *Holding the Tension: The Power of Paradox* (Albuquerque, NM: Center for Action and Contemplation, 2007), Discs 1 and 3; and Rohr, *Eager to Love,* 71–72.

3. Adapted from Rohr, *Naked Now,* 143, 144–145 and Rohr and Ingham, *Holding the Tension,* Disc 2.

4. Adapted from Rohr, *Naked Now,* 147, 154–155 and Rohr, *New Way of Seeing,* Disc 1.

5. Adapted from Rohr and Ingham, *Holding the Tension,* Discs 3 and 4.

6. Adapted from Rohr, *Eager to Love,* 68, 76–77.

7. Wiman, *My Bright Abyss,* 121.

8. Adapted from Rohr, *New Way of Seeing,* Disc 1; Rohr and Ingham, *Holding the Tension,* Disc 2; and Rohr, *Eager to Love,* 181, 183.

9. Joelle Chase, "How Change Happens," interview with Cynthia Bourgeault, *Oneing* 2 no. 1 (2014): 85.

WEEK 32: OPEN HEART, OPEN MIND, OPEN BODY

1. Adapted from Rohr, *Eager to Love*, 248; Rohr, *Breathing Under Water*, 10; and Rohr, *Dancing Standing Still*, 67.
2. Adapted from Rohr, *Naked Now*, 28, 34 and Rohr and Hudson, *Enneagram as a Tool*, Disc 7.
3. Adapted from Rohr, *Naked Now*, 126, 159–160.
4. Adapted from Rohr, *Breathing Under Water*, 8–9.
5. Adapted from Rohr, *Breathing Under Water*, 11–12.
6. Adapted from Rohr, *Breathing Under Water*, 13.
7. Brendan Doyle, trans. *Meditations with Julian of Norwich*. (Rochester, VT: Bear & Co., 1983), 70.

WEEK 33: INTIMACY

1. Adapted from Richard Rohr and James Finley, *Intimacy: The Divine Ambush* (Albuquerque, NM: Center for Action and Contemplation, 2013), Disc 2 and Rohr, *Falling Upward*, 156, 159–160.
2. Adapted from Rohr and Finley, *Intimacy*, Discs 2 and 4.
3. Dominic V. Monti, ed. *The Breviloquium: The Works of St. Bonaventure* (St. Bonaventure, NY: Franciscan Institute, 2005), 9:172.
4. Adapted from Rohr, *Eager to Love*, 239–240, xvi.
5. Adapted from Richard Rohr, James Finley, and Cynthia Bourgeault, *Following the Mystics through the Narrow Gate . . . Seeing God in All Things* (Albuquerque, NM: Center for Action and Contemplation, 2010), Disc 4.
6. Adapted from Rohr, *New Way of Seeing*, Disc 1 and Rohr, *Job*, 157.
7. Adapted from Rohr, *Dancing Standing Still*, 23–24.
8. Learn more about this process at http://www.contemplativemind.org/practices/tree/council-circle.

WEEK 34: TRINITY

1. Adapted from Richard Rohr, *The Divine Dance: Exploring the Mystery of Trinity* (Albuquerque, NM: Center for Action and Contemplation, 2004), Discs 1 and 2; Cynthia Bourgeault and Richard Rohr, *The Shape of God: Deepening the Mystery of the Trinity* (Albuquerque, NM: Center for Action and Contemplation, 2004), Disc 1; and Rohr, *Eager to Love*, 235.
2. Adapted from Rohr, *Divine Dance*, Disc 1 and Bourgeault and Rohr, *Shape of God*, Disc 1.
3. Adapted from Rohr, *Eager to Love*, 243–244.
4. Adapted from Rohr, *Divine Dance*, Disc 1; Bourgeault and Rohr, *Shape of God*, Disc 1; and Rohr, *Eager to Love*, 244.
5. Adapted from Rohr, *Eager to Love*, 232–233 and Rohr, *Divine Dance*, Disc 3.
6. Adapted from Rohr, *Divine Dance*, Disc 2 and Bourgeault and Rohr, *Shape of God*, Disc 2.

WEEK 35: THE EVOLVING JOURNEY

1. Nicola Slee explores this in depth in her book *Women's Faith Development:*

Patterns and Processes.

2. Kahlil Gibran, *The Prophet* (New York: Alfred A. Knopf, 1923), 55.
3. Nicola M. Slee, *Women's Faith Development: Patterns and Processes* (Burlington, VT: Ashgate, 2004), 21.
4. Adapted from Rohr, *Things Hidden*, 12–13.
5. G. K. Chesterton, *Orthodoxy* (London: John Lane, 1908), 84.
6. Adapted from Richard Rohr, "Living School Dean's Address" (Symposium lecture, Santa Ana Pueblo, New Mexico, August 2013).
7. Ibid.
8. Adapted from Rohr, *Dancing Standing Still*, 1, 2, 4.
9. Adapted from Rohr, *Dancing Standing Still*, 100, 103.
10. You can find labyrinths near you at http://labyrinthlocator.com/.

WEEK 36: NON-DUAL CONSCIOUSNESS
1. Adapted from Rohr, *Things Hidden*, 37–39.
2. Adapted from Richard Rohr, *Beginner's Mind* (Albuquerque, NM: Center for Action and Contemplation, 2002); Rohr and Freeman, *Transforming the World*, Disc 3; Rohr, *Divine Dance*, Disc 2; and Rohr, *Things Hidden*, 115.
3. Adapted from Rohr, *Beginner's Mind*; Richard Rohr, "Contemplation and Non-Dual Consciousness" (lecture, Tucson, Arizona, March 20, 2008); Richard Rohr, *Exploring and Experiencing the Naked Now* (Albuquerque, NM: Center for Action and Contemplation, 2010), Disc 1; and Rohr, *Naked Now*, 34–36.
4. Adapted from James Finley and Richard Rohr, *Jesus and Buddha: Paths to Awakening* (Albuquerque, NM: Center for Action and Contemplation, 2008), Disc 1 and Rohr and Freeman, *Transforming the World*, Disc 1.
5. Adapted from Finley and Rohr, *Jesus and Buddha*, Disc 1; Rohr, *Exploring Naked Now*, Disc 1; Rohr, *Naked Now*, 35–36; and Rohr, *Falling Upward*, 146.
6. Adapted from Rohr, "Contemplation and Non-Dual Consciousness."
7. Adapted from Rohr, *Naked Now*, 170–171.

WEEK 37: CONTEMPLATION
1. Adapted from Rohr and Freeman, *Transforming the World*, Disc 3 and Rohr, *Divine Dance*, Disc 2.
2. Adapted from Rohr and Freeman, *Transforming the World*, Disc 3 and Rohr, *Silent Compassion*, 5, 11, 17.
3. Teresa of Ávila, *Interior Castle*, IV, 1, 9.
4. Adapted from Rohr, *Everything Belongs*, 103–105 and Richard Rohr, *Contemplative Prayer* (Albuquerque, NM: Center for Action and Contemplation, 2003).
5. Adapted from Rohr, *Hierarchy of Truths.*
6. Adapted from Rohr, *Naked Now*, 130–131.
7. Karl Rahner, "Christian Living Formerly and Today," in *Theological Investigations VII*, trans. David Bourke (New York: Herder and Herder, 1971), 15.

8. Adapted from Rohr, *Naked Now*, 37–38; Rohr and Freeman, *Transforming the World*, Disc 4; and Rohr, *Silent Compassion*, 4, 15, 19.

WEEK 38: LIFE AS PARTICIPATION
1. Adapted from Rohr, *Great Themes of Paul*, Discs 4 and 7.
2. Adapted from Rohr, *Adam's Return*, 60–61 and Rohr, *Things Hidden*, 51.
3. Adapted from Rohr, *Adam's Return*, 65 and Rohr, *Things Hidden,* 50.
4. Adapted from Rohr, *Dancing Standing Still*, 4–5, 13–14, 18.
5. Adapted from Rohr, *Great Themes of Paul*, Discs 4 and 7 and Rohr, *Things Hidden,* 50.
6. Adapted from Rohr, *Great Themes of Paul*, Disc 7.

WEEK 39: EUCHARIST
1. Adapted from Rohr, *Things Hidden*, 215–216 and Richard Rohr, *New Great Themes of Scripture* (Cincinnati: Franciscan Media, 2012), Disc 10.
2. Adapted from Rohr, *Great Themes of Paul*, Disc 3 and Rohr and Feister, *Jesus' Plan,* 95.
3. Adapted from Rohr, *Divine Dance*, Disc 3 and Richard Rohr, *Eucharist as Touchstone* (Albuquerque, NM: Center for Action and Contemplation, 2000).
4. Adapted from Rohr, *Eucharist as Touchstone;* Finley and Rohr, *Jesus and Buddha*, Disc 1; Rohr, *Dancing Standing Still*, 15, 101; and Rohr, *Things Hidden*, 217.
5. Adapted from Rohr, *Eucharist as Touchstone*.
6. Ibid.
7. Pierre Teilhard de Chardin, *Hymn of the Universe* (New York: Harper and Row: 1961), 15–16.

WEEK 40: MUTUAL INDWELLING
1. The Jerusalem Bible and The Message.
2. Ken Wilber, *One Taste: Daily Reflections on Integral Spirituality* (Boston: Shambhala, 2000), 221.
3. Adapted from Rohr, *Things Hidden*, 207–208.
4. Adapted from Rohr, *Things Hidden*, 212–214.
5. Adapted from Rohr, *Things Hidden*, 211–212.
6. Adapted from Rohr, *Things Hidden*, 214–215.
7. Adapted from Rohr, *Eager to Love*, 68–71.
8. Adapted from Rohr, *Things Hidden*, 219–220. Poem from Stephen Mitchell, trans., *The Enlightened Heart: An Anthology of Sacred Poetry* (New York: Harper Perennial, 1993), 38–39.
9. See Mike Dash, "The Mystery of the Five Wounds," Smithsonian.com (November 18, 2011): http://www.smithsonianmag.com/history/the-mystery-of-the-five-wounds-361799/?no-ist.
10. Adapted from Rohr, *Eager to Love*, 23, 192.

WEEK 41: THE GATE OF HEAVEN IS EVERYWHERE

1. Thomas Merton, *Conjectures of a Guilty Bystander* (New York: Doubleday, 1966), 142.
2. Adapted from Rohr, *True Self/False Self,* Disc 5 and Richard Rohr, *How Do We Get Everything to Belong?* (Albuquerque, NM: Center for Action and Contemplation, 2005), Disc 3.
3. Adapted from Rohr, *Naked Now,* 25–26.
4. Adapted from Rohr, Finley, and Bourgeault, *Following the Mystics,* Disc 2 and Rohr, *Breathing Under Water,* 66.
5. Adapted from Rohr, *Eager to Love,* 5–6 and Rohr, *How Do We Get,* Disc 3.
6. Adapted from Richard Rohr, *Living the Eternal Now* (Albuquerque, NM: Center for Action and Contemplation, 2005).
7. Adapted from Rohr, *Living the Eternal Now* and Rohr, *Breathing Under Water,* 66.
8. Merton, *Conjectures,* 140–142.

WEEK 42: THE PRINCIPLE OF LIKENESS

1. Adapted from Rohr, *Naked Now,* 159 and Richard Rohr, "The Law of Attraction," *Collection of Homilies 2008* (Albuquerque, NM: Center for Action and Contemplation, 2008).
2. Adapted from Rohr, *Naked Now,* 160–162.
3. Adapted from Rohr and Hudson, *Enneagram as a Tool,* Disc 7.
4. Adapted from Rohr and Ingham, *Holding the Tension,* Disc 2 and Rohr, *Franciscan Mysticism,* Disc 2.
5. English Standard Version.
6. Adapted from Rohr, "Law of Attraction."
7. Adapted from Rohr and Ingham, *Holding the Tension,* Disc 2.

WEEK 43: LUMINOUS DARKNESS

1. *Dark Night of the Soul: St. John of the Cross*, trans. Mirabai Starr (New York: Riverhead, 2003), 10.
2. *John of the Cross: Selected Writings, The Classics of Western Spirituality*, ed. Kieran Kavanaugh (Mahwah, NJ: Paulist Press, 1988), 57.
3. Adapted from Rohr and Finley, *Intimacy,* Disc 2.
4. Starr, *Dark Night,* 11–12.
5. Adapted from Rohr and Finley, *Intimacy,* Disc 2.
6. Adapted from Rohr, *Eager to Love,* 21–22.
7. Adapted from Rohr, *Falling Upward,* 117, 119, 121–122.
8. St. Augustine, *Confessions,* Book 10, 27, largely author's paraphrase.
9. Adapted from Rohr, *Things Hidden,* 38–39 and Rohr and Finley, *Intimacy,* Disc 9.

WEEK 44: TRUST

1. Adapted from Rohr, *Divine Dance,* Disc 1 and Richard Rohr, *What Difference Does Trinity Make?* (Albuquerque, NM: Center for Action and Contemplation,

2004).

2. Adapted from Rohr, *Eager to Love,* 75–76.

3. Adapted from Rohr, *Eager to Love,* 1–2.

4. Adapted from Rohr, *Great Themes of Paul,* Disc 1.

5. Adapted from Rohr, *Dancing Standing Still,* 75–76.

6. Adapted from Rohr, *Everything Belongs,* 142–145.

WEEK 45: RIPENING

1. Adapted from Richard Rohr, "Introduction," *Oneing* 1 no. 2 (2013): 11–12.

2. T. S. Eliot, "The Hollow Men." http://allpoetry.com/The-Hollow-Men.

3. Adapted from Rohr, "Introduction," *Oneing* 1 no. 2: 11–12.

4. Adapted from Rohr, "Introduction," *Oneing* 1 no. 2: 12–13.

5. Gerard Manley Hopkins, "The Blessed Virgin compared to the Air we Breathe," *Poems* (London: Humphrey Milford, 1918), http://www.bartleby.com/122/37.html.

6. Adapted from Rohr, "Introduction," *Oneing* 1 no. 2: 13.

7. Adapted from Rohr, Rolheiser, and Gateley, *Loving the Two Halves,* Disc 5 and Rohr, *Falling Upward,* 119–120.

8. Adapted from Rohr, "Introduction," *Oneing* 1 no. 2: 14.

9. James Finley, "Ripening," *Oneing* 1 no. 2: 37.

WEEK 46: WHOLENESS

1. Adapted from Rohr, *True Self/False Self,* Disc 2 and Rohr, *Great Themes of Paul,* Disc 7.

2. Adapted from Rohr, *Eager to Love,* 177–178.

3. Adapted from Rohr, *Breathing Under Water,* 88–89.

4. John McGuckin, "Symeon the New Theologian's *Hymns of Divine Eros*: A Neglected Masterpiece of the Christian Mystical Tradition," *Spiritus* 5 (2005): 192.

5. Adapted from Rohr, *Franciscan Mysticism,* Disc 4 and Rohr, *Immortal Diamond,* 107.

6. *Bonaventure: The Soul's Journey into God, the Tree of Life, the Life of St. Francis, The Classics of Western Spirituality,* trans. Ewert Cousins (Mahwah, NJ: Paulist Press, 1978), 65.

7. Montgomery Carmichael, trans. and ed., *The Lady Poverty* (London: J. Murray, 1901), 128–129.

8. Cousins, *Bonaventure,* 100–101.

9. Adapted from Rohr, *Things Hidden,* 29–30; Rohr, *Franciscan Mysticism,* Disc 4; and Rohr, *Eager to Love,* xiv.

10. Adapted from Rohr, Rolheiser, and Gateley, *Loving the Two Halves,* Disc 5; Rohr, *Franciscan Mysticism,* Disc 1; and Rohr, *Immortal Diamond,* 56.

11. Thomas Merton, *New Seeds of Contemplation* (New York: New Directions, 1961), 227.

12. C. G. Jung, *The Archetypes and the Collective Unconscious, Collected Works of C. G. Jung* (New York: Routledge, 1991), 384.

WEEK 47: ONEING

1. Julian of Norwich, *Showings*, long text, chap. 53, author's paraphrase.
2. Adapted from Rohr and Finley, *Intimacy*, Disc 7. Quote from Julian of Norwich, *Showings*, 283–284.
3. Julian of Norwich, *Showings*, 285.
4. Ibid.
5. Adapted from Rohr and Finley, *Intimacy*, Disc 7.
6. Adapted from Rohr, *Franciscan Mysticism*, Disc 4.
7. Adapted from Cynthia Bourgeault and Richard Rohr, *God as Us! The Sacred Feminine and the Sacred Masculine* (Albuquerque, NM: Center for Action and Contemplation, 2011), Disc 6 and Richard Rohr, *Unitive Consciousness: Beyond Gender* (Cincinnati: Franciscan Media, 2013), 9.
8. Adapted from Rohr, *Eager to Love*, 70–71.
9. Adapted from Bourgeault and Rohr, *God as Us!* Disc 6.
10. James Finley, *Merton's Palace of Nowhere* (Notre Dame, IN: Ave Maria, 1978), 136.
11. Adapted from Rohr, *Franciscan Mysticism*, Disc 4.
12. Douglas Wood and Jon J. Muth, *Old Turtle and the Broken Truth* (New York: Scholastic, 2003).

WEEK 48: LOVE

1. Adapted from Richard Rohr, *Gate of the Temple: Spirituality and Sexuality* (Albuquerque, NM: Center for Action and Contemplation, 1991), Disc 1; Rohr, *Divine Dance*, Disc 4; and Rohr, *Adam's Return*, 165–166.
2. St. John of the Cross, *The Spiritual Canticle*, 32, 33, author's paraphrase.
3. Adapted from Rohr, *Naked Now*, 140–141.
4. Adapted from Rohr, *Art of Letting Go*, Disc 6; Rohr, *Franciscan Mysticism*, Disc 4; and Rohr, *Eager to Love*, 116, 242–243.
5. Adapted from Rohr, *Immortal Diamond*, 176–178.
6. Adapted from Rohr, *Immortal Diamond*, 178–179.
7. Adapted from Rohr, *Breathing Under Water*, 91–92.
8. Adapted from Finley and Rohr, *Jesus and Buddha*, Disc 4 and Rohr, *Naked Now*, 171–173.

WEEK 49: DEATH AND HEAVEN

1. Adapted from Rohr, *Eager to Love*, xxii and Rohr, *New Way of Seeing*, Disc 1.
2. Julian of Norwich, *Showings*, long text, chap. 53.
3. Adapted from Rohr and Finley, *Intimacy*, Disc 7.
4. Adapted from Rohr and Finley, *Intimacy*, Disc 9 and *In the Beginning . . . Six Hours with Rob Bell and Richard Rohr on Reclaiming the Original Christian Narrative* (Albuquerque, NM: Center for Action and Contemplation, 2014), Disc 1.
5. Adapted from Rohr, *Dancing Standing Still*, 99–100 and Rohr, *Eager to Love*, 226.
6. Finley, "Ripening," 38–39.
7. Adapted from Rohr, *Eager to Love*, 206–207, 268.

8. Excerpted from Elizabeth Lesser, "Five Ways of Practicing Dying," http://www. elizabethlesser.org/tool-box/.

WEEK 50: PRESENCE

1. Jean-Pierre de Caussade, *Abandonment to Divine Providence,* trans. John Beevers (New York: Crown/Image Classics, 1993), 50.
2. Ibid., 25.
3. Ibid., 20–21.
4. Ibid., 51.
5. Ibid., 20.
6. Adapted from Thomas Keating and Richard Rohr, *The Eternal Now—and how to be there!* (Albuquerque, NM: Center for Action and Contemplation, 2004).
7. *Augustine: Later Works*, ed. John Burnaby (Philadelphia: Westminster John Knox, 1955), 341.
8. Julian of Norwich, *Showings*, short text, chap. 4.
9. Adapted from Keating and Rohr, *Eternal Now.*
10. Adapted from Richard Rohr, "To Be Awake Is to Live in the Present," *Collection of Homilies 2008* (Albuquerque, NM: Center for Action and Contemplation, 2008).
11. Adapted from Rohr, "To Be Awake."
12. Adapted from Rohr, "To Be Awake"; Rohr, *Enneagram: Discernment of Spirits*, Disc 2; Rohr and Freeman, *Transforming the World*, Disc 3; and Rohr, *Living the Eternal Now.*
13. Adapted from Bourgeault and Rohr, *God as Us!* Disc 6.
14. Kathleen Dowling Singh, "Full Circle: The Evidence of Love," *Oneing* 2 no. 2 (2014): 63–70.
15. Daniel Ladinsky, *Love Poems from God: Twelve Sacred Voices from the East and West* (New York: Penguin, 2002), 306–307.

WEEK 51: I AM WHO I AM

1. Cousins, *Bonaventure*, 229.
2. Adapted from Rohr, *Art of Letting Go,* Disc 5.
3. Ibid.
4. Adapted from Rohr, *Franciscan Mysticism*, Disc 4.
5. Adapted from Rohr, *Art of Letting Go,* Disc 3.
6. Adapted from Rohr, *True Self/False Self,* Disc 5.
7. Adapted from Rohr, *Naked Now,* 166–168.

WEEK 52: SILENCE

1. Timothy D. Wilson, et al., "Just Think: The Challenges of the Disengaged Mind," *Science*, July 4, 2014, 345:6192, 75–77.
2. Adapted from Rohr, *Silent Compassion,* 1–2 and Richard Rohr, *Letting Go: A Spirituality of Subtraction* (Cincinnati: St. Anthony Messenger Press, 2005), Disc 3.
3. Adapted from Rohr, *Letting Go*, Disc 3 and Richard Rohr, "Finding God in

the Depths of Silence," *Sojourners* (March 2013), https://sojo.net/magazine/march-2013/finding-god-depths-silence.

4. Adapted from Rohr, *Letting Go,* Disc 3 and Rohr, *Silent Compassion,* 4–5, 9.

5. Aldous Huxley, *Huxley and God: Essays on Religious Experience* (New York: Crossroad, 2003), 62.

6. Adapted from Rohr, "Finding God."

7. Robert Sardello, *Silence: The Mystery of Wholeness* (Berkeley: Goldenstone, 2006), 10.

8. Ibid., 12.

9. Adapted from Rohr, *Letting Go,* Disc 3 and Rohr, "Finding God."

10. Adapted from Richard Rohr, "What Sustains Me: Contemplation," *Sojourners* (July 2009), https://sojo.net/articles/what-sustains-me-contemplation.

APPENDIX

Rob Bell and Richard Rohr. *In the Beginning . . . Six Hours with Rob Bell and Richard Rohr on Reclaiming the Original Christian Narrative*. Albuquerque, NM: Center for Action and Contemplation, 2014. 8 compact discs; 6.7 hours.

Cynthia Bourgeault and Richard Rohr. *God As Us! The Sacred Feminine and the Sacred Masculine*. Albuquerque, NM: Center for Action and Contemplation, 2011. 6 compact discs; 8 hours.

Cynthia Bourgeault and Richard Rohr. *The Shape of God: Deepening the Mystery of Trinity*. Albuquerque, NM: Center for Action and Contemplation, 2004. 6 compact discs; 6 hours.

"Evidence." *Oneing* 2, no. 2 (2014).

James Finley and Richard Rohr. *Jesus and Buddha: Paths to Awakening*. Albuquerque, NM: Center for Action and Contemplation, 2008. 7 compact discs; 7 hours.

"Innocence." *Oneing* 3, no. 1 (2015).

Thomas Keating and Richard Rohr. *The Eternal Now—and how to be there!* Albuquerque, NM: Center for Action and Contemplation, 2004. MP3; 9.5 hours.

"The Perennial Tradition." *Oneing* 1, no. 1 (2013).

"Ripening." *Oneing* 1, no. 2 (2013).

Ronald Rolheiser and Richard Rohr. *Adult Christianity and How to Get There*. Albuquerque, NM: Center for Action and Contemplation, 2004. 4 compact discs; 4.5 hours.

Richard Rohr. *Adam's Return: The Five Promises of Male Initiation.* New York: Crossroad, 2004.

Richard Rohr. *Are You Eager to Love? St. Francis on the Edge of the Inside.* Albuquerque, NM: Center for Action and Contemplation, 2014. 2 compact discs; 1.5 hours.

Richard Rohr. *The Art of Letting Go: Living the Wisdom of Saint Francis.* Louisville, CO: Sounds True, 2010. 6 compact discs, 5.75 hours.

Richard Rohr. *The Authority of Those Who Have Suffered.* Albuquerque, NM: Center for Action and Contemplation, 2005. MP3; 1 hour.

Richard Rohr. *Beginner's Mind.* Albuquerque, NM: Center for Action and Contemplation, 2002. Compact disc; 40 minutes.

Richard Rohr. *Beloved Sons Series: Men and Grief.* Albuquerque, NM: Center for Action and Contemplation, 2005. Compact disc; 1 hour.

Richard Rohr. *Breathing Under Water: Spirituality and the Twelve Steps.* Cincinnati: St. Anthony Messenger Press, 2011.

Richard Rohr. *CAC Foundation Set.* Albuquerque, NM: Center for Action and Contemplation, 2003. 2 compact discs; 3 hours.

Richard Rohr. *Collection of Homilies 2008.* Albuquerque, NM: Center for Action and Contemplation, 2008. Compact disc; 1.3 hours.

Richard Rohr. *Contemplative Prayer.* Albuquerque, NM: Center for Action and Contemplation, 2003. Compact disc; 1.5 hours.

Richard Rohr. *The Cosmic Christ.* Albuquerque, NM: Center for Action and Contemplation, 2009. 3 compact discs; 3 hours.

Richard Rohr. *Culture, Scapegoating, and Jesus.* Albuquerque, NM: Center for Action and Contemplation, 1998. Compact disc; 1 hour.

Richard Rohr. *Dancing Standing Still: Healing the World from a Place of Prayer.* Mahwah, NJ: Paulist Press, 2014.

Richard Rohr. *Discharging Your "Loyal Soldier."* Albuquerque, NM: Center for Action and Contemplation, 2009. Compact disc; 1.3 hours.

Richard Rohr. *The Divine Dance: Exploring the Mystery of Trinity.* Albuquerque, NM: Center for Action and Contemplation, 2004. 4 compact discs; 4 hours.

Richard Rohr. *Eager to Love: The Alternative Way of Francis of Assisi.* Cincinnati: Franciscan Media, 2014.

Richard Rohr. *Emotional Sobriety: Rewiring Our Programs for "Happiness."* Albuquerque, NM: Center for Action and Contemplation, 2011. Compact disc; 1.3 hours.

Richard Rohr. *The Enneagram: The Discernment of Spirits.* Albuquerque, NM: Center for Action and Contemplation, 2004. 7 compact discs; 7 hours.

Richard Rohr. *Eucharist as Touchstone*. Albuquerque, NM: Center for Action and Contemplation, 2000. Compact disc; 1 hour.

Richard Rohr. *Everything Belongs: The Gift of Contemplative Prayer*. New York: Crossroad, 2003.

Richard Rohr. *Exploring and Experiencing the Naked Now*. Albuquerque, NM: Center for Action and Contemplation, 2010. 3 compact discs; 4 hours.

Richard Rohr. *Falling Upward: A Spirituality of the Two Halves of Life*. San Francisco: Jossey-Bass, 2011.

Richard Rohr. *Francis: Turning the World on Its Head: Subverting the Honor/Shame System*. Albuquerque, NM: Center for Action and Contemplation, 2009. Compact disc; 1.3 hours.

Richard Rohr. *Franciscan Mysticism: I AM That Which I Am Seeking*. Albuquerque, NM: Center for Action and Contemplation, 2012. 4 compact discs; 4.75 hours.

Richard Rohr. *Gate of the Temple: Spirituality and Sexuality*. Albuquerque, NM: Center for Action and Contemplation, 1991. 3 compact discs; 3 hours.

Richard Rohr. *Great Themes of Paul: Life as Participation*. Cincinnati, Franciscan Media, 2012. 11 compact discs; 10.5 hours.

Richard Rohr. *Hierarchy of Truths: Jesus' Use of Scripture*. Albuquerque, NM: Center for Action and Contemplation, 2014. Compact disc; 1 hour.

Richard Rohr. *How Do We Breathe Under Water? The Gospel and 12-Step Spirituality*. Albuquerque, NM: Center for Action and Contemplation, 2005. 4 compact discs; 5 hours.

Richard Rohr. *How Do We Get Everything to Belong?* Albuquerque, NM: Center for Action and Contemplation, 2005. 3 compact discs; 3 hours.

Richard Rohr. *Immortal Diamond: The Search for Our True Self*. San Francisco: Jossey-Bass, 2013.

Richard Rohr. *In the Footsteps of Francis: Awakening to Creation*. Albuquerque, NM: Center for Action and Contemplation, 2010. Compact disc; 1.3 hours.

Richard Rohr. *Job and the Mystery of Suffering*. New York: Crossroad, 1998.

Richard Rohr. *Journey of Faith: Making One of Two*. Albuquerque, NM: Center for Action and Contemplation, 2007. MP3; 1.25 hours.

Richard Rohr. *Letting Go: A Spirituality of Subtraction*. Cincinnati: St. Anthony Messenger Press, 2005. 6 compact discs; 7.5 hours.

Richard Rohr. *The Little Way: A Spirituality of Imperfection*. Albuquerque, NM: Center for Action and Contemplation, 2007. MP3; 1 hour.

Richard Rohr. *Living the Eternal Now.* Albuquerque, NM: Center for Action and Contemplation, 2005. Compact disc; 1.3 hours.

Richard Rohr. *The Naked Now: Learning to See as the Mystics See.* New York: Crossroad, 2009.

Richard Rohr. *Near Occasions of Grace.* Maryknoll, NY: Orbis, 1993.

Richard Rohr. *A New Cosmology: Nature as the First Bible.* Albuquerque, NM: Center for Action and Contemplation, 2009. 2 compact discs; 2 hours.

Richard Rohr. *New Great Themes of Scripture.* Cincinnati: Franciscan Media, 2012. 10 compact discs; 13 hours.

Richard Rohr. *A New Way of Seeing, a New Way of Being: Jesus and Paul.* Albuquerque, NM: Center for Action and Contemplation, 2007. 2 compact discs; 2 hours.

Richard Rohr. *The Path of Descent.* Albuquerque, NM: Center for Action and Contemplation, 2003. 4 compact discs; 4 hours.

Richard Rohr. *Richard Rohr on Transformation: Collected Talks, Volume One.* Cincinnati: St. Anthony Messenger Press, 2005. 4 compact discs, 4.3 hours.

Richard Rohr. *St. Paul: The Misunderstood Mystic.* Albuquerque, NM: Center for Action and Contemplation, 2014. Compact disc; 1.2 hours.

Richard Rohr. *Sic et Non; Yes, And . . . .* Albuquerque, NM: Center for Action and Contemplation, 2013. MP3; 1.5 hours.

Richard Rohr. *Silent Compassion: Finding God in Contemplation.* Cincinnati: Franciscan Media, 2014.

Richard Rohr. *Simplicity: The Freedom of Letting Go.* New York: Crossroad, 1991.

Richard Rohr. *The Soul, the Natural World, and What Is.* Albuquerque, NM: Center for Action and Contemplation, 2009. MP3; 1.3 hours.

Richard Rohr. *Things Hidden: Scripture as Spirituality.* Cincinnati: St. Anthony Messenger Press, 2007.

Richard Rohr. *True Self/False Self.* Cincinnati: Franciscan Media, 2013. 5 compact discs; 6 hours.

Richard Rohr. *The Two Major Tasks of the Spiritual Life.* Albuquerque, NM: Center for Action and Contemplation, 2005. Compact disc; 1 hour.

Richard Rohr. *Unitive Consciousness: Beyond Gender.* Cincinnati: Franciscan Media, 2013.

Richard Rohr. *What Difference Does Trinity Make?* Albuquerque, NM: Center for Action and Contemplation, 2004. Compact disc; 1 hour.

Richard Rohr. *What Do You Mean "Falling Upward"?* Albuquerque, NM: Center for Action and Contemplation, 2011. Compact disc; 1.3 hours.

Richard Rohr. *Where You Are Is Where I'll Meet You.* Albuquerque, NM: Center for Action and Contemplation, 2009. 2 compact discs; 2 hours.

Richard Rohr. *Yes, And . . . : Daily Meditations.* Cincinnati: Franciscan Media, 2013.

Richard Rohr and Paula D'Arcy. *A Spirituality for the Two Halves of Life.* Cincinnati: Franciscan Media, 2012. 6 compact discs; 6 hours.

Richard Rohr and Andreas Ebert. *The Enneagram: A Christian Perspective.* New York: Crossroad, 2001.

Richard Rohr and John Feister. *Jesus' Plan for a New World: The Sermon on the Mount.* Cincinnati: St. Anthony Messenger Press, 1996.

Richard Rohr and James Finley. *Intimacy: The Divine Ambush.* Albuquerque, NM: Center for Action and Contemplation, 2013. 10 compact discs; 9.5 hours.

Richard Rohr, James Finley, and Cynthia Bourgeault. *Following the Mystics through the Narrow Gate . . . Seeing God in All Things.* Albuquerque, NM: Center for Action and Contemplation, 2010. 9 compact discs; 9 hours.

Richard Rohr and Laurence Freeman. *Transforming the World through Contemplative Prayer.* Albuquerque, NM: Center for Action and Contemplation, 2013. 6 compact discs; 7 hours.

Richard Rohr and Russ Hudson. *The Enneagram as a Tool for Your Spiritual Journey.* Albuquerque, NM: Center for Action and Contemplation, 2009. 7 compact discs; 7.5 hours.

Richard Rohr and Russ Hudson. *The Enneagram and Grace: 9 Journeys to Divine Presence.* Albuquerque, NM: Center for Action and Contemplation, 2012. 8 compact discs; 10.5 hours.

Richard Rohr and Mary Beth Ingham. *Holding the Tension: The Power of Paradox.* Albuquerque, NM: Center for Action and Contemplation, 2007. 7 compact discs; 7 hours.

Richard Rohr and Bill Plotkin. *Soul Centering through Nature.* Albuquerque, NM: Center for Action and Contemplation, 2011. 2 compact discs; 1.3 hours.

Richard Rohr, Ron Rolheiser, and Edwina Gateley. *Loving the Two Halves of Life: The Further Journey.* Albuquerque, NM: Center for Action and Contemplation, 2011. 7 compact discs; 7.7 hours.

"Transgression." *Oneing* 2, no. 1 (2014).